BECOMING QUALITATIVE
RESEARCHERS

FOURTH EDITION

BECOMING QUALITATIVE RESEARCHERS

An Introduction

CORRINE GLESNE

Boston   Columbus   Indianapolis   New York   San Francisco   Upper Saddle River
Amsterdam   Cape Town   Dubai   London   Madrid   Milan   Munich   Paris   Montreal   Toronto
Delhi   Mexico City   São Paulo   Sydney   Hong Kong   Seoul   Singapore   Taipei   Tokyo

Editor in Chief: Paul Smith
Managing Editor: Shannon Steed
Editorial Assistant: Matthew Buchholz
Marketing Manager: Erica DeLuca
Editorial Production Service: GGS Higher Education Resources,
 A division of PreMedia Global, Inc.
Manufacturing Buyer: Meghan Cochran
Electronic Composition: GGS Higher Education Resources,
 A division of PreMedia Global, Inc.
Cover Administrator: Jayne Conte
Cover Illustration: Kelly Clark/Keefe

For related titles and support materials, visit our online catalog at www.pearsonhighered.com.

Between the time Web site information is gathered and then published, it is not unusual for
some sites to have closed. Also, the transcription of URLs can result in typographical
errors. The publisher would appreciate notification where these errors occur so that they
can be corrected in subsequent editions.

Library of Congress Cataloging-in-Publication Data

Glesne, Corrine.
 Becoming qualitative researchers: an introduction / Corrine Glesne.—4th ed.
  p. cm.
 Includes bibliographical references and index.
 ISBN-13: 978-0-13-704797-0
 ISBN-10: 0-13-704797-5
 1. Social sciences—Methodology.   I. Title.
 H61.G555 2010
 300.1—dc22

                                                          2010004224

10 9 8 7 6 5 4 3   14 13 12 11

www.pearsonhighered.com

ISBN 10:   0-13-704797-5
ISBN 13: 978-0-13-704797-0

About the Author

A qualitative research methodologist and educational anthropologist, Corrine Glesne has conducted ethnographic research in St. Vincent and the Grenadines, Costa Rica, and Mexico. Author of the text *Becoming Qualitative Researchers*, she was a professor at the University of Vermont for 17 years, before her involvement with IHP, an international educational program. As a traveling professor with IHP, she taught and accompanied undergraduates to India, the Philippines, Mexico, New Zealand, and England. She coordinated the Washington, DC, portion of the "Rethinking Globalization" IHP program for several years and has worked in various capacities with the University of Vermont's semester program in Oaxaca, Mexico. Corrine did her doctoral work at the University of Illinois at Urbana/ Champaign. Her home is now in Asheville, North Carolina.

Contents

CHAPTER 3

Being There: Developing Understanding through Participant Observation   63

Introduction: A Sense of Things to Come

NEW TO THIS EDITION

"What can be involved in updating a textbook?" my non-academic friends ask me. "Can't you put in a few recent sources, talk about how technology has changed, add a couple new ideas, and be done with it? Besides, how much can research methods change in a few years?"

I reply that the situation is more intricate. Methodological perspectives do change, specifically in qualitative research, an approach noted for its variety and complexity, and especially during these times when issues of difference, plurality, justice, and meaning demand our attention. When I worked on the first edition of this text (1992), relatively few qualitative methods texts had been published, particularly in disciplines other than anthropology. Now, not yet two decades later, the qualitative research field is vast, with thick handbooks on topics barely imagined in the early 1990s. This "turn" is exciting in that it signals that people in many disciplines have sought out qualitative research methods to help them seek specific understanding or address particular issues. In so doing, approaches to and critiques of qualitative methods have proliferated. This expansion is also overwhelming for a writer of an introductory text. Compiling a comprehensive methods text for the field of qualitative inquiry could be a life's work.

What I can do is better position this text in the array of qualitative theories and methodologies, so you, the reader, are better informed about what you might be getting into through reading this book. I can point the way to other books and authors that will help you deepen your knowledge of topics only mentioned or briefly described in this text. And I can better reflect on the methods and procedures discussed, presenting ways in which they are embraced and challenged in theory and in practice. These are the goals I set for myself in creating this new edition. The following list outlines specific changes to this text since the 2006 edition.

NEW TO THIS EDITION

1. *Major reworking of Chapter 1 to include an introduction to four research paradigms and their theoretical and philosophical underpinnings.* This is meant to assist you in understanding links among beliefs about the world, the kinds of questions asked, and research methodologies.
2. *Discussion of poststructuralism and postcolonialism (Chapter 1),* which provides context for understanding some of the challenges and influences of these perspectives on interpretivism.

3. *Addition of a section on research purposes (Chapter 2).* This change will assist you in creating your personal research foci.

4. *Expanded discussion on use of Internet and virtual reality sites in data collection (Chapters 3 and 4).* These additions suggest some technological avenues that you may want to travel.

5. *Expanded section on collection and use of visual data (photographs, maps, diagrams, etc.) (Chapter 3).* This discussion could contribute to compilation of richer data.

6. *Expanded discussion on technology for recording and transcribing interviews (Chapter 4).* This provides information on technological advances that can assist in the research process.

7. *Major revisions of Chapter 5, now titled "Personal Dimensions: Field Relations and Reflexivity." More attention is given to feminist and poststructuralist challenges to prior conceptions of researcher–other relationships.* These changes are meant to assist you in thinking about the kinds of research relationships important to you in your work and alert you to ways of tracking reflexivity.

8. *Expanded ethics discussions on privacy and the Internet and on representation (Chapter 6).* These discussions are intended to increase awareness of some of the ethical challenges posed by technology and publishing.

9. *Description of more forms of data analysis besides thematic analysis (Chapter 7).* These additions provide you with more options to consider in analyzing data.

10. *Expanded discussions of autoethnography, ethnodrama, and poetic transcription that include new examples (Chapter 9).* These additions provide you with more direction in representing your work through creative analytic practices.

11. *New examples and tables throughout the text.* These additions are meant to assist you in understanding accompanying discussions.

12. *Recommended Readings sections added to the ends of chapters.* To deepen understanding of concepts introduced in each chapter, begin by reading books listed in these sections.

13. *Added exercises at the ends of chapters.* These exercises will assist you in learning the material and provide your teachers with examples of possible assignments.

14. *The addition of a glossary.* This addition will be useful for quickly refreshing your memory about the meaning and use of various terms.

PERSONAL AND TEXTUAL POSITIONING

My background and experience is in ethnographic and case study research, as well as various forms of action research, including participatory action research and collaborative research. I have lived and worked in various parts of the world and have maintained an interest in theories of development and globalization. Even though I have been reading, noting, and informing myself on paradigms and methodologies of qualitative research with which I am less familiar, I cannot do justice to them all or even to a portion of them. I have to limit what can be addressed.

This book is rooted in the interpretivist tradition of qualitative inquiry. Although I briefly introduce and make reference throughout the text to critical and postmodern/poststructural traditions, this book is not meant to be a methods book for those seeking to do research within those paradigms—although they may find some of the advice fitting and useful. Within the interpretivist tradition, different research approaches developed historically, geographically, and by discipline, including sociology (symbolic interactionism, grounded theory), psychology (phenomenology), and anthropology (ethnography). *Ethnography* is perhaps the term that is most widely used, whether correctly or not, to refer to research in the interpretivist tradition. It also carries with it a lot of baggage in its ties to colonial anthropology. Nonetheless, the research methods associated with ethnography (fieldwork, interviews, observations, document collection) are used in many other qualitative methodologies (although expectations for fieldwork, kinds of interview questions, analysis techniques, and so forth can vary widely). This book focuses on methods used in ethnographic research, including current critiques, challenges, and changes.

I believe in the wisdom of local people, whether in a farming community in Illinois or a barrio in Mexico City; I believe that there are "organic" intellectuals everywhere, working to keep traditions alive and also to shape a changing future. I continue to be partial to inquiry approaches that involve research participants more fully in the work, particularly in identifying the overarching research question and, thereby, in designing research that will be useful to the people involved. I also continue to believe that much is to be learned from conventional qualitative methods, that you can learn and practice basic techniques and then adapt them as your skills and inclinations lead. This book, therefore, is meant to continue as an introductory text to the ethnographic research techniques of data collection, analysis, and writing. Along the way, however, I have added sections that are meant to probe into and complicate some of these practices.

SUGGESTIONS FOR USING THE TEXT

Chapters tend to compartmentalize thoughts, giving the impression that data collection, for example, is distinct from data analysis. Although the activities of qualitative inquiry tend to be ongoing and overlapping, I use chapters to focus upon one research aspect at a time. My guiding principle throughout these pages has been to create a book I would want to use as a primary text to help you begin to conduct qualitative research. The book therefore guides you through the research process, with separate chapters on theoretical foundations (Chapter 1), research design (Chapter 2), participant observation (Chapter 3), interviewing (Chapter 4), data analysis (Chapter 7), and writing (Chapters 8 and 9). The chapters pose issues, questions, and quandaries with which my students and I have struggled. As students in my classes have noted, my most frequent answer to questions raised by qualitative inquiry is "It depends." In class discussions and in this book, I provide no solutions, nor absolutes. My goal is to raise questions, thereby indicating what is problematic, and suggest guidelines for developing your own judgment in order to learn from and manage the complex issues you may encounter. To become competent researchers, you must acquire the general lore associated with research processes and learn how, in light of your personal qualities and the research situation, you can best conduct your inquiry.

Because many of you will be working on theses or dissertations, I periodically address some of the particular problems that you might encounter. Many of the text examples are drawn from educational settings, but the book is not limited to the context of schools or to the needs of scholars of education. The sources of examples are the experiences of students, my own inquiries, the research of Alan Peshkin (coauthor of the first edition of this book), and published works. I am most indebted to students at the University of Vermont; they taught me much about qualitative inquiry. With permission, I identify their examples by their first names, or, for some, by pseudonyms.

From my perspective, acquiring the skill and understanding for conducting qualitative inquiry has three dimensions: reading, reflecting, and doing. Preferably, all three are done simultaneously so that the outcomes of each continually interact. Read widely and deeply about your topic *and* about the conduct of inquiry throughout the research process; begin with the Recommended Readings sections at the ends of the chapters. Practice qualitative research techniques on problems of significance to you as you read about doing qualitative research. Ideally, the course is an occasion for supervised pilot studies for theses and dissertations. Reflect before and after each step in your research journey (from developing your research statement to completing your research report) by keeping a field journal and by holding discussions with peers, supervisors, and research participants.

Keeping a field journal that describes your practices and, no less important, your critical reflections on these practices is crucial for doing good research. The field journal, in effect, becomes a personal methods book that contains the insights that result from the interaction of reading, reflecting, and doing research. Learning to reflect on your behavior and thoughts, as well as on the phenomenon under study, creates a means for continuously becoming a better researcher. *Becoming* a better researcher captures the dynamic nature of the process. Conducting research, like teaching or dancing, can be improved; it cannot be mastered.

Communicating the process of qualitative inquiry provides me some of the same kinds of rewards that teaching swimming did years ago. At the end of a semester (or, better, two semesters), students no longer fear to jump in, nor are they at risk of drowning in data. With careful, sure strokes, they stride through data collection, analysis, and writing—albeit not without the occasional stormy day. Students gain useful skills that can serve them beyond the thesis and dissertation stages. In return, I have learned much from students about both the process of doing qualitative research and their topical areas. They educate me, for example, about the social construction of developmental disabilities or about the workings of effective partner team-teaching in middle schools. I believe that qualitative research can provide a forum for reflection and communication that results in better programs, gives voice to those who have been marginalized, and assists researchers, participants, and readers to see the world in new ways. For comments, suggestions, or questions, please contact me at ceglesne@yahoo.com.

Corrine Glesne

Acknowledgments

Acknowledgements for this edition begin with Kevin Davis of Pearson Publishing, who convinced me to revise the text yet again. Although reluctant at the time, I know now that he was right. Being institutionally unaffiliated, I thank him too for making available texts that were useful to me as I reworked the book. I also appreciate the support of Shannon Steed of Pearson Publishing, who sent me kind "checking in" emails exactly when I needed them. Many thanks to the reviewers for their suggestions and insight: Beth Hatt, Illinois State University; Aimee Howley, Ohio University; Joseph A. Maxwell, George Mason University, Betsy Palmer, Montana State University; with particular gratitude to Elizabeth St. Pierre, who kindly and gently helped me become more interested in poststructural thought and its challenges to interpretivism. Her responses to drafts of several chapters were immensely useful. Appreciation goes to Gustavo Esteva, who introduced me to his work and world in Oaxaca over a decade ago and who continues to inspire me. I am grateful to ex-IHPers Catherine Austin, Chris Hayes, Jane Hodge, Johanna Silver, Elizabeth Miller, and Darryl Wong, who allowed me to use photographs of them, to Diane Yoder for her contribution, and to my brother Tom, who can solve any technological difficulty. Kelly Clark/Keefe, Marleen Pugach, and Carolyn Mears get special thanks—maybe merit badges—for their willingness to read and supportively comment on drafts at very short notice. Kelly and Marleen also helped through engaging in long discussions on concepts, processes, and ideas that few others in my current life would find as fascinating. Yet these other friends have also nourished me by fixing me dinners, periodically pulling me away from the computer, and putting up with me throughout these many months. I am grateful.

CHAPTER 1

Meeting Qualitative Inquiry

Sofie knew and taught me that everyone had some story, every house held a life that could be penetrated and known, if one took the trouble. Stories told to oneself or others could transform the world. Waiting for others to tell their stories, even helping them do so, meant no one could be regarded as completely dull, no place people lived in was without some hope of redemption, achieved by paying attention.

(Myerhoff 1979, 240)

BEGINNINGS

Anthropologist Barbara Myerhoff was talking about the grandmother who raised her and who, through her love of stories, perhaps set the course for Myerhoff's life. Learning to listen well to others' stories and to interpret and retell the accounts is integral to many kinds of qualitative research.

Because qualitative researchers often seek to make sense of actions, narratives, and the ways in which they intersect, I begin with an account of my connections to research. If you know something about my story, you may better understand and interpret the perspectives in the work that follows. This beginning also contextualizes and introduces you to different research projects that I refer to throughout the book as I draw upon my life experiences to illustrate methodological advice and reflections.

I do not remember "discovering" qualitative inquiry. The process, however, is one with which I have been familiar for some time. I grew up in a small, rural, Midwestern town where almost everyone went to church (no synagogues, no mosques) and almost everyone had European ancestry (mine was Norwegian and Welsh). I always had been interested in people whose lives were different from mine. I read each month's *National Geographic* and filled my nights with folk tales from around the world. Books such as *Arctic Wild* (Crisler 1958) and *No Room in the Ark* (Moorehead 1959) from my parents' bookshelves supplemented library books about travelers, explorers, and adventurers from Genghis Khan to Amelia Earhart.

I gravitated toward anthropology as an undergraduate, which allowed me to continue learning about the many different ways people live. For anthropologists, fieldwork—being present in others' lives—is the method to learning about another culture. The more I read, the more I wanted to experience life elsewhere. Thus began a postgraduate trek in which I traveled and worked from Wales to Afghanistan. On a kibbutz in Israel, I pollinated date palms, pruned banana plants, picked grapefruit, and grew increasingly interested in tropical agriculture. Later, I lived in Jerusalem and joined a team of archaeologists for a year. I continued with archaeological work in northern Kenya where I camped in dry riverbeds and walked over tracks of rhinos and lions as I helped to trace the southern migration of people away from the Nile 10,000 years ago. Throughout this period, I kept journals. As I read them now, I am struck by my joy about what I was learning and my frustration about how to make sense of all I was encountering. Constantly stimulated by different ways of doing things and multiple ways of understanding them, I was restless and eager to go beyond experiences. Such desires led me to graduate school with plans to apply anthropology through education. I took courses that provided theory and structure for what I had been doing haphazardly on my own.

My first qualitative research project, which was my master's thesis, was an interview and archival study of Illinois rural women who worked the land. As a doctoral student, I assisted Alan Peshkin in conducting an ethnography of a fundamentalist Christian school. Peshkin moved into the community where the school was located. The other assistant and I spent two days a week at the school throughout one academic year, observing from the back of classrooms and conducting multiple-session interviews with teachers and students.

Before beginning dissertation research, I worked as an action researcher (defined later in this chapter) in St. Vincent and the Grenadines as part of a multiple-nation Caribbean Agricultural Extension Project under the direction of Michael Quinn Patton.[1] There I assisted representatives of various farmers' groups and agricultural organizations to create a national agricultural extension plan. For my dissertation, I returned to St. Vincent to carry out ethnographic research in one rural village, focusing on young people, agriculture, and education.

As a professor at the University of Vermont (UVM), I began teaching various courses in qualitative research, among other kinds of classes. Novelists and poets lament that if they are teaching writing, they find little time to write. The same applies to teaching qualitative research. My research was limited to sabbaticals (the first in Costa Rica, the second in Oaxaca, Mexico) supplemented by short-term qualitative evaluation work and a life history project. Although I had been trained in conventional ethnographic methods, by the time I went to Costa Rica in 1993, I wanted to do research *with* and not *on* others (both conventional ethnographic methods and more collaborative research methods are discussed later in this chapter). I volunteered my research skills and worked with an environmental group in the small community in which I was living. Seven years later, my next sabbatical allowed me to continue this mode of research in Oaxaca (discussed in the next chapter).

In 2002, I received the opportunity to work as a traveling professor with the International Honors Program (IHP), a study-abroad program affiliated with the School for International Training. For nine months, thirty students and three professors lived in six countries studying issues of culture, ecology, and justice, guided by country coordinators, activists, environmentalists, and intellectuals in each country. In 2008, I directed a semester program in Oaxaca, Mexico for UVM. I continue working on short-term programs with IHP, UVM, and other groups while making my home in the mountains of western North Carolina.

From these varied research experiences and through reading works of others, I have become particularly sensitive to and interested in interactions and relationships between researchers and study participants. I readily acknowledge inquiry purposes that do not focus on serving research participants, but I am personally inclined towards research that contributes to the lives of participants as determined by them and that perspective will be evident as you continue to read.

This book focuses on approaches to qualitative research primarily within interpretivist traditions—with frequent references to challenges to and quandaries within interpretivism. A quotation from *The Tao of Painting* represents my perspective on learning to do qualitative inquiry:

> Some set great value on method, while others pride themselves on dispensing with method. To be without method is deplorable, but to depend on method entirely is worse. You must first learn to observe the rules faithfully; afterwards, modify them according to your intelligence and capacity. (Sze and Wang 1963/1701, 17)

Learning to do qualitative research is like learning to paint. Study the masters, learn techniques and methods, practice them faithfully, and then revise and adapt them to your own persuasions when you know enough to describe the work of those who have influenced you and the ways in which your modifications create new possibilities.

SEARCHING

Dictionaries define *research* as a careful and diligent search. We have all been engaged in a variety of careful and diligent searches without necessarily labeling the process *research*, let alone a particular type of research. My mother's interest in our family's genealogy is one example of searching. In her pursuits to develop the family tree, she asked questions of great aunts and second cousins; requested that they and other relatives share letters and photo albums; wandered in cemeteries in towns where ancestors had lived; and sent for documents from hospitals, town clerks, and churches. From the formal and informal documents and the words of her relatives, she carefully and diligently traced our family's history, recording both the dates of significant events (births, marriages, deaths) and the stories she heard.

As students some of you may have conducted searches without having been assigned to do so. For example, a group of undergraduates living in a residence hall became increasingly dissatisfied with the selection of food provided by the food service. They complained, but nothing changed. Over a particularly unsatisfactory meal, they decided to develop a survey that took shape as a series of statements followed by a five-point scale ranging from strongly agree to strongly disagree. They typed it up, discussed it at a hall meeting, and got the resident hall advisor to make copies, which were distributed via mailboxes. Respondents were asked to deposit the survey in a designated box by a certain date. On that date, the students collected the surveys and tallied the numbers, learning what proportion of residents responded and how those residents felt about certain aspects of the food service. Armed with facts in the form of a written summary, they distributed a copy to the school newspaper, the university president, and the food service.

As professionals, you may have continued to conduct searches. A middle school English teacher was struck each September by a pattern of frightened, uncertain new students. She had a hunch that teachers, administrators, and older students could do something to ease the transition, but she was not sure what. So she asked her sixth-, seventh-, and eighth-grade classes to write essays about how they felt during their first few days as sixth graders, what made the experience good, what made the experience bad, and what could be changed to make it better. Then, working with the students, the teacher prepared a report for presentation to staff and administration, suggesting steps that the school could take.

In all three of these examples, people are engaged in research. They deliberately set out to collect data for specified purposes. In all three cases, data might have been collected more carefully, but the point is that people carry out research of all sorts in their everyday lives—even though they may not name the methods they use or be aware of how to improve the process so the results are more trustworthy or of greater use. This book is meant to help you approach qualitative research in ways that are thoughtful and useful.

Most likely, some of you have been conditioned to think of research as a process that uses an instrument such as a survey, involves a large number of people, and is analyzed by reducing data to numbers. This mode of inquiry, as demonstrated by the food survey, uses *quantitative* research methods. The middle school example and parts of the genealogical search show the researcher gathering words by talking with a small number of people, collecting a variety of documents, and, in the middle school example, observing behavior. Both of these cases use *qualitative* approaches.

The two modes of inquiry are frequently contrasted. Quantitative and qualitative researchers, however, use similar elements in their work and their methods should be viewed as more on a continuum than as a dichotomy. They state a purpose, pose a problem or raise a question, define a research population, select research methods, develop a time frame, collect and analyze data, and present outcomes. They also rely (explicitly or implicitly) on theory and are concerned with rigor. Nonetheless, how researchers go about putting these elements together makes for distinctive differences in the research processes and products as discussed in the next section on research paradigms.

WAYS OF KNOWING: PARADIGMS OF RESEARCH

> Paradigms are frameworks that function as maps or guides for scientific communities, determining important problems or issues for its members to address and defining acceptable theories or explanations, methods, and techniques to solve defined problems.
>
> (R. Usher 1996, 15)

The concept of research paradigms grew out of work by Thomas Kuhn, who published *The Structure of Scientific Revolutions* in 1962. Kuhn, trained as a theoretical physicist, had a strong interest in philosophy. While a doctoral candidate, he became intrigued by how history informed the philosophy of science (Loving 1997, 430). The book that resulted from this exploration began a philosophical revolution in the practice of science. Before its publication, Western scientists tended to believe that research built upon itself, progressively increasing the "body of knowledge" until they could come to know how the world worked. Referred to as *logical positivism,* this paradigm held that knowledge was "limited to what could be logically deduced from theory, operationally measured, and empirically replicated" (Patton 2002, 92). Although science, at the time, was viewed as objective, neutral, and value-free, Kuhn demonstrated how science was often an ideological battleground where ideas and explanations competed, and those that "won" tended to be those of the scientists with the most power (economically, politically, socially, etc.). From Kuhn and others came the argument that "data and observations are theory-led, that theory is paradigm-led, and that paradigms are historically and culturally located" (R. Usher 1996, 16).

A paradigm, then, is a framework or philosophy of science that makes assumptions about the nature of reality and truth, the kinds of questions to explore, and how to go about doing so. The word *ontology* is often used to refer to beliefs regarding reality or what kinds of things make up the world. "Ontology," states Potter (1996, 36), "is the concern about whether the world exists, and if so, in what form." You might think of the world as one of matter, for example, things you can observe and measure. Or you might see the world as more shaped by the mind, by how the mind perceives, categorizes, and interprets things. What you believe about the nature of reality, in turn, affects the kinds of questions you ask of it, what you consider knowledge to be. *Epistemology* is the word used to refer to the study of the nature of knowledge. What you believe knowledge to be, in turn, shapes and serves to justify the methodology you choose to answer your questions.

Every research study is, therefore, informed by higher-level theory, even though researchers sometimes are not aware of these theories because they are embedded in their assumptions about the nature of reality and knowledge. Part of your duty as a researcher is to figure out what philosophical and theoretical perspectives inform the kind of work you choose to do. This introduction is meant to initiate that process, but it is only a beginning. Some sources to help you become more familiar with the thought and language of theories and philosophies that inform research are suggested at the end of this chapter.

For ease of discussion, I classify the higher-level theories and philosophies that guide the work of social scientists into four paradigmatic families: positivism, interpretivism, critical theory, and poststructuralism. Each should be viewed as a loosely bonded grouping of assumptions, philosophies, and theories, containing several related schools of thought. They are not rigid, well-defined categories. These paradigms have developed and changed over time, influenced by socio-historical contexts as well as by thought from both within their own traditions and also within other paradigms. To complicate matters, different theorists and authors use diverse labels for the paradigms, and some labels, such as *postpositivism*, get associated with various paradigms. Nor is there agreement among social scientists on how many paradigms there are or on how associated methodologies should be divided. My purpose in using the categories proposed here is as a heuristic for making clearer the ways in which research is theory-driven, ensconced in belief systems that offer different purposes for doing research and different ways of making meaning.

As you reflect upon the various paradigms described in the sections to follow, you may find it useful to refer to Table 1.1.

Logical Positivism/Logical Empiricism Paradigm

Empiricism developed and flourished with the Renaissance (1450–1600), as a response, in part, to the power of religion during the Middle Ages. Rather than explanations based on religious texts, the empiricists believe they could explain the world and find truth through observations and experimentation. During the Age of Enlightenment (1600–1800), empiricism became viewed as *the* way to do research, contributing to rapid expansion of knowledge in the physical and natural sciences in Europe.

The term *positivism* came from Auguste Comte, a nineteenth-century French philosopher, as he advocated "an approach to social science . . . that would emulate the natural science and would be *positive* in its attempts to achieve reliable, concrete knowledge on which we could act to change the social world for the better" (O'Reilly 2005, 45). Social scientists from many disciplines applied positivist methods and concepts (such as validity, reliability, objectivity, generalizability, etc.) to their research. By the 1930s and 1940s, however, the ontology on which logical positivism was built—that a fixed reality existed that could be measured and known—received much criticism. Most who work within this paradigm today would agree that the world is not knowable with certainty, but they continue to use and value procedures and language associated with the scientific method and to assert that research can reveal "good enough" objective facts that can assist in making generalizations and predictions regarding social behavior. This modification of positivism is referred to as *logical empiricism* and, sometimes, as *postpositivism*. I use the term *positivism* as a kind of shorthand in this text but intend it to denote this less rigid version of empirical thought.

If you are a positivist researcher, your ontological beliefs include a fixed reality external to people that can be measured and apprehended to some degree of

TABLE 1.1   Paradigms, Purposes, and Methodologies/Analyses

PARADIGM* OR THEORETICAL FRAMEWORK	OTHER TERMS OR LABELS	A FEW ASSOCIATED THEORISTS OR PHILOSOPHERS	CENTRAL PURPOSES FOR RESEARCH WITHIN THE PARADIGM	SOME ASSOCIATED RESEARCH METHODOLOGIES OR ANALYSES
Positivism	Postpositivism** Logical empiricism	August Comte	Predict	Experimental Quasi-experimental Causal comparative
Interpretivism	Constructivism Naturalism Phenomenological Hermaneutical	Clifford Geertz Jurgen Habermas Edmund Husserl Immanuel Kant George Herbert Mead	Understand	Ethnography Phenomenology Symbolic interactionism Narrative analysis Grounded theory
Critical Theory	Feminist theory Critical race theory	Karl Marx Antonio Gramsci Max Weber Herbert Marcuse Luce Irigiray	Emancipate	Critical ethnography Feminist research Participatory action research (Freire) Critical discourse analysis
Poststructuralism	Postmodernism Postcolonialism Post-Fordist	Michel Foucault Jacques Derrida Jean F. Lyotard Gayatri Spivak Edward Said Arun Appadurai Homi Bhabha	Deconstruct	Deconstruction (Derrida) Genealogy (Nietzsche, Foucault) Rhizoanalysis (Deleuze, Guattari) Paralogic legitimation (Lyotard)

*Term frequently used to describe the family of theoretical frameworks.

**Postpositivism* is used by some to refer a less strict form of positivism, and by others to refer to anything other than the early form of positivism. In the latter use of the term, all the paradigms other than early positivism would be forms of postpositivist thought.

Source: Aspects of this table were informed by Patti Lather and Elizabeth A. St. Pierre's table "Postpositivist New Paradigm Inquiry," on p. 164 of Lather, P. (2007). *Getting lost: Feminist efforts toward a double(d) science.* Albany, NY: SUNY Press.

accuracy. Because the world is at least approximately knowable, you seek to do research in order to make generalizations about social phenomena, to provide explanations about their causes, and to create predictions concerning those phenomena. You work to gain this knowledge through objective observations, measurements, and carefully designed experiments. Your research methods generally begin with a theory about the phenomena in question. Using that theory, you pose several hypotheses, and then test your hypotheses through methods designed to be objective and to keep you removed from subjects to avoid your influencing their behavior and responses. The data you collect are reduced to numerical indices or quantifiable bits of information and analyzed statistically. These procedures tend to be called *quantitative* methods.

Interpretivist Paradigm

Although ideas found in interpretivism can be traced back to Greek and Roman philosophies, interpretivism as a form of social science research grew out of the work of eighteenth century German philosopher Immanuel Kant and was expanded on by Wilhelm Dilthey, Max Weber, Edmund Husserl, and others. These philosophers are referred to as *idealists* in that, unlike *realists,* who believe a world exists independently of the knower, *idealists* believe that the world cannot exist independently of the mind—or of *ideas.* "An idealist does not necessarily hold that the natural and social worlds are unreal or nonexistent, but that there is . . . no direct understanding of the world. The world is always interpreted through mind" (Schwandt 2007, 143). The role of the social scientist then becomes that of accessing others' interpretations of some social phenomenon and of interpreting, themselves, other's actions and intentions. Many different traditions of interpretivism have developed (some of which are discussed later in this chapter), but they share the goal of understanding human ideas, actions, and interactions in specific contexts or in terms of the wider culture.

The ontological belief that tends to accompany interpretivist traditions portrays a world in which reality is socially constructed, complex, and ever changing. What is of importance to know, then, is how people interpret and make meaning of some object, event, action, perception, etc. These constructed realities are viewed as existing, however, not only in the mind of the individual, but also as *social constructions* in that individualistic perspectives interact with the language and thought of the wider society. Thus, accessing the perspectives of several members of the same social group about some phenomena can begin to say something about cultural patterns of thought and action for that group.

With the research goal of interpreting the social world from the perspectives of those who are actors in that social world, it follows that the research methods include interacting with people in their social contexts and talking with them about their perceptions. If your higher-level theoretical perspective is interpretivism, your study design will tend to focus on in-depth, long-term interactions with relevant people in one or several sites. Although site-specific hypotheses may be a result of your study, you probably will not begin with them, but rather with an exploratory, open mindset to the variety of perspectives and issues that might arise. You observe, ask questions, and interact with research participants. You may look for patterns in your analyses, but you do not try to reduce the multiple interpretations to numbers, nor to a norm. Your final write-up will be quite descriptive in nature. These methods tend to be called *qualitative.*

Because some of you may be more familiar with positivist traditions of research and are trying to figure out exactly how interpretivist traditions differ, I have

POSITIVIST APPROACH	INTERPRETIVIST APPROACH
Assumptions • Social facts have an objective reality • Variables can be identified and relationships measured	*Assumptions* • Reality is socially constructed • Variables are complex, interwoven, and difficult to measure
Research Purposes • Generalizability • Causal explanations • Prediction	*Research Purposes* • Contextualization • Understanding • Interpretation
Research Approach • Begins with hypotheses and theory • Uses formal instruments • Experimental • Deductive • Component analysis • Seeks the norm • Reduces data to numerical indices • Uses abstract language in write-up	*Research Approach* • May result in hypotheses and theory • Researcher as instrument • Naturalistic • Inductive • Searches for patterns • Seeks pluralism, complexity • Makes minor use of numerical indices • Descriptive write-up
Researcher Role • Detachment • Objective portrayal	*Researcher Role* • Personal involvement • Empathic understanding

EXHIBIT 1.1   Predispositions of Positivist and Interpretivist Approaches to Research

included Exhibit 1.1. The differences suggested should not be taken as hard and fast distinctions but rather as predispositions of the different inquiry approaches.

Critical Theory Paradigm

Critical theory research takes you beyond describing "what is," the intention of interpretivists, and toward describing, "what could be" (Thomas 1993). In critical theory, the term critical refers to "the detecting and unmasking of beliefs and practices that limit human freedom, justice, and democracy" (R. Usher 1996, 22). Critical theory research critiques historical and structural conditions of oppression and seeks transformation of those conditions.

Critical theory research is guided by a *historical realism* ontology: that life is a "virtual reality shaped by social, political, cultural, economic, ethnic, and gender values crystallized over time" (Lincoln and Guba 2000, 168). A central concept in critical theory work is that ideologies work to distort reality. The role of critical theorists is to reveal and critique these distorting ideologies and the associated structures, mechanisms, and processes that help to keep them in place (Prasad 2005).

In particular, they work to situate the experiences and perspectives of the oppressed group in a social, historical context, revealing how conditions serve certain groups and not others.

Critical theory researchers often make use of (and make others aware of) *standpoint epistemologies*. Standpoint epistemologies are positioned in the experiences, values, and interests of a group that has traditionally been oppressed or excluded (women, gays, lesbians, people of color, colonized, etc.). From those standpoints, researchers critique and reconstruct narratives of dominant groups, exposing ways in which they have been racists, masculinist, straight, Eurocentric, and so forth (Schwandt 2007). Two examples of standpoint epistemologies are critical race theory and queer theory. *Critical race theory* focuses on ways in which racism is so embedded in society that it appears "normal" for many, and portrays race as a socially constructed means to identify and classify people. With emphasis placed on social and political forms of power, critical race theory looks at how both work to include and exclude people of color (Madison 2005; Schram 2006). *Queer theory* challenges the concept of heteronormativity, the perspective that heterosexuality is/should be the normal (and legal) way for interactions. Queer theory views heterosexuality as a social construct and works to bring under suspicion any views considered "normal" by dominant society (Madison 2005).

Although critical theory research does not follow any particular set of methods, a few general aspects of research design are characteristic:

- Critical theory researchers see research as a political act because it not only relies on values systems, but challenges value systems (R. Usher 1996). Critical theory research tends to focus on issues of power and domination and to advocate understanding from perspective of the exploited and oppressed.
- Critical theory researchers often focus upon language or the "tacit rules that regulate what can and cannot be said, who can speak with the blessings of authority and who must listen, whose social constructions are valid and whose are erroneous and unimportant" (Kinchelow and McLaren 2000, 284). As such, their interests lie in exposing ways in which discourses are socially and historically constructed and how these discourses support and maintain conditions of inequality, oppression, and exploitation.
- Critical theory researchers are often interested in *praxis*, or the relationships between thought and action, theory and practice. As such, some incorporate dialogue and critical reflection as part of the research process in an effort to reveal unexamined assumptions among participants and the ways in which people may be accepting explanations of the dominant cultural group that serve to oppress. This process "enables people to challenge learned restrictions, compulsions or dictates of habit" (Higgs 2001, 49) and can point the way to changing current relationships or structures.

Weis and Fine (2004) provide engaging examples of the possibilities associated with critical research. They demonstrate how research can go beyond description to reveal ways in which certain groups are subjugated, and then to raise awareness among participants of those processes. In one of their studies, Weis and Fine created "research camps" for New York City high school students from a variety of identities (racial, class, gender, ethnic, etc.). In the camps, students learned about critical race theory as well as research methods. The students created a school survey, administered it, and then analyzed and interpreted the data. Using critical race theory, Weis and Fine urged students to look at ways in which dominant perspectives were perpetuated through their own analyses, and at how certain groups got silenced in the process. For many of the students, the work was empowering as they gained authority and confidence to speak out about school inequities and societal injustice.

Critical Feminist Research.   Feminist theory can guide research in each of the paradigms, but feminist research is often allied with critical theory research. An underlying assumption to critical feminist work is the belief that women experience oppression and exploitation, and that this experience varies, considering the multiple identities each person holds (Maguire 1996). As with critical theory researchers in general, critical feminist researchers focus on issues of justice and power, and are committed to uncovering and understanding the forces that cause and sustain oppression (Maguire 1996). They hold as a primary focus of their work the transformation of asymmetrical power relations, particularly as applied to women. This does not mean, however, that the focus is exclusively on gender because "gender oppression is not experienced or structured in isolation from other oppressions" (Maguire 1996, 108). Rather, women's identities are understood as *intersectional* (McCall 2005), making it imperative that consideration and analysis of race, class, culture, ethnicity, sexual preference, and other identities play a primary role in feminist research.

Beginning with the research question, the feminist position is that research with women must ask research questions that are of interest and importance to women (Bloom 1998). Second, "the most critical components of feminist methodology and perhaps its most distinguishing features are the concern for the research relationship and the enlargement of the definition of rapport in the fieldwork process" (Bloom 1998, 150). Whether or not researcher and participants become friends, the researcher acknowledges and is aware that a relationship exists and works to honor that relationship. Third, feminist researchers advocate critical self-reflections of their own roles as researchers and of their histories, values, and assumptions in relationship to the research. Feminist researchers extend their attention to interactions among subjectivities of researcher and participants and to the role power and authority might play in the research process. Fourth, feminist researchers tend to position themselves in the inquiry process as activist scholars, committing themselves to using their privileged positions and research products for social justice ends, particularly on behalf of those most disadvantaged (Bloom and Sawin 2009).

Feminist research has made lasting changes in how qualitative inquiry in general is conducted. By feminist researchers moving to create less hierarchical or collaborative research relationships, other researchers revise their perspectives on ways to be with research participants and ask new questions about how the nature of research relationships affects the kind of data obtained. Feminists' focus on interrogating their own actions, interactions, power, and authority in the research process has also contributed to general discussions of reflexivity in research and its expected incorporation into most forms of qualitative inquiry (see Chapter 5 for more discussion on this topic.)

Postmodern/Postcolonial/Poststructural Paradigm

> . . . when we white Western males can no longer define the truth we claim there is no truth.
>
> (Bruner 1993, 23)

The term *postmodernity* indicates a break from modernity, a historical period of time marked, in part, by industrialization. Characteristics of modernity included a belief in formal logic as necessary for reason, the bureaucratization of society, and a belief in science and technology as means to solving problems (Harker 1993). Postmodernity is marked by globalization, the spread of information technologies, and the fragmentation of nation-states. Under postmodernism, the grand theories that have been relied upon as explaining how societies work and how people develop and interact are subjected to critique and distrust (Schwandt 1997, 120). "Postmodernism argues that there are no universal truths to be discovered, because all human investigators are grounded in human society and can only produce partial locally and historically specific insights" (Delamont 2002, 157). Rather than questions about social coherence or causality, concepts that are relevant to postmodernism include plurality, fragmentation, and indeterminacy (Prasad 2005).

The paradigm of inquiry that is informed by postmodern thought is variably referred to as postmodern, poststructural, postcolonial, and post-Fordist, among others. These traditions can be distinguished from each other and yet share similar perspectives or philosophies and are used, therefore, somewhat interchangeably by many. Researchers within these traditions "offer a radical critique of the entire fabric of modern Western thinking from both within and outside it" (Prasad 2005, 211). For each, the term *post* is more than a marker of time. It refers to a break with the past and to "the *regeneration* and *reconstellation* of new ideas and social practices" (Prasad 2005, 213).

Postcolonialism.   Postcolonialism theory has emerged from throughout the world—in previously colonized countries as well as in Europe and the United States. Postcolonialism is concerned with legacies of colonialism and how they work "to subjugate entire populations on basis of race and geography" (Prasad 2005, 212). It focuses upon the multiple ways (language, values, customs, positions of power, borders) colonialism continues in the everyday lives of people, and how it is resisted and challenged. Postcolonialism critiques ways in which Western thinking (liberal humanism and modernist ideals) dominates lives of people throughout the world and it works to bring the voices of the margins to the center, to displace the Western hegemony. Important postcolonial scholars include Edward Said, Gayatri Spivak, Homi Bhabha, and Arjun Appadurai, among others.

Poststructuralism.   Much of the thinking regarding poststructuralism emerged out of French intellectual thought, particularly the work of Jacques Derrida and Michel Foucault. Reacting to the socio-linguistic work of structuralists who sought underlying linguistic codes or grammars to understand social interactions and cultures, poststructuralists were more interested in how texts resisted "order and systematization"(Prasad 2005, 238). Viewing speech and human behavior as textual productions (not only written words), poststructuralists tend to focus on deconstructing texts, showing how they systematically include and exclude people and ideas. Anything occupying a central position in a society, such as the notions of progress and liberal democracy in the United States, is suspect as discourses of control and power. The poststructuralist works to decenter and to destabilize such ways of thinking, "replacing them with a stream of ideas from the margin" (Prasad 2005, 243). Because these central discourses are seen as insidious, penetrating most venues of social thought, including that of researchers, "poststructuralism does not allow us to place the blame elsewhere, outside our own daily activities, but demands that we examine our own complicity in the maintenance of social injustice" (St. Pierre 2000, 484).

The central purpose of these various "post" traditions, can be described as that of *deconstruction*. Jane Flax (1990, 41) writes that "postmodern discourses are all deconstructive in that they seek to distance us from and make us skeptical about beliefs concerning truth, knowledge, power, the self, and language that are often taken for granted within and serve as legitimation for contemporary Western culture." Elizabeth St. Pierre (2000, 483) elaborates on *deconstruction*:

> One of the most significant effects of deconstruction is that it foregrounds the idea that language does not simply point to pre-existing things and ideas but rather helps to construct them and, by extension, the world as we know it. In other words, we word the world. The "way it is" is not "natural." We have constructed the world as it is through language and cultural practice, and we can also deconstruct and reconstruct it.

Postmodernism, poststructuralism, and postcolonialism challenge virtually every aspect of Western philosophy and science that has developed since the period of Enlightenment. Its reach has quickly expanded, influencing thought around the world, across many disciplines, and the research that is done.

Mixed Methods

A question that often arises in research discussions is whether or not you can combine approaches, usually meaning can you combine quantitative and qualitative research techniques within one study. To address this question, I need to clarify the terms *methodology* and *methods*. Methodology, drawing from Schwandt's (2007, 193) useful dictionary of qualitative inquiry terms, refers to "a theory of how inquiry should proceed. It involves analysis of the assumptions, principles, and procedures in a particular approach to inquiry." The term *methods* generally refers to "a procedure, tool, or technique used by the inquirer to generate and analyze data" (Schwandt 2007, 191). If you were to attempt to combine a positivist methodology that relies heavily on quantitative methods such as experimental design with an interpretivist methodology that relies on qualitative methods such ethnography, you would end up doing two studies. These methodologies make different assumptions about the nature of the world and about what counts as valuable knowledge. Each require different procedures or methods to find the type of data needed.

If, however, you wanted to combine quantitative and qualitative methods or techniques, you could. The experimental researcher sometimes uses interviews and the ethnographer sometimes uses surveys. One method tends to be supplementary to the dominant mode of gathering data. That is, if doing ethnography, you might include a quantifiable survey in your study, but most of your methods would be qualitative.

Even if you combine qualitative and quantitative methods in some way, you still situate yourself within particular paradigms of research that tend to match your way of viewing the world. The particular research approach with which you will find greatest comfort, satisfaction, and meaning will depend on your personality, background, values, and on what you believe is important to know about the world around you.

HOW THEORETICAL FRAMEWORKS SHAPE INQUIRY QUESTIONS AND METHODS

This section demonstrates how specific theoretical frameworks help to shape the kind of research questions asked and the methods used. For comparisons, I focus on ethnography (interpretivism), critical ethnography (critical theory), and collaborative action research.

In 1992–1993, I lived for eight months in Costa Rica. For much of that time, I was in a small fishing village, working with a local environmental group. They were training young men and women as nature guides and working to educate national and international tourists as well as members of the broader community about the environments and cultures of the area. The organization was a grassroots group, developed by local people for local environmental efforts. It was headed by an indigenous man and drew members from all the ethnic and cultural groups in the area—African Caribbean, Indigenous, Hispanic, and European.

Through a mutual contact, I was introduced to the president of the environmental organization to discuss possibilities of my doing research with the group. He suggested that I draft a proposal for the group's board to discuss. The proposal was accepted and I rented a small house in the village. Within this one setting, my research could have taken a variety of forms.

I might have done conventional ethnography. After working with and hanging out with the group for a month or so, I began to see the leaders and activists of the group as "bridges" between several different cultural or value systems. In my journal, I was forming an ethnographic research statement: I wanted to understand (1) the motivations of and perceived rewards for those who give of themselves for a greater good; (2) the cultural and historical contexts that nurture or provoke such a gathering of varied, talented, committed individuals; and (3) the role of cross-cultural experiences in the philosophical orientations of the leaders/ activists.

For such a study, I would have developed criteria for selection of leaders/ activists, set up a series of interviews, and continued "hanging out" with the group, observing actions and interactions. To help in understanding the sociocultural context of the leaders, I may have set up interviews with family members and significant others. Eventually, I would analyze the interview and observation data for patterns and themes and write a descriptive account meant to contribute to the scholarly understanding of activists/leaders. But I did not do conventional ethnography, as much as those research questions interested me.

I might have done critical ethnography. Most of the inhabitants of the area were either African Caribbean in heritage or Indigenous. Although patterns of racial and ethnic oppression have taken different forms in Costa Rica than in the United States, both African Caribbean and the Indigenous suffer discrimination. While in the village, I began to hear stories about the ways outsiders (Costa Rican and foreign) were gaining access to land because the local people lacked legal title, in spite of traditional claims to the land.

I could have done research to understand local customs of land tenure and Costa Rican legislature regarding owning land. Then, I might have formed a critical ethnography research statement such as the following: I want to (1) uncover ways in which current systems of power and privilege (class, ethnicity, gender) allow locals to lose claim to their coastal and rain forest land and (2) work with local groups to develop strategies to retain control over their land. Research methods might include creating dialogue groups to discuss experiences with land tenure, pressures to sell land if title is held, and possible strategies to defend rights and retain land. I would act as a group facilitator and resource person, providing information about legalities where needed. My primary intent would be to help develop strategies and raise awareness of ways to challenge the ongoing loss of land. But I did not do critical ethnography.

Critical ethnography can be a kind of action research, but it isn't necessarily action research. Action research has at its essence the intent to change something, to solve some sort of problem, to take action. Through preliminary discussions with the environmental group, action research was the preferred inquiry mode. If I, with my skills as a researcher, was going to be involved with the group, they wanted me to use my abilities to help their organization in its efforts, not to do research on them for use elsewhere. And I wanted to be of use to the people with whom I was living and from whom I was learning. I described my role as that of a *volunteer researcher*.

We set up a series of meetings to discuss small-scale research projects that the board desired. I took on these projects, often in concert with another member or two. For example, as part of the educational mission of the group, they asked me to investigate the area's environmental and cultural history and diversity, paying specific attention to items that visitors often asked about, such as indigenous uses of the rainforest. Such projects allowed me to learn from others about the area and their lives, sponsored by the group's introductions. I accompanied locals as they demonstrated everyday work and hiked in the rainforest as they pointed out and discussed their relationship to specific flora and fauna. The resulting document was illustrated by a local artist and made available in both English and Spanish.

Another issue they asked me to assist with was determining how to prioritize program-related projects and manage time demands, since most members were not paid staff. After facilitating (and taking notes on) a series of discussions with the whole group, smaller groups, and individuals, I drafted a plan for the year that reflected people's interests, commitments, and possible schedules. The plan then went through several iterations with the group as a whole before being put into action.

As these examples show, research can take a variety of shapes within the same context. The possibilities can sometimes feel overwhelming. In the midst of critiques of fieldwork, some researchers have abandoned such research altogether, choosing to inquire into society and culture through a focus on their own experiences (autoethnography). Others emphasize how their interpretations are limited and work to present multiple ways of construing the research. Some involve themselves only in research that is developed with locals as co-researchers, addressing local concerns. Yet others defend the view that well-done research, no matter what the paradigm, can make a contribution and is a worthy enterprise. Your task is to figure out for yourself where you stand philosophically and politically on doing research. Your position will help you determine not only what you study but also how you design your study and what techniques or methods you use. Because this text focuses primarily on qualitative research within the interpretivist paradigm, a bit more introduction to interpretivist inquiry is presented in the remainder of this chapter.

INTERPRETIVIST TRADITIONS OF QUALITATIVE INQUIRY

> Novice researchers often get lost in the literature on interpretive research. It's conceptually dense, can be conceptually foreign, and has conflicting use of terminology.
>
> (Higgs and McAllister 2001, 34)

By this point, I assume you are not surprised by the proceeding quotation. Researchers differentiate among various types of interpretivist inquiry, but approaches are multiple and distinctions are not clear-cut. For example, you might call your research autoethnography, case study, conversation analysis, cognitive anthropology, critical ethnography, discourse analysis, educational connoisseurship, ethnography, ethnomethodology, ethnoscience, grounded theory, hermeneutics, heuristic inquiry, life history, narrative analysis, oral history, phenomenology, symbolic interactionism, and several other possibilities. Each approach carries with it philosophical assumptions, emphasizes certain foci (culture, language, etc.), is associated with particular disciplines (sociology, anthropology, psychology, etc.), and tends to rely upon select methods (in-depth interviews, cross-case analysis, etc.). Nonetheless, it may be best to think of the various approaches as orientations rather than distinct, separate categories, in that each approach primarily seeks to understand and describe social phenomena from perspectives of participants.

Because much of the information in this book is grounded in interpretivism, this section delves a bit into the history and complexity found within some aspects of the interpretivist paradigm. This discussion is not comprehensive; rather, it is provided to alert you to some of the variety within the interpretivist paradigm and to your need to seek out sources that can inform you on approaches of particular use to you for the questions you desire to ask. Of the many possible interpretivist methodologies, I briefly introduce five: ethnography, life history, grounded theory, case study, and action research. They are presented to demonstrate ways each mode differs and yet makes use of some of the same methods (in-depth interviews, participant-observation, document collection) discussed in this book.

Ethnography

> "Sciences and their societies . . . co-constructed each other"
>
> (Harding 1998, 2)

Through my anthropological background and interests, the interpretivist tradition with which I am most familiar is *ethnography*, an approach widely used in other disciplines as well, particularly in applied fields such as education and nursing. Since I refer to ethnographic methods throughout the text, I discuss it more fully than other interpretivist methodologies. I also provide more of a historical context for the ways in which ethnography has been and continues to be used so that you can better understand and consider critiques of ethnography at home and around the world.

Ethnography comes from the Greek *ethnos*, meaning a people or cultural group, and *graphic*, meaning to describe. *Ethnographic* literally means to describe a people or cultural group. Using *culture* as the theoretical framework for studying and describing a group, ethnography's origins are associated with anthropology and, to some extent, with sociology. Although social scientists do not necessarily agree on what culture is, they do see it as the organizing principle for doing ethnography. Some, for example, focus on shared meanings within a group while others focus on what one needs to know to behave appropriately in some context. Through long-term immersion in the field, collecting data primarily by participant-observation and interviewing, the researcher develops the "thick description" (Geertz 1973) needed for getting at how people within a cultural group construct and share meaning.

Ethnography's Historical Context.   Many forms of Western science expanded and advanced through colonialism. Colonial interests, for example, led to a need for navigation knowledge, and the science of cartography developed. As colonization put explorers, bureaucrats, and settlers in contact with new diseases, the science of tropical medicine grew. Agricultural knowledge expanded because of colonists' exposure to new plants such as maize, potatoes, and sugar cane. These new sciences benefited Europeans, contributing to higher standards of living in the home countries. While colonialists appropriated some local knowledge such as tobacco cultivation, they imposed their own ways of knowing upon the people they subjugated. As they destroyed local industries, trades, and cultural traditions, they effectively slowed the growth of non-Western sciences (Harding 1998).

Throughout the colonial period, explorers, missionaries, and colonial administrators wrote reports and descriptions of people encountered, but they were more interested in how to best exploit the new territories and the labor of the people than in describing their ways of life. Most reports "were written from the perspective of, or by the representatives of, a conquering civilization, confident in its mission to civilize the world" (Vidich and Lyman 2000, 41).

During the later part of the Victorian era (late 1800s), anthropology developed as a discipline. In this "armchair anthropology" period, scholars compiled descriptions of people's cultures through information from colonial reports, missionaries, and adventurer-scholars. Influenced by Darwin's publication *On the Origin of Species* in 1859, these early anthropologists tended to embrace a theory of social evolution. This theory posited a continuum of societal development from "primitive" to "civilized." A major task of anthropologists was to collect and compare enough information so that they could determine the indicators for placing people and their societies at different stages along the societal development continuum. Unsurprisingly, Europe was the standard for "civilization" and this anthropological "science" was often used to further racist, Eurocentric causes (Vidich and Lyman 2000).

The "Classic Anthropology" period began in the 1920s, after Bronislaw Malinowski carried out long-term fieldwork (which he called *ethnography*) in New Guinea and the Trobriand Islands between 1914 and 1918. Fieldwork soon became associated with anthropological research. Major scholars of the early part of this period include A. L. Kroeber, Margaret Mead, and Ruth Benedict in the United States and Malinowski and Alfred Radcliffe-Brown in England. Since much of the world was colonized in the first half of the twentieth century, the work of anthropologists was bound up with the colonial enterprise as young people from Europe and the United States set off to study "natives" or "tribals," often in areas of the world remote to them. Their attitudes towards the role of colonialism varied widely. Some anthropologists supported cultural and political self-determination, while others saw assimilation as the direction of the inevitable future if those who had been colonized hoped to survive in a modernizing world. On the one hand, a number of horror stories can be told of anthropology's role in colonization. On the other hand, the contributions of some anthropologists in refuting racist theories, in affirming non-Western values, and in opposing Western national development models also should be recognized (Benthall 1995).

By the end of World War II and the cessation of colonial control in much of the world, anthropologists had abandoned the theory of social evolution. The discipline suffered, however, from a collective guilt over its connection to colonialism. Because of this guilt and, most likely, because of less access to ex-colonial countries, many anthropologists began studying their own people, often looking for the "exotic" or "marginal" in their own societies, as a group of sociologists from the University of Chicago were already doing.

Referred to as the *Chicago School*, these sociologists from the University of Chicago undertook what they simply called *fieldwork* (Tesch 1990). Influenced by British social anthropology, they began applying participant-observation techniques to the study of groups within their own communities. Robert Park and Ernest Burgess were two of the influential sociologists guiding the Chicago School movement, which attracted a number of young sociologists between 1920 and 1960. Viewing Chicago as their laboratory, these young sociologists conducted urban fieldwork focused on individuals, groups, and organizations and wrote ethnographic texts now considered classics, including Anderson's *The Hobo,* 1923; Cressey's *The Taxi-Dance Hall,* 1932; Shaw's *The Jack Roller,* 1930; and Zorbaugh's *The Gold Coast and the Slum,* 1929.

Current Ethnography.   Not only have the social context and times changed for ethnographers, but also who ethnographers are has changed (Tedlock 2000). Rather than men, many ethnographers tend to be women; rather than from primarily privileged classes, they come from many different socioeconomic, ethnic, gay and lesbian, and non-Western groups. Along with the diversity in researchers, the reasons for doing ethnography are many. The conversations and challenges within anthropology, particularly in addressing its historical associations with colonialism, have contributed to thoughts and debates within interpretive, critical, and poststructural paradigms. For example, former subjects of colonization not only have critiqued what was written about their cultures, but also have become ethnographers and taken up representing themselves in ways that reveal the assumptions of the gaze from outside, bringing attention to issues of interpretation and representation. Anthropologists and ethnographers have been at the forefront of discussions about how representations are all fictions of sorts, produced by the experiences and theoretical lenses of the authors, conventions of scholarly rhetoric, types of field relationships, and so forth.

Perhaps because ethnography was one of the early qualitative research methodologies, the methods of participant-observation and in-depth interviewing are often referred to as ethnographic field methods whether or not one is doing ethnography. I tend to adopt this broad-brush use of the term. Throughout the book, I use *ethnographic* somewhat interchangeably with both *interpretivist* and *qualitative* to refer to practices that seek to interpret people's constructions of reality and identify uniqueness and patterns in their perspectives and behaviors.

Life History

> One may merely know that no one is alone and hope that a singular story, as every true story is singular, will in the magic way of some things apply, connect, resonate, touch a major chord.
>
> (Wolff 1981, 72)

In life history research (also sometimes referred to as *life story, oral history, biography,* or *narrative research,* although distinctions can be made among these terms), the researcher conducts a series of interviews to create a narrative of a life or lives. This life is sometimes used as a way of discussing a whole culture or group. For example, Oscar Lewis's work in Mexico tended to be cultural portrayals through focusing on the lives of members of one family (Tedlock 2000). Sometimes the life story is used more to illustrate perceptions and effects of particular historical events, as Linden (1993) does in her work with women reflecting on the Holocaust. The project can also be biographic, with researchers seeking some foci for interpretations, such as inquiring into key incidents that shaped the creative life of artists or that contributed to identity formation of activists.

A good life history illustrates the uniqueness, dilemmas, and complexities of a person in such a way that it causes readers to reflect upon themselves and to bring their own situations and questions to the story. In some cases, the whole research project focuses on one person and the researcher carries out many interviews over time with that person (see Behar 1993; Shostak 1981; Teran 2002). In other cases, life stories are focused vignettes, exemplary of particular perspectives, incidents, or interactions. The researcher may interview several people and compile shorter life stories as chapters in a text (see Bateson 1990; Linden 1993; Myerhoff 1979).

Life history researchers draw upon many of the same data sources as the ethnographer—interviews, personal letters or diaries, and other documents and archives. Although less intensely used than in ethnography, they also employ participant observation to note context-setting details and to better interpret meanings of interviewees' words. In recent years, interest in linking the biographical with social theory has led to the growth in popularity of *narrative analysis.* Narrative analysis extends the idea of analyzing written text to that of viewing narrations as text, whether in naturally occurring conversations or in interviews. These spoken texts are recorded and analyzed for how they are told (conventions of beginning, middle, end, plot, rhetoric, pauses, overlaps in talk, nuances of speech, etc.) as well as for what they say about the social life and cultures of which the narrators are a part (see Gubrium and Holstein's 2009 text *Analyzing Narrative Reality*).

The representation of the life is often more holistic and embodied than writing in ethnographic reports, although the life history researcher may use some of the same analytical tools. As with ethnography, interpretations go beyond the individual: Because researchers "assume that the subjective world of experience is at once intersubjectively constituted, life-history approaches seek to interrelate the private and the public, the personal and the social" (Schwandt 2007, 22).

A form of life history research that could be classified in the critical paradigm is the *testimonio*. Developed in large part in Latin America, the *testimonio* is often used to tell a story of social marginalization or oppression (Tierney 2000). It differs from traditional procedures for doing life history in that "the testimonio is developed by the one who testifies in the hope that his or her life's story will move the reader to action in concert with the group with which the testifier identifies" (Tierney 2000, 540). A testimonio sometimes results from collaborative work. For example, *Let Me Speak! Testimony of Domitila, a Woman of the Bolivian Mines* (Barrios de Chungara with Viezzer, 1978) was written after Moema Viezzer heard Domitila Barrios de Chungara speak at a political event. Viezzer conducted numerous interviews with Barrios de Chungara and they then organized and revised the work together.

Grounded Theory

Anselm Strauss and Barney Glaser (1967) receive credit as the founders of grounded theory research. Their work has been extended by Strauss and Corbin (1998) and Charmaz (2002), in particular. Grounded theory is not a theory in itself, but a methodology for developing theory that is "grounded" in data. The purpose of this research approach is to "demonstrate relations between conceptual categories and to specify the conditions under which theoretical relationships emerge, change, or are maintained" (Charmaz 2002, 675). Grounded theory work involves specific procedures for data collection and analysis that include continual data sampling, coding, categorizing, and comparing in order to generate theory about social phenomena. In very simplified terms, the grounded theorist collects data (through interviews and observations) on a topic, analyzes that data for conceptual categories, links the categories into a tentative theory, and then collects more data to see how the theory fits. This process repeats and continues with the researcher further developing conceptual categories and modifying the theory with each new set of data. The developing theory itself suggests different settings or people to sample (referred to as *theoretical sampling*) in order to compare and contrast aspects of the theory. Grounded theory researchers use many of the tools of the ethnographer to collect their data, but they select their cases, code, compare, and test emergent concepts in specialized ways.

Grounded theory helped to move social science research away from positivism and supported qualitative research methods at a time when many in academe endorsed quantitative methods. Terms, concepts, and procedures that originated in grounded theory (such as *theoretical sampling* or *data saturation*) often are used by researchers employing methodologies other than grounded theory. A problem arises, however, when researchers claim to be doing grounded theory or to have developed "grounded theory," but they are merely using such words because they appeal to committee members or proposal reviewers with positivists leanings. Before calling your research *grounded theory*, learn more about it. Some books to begin with include Glaser and Strauss's *The Discovery of Grounded Theory* (1967), Glaser's *Theoretical Sensitivity* (1978), and Strauss and Corbin's *Grounded Theory in Practice* (1997).

Case Study

Case study has been used to mean different things in different disciplines. Case studies in the Harvard Business School are created as pedagogical tools for discussion in business classes. In qualitative inquiry, case study research refers to the intensive study of a case, but what a "case" means can vary, from one person to a village or from an event to a set of procedures such as the implementation of a particular program. The common denominator is that each—the person, the village, the event, the program—is a *bounded* integrated system with working parts (Stake 1995). Defining something as "bounded" often remains ambiguous, though, with the researcher deciding what will and will not be included within the boundaries. The study of the case, however defined, tends to involve in-depth and often longitudinal examination with data gathered through participant observation, in-depth interviewing, and document collection and analysis. The write-up is often descriptive and holistic, rather than thematic, although comparisons of more than one case frequently lend themselves to a search for patterns.

Stake (2000, 437) differentiates three types of case studies: intrinsic, instrumental, and collective. The intrinsic case study contributes to better understanding of that particular case such as of a specific child diagnosed with attention-deficit/hyperactivity disorder (ADHD). An instrumental case study refers to studying a particular case to "provide insight into an issue or to redraw a generalization" such as focusing on the child diagnosed with ADHD to provide insight into how schooling and the labeling of ADHD interact. When the instrumental case study involves looking at several cases—at several children diagnosed with ADHD, it becomes a "collective case study," and allows investigation of "a phenomenon, population, or general condition."

Although some see case study as a research strategy, Stake (2000, 435) observes that "case study is not a methodological choice but a choice of what is to be studied." Various methods and methodologies can be employed to do case study research, including quantitative methods. But, as Schram (2006, 107) reminds us, "Whether you consider case study as a way of conceptualizing human social behavior or merely as a way of encapsulating it, its strategic value lies in its ability to draw attention to what can be learned from the single case." You focus on the complexity within the case, on its uniqueness, and its linkages to the social context of which it is a part.

Action Research

In general, as has been discussed, particular methodologies (i.e., experimental, narrative analysis, critical ethnography) are associated with specific research paradigms. It's important to remember, however, that these are permeable categories. Paradigmatic thought and categorization has changed in response to historical moments and to previous ways of thinking about the world and knowledge. Similarly, methodologies are not stable entities, and the thinking and procedures associated with them change over time, across disciplines, and, sometimes, with locations. Thus, the same label might indicate several different ways of going about doing research, depending upon the times and/or practitioners. Action research is a good example.

Action research grew out of the work of Kurt Lewin in the mid-1900s. His model of action research was grounded in the positivist paradigm with clear separation between the researcher and the researched and with cycles of discovery, intervention, and evaluation (Bryant 1996). It was used particularly in industry research as ways to make businesses more efficient.

Action research has experienced popularity again, particularly in education, as a way to improve practice. Based in interpretivism, however, the cycles of research have evolved to observing, reflecting, and acting (Kemmis and McTaggart 1988; Stringer 1999), using primarily qualitative interviews and observations, as well as surveys and quantifiable data. During the reflection phase, the researcher or co-researchers interpret the data and communicate the multiple viewpoints to those with a stake in the process (the *stakeholders*). This is followed by discussions of what actions need to be taken and then, the action phase that involves planning, implementation, and evaluation.

In this form of action research, the researcher works with others as agents of change. Stringer (1999) elaborates on what he calls community-based action research which assists a group, community, or organization in defining a problem; better understanding the situation; and then in resolving their problems. The research process is collaborative and inclusive of all major stakeholders with the researcher acting as a facilitator who keeps the research cycles moving.

Participatory action research (PAR) sounds as though it could be another term for community-based action research, and, indeed, some use it this way, but PAR is usually linked to the theories and work of Brazilian activist and educator Paolo Freire (1970/2000). Evolving since the early 1970s, PAR is associated with critical theory in that it is action research committed to social transformation through active involvement of marginalized or disfranchised groups. PAR includes the objective of *concientization* or consciousness-raising in that the group, as a whole, works to generate and analyze information that helps to transform the thinking and realities of that group (Kindon 2005).

When the primary researcher/facilitator is an outsider to the community or organization, difficulties in carrying out action research are often associated with defining the research focus, creating action groups where no formal organization exists, and knowing when and how to leave or end the research project. The problems and strengths associated with action research (whether interpretive or critical) suggests that the concept of practitioners as researchers (e.g., teachers, nurses, social workers) who investigate, with others in their community, their own "backyard" carries much potential. Insiders who couple research theories and techniques with an action-oriented mode can develop collaborative, reflective data collecting and analysis procedures for their own practices and thereby contribute to the sociopolitical context in which they dwell.

Possibilities of Interpretivist Inquiry

In practice, neither research paradigms nor methodologies are as neatly segregated as they might appear by the headings in this chapter. Think of them as philosophies in dialogue with each other and with prevailing intellectual and cultural thought. Each paradigm has influenced and will continue to affect the theories and approaches in others. Each has different strengths, challenges, and possibilities. I end this section with a list of some of the possible contributions associated with doing research within interpretivist qualitative traditions:

- From what you see and hear, you interpret others' perspectives of some aspect of the world, contributing to the multiplicity of voices and visions and the plurality of our knowing.
- The act of listening can be, in itself, a radical action when you use your inquiry to witness the stories and lives of those whose voices are ignored or silenced.
- Your interpretations can point out some significance or meaning in the world that through your representations, can inspire others to perceive, believe, or act in different ways.
- Interpretive inquiry attunes your senses, your eyes and ears in particular, to the richness of the lives around you, to the complexities and particularities of people's actions and words which you communicate to others. This way of being also can become part of who you are beyond your researcher self.
- Seeking to interpret a context not your own can work to reveal you to yourself. You will more easily see your own assumptions, stereotypes, and subjectivities.
- Ideally, you are researching in situations where you can take on Maria Lugones notion of being *playful:* "to be playful means that one is free to not worry about competence and to abandon competition and self-importance" (as quoted in Madison 2005, 101). Without attaching expectations, you give of yourself as you take delight in learning about those around you and yourself. In the process, you develop meaningful relationships.

WHAT IS TO COME

After collecting data for a semester, Susan, an environmental science master's student, stated, "I'm ready to throw the whole project out because I've come up with so many new questions. This process has blown me away. I feel like I need to go back and begin all over again." Susan is right. You know best what you should look for, what questions you should ask, and what methods you should use at the end of your study. The process of getting to that end, however, takes you through a terrain that eventually becomes clearer overall, while growing more dense in detail. The combination of your own inquiry, field log, and reading of this text and others should help you to grasp the phenomenon of your research with the clearer understanding and sense of complexity that are the gifts of qualitative inquiry.

The open, emergent nature of qualitative inquiry means a lack of standardization; there are no clear criteria to package into neat research steps. The openness sets the stage for understanding as well as for ambiguity that can engender a sometimes overwhelming sense of anxiety: "Who else should I be seeing?" "What else should I be asking?" "How can I ever assemble all of the pieces into something meaningful?" The openness allows the researcher to approach the inherent intricacies of social interaction, to honor complexity, and to respect it in its own right. As Eisner (1981, 9) states, "To know a rose by its Latin name and yet to miss its fragrance is to miss much of the rose's meaning."

This chapter has introduced you to some of the philosophical and theoretical contexts of qualitative research. The chapters to come focus more on process—on some methods used in qualitative inquiry. They take you through procedures of research design, data collection, data analysis, and writing, as well as into discussions of reflexivity and ethics. Like learning to paint or swim, you will gain skills that can be enhanced only through practice. Wolcott (2001, 7) states, "Qualitative approaches beckon because they appear natural, straight-forward, even 'obvious,' and thus easy to accomplish. Were it not for the complexity of conceptualizing a qualitative study, conducting the research, analyzing it, and writing it up, perhaps they would be." It is to the complexity of conceptualizing the studies that we now turn.

RECOMMENDED READINGS

Historical, Theoretical, and Philosophical Introductions to Research Paradigms and Methodologies
Crotty, M. 1998. *The foundations of social research.* Thousand Oaks, CA: Sage.
Prasad, P. 2005. *Crafting qualitative research: Working in the postpositivist traditions.* Armonk, NY: M. E. Sharpe.
Willis, J. 2007. *Foundations of qualitative research.* Thousand Oaks, CA: Sage.

Interpretivist and Action Research
Cresswell, J. 2007. *Qualitative Inquiry and Research Design,* 2nd ed. Thousand Oaks, CA: Sage.
Patton, M. Q. 2002. *Qualitative Research & Evaluation Methods,* 3rd ed. Thousand Oaks, CA: Sage.
Stringer, E. 2007. *Action Research,* 3rd ed. Thousand Oaks, CA: Sage.

Critical and Feminist Qualitative Inquiry
Hesse-Biber, S. N. (Ed.). 2007. *Handbook of Feminist Research: Theory and Praxis.* Thousand Oaks, CA: Sage.
Madison, D. S. (2005). *Critical Ethnography: Method, Ethics, and Performance.* Thousand Oaks, CA: Sage.
Thomas, J. (1993). *Doing Critical Ethnography.* Newbury Park, CA: Sage.

Poststructuralist, Postcolonial Inquiry
Foucault, M. (1979). *Discipline and Punish: The Birth of the Prison* (A. Sheridan, trans.). New York: Vintage Books. (Original work published 1975.)
Lyotard, J.-G. (1984/1979). *The Postmodern Condition: A Report on Knowledge* (G. Bennington & B. Massumi, trans.). Minneapolis: University of Minnesota Press.
Said, E. (1978). *Orientalism.* New York: Vintage.

EXERCISES

1. Broaden your understanding of critical, feminist, poststructural, and postcolonial approaches to qualitative inquiry. Individually or in small groups, do some more reading on the theories and philosophies associated with one of these approaches. Share what you learn with the class.

2. Broaden your understanding of the diversity within the interpretivist qualitative paradigm. Individually or in small groups, choose an interpretivist research approach other than ethnography (such as phenomenology, narrative analysis, symbolic interactionism, etc.) and do some reading on that approach. Share your understandings with the class.

ENDNOTE

1. Michael Quinn Patton has received a number of awards for his work in evaluation and sociology. He is author of many evaluation and research books, including *Qualitative Research and Evaluation Methods*, an excellent resource and guide for qualitative research.

CHAPTER 2

Prestudy Tasks: Doing What Is Good for You

Change permeated my pilot project. I changed focus, questions and sampling strategies. I changed the way I framed, worded and ordered questions, how I thought about my topic and the motivating force behind it. And I changed the theoretical lens I used to view my research, eventually changing it back again.

(Tabitha, UVM student)

In late 1999, I was planning to go to Mexico for a sabbatical year of research. Having taken students to Oaxaca for several years, I knew broadly "where" I wanted to do research (the state of Oaxaca), vaguely "what" (community grassroots organizing and nonformal education), and generally "how" (a collaborative undertaking). Working on the sabbatical proposal helped me think through questions of research design and to focus the study. In introducing the context to the study, I wrote:

> In *Grassroots Post-Modernism*, Esteva and Prakash (1998) urge local thinking and action. They illustrate how the strength of grassroots efforts lies in community. Their book is ultimately about how some communities in the "Two-thirds World" (a term they offer as replacement for "Third World") have resisted Western notions of "development" and worked to form culturally appropriate solutions to their own problems. In presenting examples from both Mexico and India, Esteva and Prakash challenge readers to examine their assumptions of the "good life" and to reconsider what it means to be "developed."

This helped me to begin to set a theoretical context for my proposed work (fleshed out in the literature review), and also to focus in on the notion of "culturally-appropriate solutions" as I struggled to create a research question based upon both my interests and those of Esteva with whom I had been discussing research plans. I developed three questions:

1. In what ways do various grassroots projects (whether an iguana farm or development of school texts in indigenous languages) reflect local knowledge and customs?

2. In what ways do the decision-making processes and project implementation procedures reflect local knowledge and customs?
3. What philosophical (economic/sociopolitical) challenges do local grassroots efforts raise for dominant (Western, capitalist, individualist, etc.) ideologies?

I continued by introducing Esteva and describing how our conversations had set the stage for the work:

> Esteva will be my collaborator in the sense that I am "volunteering" to work with him to do research that is of use to him and the communities with which he works. I cannot do this research without his direction and without his introduction to the various communities where I will spend time documenting grassroots efforts.

Exactly which communities and how many was left undetermined. Instead, I indicated a minimum number:

> **SITES AND PARTICIPANTS**
> Research sites will be various indigenous communities within the state of Oaxaca where grassroots organizations are involved in addressing local issues in innovative ways. Esteva and his colleagues who live and work with communities throughout southern Mexico will identify these sites. The number of sites studied will depend upon access and the amount of time needed at each site . . . At the minimum, I expect to be involved with six different communities.

The proposal continued, describing data gathering methods, data analysis techniques, and possible products and contributions of the research. As I revisit the proposal, I see many ways in which the plan changed as the year unfolded. I began working with a youth group that I had met previously through Esteva and his programs for our students. The group was assisting other youth groups to find ways to stay in their home communities rather than having to migrate for work. Together we engaged in action research to look at what was happening with various youth groups and to suggest ways each could be better supported. Through this work, I interacted with young people from 10 different communities, and, ultimately, was able to address each of the research questions. Would all this have happened anyway, without the proposal? Perhaps. Even with the proposal, however, I felt as though I were flailing around, trying to find firm research ground the first several months in Oaxaca. Without the proposal and a sense of direction, I would have floundered more.

The sections of this chapter raise issues for discussion in preparing the research proposal. Researchers make numerous decisions before they begin fieldwork. These decisions generally are embodied in a research proposal prepared for a thesis or dissertation committee or a funding agency. Appendix A may assist in your work on a proposal. A note of caution is needed here: The decisions you make will be linked to the kind of qualitative research you choose to do. For example, if doing grounded theory research your sampling strategies will be different than if choosing critical theory participatory research. The purpose of this chapter is to alert you to the general kinds of decisions you will want to make as you prepare to move into the field. The specific choices you make will depend upon various factors, including your methodological choice.

Start getting used to writing in your research journal now. Use it at this stage in your research to generate and keep track of your thoughts and ideas about what it is you want to do. Such notes are often referred to as research memos or "memos to yourself." They are writings that you do to help you think, to produce new ideas, and work through ideas. They are not meant for anyone other than for yourself. Lots of the things you write in your research journal will not find their way into the proposal or final project, but these writings help you get to that proposal and final project and are often useful when you do begin the more formal writing.

As you work on crafting your study, you will find helpful Thomas Schram's (2006) text *Conceptualizing and Proposing Qualitative Research* and Joseph Maxwell's (2005) text *Qualitative Research Design: An Interactive Approach*. Schram's book will help you think through your theoretical and philosophical approaches and to see how these perspectives interact with the research methods you choose. Maxwell's text helps you to create a well-designed study and is full of useful exercises. These books complement and extend the information you will find in this chapter.

THE RESEARCH TOPIC

The first research decision is to determine what you want to study. Unless you are working on a project conceptualized by someone else, you must figure out which issues, uncertainties, dilemmas, or paradoxes intrigue you. Your passion for your chosen topic will be a motivating factor throughout the various research aspects, some of which are intrinsically more interesting than others. You tap into your subjectivity, of which passion is a part, to find topics appropriate to your interests. The topic, however, should not be so personal that it is of little interest to anyone else; nor, as Douglas (1976) warns, should it be in an area where you have major emotional worries. You must be able to distinguish the line between your passion to understand some phenomenon and your over involvement in very personal issues that need resolution.

Distinguishing the difference between a topic for research and one for therapy is not always easy. For example, one student, who was also an instructor in a small community college, was about to begin a research class when he received word that his teaching contract was not renewed. Understandably, he was angry and disturbed. Consumed with thoughts on this matter, he decided that for his research project he would interview people at his institution to develop a better understanding of why he was dismissed. The class convinced him not only that such an investigation would be limited in scope, but also that he was unlikely to get honest and complete answers from interviewees. In the end, he explored another interest: attitudes of prison guards toward the private tutoring of inmates, a topic that, as he gathered and analyzed his data, brimmed with fascinating possibilities for continued study.

Asking yourself how your proposed research intersects with your life history and whether you are setting out to prove something that you already believe to be true helps to test your emotional attachment to particular outcomes. Ken, an elementary school principal who had held several different principalships, wanted to investigate the relationship of job stress to administrative turnover. Reflecting on the role of subjectivity in his research, Ken wrote:

> My topic is perfect, I thought. The turnover rate for school administrators is incredible, I know the subject firsthand, I have dozens of contacts in the field, and stress is on everybody's agenda, both public and private sector.
>
> So what's the problem? I care too passionately about the results. I desperately want the study to prove that school boards and superintendents should show some compassion for building administrators. I want taxpayers to recognize the limitations of personnel, resources, and supplies, which make the job of principal so frustrating. I want parents to see that a partnership between school and home is in the best interests of the children. I want to prove that the narrow-minded bigots who persecuted, criticized, harassed, and hounded me were wrong. This is clearly no way to begin a study.
>
> Interestingly, however, I did not realize the full extent of my personal prejudices until I presented my initial ideas to the qualitative methods class. I was angered and shocked to be accused of having an ax to grind—of having reached my conclusions before I began my research. I was particularly angry because I recognized that they were right.

Ken wanted to justify his own experience. Although he needed to be interested in his research topic, his emotional attachment precluded the open, exploratory learner's attitude that is necessary for good data collection and analysis.

Emotional attachment may manifest itself in other ways. If the very thought of approaching your research participants causes severe anxiety attacks, then you should ask yourself why. Debbie, a special education teacher, new to her school and district, was feeling uncomfortable when designing a project that involved interviewing administrators and supervisors. Finally, she realized that she was threatened by the thought of exposing herself to her bosses in her novice researcher role. She considered alternatives, shifted her focus, and set up a study that required obtaining data from teachers rather than from administrators.

Not everyone works effectively under the same conditions. If you are overly intimidated by the thought of going into the field, then consider reshaping your study in a more inviting way. Some of your intimidation may be the result of feelings or problems that you need to overcome; others may represent feelings and problems beyond your capacity to remedy. The qualitative inquiry process, by nature, is replete with anxiety-producing occasions without the researcher's unwittingly setting up more.

Practical issues such as time and money must also be considered. The conceived study may be appropriate in academic terms but impossible to conduct given practical limitations. Do not begin with a topic so vast in scope that you could never reasonably afford the time or money to complete it.

Although the planned scope for a research topic should be realistic, neither too broad nor too narrow, the researcher cannot always know the ideal scope until data collection is underway. For example, Purvis (1985) originally planned historical research to look at all forms of adult education provisions for working-class women in nineteenth-century England. As she collected and examined documents, however, she realized she had to narrow her study, but how she should focus her research was unclear. Should she investigate forms of adult education provided by the middle class, or types of adult education organized by working-class women themselves? Should she look at all forms of adult education, or concentrate on specific areas? Should she limit her inquiry to education in rural areas or in urban areas, or should she address regional differences? Purvis's range of choices suggests the alternatives available as you consider a research focus; you will find good arguments for supporting many different focuses within the same general area of study. Reading related literature and theory facilitates developing the research focus. It is part of getting started.

REVIEW OF LITERATURE

> Preconceived ideas are pernicious in any scientific work, but foreshadowed problems are the main endowment of a scientific thinker, and these problems are first revealed to the observer by his theoretical studies.
>
> (Malinowski 1922, 9)

Knowledge of associated literature will help you to judge whether your research plans go beyond existing findings and theories and may thereby contribute to your field of study. In the past, some qualitative researchers argued against reviewing literature until after data collection had begun, for fear that the conceptual frameworks, research designs, techniques, and theories of others would unduly influence the researcher. Most researchers today agree that literature should be read throughout the research process, including a thorough search before data collection begins. This perspective acknowledges that we never enter into research as a "blank slate," but rather carry with us guiding theories and assumptions, even if not conscious of them.

Reading about the studies of others in a way that is useful to your work requires a particular frame of mind. First, collect, scan, and read literature to verify that you have chosen a justifiable topic. For example, the many dissertation studies that have investigated why parents send their children to fundamentalist Christian schools have identified and discussed a range of explanations. Another study on this topic, even in a state where no such studies have taken place, most likely, would contribute little more of interest. Try to warrant your own project on the basis of what has been done and what has not been done.

Second, use relevant literature to help find focus for your topic. When you find an article that applies to your area of interest, study the references carefully and seek out the ones that may inform you more. Existing studies show what is known about a general area of inquiry and what is missing. A review of Christian school literature suggests that very little is known about the lives of adults who as children attended a fundamentalist Christian school. To what extent do they live within the boundaries of the doctrine espoused by their schools? Someone interested in Christian schooling could make a significant contribution by studying this population.

Third, literature can help to inform your research design and interview questions. Read critically and learn from the successes and failures of other researchers investigating similar phenomena. Did the researcher spend enough time interviewing each participant to obtain more than surface responses? Were the questions asked of a usefully varied group of people? What questions were not asked at all? What situations were (and were not) observed? What directions for future studies did researchers recommend?

Fourth, remember that in qualitative inquiry reviewing literature is an ongoing process that cannot be completed before data collection and analysis. As you reflect upon the data you collect, you will realize the need to review previously unexamined literature of both substantive and theoretical nature. For example, before I began fieldwork in the Caribbean (Glesne 1985), I reviewed rural development literature in addition to agricultural and educational studies and documents pertaining to the eastern Caribbean. During my time in the field, but particularly after focused time on data analysis, I began to read extensively about dependency theory, which explained economic and power relationships between nation states. Dependency theory became central to my data analysis and discussion, while rural development literature receded, used primarily to contrast a dominant Western perspective of development with that of various Latin American scholars at the time. Regard reviewing literature in interactive terms. You can learn different things from the work of others depending on what you already have learned and what you need to know. You may find yourself both dismayed and pleased to benefit later from material read earlier but overlooked because you lacked the experience to recognize it as beneficial.

Fifth, in conducting your literature search, cast a wide net. Do not confine yourself to your topic, nor to your discipline. If, for instance, your topic involves the use of French in U.S. schools near the border with Quebec, then you will want to collect literature on schooling and bilingualism in general. Delamont (1992) suggests reading for contrast. That is, if you are interested in women in science, then you might also want to read about men in predominantly female professions such as nursing to help generate questions for your study. Sociologists, anthropologists, psychologists, and educators often write on the same topics, but from different perspectives. Try to seek sources from all possible disciplines.

You should not, however, let the widening circles of possibly applicable literature preclude your entry into the field. Remember that data collection and data analysis will also inform your literature search. Ernie was preparing to collect data on professionalization in the field of physical therapy. He reflected on his dance with literature:

> First of all, I needed to define what professionalization was. Then I felt the need to read enough sociology to understand how people achieved it, which got me into the field of professional socialization. Then if you do achieve it and act it out, you are into the area of professional power and influence. After reading literature about that, I thought I needed to understand professional ethics and how that linked with the idea of the development of community. Finally, I realized that if I didn't go out to the field, I'd spend the rest of my life saying, "Next month, I'll be ready."

Remember that being ready to go to the field is often a state of mind, affected by, but not necessarily related to, having completed the preliminaries.

After you have collected and read a variety of works on your topic, you usually need to write a literature review or conceptual context for your proposal. In doing so, organize the review around understandings that come from investigating specific questions of studies and theory that relate to your topic. A literature review is not a summary of various studies, but rather an integration of reviewed sources around particular trends and themes. Point out gaps in the literature that relate to your area of interest, thereby using the literature to establish need for more or different kinds of studies. And quote sparingly—when something is said uniquely and when how it is said contributes to the text.

Creswell (1998) suggests creating a diagram as a visual picture of the literature to help organize the review and to figure out how one's own study relates to the larger body of literature. For example, Susan, a student in natural resources, had received the opportunity to teach environmental science to a group of middle school students. She decided to do *teacher research*, reflecting upon what happened in her own class over a semester to understand how integrating the arts into the curriculum assists students in learning environmental science. Exhibit 2.1 is a beginning visual of the relationship of her research interests to the literature.

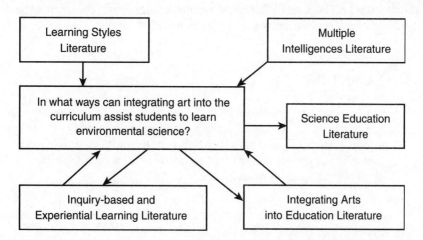

EXHIBIT 2.1   Relating Study Interests to Literature Through a Diagram.

Susan felt she needed to read literature regarding learning styles, multiple intelligences, inquiry-based learning, experiential learning, and integrating arts into education curriculum in order to help her plan and analyze her study. In turn, she hoped her study would contribute to the literature on inquiry-based and experiential learning, integrating arts into education curriculum, and, in particular, to science education literature. She entered into an intense period of reading and noting, aware that some areas might become more important than others and that she may realize the need to look at yet other areas of literature.

It may be useful to think about creating the "conceptual context" for your study, rather than doing a "review of literature" (Schram 2006; Maxwell 2005). This keeps the focus on your proposed work, instead of becoming a task in which you feel the need to touch upon every study somewhat related to your work. It may also help you to think more broadly and more focused at the same time. You think broadly about how your work fits into larger theories or significant ideas. And you think more specifically about the possible significance of what you want to research and how. By thinking about "concepts" that inform your work, you create a useful organizational schema into which you can integrate theories and perspectives from multiple disciplines and perspectives (Schram 2006).

Some novice qualitative researchers assume that when they have written their literature review or conceptual context for their proposal, they can check off one chapter of the dissertation from their "to do" list. Literature reviewed as a prestudy task often finds its way into the final write-up, but not usually as a chapter in itself. As indicated earlier, expect to read articles, reports, and books throughout the research process. Even with all these additional resources, a chapter titled, "Review of the Literature" is not necessarily appropriate. Wolcott (1990) states that he expects his students to know the literature related to their topics, but he does not want them "to lump (dump?) it all into a chapter that remains unconnected to the rest of the study" (17). He suggests incorporating literature throughout the telling of the story: "Ordinarily this calls for introducing related research toward the end of a study rather than at the beginning, except for the necessary 'nesting' of the problem in the introduction" (17).

THEORETICAL CONTEXT

I find it instructive that the word "theory" comes from the same Greek root as the word "theatre." A tragedy or comedy is, after all, no less an inquiry into reality, no less a distillation of perceptions and experiences, than a hypothesis or theory that undertakes to account for the variable incidences of murder or marriage.

(Nisbet 1976, 12)

. . . distinguish between having a grip and being in the grip of existing theories . . .

(Schram 2006, 61)

Social scientists define theory in different ways. A prevalent definition comes from Homans, paraphrased by Denzin (1989a, 49): "Theory refers to a set of propositions that are interrelated in an ordered fashion such that some may be deducible from others, thus permitting an explanation to be developed for the phenomenon under consideration." The ultimate goal of this form of theorizing is to develop universal laws of human behavior and societal functioning as found in theories of kinship, behavior modification, and economic development.

Glaser and Strauss (1967) took issue with the conventional deductive approach to research and focused on verification for theory development. In *The Discovery of Grounded Theory,* they proposed an inductive strategy whereby the researcher discovers concepts and hypotheses through constant comparative analysis. They advocated theory generation through inquiry and called the results *grounded theory.* For Glaser and Strauss, the ultimate function of theory is still explanation and prediction. They and others agree that it is "important to be able to go beyond the local setting of the research and to engage with formal ideas at a more general level" (Coffey and Atkinson 1996, 14). Whether or not theory formation as described so far should be a goal of social science is a contested issue in qualitative scholarship.

Interpretivists such as Geertz (1973) offer yet a different understanding of theory based on interpretation, or the act of making sense out of a social interaction. Theory building proceeds by *thick description* (Geertz 1973), defined as "description that goes beyond the mere or bare reporting of an act (thin description), but describes and probes the intentions, motives, meanings, contexts, situations and circumstances of action" (Denzin 1989a, 39). The goal of theorizing, then, becomes that of providing an understanding of direct lived experience instead of abstract generalizations. Interpretivists consider every human situation as novel, emergent, and filled with multiple, often conflicting, meanings and interpretations. Theoretical work thus becomes observing, eliciting, and describing these meanings and contradictions.

What researchers believe theory to be and how to go about creating it links directly, therefore, to their methodological choices and study design. Researchers also use theory both implicitly and explicitly within those studies. Implicitly, your theoretical perspectives (behaviorism, feminism, liberalism, etc.) and values often affect your choice of research topic, the questions you ask of that topic, and how you describe what you "find." Increasingly, researchers are asked to reflect upon and reveal these theoretical predispositions that traditionally remained hidden from participants and readers alike, and, sometimes, to the researcher as well.

Explicit theories—the theories you write about in your proposal and research report—also help to situate your study, develop research questions, select research participants, create interview questions, provide an analytical framework, and make sense of your findings. These theories may be at various levels of abstraction, from *empirical generalizations* to *formal theories.*

Empirical generalizations or *substantive theories* are at a low level of abstraction and refer to outcomes from related studies. You might use these theories to help provide the rationale or to raise questions for your study in your proposal, and you might use them later on to compare and contrast with findings from your own work. Reviewing the literature related to your study's main concepts provides the base for working with empirical generalizations.

Formal theory (Strauss 1987) is sometimes referred to as *general theory* or as *middle-range propositions* (Turner 1985). "Middle range theories try to explain a whole class of phenomena—say, for example, delinquency, revolutions, ethnic antagonism . . . They are therefore broader in scope than empirical generalizations and causal models" (Turner 1985, 27). Qualitative researchers often make use of these more general theories as a framework for both asking questions of their study and discussing aspects of their findings.

Guiding theories, whether at a low or high level of abstraction can help you design your research in many ways. It's important to remember, however, that while theories help to illuminate some things, they also conceal other aspects. They can be restrictive at best and misleading at worst. As Schram (2006, 60) states, "Imposing a well-established theory on your developing inquiry may set you up with a neat and satisfying framework for your study, but it may also prematurely shut down avenues of meaningful questioning or prevent you from seeing events and relationships that don't fit the theory." One way to address this is to use several different theories as guiding frameworks for the study. Another is to look for the gaps between what a guiding theory does and does not explain in your own work and to add new propositions to prevailing theories or point out the contradictions or incompleteness of prevailing ones. Mills and Bettis (2006, 83) assert that if as researchers we constantly seek out alternative interpretations that contradict our own expectations and the theories we are using, then we "can push our analyses to more nuanced stages that go beyond what our frameworks provide us."

Rebecca Esch (1996) provides an example of using theory in developing the conceptual context for a research proposal. Rebecca was interested in studying adolescent girls' development. After describing the basis for her interest in adolescent girls, she wrote:

> This interest in adolescent girls led me to an exploration of the theories which sought to describe girls' experience of the transition from childhood to adolescence, in addition to theories outlining girls' development, particularly as their development was believed to diverge from traditional theories of adolescent development. My research focused on the ideas of the Stone Center for Developmental Services and Studies at Wellesley College, and the Harvard Project on Women's Psychology and Girls' Development. Both of these groups place the experience of relationship at the center of girls' development. This is in contrast to traditional theories of development that stress individuation and separation.

Rebecca discussed these contrasting theories of adolescent development. Then, she transitioned to literature on friendship, situating the inclusion of this literature in a perceived gap in human development theories:

> My perspective is that although many girls struggle during this period, and perhaps all face the possibility of suffering some ill effects due to cultural, school, and peer pressures, many girls thrive. Thus, one goal of my research is to re-define or

re-label the experience of girls' development during this transitional period. Much of this moving away, on my part, from a crisis philosophy, has been generated by my own reflexive search through my adolescent memories, during which I can find little evidence of a similar "crisis." . . . Thus, the question began to form, what of those of us who did not suffer a traumatic transition from childhood to adolescence? What of those of us who did not lose our voice or our sense of self?...In thinking about these questions I keep coming back to the idea of growth within relationship and what role my friends have played during the changes and difficulties of my life . . . I began to wonder if perhaps girls' friendship might play an important role during this transitional period.

With this introduction and rationale, Rebecca then explored literature and theory on women's and girls' friendships, and their relationship to the concepts of *developing a sense of self* and *resilience*.

In summary, theory, sometimes referred to as the latest version of what we call truth, is used in a variety of ways in qualitative research. Typically, qualitative research is not explicitly driven by theory, but it is situated within theoretical perspectives. Researchers often use empirical generalizations and formal theory to help situate their research within a larger configuration of thought and to form initial questions and working hypotheses during the beginning stages of data collections. Later, as they focus more on data analysis, they often seek out yet other theories to help examine the data from different perspectives. Their work may or may not eventuate in statements of theory that are grounded in the data.

RESEARCH PURPOSES

This section and the one that follows discuss how to go about determining your *research purposes* and *research questions*. They are not the same thing. Research purposes address your practical and intellectual (and possibly personal) goals. Research questions or your "problem statement" focuses your inquiry by posing a question or set of questions that, through your study, you plan to address.

Figuring out research purposes can help you in a variety of ways. First of all, they help you to justify your research as something worth doing by pointing out what is potentially significant about it. Second, your research purposes help you to figure out the kind of research you need to do to achieve your purposes. If a goal is to raise consciousness among teens of how educational opportunities intersect with class and race, then you will design your study differently than a study with a purpose of contributing to teacher training by demonstrating how teacher talk differs in rural and urban schools. Third, figuring out your intellectual goals helps you focus your research questions. Fourth, your purposes, along with your research statement, can act as a touchstone and help to keep you focused when, in the midst of fieldwork, you become overwhelmed by the multiple directions you could pursue.

Maxwell (2005) suggests you work to distinguish between personal, practical, and intellectual goals. Your personal goals are what motivate you to do the study. If the only personal goal you can come up with is associated with completing a degree requirement, then you should probably rethink your study since that may not be a sufficient motivating factor for taking you through qualitative inquiry. Personal goals relate to personal experiences. For example, I grew up with a brother who was mentally handicapped in a time when little resources were available for him or his family. In fact, the ideology at the time (1950s) was more one of hiding such "problems," if not institutionalizing. This personal experience could be part of a motivating purpose to want to investigate difference and stigmatization in a variety of ways. As you work to figure out your personal goals, write about what motivates you in your research journal. As you write your proposal, include those motivating factors that help build the case for the research and perhaps help justify why you are an appropriate person to conduct the study.

Those of you in applied fields such as education, social work, nursing, and physical therapy will probably be motivated by practical goals. That is, you hope that the research will help to change or accomplish something—that teachers will become more aware of how their talk and actions encourage or discourage girls to like mathematics or that hospital administrators will implement a policy for a team-approach to medical care. Practical goals also help to justify your research, but are not usually outcomes that you can claim that your research will achieve. Rather they can help situate the potential significance of your work.

It is your intellectual goals that lend themselves to helping you define your research statement or questions. "Intellectual goals . . . are focused on understanding something—gaining insight into what is going on and why this is happening, or answering some question that previous research has not adequately addressed" (Maxwell 2005, 21). Making sure teachers encourage girls to like mathematics is not, in itself, a researchable topic. But based on your own experiences and your reading about girls, mathematics, and teaching, you might become intrigued with, for example, the role of teacher talk in girls pursuit of and attitudes towards mathematics. You then form this interest into a research statement and questions, linking tightly the research statement to your intellectual goals.

To help you figure out your intellectual goals, think about what it is that you want to describe, interpret, and/or explain (Schram 2006). Descriptive purposes involve documenting day-to-day interactions or the ways in which people talk about and do things. Interpretive purposes focus on how things work in particular settings and on how people make meaning of particular phenomena. Explanatory purposes include identifying patterns and possible relationships among behavior, settings, and phenomena. Another purpose that has gained increased attention in qualitative research, particularly with critical and poststructural work, is the emancipatory goal with desires "to raise awareness, foster self-understanding and self-determination, and create opportunities to engage in social action and seek social justice" (Schram 2006, 32). Research purposes as with other aspects of your design are closely aligned with your beliefs on what counts as meaningful knowledge and how you go about knowing.

RESEARCH STATEMENT AND QUESTIONS

Researchers often know from the beginning where they want to do research and with what group of people. John, a middle-school teacher working with an innovative teacher summer institute that invites middle-school students to be discussants and participants, knew he wanted to do research with this institute. Dorianne, who taught English in an urban public school, wanted to do research with English teachers in other urban schools. Schram (2006, 29), however, warns, "do not confuse where you are looking (or what you are looking at) with what you are looking for." In other words, you have to have a conceptual issue at the core of your research.

Qualitative researchers tend to be concerned with social structures, individual experiences, and/or the relationship between them (Winchester 2005). Extending this useful observation, Winchester (2005) poses two kinds of overarching questions that are often starting places for qualitative inquiry:

- "What is the shape of societal structures and by what processes are they constructed, maintained, legitimized, and resisted?" (5)
- "What are individual' experiences of places and events?" (6)

Structures tend to be viewed through social, cultural, economic, political, and/or environmental lenses. Within these structures, individuals' experiences are assumed to be varied and multiple. The interpretivist researcher seeks to describe and interpret this complexity by documenting how structures shape individual experiences, and also how individuals create, change, or penetrate the structures that exist. Research statements often focus on some aspect or aspects of questions like these.

Unlike quantitative studies, which identify sets of variables and seek to determine their relationship, qualitative studies are best at contributing to a greater understanding of perceptions, attitudes, and processes. As Creswell (1998) states, "the research question often starts with a *how* or a *what* so that initial forays into the topic describe what is going on" (17). Your statement presents the overall intent of your study and indicates how open or closed it will be. It provides a focus for thinking about data collection and analysis. In one clear sentence, try to describe what it is that you want to understand. After working on your research statement, look at all the questions you have generated and consider which ones to put on hold for another study and which ones to categorize into subquestions that will assist in investigating your central issue.

Rebecca's and Ashley's works are drawn upon here to provide examples of research statements and questions. Rebecca focused her research on individuals' experiences with the following statement:

Through my research I will explore the intersection of girls' friendship and the development of self during the transition from childhood to adolescence.

Rebecca felt compelled to clarify this general statement with several more statements:

> I hope to begin to understand what role friendship plays in girls' developing sense of self. Further, I hope to begin to illuminate whether girls' friendship provides a form of resilience, and/or fosters resistance for girls as they negotiate the transition from childhood to adolescence.

She then created four categories of research questions to help guide her work on girls' friendship and the development of self:

1. How do girls describe the development of their sense of self during this transitional period?
2. What is the experience of friendship for girls during this transitional period?
3. How do girls describe their experiences during this transitional period?
   - What can be understood of a girl's world during this period with respect to family, school, peers/friends, culture, etc.?
   - How does the term crisis apply to this period of girls' development? Is there a more positive and proactive way to define, describe, and understand this transitional period?
4. How does an understanding of girls' development and friendships during this transitional period contribute to relational theories of development, and/or other developmental theories?

Ashley was working on a master's thesis in the School of Natural Resources. Her research statement took the following form:

> In this research, I seek to understand how stakeholders involved with the relicensing of hydroelectric projects enter into negotiations and reach consensus concerning resource use and ecosystem protection.

Ashley's research statement is an example of a qualitative study focused upon understanding a process, in this case, the process of negotiating and reaching consensus within a particular social structure. She developed four research questions to guide her work:

1. How do stakeholders enter into negotiations and what motivates and constrains them in the negotiation process?
2. What stages are involved in the process of reaching consensus?
3. How do stakeholders perceive the final agreement/outcome?
4. How does legislative context affect the stakeholders (from their perspectives) and the negotiation process?

With research purposes clear and research statement and questions developed, both Rebecca and Ashley were ready to consider how they would go about designing their studies to get the data they needed.

SITE SELECTION

With your topic selected and the process of reviewing relevant literature and theories begun, you must decide where to conduct the study, who the study's participants should be, what techniques to use to gather data, and how long to spend in the field. Each decision needs careful prestudy thought, but, as with the research statement, each is subject to change as data collection proceeds and informs you. No guiding list of rules exists for these decisions, but that does not mean that anything goes. Literature, documents, your methodological philosophical position, discussions with potential research participants, guidance of experienced researchers, and your own good judgment all contribute to sound decisions.

In the past, part of the rite of passage for anthropology students was to do research in cultures different from their own. Immersion in a foreign culture was a test, of sorts, of one's ability to learn new modes of behavior and perception. In some ways, moving into a new culture is easier than studying your own. When everything is different, you are more open to new understandings. When you are already familiar with a culture or group or school, your angles of vision are narrowed by preformed assumptions about what is going on. Preformed assumptions can also accompany you into new settings or cultures as evidenced by Western agricultural researchers who, for many years, ignored the role of women in agriculture around the world. Assumptions are, however, more readily challenged in settings new to you, even if within your own city.

Currently, many researchers are drawn to studying their own institution or agency, to doing *backyard* research. Doing so is attractive for a number of reasons: They have relatively easy access; the groundwork for rapport is already established; the research would be useful for their professional or personal life; and the amount of time and money needed for various research steps would be reduced. As a novice researcher, you may be understandably tempted to undertake backyard studies, but you should do so fully aware of the possible problems generated by your involvement in and commitment to your familiar territory. Previous experiences with settings or peoples can set up expectations for certain types of interactions that will constrain effective data collection. When you enter a new culture as a researcher, that is your role, although research participants often assign other roles to you. When studying in your own backyard, you often already have a role—as teacher or principal or caseworker or friend. When you add on the researcher role, both you and those around you may experience confusion at times over which role you are or should be playing.

Carolyn, for example, was interested in physically disabled children and interviewed special education supervisors in her own community about their work. She herself was a mother of a disabled child. She said of her interviewees, "They couldn't disassociate my research role from my role as a parent of a handicapped child." Instead of giving careful answers to her questions, they tended to say, "Well, you know what it's like," or "We've talked about this before."

Gordon was a school principal whose pilot project involved interviewing students in his school:

Ah! the innocence of the novice researcher! Feeling smug with my own cleverness for choosing a subject both near and dear, I set out to do my research. What could be easier? I was a well-established, well-regarded principal in a small community. Principals are supposed to study student achievement. Thus I had not only the right, but also the professional imperative to visit classrooms and interview students if these activities would bring about improvement in the educational program. I knew each subject individually, my teachers respected me (I had hired most of them), and I had control of scheduling. Best of all, I was the main gatekeeper for the school. Thus, through my role as principal, I had the opportunity, the right, and the resources to make short work of interviews and observations. What could go wrong?

Well, several things. First of all, as principal I was on duty anytime I was in the building and crises didn't go away just because I was doing qualitative research. Thus my good intentions to make observations and do interviews were regularly shattered by irate parents, students with personal problems, broken boilers, and wayward buses. Second, as a principal it was my responsibility to protect the education of children wherever possible. How, then, could I justify taking children out of class to interview them about achievement when half of them were reputed to be underachievers? Third, as the primary disciplinarian in the school, I became involved in a long-term disciplinary process with two of my subjects, and I lost valuable data because I was unable to interview them. Finally, as principal, I felt pressure not to upset rapport with teachers, so I found that I tried not to rock the boat any more than I had to. I think I lost valuable data by not interviewing them about their views on the underachievement of students.

What did I learn from all this? First of all, I've found that it's a good idea to go away from home to do your research. Research should be undertaken at least far enough away so that your job role does not interfere with your activities. Second, conduct your research where you are not so emotionally close to your subjects that it distorts your design, preferably someplace where you have not worked and lived for many years.

In addition to the potential access and research design problems that Gordon identified, backyard research can create ethical and political dilemmas. As an established insider, your observations of colleagues may lead to guilt or anxiety. Politically charged situations can leave you feeling vulnerable. Anne, for example, decided to inquire into the use of a particular educational computer program in area schools. What she did not take into consideration at the outset of her research were the people invested in keeping the program in the schools. She states:

My worst fear of affecting my professional relationships as a result of research came true. Mike . . . was offended by the analysis. I have now had to edit my analysis to create a less in-depth and more toned down version of the original. My eyes are open to the political ramifications of research. And I have learned to not do research in my own "backyard."

Also, interviews frequently uncover what can be termed *dangerous knowledge*, or information that is politically risky to hold, particularly for an insider. Such problems are not limited to backyard research, but they do seem to proliferate there.

Ending the research is also different in backyard versus other settings. When inquiring into a phenomenon set in an unfamiliar local, a researcher eventually leaves the town, agency, or culture even though connections may remain for life. You don't usually leave your own "backyard," although you may want to as a result of the "dangerous knowledge" you received in your researcher role.

These warnings against research in your own backyard apply, in general, to interpretivist qualitative studies where the researcher is the primary investigator. The situation is different in action research, teacher research, and some critical and poststructural research. Action researchers work with groups of people to make organizations, projects, curriculum, etc., "better." Teacher researchers often study their own classrooms with the purpose to improve schooling experiences for students. These kinds of backyard research generally remove the confusion over role; either your research role is personal in that it is centered upon your own behaviors and thoughts and those of students in your classes or the role is assigned or acknowledged by colleagues as an important role for the organization. Action-oriented research lessens the political challenges common to backyard interpretivist research because the knowledge gained is either personal knowledge to guide your own behaviors or open knowledge from which the group as a whole learns and forms new directions. Finally, in action and teacher research, your being part of the organization is vital because the research is generally a beginning step in a longer, change-oriented process. Indeed, action research is difficult to carry out when you are not part of the organization because the people involved in the research are often those most invested in carrying out the needed changes.

Glen chose, with blessings from his school, to do a formative evaluation of an alternative education program in the high school where he taught science. Reflecting upon his work, he states:

> I cannot imagine a more effective way to learn qualitative research than being able to do it in a culture and field in which I have some knowledge. This project is more than an individual effort, it is a social journey into my own, and my school's, zone of proximal development. Being able to choose my topic of interest situated in my passion, anchoring it to theory in which I am conversant, not only made it meaningful but also made it worthwhile for my institution and community.

Backyard research can be extremely valuable, but it needs to be entered with heightened consciousness of potential difficulties. Qualitative research classes often include a pilot research project as a semester assignment. Because of the apparent ease involved in accessing and talking with people you already know, you may be inclined to design a project around interviewing colleagues, partners, or friends for the assignment. Making this choice is understandable, but you are likely to learn more about doing qualitative research *and* about a new topic if you create a project that takes you to strangers or people you don't know well.

If you do not research your own backyard, then how do you go about selecting a site? Often, the selection of research place or places is built into the research problem. A colleague, for example, studied what happened when a Japanese firm moved into a predominantly white, small American city. His interest grew out of yearlong negotiations that took place in several small Midwestern cities before a Japanese car industry selected one as its base. He then knew where his site would be.

Some research problems do not call for a specific research site; they simply require a setting within some specified geographical boundaries. For example, a study focused on an issue concerning working single mothers who had been on welfare within the past year does not necessarily involve selecting a single study site, but travel constraints suggest limiting the selection of study participants to nearby locations. Similarly, Rebecca, with her focus on adolescent girls' friendships and development, selected her own community as the site for observations and interviews.

Commonly, however, researchers need to develop a rationale for selecting one or more sites for data collection. Perhaps the phenomenon you wish to investigate exists to some extent everywhere. Do you choose an exemplary site or a typical site? What criteria determine exemplary, typical, or other classifiers? If you select a rural school, must you also look at an urban school? How many sites should you select? To make such decisions, you must look again at your research interests and carefully reflect on what you want to learn. You may also need to try out, or pilot, tentative site selections. The next section, "Selection of Study Participants," discusses some sampling strategies that apply to selecting sites as well as study participants.

SELECTION OF STUDY PARTICIPANTS

Since most research situations are too vast to interview everyone or to observe everything associated with the topic, you need a justifiable selection strategy by which to choose people, events, and times. Random sampling, the strategy often used in quantitative research, is appropriate for selecting a large, statistically representative sample from which generalizations can be drawn. Qualitative researchers neither work (usually) with populations large enough to make random sampling meaningful, nor is their purpose that of producing generalizations. Interpretivist researchers tend to select each of their cases *purposefully* (Patton 2002). "The logic and power of purposeful sampling...leads to selecting *information-rich cases* for study in depth. Information-rich cases are those from which one can learn a great deal about issues of central importance to the purpose of the research . . ." (Patton 2002, 46).

Patton (2002) identifies and discusses 16 different purposeful sampling strategies. Several of these strategies are presented here (see Exhibit 2.2) as examples of ways in which you might think about what you want to know and, accordingly, the sampling decisions you need to make. Different sampling strategies allow you to learn different things about your topic because each strategy you choose leads you to particular kinds of sites and people.

Typical case sampling	Illustrates or highlights what is typical, normal.
Extreme or deviant case sampling	Selects cases from the extremes, cases that are unusual or special in some way, such as high school valedictorians and dropouts; or female scientists who work in Antarctica.
Homogeneous sampling	Selects all similar cases in order to describe some subgroup in depth such as a study of female professors from working-class backgrounds who were the first generation in their families to receive a college education (Clark 1999).
Maximum variation sampling	Selects cases that cut across some range of variation such as students of different ethnic backgrounds enrolled in an environmental studies program. Searches for common patterns across great variation.
Theoretical sampling	Selects cases, people, events, activities, etc. through evolving theoretical constructs in one's research. Associated with grounded theory, but also used by others working within interpretivist traditions.
Snowball, chain, or network sampling	Obtains knowledge of potential cases from people who know people who meet research interests. Wright and Decker (1997) used this approach to find men and women who were active armed robbers at the time of their research. Snowball sampling is useful for getting started when you have *no other way* to find the participants you want, but it is not always a sufficient strategy in itself for participant selection.
Convenience sampling	Selects cases on the basis of convenience. This strategy has low credibility and is inappropriate for anything other than "practice."

EXHIBIT 2.2   Some Selection Strategies for Research Sites and Participants.

Informed by Exhibit 5.6 in Patton, M. Q. (2002). *Qualitative Research & Evaluation Methods,* 3rd ed. Thousand Oaks, CA: Sage.

Committee members and funding agencies often expect the research proposal to delineate clearly how many and which persons will be interviewed, as well as how many and which situations will be observed. The researcher, therefore, is tempted to develop complex selection matrices. Thinking of important stratification criteria is a good place to begin, but do not get overinvested in including all the possible configurations of such variables as ethnicity, gender, socioeconomic class, educational level, sexual orientation, age, etc. in your study. Select only those criteria that the literature and your experience suggest are particularly important and remember that the selection strategy is often refined as the researcher collects data.

For example, as Carol began her study of the leisure styles of later-life widows, she assumed that leisure was affected by social class, years of education, employment status, and leisure options locally available. Varying her selection of study participants by these attributes would help her to learn more about her topic. Nonetheless, as Carol began collecting data, she learned of other criteria that appeared to affect leisure styles—such as how recently the women were widowed—and knew she had to include these attributes in her selection strategy.

As she spent time in the field, Carol decided that there was too much variation for her to understand the leisure styles of all later-life widows. She narrowed her focus to one group: high school educated, working, recently widowed, urban women. Doing so simplified her selection of participants and allowed her to go deeply into the leisure behavior of a reasonably homogeneous group. What struck Carol as ideal at the planning stage of her project was replaced by something both useful and feasible.

Rebecca also chose a fairly homogeneous sampling strategy since she was choosing depth rather than breadth of understanding. She described her rationale for her selection of adolescent girl participants:

> I am not as concerned about studying a broad spectrum of girls so much as gaining a preliminary understanding of the intersection of girls' friendship and the development of self . . . Once I have gained an understanding of this issue, I can then move on to exploring how it plays out across a broad spectrum of girls. . . .
>
> By definition, my study requires the engagement of girls who are quite young. To have any breadth of access, I will require the full support and cooperation of their families. Given these considerations, I will choose for my case studies six girls who I either already know, or know of, through my circle of academic relationships and I will ask each girl to invite a best friend to participate with her. . . . Engaging this rather homogeneous circle of girls will allow me to describe their collective understanding of friendship and the development of self with somewhat less confusion from factors such as SES, education [of family], significant family differences, etc. Although drawing on this circle of girls will allow me to gain depth in my understanding and description of girls' friendship, I realize I will lose diversity. . . .

As Rebecca's discussion suggests, in the numbers game, depth is traded for breadth. How many persons must you interview? How much must you observe? How do you know when to stop? There are no magic answers, although Morse (1994, 225) suggests that between 30 and 50 interviews are needed for ethnographic and grounded theory research.

For depth understanding, you repeatedly spend extended periods with fewer respondents and observation sites. For greater breadth, but a more superficial understanding, carry out one-time interviews with more people and fewer observations in more situations. The strategy of participant selection in qualitative inquiry rests on the multiple purposes of illuminating, interpreting, and understanding—and on your own imagination and judgment. Develop an explicit rationale, however, for participant selection based upon theory, methodological perspective, personal hunches, and your pilot study.

SELECTION OF RESEARCH TECHNIQUES

Although researchers tend to use the term *data collection,* as I have throughout this section and, indeed, the book, it isn't, perhaps, the best term. Dicks et al. (2005, 115) suggest *data recording* as a better term because data are not "simply inert materials lying around in the field, waiting for the researcher to come along and 'collect' them." Qualitative researchers have an active role in producing the data they record through the questions they ask and the social interactions in which they take part, so perhaps "data recording" isn't exactly the right term either because it does not convey ways in which qualitative information is co-constructed. Be aware of such problems with the language accompanying qualitative research, much of it inherited from more positivist traditions. I have continued using the term *data collection* for want of a better term but also occasionally use *data production.*

Most qualitative approaches depend on a variety of methods for obtaining data. This practice of relying on multiple methods is commonly called *triangulation,* a term taken from surveying and navigation. Although multiple data-collection methods is the most common form of triangulation in qualitative research, triangulation also refers to the incorporation of multiple kinds of data sources (i.e., not just teachers, but students and parents as well), multiple investigators, and multiple theoretical perspectives.

In the past, qualitative researchers, influenced by positivism, tended to view triangulation as a way to "validate" claims. The reasoning went that if you heard something from multiple sources, saw it enacted, and perhaps had a co-researcher who heard and saw it as well, then you could feel confident in claiming things were the way you were seeing and hearing them. From a positivist perspective, describing things as they really are is important. From an interpretivist perspective, you are not seeking to elucidate the "truth" of a setting or situation since you believe in no underlying reality, but rather you are trying to understand the multiple perspectives available.

You might raise the questions, then, "Why use multiple methods or why talk to different sets of people about some concept?" and "Why is triangulation still important?" Gibbs (2007, 94) provides two good reasons: "It is always possible to make mistakes in your interpretation and a different view on the situation can illuminate limitations or suggest which of competing versions is more likely" and, when what people say is inconsistent with what people do, "forms of data triangulation (e.g., observing actions as well as interviewing respondents) are useful . . ., not to show that informants are lying or wrong, but to reveal new dimensions of social reality where people do not always act consistently." Inconsistencies can help to reveal the complexity of a situation. Richardson (2000, 934) suggests *crystallization* as a more useful metaphor than *triangulation*: "I propose that the central image for 'validity' for postmodern texts is not the triangle—a rigid, fixed, two-dimensional object. Rather, the central imaginary is the crystal, which combines symmetry and substance with an infinite variety of shapes, substances, transmutations, multidimensionalities, and angles of approach."

To try to get at the deepened, complex understanding, three data-gathering techniques dominate in qualitative inquiry: observation, interviewing, and document collection. Within each technique, a wide variety of practices can be carried out, some more common than others. For example, when observing, some researchers use videotaping as a means to replay, slow down, and freeze observed interactions. Many, however, rely on their senses, the results of which are relayed through their pens and stored in field logs. Some researchers use props such as card sorts or pictures as stimuli for specific information in interviews. Most only ask questions.

These data-gathering techniques are discussed in later chapters; the point here is that, ideally, the qualitative researcher draws on some combination of techniques to record and construct research data, rather than a single technique. This is not to negate the utility of, say, a study based solely on interviews, but rather to indicate that the more sources contributing, the richer the data and the more complex the findings.

To figure out which techniques to use, once again contemplate carefully what you want to learn. Different research questions have different implications for data collection. In considering options, choose techniques that are likely to (1) elicit data needed to gain understanding of the phenomenon in question, (2) contribute different perspectives on the issue, and (3) make effective use of the time available. In your research proposal, discuss each data production technique that you select as Rebecca did in the following example:

1. *Interviews.* Through the use of interviews . . . I will explore each individual's understanding and experience of friendship . . . As highlighted in previous sections, my research, by design and by philosophy, requires the involvement of my "others" as colearners in this study, and the development of a relationship based on trust and rapport . . . I will engage in multiple interviews across which I and my colearners will collaboratively design, and redesign, the interview structure as we proceed. Given that our relationship will be evolving across these interviews, my hope is that the quality of the information we exchange will also evolve.

2. *Participant Observation and Document Collection.* To create an in-depth case study of each of the girls, I will not only interview them individually, but also spend time with them and their friends at home, at school, and in other settings. I will bring the girls together in groups . . . for conversations about friendship, and, if possible, employ a video camera to aid me in analyzing more deeply their interactions and conversations . . . I will encourage them to keep a journal, draw, paint, take pictures, or engage in any other medium they feel allows them full expression of their ideas. To initiate this exploration, I plan to give each girl . . . a journal upon the embarkation of our journey . . .

3. *Open-ended "Survey."* With the *New Moon* [magazine] girls I plan to suggest the same sort of creative means of expression as I do with the case study girls . . . I will ask them to submit a paragraph, essay, picture, photograph, collage, or other creative form that best expresses their feelings about friendship.

Multiple means of data development can contribute to research trustworthiness and verisimilitude, or sense of authenticity. Design into your research plans, as well, other ways of making your research rigorous, trustworthy, and plausible, the topic of the next section.

TRUSTWORTHINESS

"You must learn to sit with people," he told me. "You must learn to sit and listen. As we say in Songhay: 'One kills something thin only to discover that [inside] it is fat.'"

(Stoller 1989, 128)

Validity is another debated topic in qualitative research scholarship. Most agree that we cannot create criteria to ensure that something is "true" or "accurate" if we believe concepts are socially constructed. Yet, what this belief implies for research methods is not agreed upon. Some use the concept of "trustworthiness" and create criteria as described below to demonstrate ways in which the researchers can claim that their work is plausible or credible. At the other end of the spectrum are scholars who reject attempts at such claims and focus on whether the inquiry "advances a social agenda or offers cultural criticism" (Schwandt 2007, 311), in addition to other concerns.

Research committees often expect the proposal to address issues of validity. This section, therefore, touches on ways in which the researcher can increase credibility or trustworthiness. Creswell (1998, 201–203) describes eight procedures (summarized here) often used in qualitative research to contribute to trustworthiness:

1. prolonged engagement and persistent observation—extended time in the field so that you are able to develop trust, learn the culture, and check out your hunches,
2. triangulation (or crystallization)—use of multiple data-collection methods, multiple sources, multiple investigators, and/or multiple theoretical perspectives,
3. peer review and debriefing—external reflection and input on your work,
4. negative case analysis—conscious search for negative cases and unconfirming evidence so that you can refine your working hypotheses,
5. clarification of researcher bias—reflection upon your own subjectivity and how you will use and monitor it in your research,
6. member checking—sharing interview transcripts, analytical thoughts, and/or drafts of the final report with research participants to make sure you are representing them and their ideas accurately,
7. rich, thick description—writing that allows the reader to enter the research context,
8. external audit—an outside person examines the research process and product through "auditing" your field notes, research journal, analytic coding scheme, etc.

Attending to all of these means of increasing trustworthiness is not necessary in any one study, but validity issues are often aspects to consider and discuss in your research proposal. Lorraine's work provides an example. She was researching ways in which physical therapists work with elders with dementia:

Bias.   I am very invested in the search for a better understanding of how physical therapists work with elders with dementia. My attachment to this field of study may lead me to data that support my own working hypothesis. I may hear what I want to hear and see what I want to see. I may easily find ways of discrediting those that disagree. I will address researcher bias by continuously exploring my own subjectivity. By writing both before and after my interviews and observations, I will be able to address pre-conceived opinions and reflect upon my biases.

Negative Cases.   My biases may be more apparent to me if I seek out interviews with colleagues that I know to hold differing opinions. These discussions with colleagues will be another method that will allow me to explore my topic, as well as my subjectivity.

Multiple-Session Interviews.   I need to address the possibility of therapists telling me that they treat patients one way when they actually do not. Truthfulness may be a problem for some therapists since certain opinions or behaviors are not socially accepted . . . Repeat interviews throughout the course of the study will aid in developing rapport and increasing the possibility that interviewees tell me how they really feel and act. They will also allow the participant time to think more deeply about their own feelings, reactions, and beliefs.

Persistent Observation.   It may also be difficult to determine whether therapists are performing in their best behavior rather than their usual behavior, because people act differently when they are being watched. This reactivity phenomenon will be addressed by spending long periods of time in a facility. This will allow therapists to get used to the researcher's presence. By increasing the therapists' comfort with an outsider, they will soon be behaving in their normal fashion.

Multiple Sites.   I have chosen to observe and interview in three facilities. Therapists often adopt similar techniques and behaviors of those around them. Looking at three different sites should increase the trustworthiness of common themes.

Some of these procedures for revealing the complexities in and increasing the trustworthiness of your findings receive attention elsewhere in this text. They are introduced here to signal another prestudy area for thought.

THE TIME FRAME

You cannot know with certainty how long your research will take. Invariably, you will underestimate the amount of time needed. For example, gaining access to a school may drag on because the school board did not address the researcher's plans on the evening scheduled. Introduction to the school's teachers is delayed because the teacher's meeting was canceled. People reschedule interviews at the last moment, or they don't show up. Unexpected assemblies or field trips change observation schedules.

That things simply take longer than planned is a basic given in qualitative research. Terry Denny advised students at the University of Illinois to figure how much time each step should take and multiply by two and a half. It took even longer than that for Mark, who was studying attitudes of correctional officers toward educational programs for inmates:

I had expected that contacting the officers and arranging for interviews would have taken a day or two at most. It was over a month between when I scheduled my first interview until I arranged the last one. I had not counted on vacations, weddings, changing shifts, or even officers changing job sites. Not a single interview happened at the time it was originally scheduled. One officer was ordered to work back-to-back shifts because of lack of staff. Twice, officers were ordered to transport offenders to other facilities. One officer was ordered to work an hour longer than her normal shift (due to understaffing) so she could guard the perimeter fence while inmates enjoyed their outside recreation period. No wonder another officer complained in his interview that inmates have more freedom than the officers who guard them.

Despite the delays, do not become discouraged. Rather, remember that unless you are researching your own backyard or doing some form of collaborative research, you are external, if not alien, to the lives of research participants. You are not necessarily unwanted, but, because you are not integral to the lives of your others, you are dispensable. You will complete your research tasks, but normally later than you expect.

Institutional structures affect schedule planning. For example, the elementary and high school setting is more structured than the university setting. The scheduling of bells to demarcate set periods assists researchers in planning whom they can interview or when they can observe and for how long. Institutional frameworks also affect the control respondents have over their time. In general, it appears that individuals who hold higher places in the institutional hierarchy have greater autonomy to declare when they are free. Yet they often are busy individuals who reschedule appointments as a matter of course. Those lower in the hierarchy often have little autonomy to set a time to talk. When Lynne interviewed the custodial staff of a university, she had to work through the physical plant manager. He helped develop a schedule, communicate the research intent to the staff, and release individuals for interviews. As a result, Lynne felt caught between management and the workers, grateful to the manager for access and to the workers for their stories, but unsure of how to report the data she received. A way around this situation would be to interview people when they are not at work, although that can create other challenges.

In thinking about the time needed for observations, find out whether the institution has cycles or seasons of activity, and if it has episodic occasions that affect what goes on. If so, your observations should take account of the different phases of the cycle, as well as the different occasions. This does not mean that observations need to occur every day, but it does mean that time, as well as places and people, must be sampled. Findings from classroom observations made during the first quarter of a school year are likely to differ from those made in the fourth quarter. Classroom observations made only on Mondays may present a very different picture from observations made on other days of the week. Teachers and their students may interact quite differently in September than they do in December, as they may before football games, proms, and all the other big events that temporarily stand a school on end.

Despite the problems that individual researchers face in estimating the time they need to carry out their research, developing a timetable is a good idea. Doing so helps to assess the proposed aspects of the research and to anticipate the requirements of each: arrangements to be made, letters to be written, people to be phoned, and places to be visited. Although somewhat integrated with data collection, analysis and writing should receive at least as much scheduled time as data collection; it is relatively easier to collect data than it is to shape them satisfactorily as words on a page. Finally, the timetable serves as a reality check on the feasibility—given the inevitable constraints of time and finances—of your choice of research topic, methods, sites, and participants. See Exhibit 2.3 for an example of a dissertation timetable.

The timetable is a useful tool, but, like other qualitative research tools, it must remain flexible. In face-to-face interactions, unforeseen circumstances occur that can considerably delay your plans. On one hand, this can be perceived as a source of frustration and anxiety. On the other, the unforeseen is part of the world of exploration, and researchers, if open to what one can learn from occurrences

Task	2009 June	July	Aug	Sept	Oct	Nov	Dec	2010 Jan	Feb	March	April	May	June	July	Aug	Sept	Oct	Nov	Dec	2011 Jan	Feb	March	April	May	June	July	Aug	Sept	Oct	Nov	Dec
Read Associated Literature	■	■	■										■	■	■	■										■	■				
Conduct Research Pilot				■	■																										
Draft Proposal					■	■	■																								
Proposal Hearing & Revisions									■	■																					
Gain Access to Site/s & Participants										■	■					■															
Document Collection/Analysis											■	■	■	■	■																
Participant Observations											■	■	■	■																	
Set Up & Conduct Interviews												■	■	■	■	■															
Data Transcription													■	■	■	■	■														
Preliminary Data Analysis														■	■	■	■	■													
Journaling & Writing Preliminary Interpretations											■	■	■	■	■	■	■	■	■												
Assessment of Further Data Needs & Gathering of Info																	■	■	■												
Focused Data Analysis																			■	■	■										
Outline Dissertation Chapters and Sub-Sections																					■	■									
Draft Dissertation																						■	■	■	■	■	■				
Discuss/Revise/Edit																												■	■	■	
Dissertation Defense																															■

EXHIBIT 2.3   **Example of a Dissertation Timetable.**

that deviate from their plans, may use it to acquire better data and a better understanding of the people and setting under study.

RESEARCH SUMMARY

Pre-data-collection tasks are not complete without a developed research summary for your participants, which Institutional Review Boards (IRBs) often refer to as the *lay summary* that accompanies a consent form. Research summaries are written or verbal presentations of your research that you give to research participants to help explain who you are, what you are doing, and what role you would like them to play in your research. In general, research summaries address the following points:

1. Who you are
2. What you are doing and why
3. What you will do with the results
4. How the study site and participants were selected
5. Any possible benefits as well as risks to the participant
6. If applicable, the promise of confidentiality and anonymity to participants and site
7. How often you would like to observe or hope to meet for interviews
8. How long you expect each session to last
9. Requests to record observations and words (by notes, tape recording, or videotaping)

There is no one way to construct a research summary. What you develop depends upon the context and needs of your research. You do, however, have the responsibility to be as clear and honest as possible in telling your research participants who you are, what you want to do and why, how you plan to go about it, and what you will do with the information you receive.

In addition to the summary, interactions with your participants may require other discussions as well. The teacher being observed from the back of the room may receive different reassurances than the teacher being interviewed. The observed teacher needs to feel reassured about what the researcher is doing "back there," what is being scribbled, and what will happen to the scribblings. Interviewing makes confidentiality and anonymity more palpable issues. Also, for some respondents, interviewing may resemble a test and can cause interviewee anxiety about "right answers." Reassuring participants that they cannot be wrong is necessary. They need to be told that to "do right" they must simply verbalize their stories, opinions, and feelings, and remain comfortable when they do not remember something or have nothing to say to a question.

You should be prepared also for questions that participants might have, such as, "Can I see the data?" or "Will I get a copy of the final report?" Anticipate such questions and be able to give reasonable answers and explanations without promising more than you can deliver.

Following is the research summary that Rebecca gave her adolescent participants:

REBECCA'S RESEARCH SUMMARY

You are invited to participate in a research study to learn about girls' friendship and development of their "self" (ideas about who you are and what you are like). This research is being done as part of my program as a doctoral student at the University of Vermont.

I am asking you to participate because I believe that your ideas and feelings about friendship and self would help me to better understand girls' friendship during this time of their growing up. The benefits to you of doing this study is that you might learn some new things about yourself, you might enjoy sharing your ideas and feelings about friendship and self with other girls like you, and you might even make some new friends. In addition, your participation in this study may help me and others better understand how to help girls have good friendships and help them feel good about themselves. There is, however, a risk that sometimes, for some people, talking about relationships and how you see yourself can be upsetting.

I will be the only person (other than your parents) who knows that you are participating in this study. Anytime I use the information you give me, I will always identify you with a fake name (if you would like you can decide what name I use for you). When I interview you I would like your permission to tape-record our interviews, sometimes videotape them, take photographs, and also take notes to remind me about what we talked about. I will be the only one who gets to listen to or see these tapes, videos, and notes, and when I am not using them they will be kept in a locked cabinet that only I have the key to. After I have finished with this study, all of these tapes will be destroyed. I would, however, like to take photographs to include in my presentation of my dissertation. If I use a photograph of you, I will use your fake name to identify the picture, and I will not pair your photograph with what you said about friendship and self. You may choose not to allow me to take photographs of you while you participate in this study. At the end of this consent I will ask you to check off whether you do or do not give me permission to take and use your photograph.

As part of your participation in this study, I will spend time with you and talk with you over the course of a number of weeks. I will first talk with you by yourself for an hour or two and ask you questions about friendship and yourself. During this interview I will also ask you for the name of a friend you would like to have participate in this study with you. After I have arranged for your friend to be part of this study, I will talk with you both together and ask you questions about your friendship and how this friendship makes you feel (about 1–2 hours). Next, I will spend several periods of time with you and your friend so I can see what you and your friend do together and what you talk about (about 3–9 hours altogether depending on what you and your friend feel comfortable with). Then I will have you get together with the other girls like you who are participating in this study and ask you as a group to talk about friendship and self (I think this part will be some sort of pizza party at my house—about 3 hours). This may be the last part of this study, but my plan is to talk with all of you at this point and see if it might be helpful for me to talk to all or some of you some more.

The most important thing for you to remember while you are participating in this study with me is that there are no right or wrong answers to the questions I ask you. All I am looking for is your opinion or ideas or feelings and if I ask you to tell me more, or explain your answer, it is because I want to be really sure I understand what you are telling me. Always remember that in this situation you are the expert, or teacher, and you are explaining to me what friendship and self is like for you and girls like you.

You should also know that you can decide to not participate in this study, or stop doing it at any time after you have started—this is your decision. If you decide to stop doing this study, your decision will not affect any future contact you have with the University of Vermont.

IRBs have the responsibility of reviewing all research conducted in an institution receiving funds from the U.S. Department of Health, Education, and Welfare, whether or not any of the funds go to a specific study. (Other parts of the world have parallel institutions with different names, such as University Ethics Committees in England.) IRBs are charged with making sure research participants are aware of both potential risks and benefits related to taking part in a study. IRB committees look specifically for research summaries, consent forms, and examples of interview protocols or other research "instruments" in addition to generally assessing the overall design of a study. (The role of IRBs is discussed further in Chapter 6.)

The IRB received Rebecca's research proposal, research summary, and consent letter. Because she wanted to do research with adolescents, her proposal underwent full committee review. The committee sent her a memo, asking for clarifications and research summary/consent form revisions. In particular, committee members requested that she provide examples of questions to be asked during the interviews and that she develop a mechanism for obtaining consent from the parents of the girls recruited through *New Moon*. They also worried about her use of photographs and stated,

> There should be two points at which subjects and parents make a decision regarding the photographs: in the initial consent form, they should be asked for consent to take the pictures; and after the text is complete, they should sign a release for the use of the pictures in the document and presentation. Please revise the initial consent form accordingly and develop a second form for the use of the photographs. You also need to make it very clear that the photographs will be part of a permanent, public document.

The time Rebecca submitted her original proposal to the IRB to the time she received a confirmation letter from the IRB was nearly three months. Because of her work with adolescents, the committee was particularly careful that the project would not result in any harm to participants. Rebecca eventually got all the pieces in place to everyone's satisfaction, but such are the unforeseen extensions of time that can take place in any research project.

Another student came to me with a proposal focused on asking teachers and parents about their experiences with children learning to read. As we talked, it became clear that she really wanted to observe children who were beginning to read and to talk with the children about it. When I asked why she didn't design her study this way, she replied, "I've heard that it's difficult to get through the IRB process if children are in your study." I responded that it might take longer, but that any good proposal should include the plans that the IRB will want to see, with or without children as participants. Because the research you want to do includes the IRB category of "potentially vulnerable populations" should not cause you to change your topic, but rather it should be a catalyst to make your work as well thought out and as ethically sound as possible.

THE PILOT STUDY

A pilot study is useful for trying out many aspects of your proposed research. It can help you learn whether the concept of interest to you is of interest to participants. It can assist in clarifying research statement and questions. It can begin to challenge and uncover some of your assumptions about your proposed topic and context. Finally, a pilot study is an important place to try out research methods. Conduct your pilot study in situations and with people as close to the realities of your actual study as possible. Ideally, pilot study participants are drawn from your target population.

Researchers enter a pilot study with a different frame of mind from the one they have when going into the full-scale study. The idea is not to get data per se but to learn about your research process, interview questions, observation techniques, and yourself. Clarify your piloting intentions for respondents. For example, "I would like to interview you with these questions and then talk to you afterward about the questions themselves: How clear are they? Are they appropriate? What else should I be asking?" The pilot participants need to know that they are part of a pilot and that, as such, their role is to answer the questions you ask, but with the intent to improve them. Use the pilot study to test the language and substance of your questions, and the overall length of your interview. Use it to determine how your introduction to the study works: Is it too long or not detailed enough? What else do people want to know? Does it inform as broadly as necessary to reassure others about your proposed project?

Use the pilot study to assess your observation techniques: How do those who are observed respond? What would make them feel more comfortable? Can you take field notes as you observe, or should you write them up after observation periods? Less obvious than learning about your interview questions and getting a general sense of the nature of your research setting is the need to learn how to be present in that setting. What roles can and should you play in addition to that of researcher? Does the researcher role itself have ramifications that are peculiar to a particular place, ranging from the serious matter of needing clearance from the institution's head for each change in research routine, to the less serious but still important matter of how to dress? Learning an institution's rules and expectations, its major actors, and its taboos can direct you to personal behavior that will help you to gain access and keep it.

Finally, use the pilot as a chance to inform yourself about the topic itself. How does your research statement hold up? Do new research questions arise?

Changes in research focus may indicate poor planning, but they are also likely to indicate new learning. As Carol noted after her pilot project, "qualitative research is like the game of twister. You spin the dial and end up somewhere else." It is important to be open to changes so that the best possible connections among researcher, research participants, and topic will result.

A pilot study readies you for gathering data. How many people need to be in the pilot? Again, there is no specific answer. The number and variability should be sufficient to allow you to explore likely problems, as well as to give you clues on stratification criteria for selection of participants. With the results of the pilot, you may revise your research statement, research plans, interview questions, and even your way of presenting yourself.

In your research proposal, make use of your pilot by describing how your research plans have been influenced by the pilot, but do not view the pilot as a study in itself. I have seen dissertation proposals in which students cited their pilot (APA format) along with statements such as "Previous research (student's name 2005) with women's shelters showed that. . . ." You cannot make such claims from a pilot, but you can describe how your pilot indicated specific topics or directions to pursue. The pilot, as with your research memos, is helpful in developing your ideas and research plans and should be viewed as such.

GAINING ACCESS

With all these preliminary tasks taken care of, you are almost ready to begin your research. But first, you must gain access—sometimes a simple matter, sometimes not. This section discusses the process of gaining access in general. As with the other aspects of qualitative research, what you do in practice will depend on the context, the researcher-participant relationship, and the theoretical orientation of your methodology.

Gaining access is a process. It involves acquisition of consent to go where you want, observe what you want, talk to whomever you want, obtain and read whatever documents you require, and do all of this for whatever period of time is necessary to satisfy your research purposes. If you receive full and unqualified consent, then you have obtained total access. If your access is qualified somehow, then you must explore the meaning of the qualifications for meeting research expectations: Should you redefine your research? Should you select another site?

If the study involves some sort of organization or agency, then you must first make contact with its *gatekeepers*, the person or persons who must give their consent before you may enter a research setting, and with whom you must negotiate the conditions of access. Since there may be several different gatekeepers, making contact can be complicated, involving different persons at different times. If, for example, you want to study a particular elementary school, do you go first to the principal, the superintendent, or the school board? Starting anywhere but at the top of the hierarchy can be risky because acceptance by those in the lower ranks may be negated by supervisors. Yet gaining acceptance at the top is also risky because others may feel ordered to cooperate or may think that you are somehow politically aligned with one of several factions. It helps to know an insider who is familiar with the individuals and the politics involved who can advise you in making access decisions.

If you are interested in individuals unrelated to any organizational structure, then you must make direct contact with these potential participants. Whether approaching gatekeepers or a series of individuals, you want them to say, "Yes, your study sounds interesting. You are welcome." Such a response is more likely if an intermediary whom the gatekeepers or potential participants know and respect introduces you. Others then have a way to check you out—to find out informally who you are, what you are like, and whether they would mind having you around. When there is not an intermediary, and even sometimes when there is, gaining access to people within a site is best achieved by first *logging time*. Just being around, participating in activities, and talking informally with people gives them time to get used to you and learn that you are okay. This approach leads to better data than one in which a superior requests a subordinate to cooperate with you. For example, asking the principal to arrange a schedule for interviewing the school's teachers can be an efficient way to obtain teacher cooperation, but not necessarily an effective one. Gaining access is also more probably if you are doing work that will benefit participants and/or their community in some way.

When meeting the gatekeeper, be prepared to negotiate your access. This involves presenting your research summary, listening and responding to concerns and demands, and clarifying overarching issues. First, make clear that your data— field notes and interview transcripts—belong to you (or to you and the respondent); claim this ownership in the interest of preserving the anonymity and confidentiality that you promise. Second, make clear what you will deliver. This relates to your responsibility to meet respondents' expectations for things such as receiving drafts that they may review and critique, final reports, or consultation

This student had just arrived in a Filipino village where he was to live in a "homestay" with a local family. He needed to learn where he could and could not go, what he could and could not do, and ways in which he could "give back"— all parts of gaining and maintaining access. What kinds of things would you be thinking about if you were in his place?

about certain issues. Third, make clear the emergent possibilities of qualitative research. In other words, make sure the gatekeeper understands that during the course of research, new issues may surface that could require more discussion, initiated by either party. Gaining access is an initial undertaking. Maintaining access is another matter, occasioned by changes in the expectations and needs of both researcher and researched at any time during the research process.

Just as research statements and interview questions may change over the course of fieldwork, so, too, does trust. Trust needs to be developed before people can be willing to provide certain kinds of information. For instance, if you are interested in college students on academic probation, then you should probably wait until after several interviews before requesting access to their academic files. You do not want to put research participants in the uncomfortable position of saying "no" to you, nor do you want to be told "no."

Despite utmost care, rejections do occur. It is easy to overreact and become paranoid when faced with negative responses to requests to interview, sit in class, or attend a meeting. Although the negative response may be real, resist concluding that you will not be allowed to do the other things you have requested. The rejection may be unrelated to anything you have done or could have done, but it is, nonetheless, a signal to reflect on what you are doing and perhaps, to rethink your approach.

Sometimes denied access may turn out for the best as it did in Lorna's pilot study of inclusion of special needs children in schools:

> I initially wanted to observe more than two schools. This was probably totally unrealistic, since I very much underestimated the time involved in all aspects of the project. However, I immediately encountered some access problems. I was unable to connect with one building principal to get permission to observe in that school. Multiple phone calls where I did not get further than the secretary left me frustrated. I finally gave up, and focused on the other two classrooms. This is probably the "old blessing in disguise" since I would have felt even more inundated with too much data to deal with.

RESEARCHER ROLES

As a researcher, you need to clearly define your research roles. This definition is situationally determined, depending on your philosophical perspective, the context, the identities of your participants, and your own personality and values. There are, however, predispositions that qualitative researchers carry with them into research situations. First is the researcher's role as researcher. You are a researcher when you are sitting in the nurse station of a hospital taking notes or in the midst of a lengthy interview; you are also a researcher when you talk informally in the grocery store with someone in your study. All of the places in which you present yourself communicate to your others how a researcher acts. As a researcher, ever conscious of your verbal and nonverbal behavior, you are more than usually attuned to your behavior and its impact. This degree of awareness may be uncomfortable to manage, particularly in the early days of your field contacts. Developing a level of self-consciousness that has you habitually attending to your behavior and its consequences, however, is useful. You may want to also seek feedback from trusted persons in the research setting who can see you as you cannot see yourself.

Although often anxiety producing, the researcher's role can also be ego gratifying. Students in research classes discuss how they deal with their new credentials as researchers. After being in the field for a while, they find themselves saying to colleagues, "Well, my research suggests that . . ." They are asked to give presentations; they begin receiving clips of relevant articles and notices from colleagues and friends; and they begin to gain pleasure from their research role.

The second research role is the researcher as learner. Having this sense of self from the beginning is important. The learner's perspective will lead you to reflect on all aspects of research procedures and findings. It also will set you up for particular kinds of interactions. As a researcher, you are a curious student who comes to learn from and with research participants. You do not come as an expert or authority. If you are so perceived, then your respondents will not feel encouraged to be as forthcoming as they can be. As a learner, you are expected to listen; as an expert or authority, you are expected to talk. The differences between these two roles are enormous.

During data collection, expect to feel—at the same time or in close sequence— that you are not learning enough, that you are learning more than you can ever deal with, that you are not learning the right stuff, and that you are learning great stuff but do not know where it will lead or how it will all fit together. Anxieties about your research will change as you engage in each aspect of the process. Anxieties about how everything will fit together signal that you have begun seriously to consider the meaning of the data. As coding and data analysis progress, you will invariably become anxious about how to organize everything into written form.

Accompanying all of the various forms of anxiety is the feeling that your research is running your life. In this research-heightened condition, you will see nonresearch settings as potential research sites. Informal events will trigger thoughts about your research, and those near to you may come to know another person. "I learned about creative chaos," said Andrea, in the midst of her research; "I was organized in my research, but my house was a total mess. One day I took my son to school without his shoes. My mind was simply on other things."

I have been asked more than once to provide a "map" for the qualitative research process, so that newcomers can begin to grasp what is involved. I resist because diagrams often create the illusion of a static or prescribed process. Qualitative research can take many shapes. Nonetheless, I understand the value of being able to "see" the whole process on one page, and, indeed, am often asking students to draw or chart their literature review or research understandings at various moments. Figure 2.1 is my attempt to diagram the ethnographic research process. It should be seen as a kind of spiral that, through reflexive moments, continually moves to another place.

Neither this chapter nor any other specification of prestudy tasks can exhaust the possibilities of what you personally might anticipate and do before you begin to collect data. You may engage in exhaustive, detailed planning; or you may be

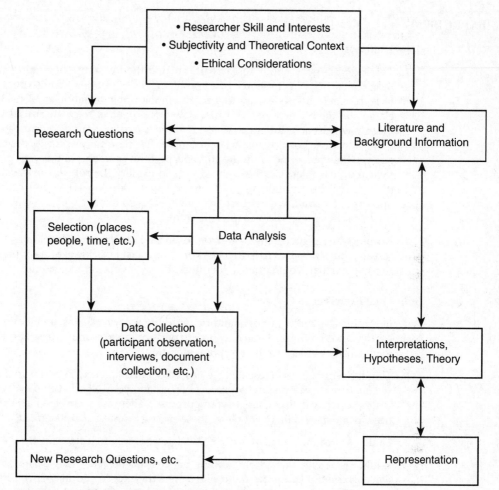

FIGURE 2.1   The Qualitative Research Spiral.

comfortable with preparations well short of exhaustiveness. In this, as in so much of research, you need to find your own style, so that you will learn what works for you. Getting ready to conduct your study is not an end in itself. It is a means to the end of data collection. The next two chapters address such activity: participant observation and interviewing.

RECOMMENDED READINGS

Maxwell, J. 2005. *Qualitative Research Design: An Interactive Approach,* 2nd ed. Thousand Oaks, CA: Sage.

Schram, T. 2006. *Conceptualizing and Proposing Qualitative Research,* 2nd ed. Upper Saddle River, NJ: Pearson Education, Inc.

EXERCISES

Class Exercises

1. This exercise goes about research in an unorthodox way—beginning with the research participants in search of a "problem." I suggest this exercise not as a way to *do* research, but as a way to *practice* ethnographic techniques. Consider your classmates the research participants. Now work together to create a research statement to which each student could bring some expertise. Frame your research statement in a clear, focused way. For example, the class may want to describe and analyze how part-time graduate students perceive, manage, and assign priority to their multiple roles. Or, they may decide to explore the role "peer learning" has played in the education of graduate students. Develop what you consider an appropriate qualitative research statement. This statement will serve as the basis for more class exercises in chapters to come.

2. Keeping the research statement (from Exercise 1) as the core, develop three to five research questions that help to focus your topic. List possible aspects of the conceptual context that would guide a literature review if you were to do one.

Individual Exercises

1. Diagram your current understanding (working theory) of a research issue of interest to you. What important concepts are parts of this research interest and how do they relate? Begin a search of relevant literature.

2. Through writing a set of research memos, work out differences between your research statement and your research purposes. Try asking yourself what it is that you hope your research will do or change (your purposes). Then, ask yourself what is it that you need to understand that might have these effects (your research statement).

3. Draft research questions to further elucidate your research statement.

4. While discussing metaphors, author Bill Roorbach (1998, 126) quotes comedian Steven Wright: "I've got a mind like a steel trap: rusty and illegal in thirty-seven states." This following exercise is adapted from one of Roorbach's writing exercises.

   In a long paragraph, compare your project focus to something else. You can use what you might see as "obvious" metaphors—the school is like a factory or implementing a new program is like constructing a building. You could also use a less obvious metaphor—the school is like a rodeo or implementing the new program is like fishing. Extend the metaphor as far as you can go, to the absurd, while posing questions about your topic. Here's from Roorbach asking questions of the mind like a steel trap:

   > If your mind is like a steep trap, what is the spring? What is the steel plate that triggers the release mechanism? If animals are ideas and minds are traps, do minds destroy ideas? Do ideas have lives separate from minds? Do ideas roam the wilderness? What are the furs of ideas? And tell me this: Who is the trapper running the trap line? What's the chain? What's the stake?

   Finally, write a second paragraph reflecting upon how this metaphor activity may have led you to think differently about or ask some new questions of your topic.

CHAPTER 3

Being There: Developing Understanding through Participant Observation

After a hot, still day, the evening was delightfully cool. Ina, Elija, and Marcus had just entered my house in the Caribbean valley. They had been to a "sing" up on Mango Ridge. A Methodist missionary group from the United States was in the valley for the evening to preach and spread the Word. It was an occasion for a gathering—something out of the ordinary—and many attended. Ina told how a young woman asked him if he had accepted the Lord as his personal savior. Ina had said yes and produced a detailed conversion story when asked for the particulars. All three friends laughed at this and the other invented tales they had told of evil deeds and repentance.

I laughed with them but felt uneasy. After several months in the Caribbean valley, I suddenly wondered what was real and what was made up in the stories I had been told. Ina, Elija, and Marcus assured me that, although they made up names and made up jobs in their earliest conversations, they no longer did this. After all, I was living in the valley with them; I was "practically Vincentian."

Whether you are in a village in another country or in a school in your home-town, participant observation provides the opportunity for acquiring the status of "trusted person." Through being a part of a social setting, you learn firsthand how the actions of research participants correspond to their words; see patterns of behavior; experience the unexpected, as well as the expected; and develop a quality of trust, relationship, and obligation with others in the setting. Interview questions that develop through observations are connected to known behavior, and their answers can therefore be better interpreted. Although participant observation ideally continues throughout the period of data collection, it is particularly important in the beginning stages because of its role in informing you about appropriate areas of investigation and in developing a sound researcher-researched relationship. This discussion on participant observation focuses first on the process and then on the researcher.

THE PARTICIPANT–OBSERVATION CONTINUUM

> A psychotherapy clinic, for example, provides a different situation for storytelling than a retirement party.
>
> (Gubrium and Holstein 2009, 32)

Participant observation is a problematic term. First, it is used in different ways (O'Reilly 2005). Some use *participant observation* as a synonym for the whole process of doing fieldwork (observations, conversations, interviews, document collection). Others (and I) distinguish participant observation as a research method different from interviewing, although I readily acknowledge that while interviewing, the researcher often makes observations and may be participating in the social life of the community. The differentiation is more for the ease of focused discussion of associated techniques and issues, than to separate as distinct entities.

Second, the term *participant observation* is troubling because it is an oxymoron. The words contradict themselves, urging engagement and distance, involvement and detachment (Tedlock 2000, 465). The participant observer stance can create tension within the researcher and between researcher and participants. As a researcher, your observer stance can make you and others feel as though you are a spy of sorts, while your participant stance can indicate a closeness or an involvement that may be suspect because of your role as researcher (and observer). In some forms of qualitative research, such as collaborative and action research, tensions in the participant–observer role are lessened because the researcher is either already an insider or is invited to work with insiders on the research project. Both observations and participation contribute to what you can learn about a site, a process, and insider perspectives. You need to decide, in relationship to the kind of research you choose to do, how much of a participant and how much of an observer you want to be.

You can think about participant observation as ranging across a continuum from mostly observation to mostly participation. It can be the sole means of data collection or one of several. Although your actual participant–observer role may fall at any point along this continuum, you will most likely find yourself at different points at different times in the data collection process.

Psychologists often carry out research entirely at the *observer* end of the continuum. This role is more in keeping with the positivist paradigm, wherein the researcher has little to no interaction with those being studied. For example, the researcher may observe children in a university day-care program through a one-way glass. Similarly, the observer may sit on a city park bench, notebook in hand, observing town square activities. At the complete observer end of the continuum, people do not know that they are being observed.

Observer as participant is the next point on the continuum. The researcher remains primarily an observer but has some interaction with study participants. When another graduate student and I assisted Alan Peshkin in a study of a fundamentalist Christian school (Peshkin 1986), we interacted with students and teachers, but for a semester we were primarily observers, taking notes from the back of a classroom. We did not teach; give advice; or assist teachers, students, or administrators.

In contrast, I was more of a *participant as observer* during my work in Saint Vincent (Glesne 1985). I was interested in nonformal education and interacted extensively with others throughout my year's residency in their village. I assisted in agricultural work, socialized, and became an intermediary, if not an advocate, in interactions with agricultural agencies. A paradox develops as you become more of a participant and less of an observer. The more you function as a member of the everyday world of the researched, the more you risk losing the eye of the uninvolved outsider; yet, the more you participate, the greater your opportunity to learn.

The *full participant* is simultaneously a functioning member of the community undergoing investigation and an investigator. You may already be part of the community, or you may decide to join it. In order to learn about the politics and workings of a social welfare agency, for example, you might seek employment with such an agency. Researching in your own community is not always as easy as first perceived because you may have to manage two, sometimes conflicting, roles. Jan Yoors, in his book *The Gypsies,* describes the dilemma of becoming a full participant: "I was torn between two worlds and unable to choose between them despite the Romany saying that *Yekka buliasa nashti beshes pe done grastende* (with one behind you cannot sit on two horses)" (Yoors 1967, 47).

Where on this continuum *should* you place yourself? Your answer depends on the question you are investigating, the context of your study, and your theoretical perspective—to restate some of the contingencies underlying this much-used response. What applies to so much of the conduct of qualitative inquiry applies here: What is best done is less a case of what is established as right than of what your judgment tells you is fitting. If you are interested, as Woolfson (1988) was, in the nonverbal interaction between medical doctors and their patients during the initial, symptom-description phase, then you need to observe as unobtrusively as possible. Woolfson operated a video camera from outside the room where doctor and patient sat.

The context of the study can also affect your position on the participant–observer continuum. Because neither Peshkin nor I was fundamentalist Christian, we could never, without more deception than we could justify, be full participants in the study of the Christian day school. In his study of ethnicity in a California high school, Peshkin (1991) found himself moving from his usual "observer as participant" role to more of a "participant as observer" because he was easily and readily incorporated into the lives of the people there. Your place on the continuum also depends on your theoretical perspective. If you are doing action research, you are more likely to be a full participant than if you are doing conventional ethnography.

For some, observation and participation have moved into virtual realms. Multi-player computer games involve virtual reality sites that combine elements of role-playing. Dungeons and Dragons was the classic virtual fantasy world, and such games were referred to as MUDs, for "multi-user dungeons" (which later became multi-user domains or dimensions). The next iteration of MUDs was social virtual worlds such as World of Warcraft, in which a large number of players could interact, with each assuming the role of a fictional character that became an inhabitant in a virtual world. Some qualitative researchers have focused on aspects of these virtual worlds, observing and participating within them. For example, anthropologist Frank Schaap (2002) spent up to sixteen hours a day for two years participating in a virtual reality called New Carthage. He states that he "studied the daily life of the citizens of New Carthage as I might have done in any other town" (16), taking notes as his character (he took on the identity of a woman named Eveline) lived in the virtual city: "In this violent city I have worked, eaten, slept, gotten drunk and fallen in love. I have loved and lost those I loved. I have killed to survive and barely survived the attack of a psychotic gang leader myself" (16). His ethnographic study focuses on the social and cultural conventions participants use to construct and perform their characters. See his ethnography *The Words That Took Us There: Ethnography in a Virtual Reality.*

PARTICIPANT–OBSERVATION GOALS

Some people and some places are much studied. People can become jaundiced by the presence of outsiders who stay too short a time to get the picture that local folks have of themselves. Robert Caro, author of a book on Lyndon Johnson, describes his entry into the thinly populated county where Johnson grew up. At first the local people did not trust him. Too many reporters and journalists had already come for a day or a month and had invariably misrepresented the place and its people. Caro (1988) says,

> The people felt—and they were right—that they were being used, and that the things that were being written didn't accurately reflect and convey the country they loved. When I moved there, as soon as I said "I love it here and I'm going to live here and I'm going to stay here as long as it takes to truly understand it," their attitude really changed. (227)

In contrast to the journalistic tendency to swoop in and swoop out, the ethnographic researcher means to stay long enough to get a full description and a deep understanding.

The main outcome of participant observation is to better understand the research setting, its participants, and their behavior. Achieving this outcome requires time and a learner's stance. Hymes (1982) states:

> Much of what we seek to find out in ethnography is knowledge that others already have. Our ability to learn ethnographically is an extension of what every human being must do, that is, learn the meanings, norms, patterns of a way of life. (29)

"Rather than studying people," agrees Spradley, "ethnography means learning from people" (Spradley 1979, 3).

As a learner, you are not in the research setting to preach or evaluate, nor to compete for prestige or status. Your focus is on research participants and their perspectives and behaviors. To maintain this stance, you need to be flexible and open to changing your point of view. Mary Catherine Bateson (1984) describes the importance of this attitude in the lives of her parents (Gregory Bateson and Margaret Mead) and in anthropological fieldwork in general:

> ... even when you take with you certain questions you want answered or certain expectations about how a society functions, you must be willing to turn your attention from one focus to another, depending on what you are offered by events, looking for clues to patterns and not knowing what will prove to be important or how your own attention and responsiveness have been shaped. (164)

Through participant observation, you also seek to make the strange familiar and the familiar strange (Erickson 1973). The strange becomes familiar in the process of understanding it. To make the familiar strange is often more difficult because you must continually question your own assumptions and perceptions, asking yourself: Why is it this way and not different? Overcome your disposition to settle into a way of seeing and understanding that gives you the comfort of closure at the price of shutting down thought. Philosopher Raimon Panikkar (1979, 20) refers to preconceived assumptions and socialized viewpoints as guiding myths: "The myth you live is comprised of the ensemble of contexts you take for granted." As participant observers, you want to be open to exposing and rethinking that which you have taken for granted. Only then can you begin to expand on what you are capable of seeing and understanding. Panikkar describes the myths we live as "the accepted horizon within which we place our experience of truth." You want your horizons to be wide.

In the end, your new understandings—achieved through your learner's stance, your flexibility, and your emphasis on making the strange familiar and the familiar strange—provide new vantage points with wider horizons, new ways of thinking about some aspect of social interaction.

THE PARTICIPANT–OBSERVATION PROCESS

> Seeing, being surrounded by the visual, doesn't always or necessarily mean that we notice what we see. It is the paying attention, the looking and the taking note of what we see that makes images especially important to art, scholarship, and research.
>
> (Weber 2008, 42)

In everyday life you observe people, interactions, and events. Participant observation in a research setting, however, differs in that the researcher carefully observes, systematically experiences, and consciously records in detail the many aspects of a situation. Moreover, a participant observer must constantly analyze his or her observations for meaning (What is going on here?) and for evidence of personal bias (Am I seeing what I hoped to see and nothing else? Am I being judgmental and evaluative?). Finally, a participant observer does all of this because it is instrumental to the research goals, which is to say that the observer is present somewhere for particular reasons. In your ordinary, everyday life, you may be a good observer of the interaction around you, but you do not consciously record and analyze what you hear and see in the context of particular goals that direct your behavior.

Research goals are often varied. No matter what the specific goals, one general goal that accompanies research is the need to write or communicate "findings." Perhaps you are collecting data so that you can compose a thesis or dissertation. Maybe you will create an article or prepare a report for a funding agency. You might be documenting some process as a basis for action. Thinking about this communicating goal from the beginning helps in the end. Novelist Stephen King (2000, 103) refers to writing as a form of telepathy. One person puts words on a page, describing a setting or an event. In a different time, in a different place, another person reads those words and, if the transmission is good, sees and feels nearly the same thing as the writer. Realizing the possibilities of good telepathy, you need to note details, reflections, and emotional responses as you experience them. If you don't, you will transmit (and have received) only vague images with fuzzy edges.

Early Days of Fieldwork

If you are in a setting somewhat new to you, the first days in the field are the most anxiety-producing, as you question whether people will accept you and whether what you are doing is "right." The early days are also exciting and full of new learnings, but the many unknowns can create stressful situations.

After you've received overall permission to do your study, figure out where you can hang out and begin to get to know people without having to get any one person's permission to be there. If in a school or hospital, this might be the cafeteria, picnic grounds, or staff lounge. Spend time in these places, getting to know people and letting them get to know you, so that they will feel comfortable with you and will welcome you in "their" space.

If doing research in sites unfamiliar to you, do not feel the need to "get in" with everyone, everywhere. Look for easy openings, that is, with friendly, welcoming people. Spend enough time with them so they get to know what you are doing, how you will be present, and what it is like to have you present—so that they can reassure others about you. But try to not spend so much time with one group that you neglect others at the site.

Look for entry into closed places that in some ways are controlled by a person or group, possibly by arranging for introductions through mutual friends. Do not seek administrative-ordered permission to enter closed places in institutions, such as schools, clinics, or offices; if formal permission is given, do not take it as a proper invitation. Instead, arrange for the administration to announce your presence; then, address all of those present with your research intentions, clarifying that you want to come to their spaces but that you will not do so unless they agree.

If in a school, ask teachers if you can introduce yourself the first time you come to a class. This allows you to reassure the teacher and the students that you are there to observe, not to judge or evaluate. You can also more easily interact with students because they know who you are and why you are there.

Finally, guard against bringing preconceived opinions to your observations. This is particularly easy to do if you are or have been a teacher, nurse, or social worker yourself and then become a participant observer in a similar site. Even though you were once "there," you cannot safely assume that you know what the people are like in your research site. All schools, hospitals, and social work agencies are not the same. For example, Sandy taught in a school where teachers were very critical of professors from a nearby university. Therefore, when she began participant observation in a school in another university town, she was hesitant to identify herself with the university—when in fact the school chosen for her study had a good working relationship with the university. Do not assume that you know nothing about schools, hospitals, or village life, but do assume that you have much to learn about the particular site and its people.

Observations

The focus of your observations will vary with the kind of research approach you are taking. For example, if doing narrative ethnography, you will concentrate more on the details surrounding conversations and means of communicating than if doing general ethnography (Gubrium and Holstein 2009). The advice that follows is for those involved in general ethnographic or case study work, but much applies to other qualitative research approaches as well.

When you begin your role as a participant observer, try to observe everything that is happening: make notes and jot down thoughts without narrow, specific regard for your research problem. Study the *setting* and describe it in words and in sketches, using all your senses. How does the setting sound and smell? In what ways does the setting change from place to place throughout your research site? For instance, if you are doing research in a K–12 school, then in what ways is the first grade setting similar to and different from a twelfth grade classroom? Work on making the familiar strange. For example, if you notice that classroom doors tend to be left open (or closed), then ask yourself what this signifies.

Take note of the *participants* in the setting. Who are they in terms of age, gender, social class, ethnicity? What do they do and say? Who interacts with whom? Human beings communicate nonverbally in many ways. They send messages through what they wear, through their hair styles, through their accessories. They make announcements through how close they stand to another, through their use of space when around others, referred to as *proxemics*. Remember that "the body is not just a physical object; it is a social object" (Sunstein and Chiseri-Strater 2002, 295). So take field notes that describe not only what people are doing and saying but also what they are wearing, how they decorate themselves, and how they use and share space with others.

Take note of *events*, differentiating between special events and daily events; then look for *acts* within those events. In the fundamentalist Christian school, for example, the first event of every day was a teachers' meeting. What kind of greetings do teachers offer during teachers' meetings, and to whom do they offer them? What do they informally talk about with one another? What kinds of questions do they ask of the principal? In other words, what "acts" make up the "event" of a teachers' meeting?

Another category for observation is people's *gestures*—their postures, positions, and movement, also known as *kinesis*. How do students show enthusiasm and boredom? How does the teacher? What gestures help the principal to deliver his or her points? Observe which gestures jump out at you, which you take for granted, and which you might be misinterpreting. If a child lies with her head on the desk while the teacher is talking, is she sleepy, bored, or concentrating?

Cross-cultural research brings with it the recognition of either new gestures or new meanings to familiar gestures. A whispered "pssst" in the Caribbean can be a friendly "hello." Sucking air in through one's teeth with an upward motion of the head, however, is not the desired reaction to one of your serious comments—it signifies disregard, disagreement, or disdain. But you need not go to another country to find differences in how gestures are used, as those of you from marginalized groups are aware. Compared to European American children, Native American children may opt for collaborative work assignments and avoid ones that draw attention to individual success (Sindell 1987). African American children may seek eye contact with the teacher but at a different rate than white children do (McDermott 1987). Just as teachers, to be effective, need to be aware of cultural differences in gestures, so, too, do researchers.

As a participant observer, then, consciously observe the research setting; its participants; and the events, acts, and gestures that occur within them. In the process, note what you see, hear, feel, and think. Begin to look for patterns and to abstract similarities and differences across individuals and events. For example, Ginny chose to practice her observation skills in the lounge of a squash facility during a men's round-robin tournament. After a period of jotting notes, she began to see a pattern:

> The winners of matches seem to stand or walk around after the match is complete. The losers always sit immediately. Blue headband wins. Red sits. Blue goes off to find a towel and water. Blondy, who had mentioned a head problem earlier, wins a match with Glasses. Glasses sits down. Blondy walks around and asks the director who is winning.

Ginny continued with more examples and concluded with questions about the behavior of male winners and losers during sports competition. She was able to move from the individuals in her observation, to their behavior, to thoughts about the more general behavior of men in sports events.

Wolcott (1981) suggests four more strategies to guide observations: (1) observations by a broad sweep, (2) observations of nothing in particular, (3) observations that search for paradoxes, and (4) observations that search for problems facing the group.

In the broad sweep observations, you try to observe and record everything. Since doing so is impossible, you begin to be selective about what to observe and record, and then need to reflect upon your choices. When you search for nothing in particular, you begin to note what stands out, what appears as unusual. And when you search for paradoxes and for problems, you begin to look deeper into the interactions before you. All these strategies help to make the familiar strange, make the strange familiar, and ground you in the research context.

Field Notes

> The difference between doing fieldwork and just "hanging out" is the writing. Without writing, the sharp, incisive details about people, places, and cultures are lost to us.
>
> (Sunstein and Chiseri-Strater 2002, 56)

Notebook Form. The field notebook or field log is the primary recording tool of the qualitative researcher. It becomes filled with descriptions of people, places, events, activities, and conversations; and it becomes a place for ideas, reflections, hunches, and notes about patterns that seem to be emerging. It also becomes a place for exploring the researcher's personal reactions.

The actual form of the field notebook varies with the preferences of the individual researcher. Some arrange everything chronologically in spiral-bound notebooks; others keep loose-leaf notebooks so that different kinds of notes can be easily separated; yet others take notes directly onto their laptops when in settings where that is possible, shortcutting the transcription step of typing field notes into computer files. What form you choose for keeping notes is not important. That you keep field notes, however, is vital.

Making Notes. Lofland and Lofland (1995) distinguish among mental, jotted, and full field notes. Mental notes are made of discussions or observations when pulling out one's notebook would not be prudent. In the fundamentalist Christian school, since Peshkin, the other research assistant, and I did not take notes during chapel, we made mental notes and wrote them up later. Jotted notes may be done in private or in public. They are the few words jotted down to help remember a thought or a description that will be completed later on. The full field notes are the running notes written preferably throughout the day, but sometimes, depending on the circumstances, after the observational period.

If possible, carry a notebook with you at all times and make it known that, as a researcher, you will write in your notebook. Your role will become that of inscriber, and soon it will be expected that if anything at all is going on, you will write it down. Of course, not all situations lend themselves to full note taking.

Carry a field notebook with you all the time, if possible. You never know when or where you will see something, talk with someone, or have a thought that you want to record.

Agar (1973) could not take his notebook with him when doing research on drug addiction in New York City. Other settings are more conducive. Pens, paper, and clipboards are standard equipment of nurses and doctors. Researchers in these settings often find their note taking an expected action, even if they have no medical training. If unsure about how your note taking will be received, you may want to spend a few days to a few weeks just hanging out, getting to know the people and the place before you determine just when and where it is acceptable to take notes.

All notes should be expanded later, preferably the same evening. When you review your notes, you add in things you hadn't taken the time to note while at the site and also reflect on what you've seen. These reflections help you construct your beginning theories on what's going on and help to shape the direction for more observations and questions. Some studies indicate that you can sleep on a day's events and retain your recall abilities, so that you could write up field notes the morning after participant observation. Ability to remember the details needed for field notes declines rapidly after that period of time, however.

Allot ample time for working on field notes. If you are making only mental or jotted notes, some researchers suggest that you give as much time to writing up your notes as you did to being in the field. If you are taking full field notes, then allow several hours to read through your notes to clarify and expand on them and to add your reflective thoughts and ideas. If this all seems rather much, be assured that your ability to write quickly and to observe and remember what you saw and heard does improve with practice. You will be pleased with the trouble you take to prepare clear, ample notes when later you sit down to analyze and write. One caveat: Your comfort zone may be breached by the demands of note keeping. Find a balance between preparing notes that support your research needs and preparing them to an extent that makes research an aversive act.

Descriptive Notes.   Your field notes should be both descriptive and analytic. In recording details, strive for accuracy but avoid being judgmental. Make sure that your notes will enable you, a year later, to visualize the moment, the person, the setting, the day. Summarizing observations into succinct abstract statements will not do the job. For example, after observing a class, you might be tempted to write, "The class was disorderly and noisy." This statement does not present a clear picture of the classroom, and it is judgmental because it relies on the researcher's conceptions of "disorder" and "noise." The following statements are more concrete in their descriptiveness:

> The fifth grade class contained fifteen girls and twelve boys. When I entered, they were clustered loosely into six groups. One group of four girls was trying to see who could blow the biggest bubble with their gum. A group of five boys was imitating a Kung Fu movie they had seen on TV the evening before. . . .

When you observe and describe the interactions taking place, you invariably look for patterns in what at first you might perceive as chaos and disorder. Check your field notes for vague adjectives such as *many* or *some* and replace them with more descriptive words. Look for and replace with descriptions words that convey an evaluative impression, that obscure rather than clarify, such as *wonderful, mundane, interesting, doing nothing, nice,* or *good.*

Make note of the dialogue that occurs. In particular, focus on words frequently used in or unique to the setting. Such terms help in wording interview questions and often become *insider* or participant-generated analytic categories in the final write-up. Be alert for familiar words that assume very different meanings from your usual understanding. I spent a month in Saint Vincent before I understood that Vincentians did not use the word *country* to describe any nonurban area. Instead, they used *up country* to refer to the windward, or eastern, side of the island. A young man who lived in the capital city, Kingstown, but went *down leeward* (to the western side of the island) every weekend to help his grandmother on her land could honestly answer that he could not remember when he was last *in the country.*

Drawing sketches also helps you to visualize a setting. Focus on where people and inanimate objects are located in space. Are there patterns? Do they change over time?

Your eyes, ears, and hands work together to portray the details of a setting in your field notes, particularly early on in your fieldwork, when you are trying to draft an overall picture of the setting and its people. Through note taking, you reflect on the appropriateness of your problem statement and become increasingly focused. Then, what you record and what you omit will begin to depend on your ever-refined, ever-clarified purpose. If you decide to emphasize, for instance, the interactions of international children in a university day-care center, then you do not need to describe in detail the teacher's curriculum. If, however, you are looking at the role religion plays in Christian schools, then you do note where in the curriculum religion does and does not play a part.

The following is an example of descriptive notes from my field log that I wrote one early morning in Saint Vincent, after I had walked the mile to the sea from the house I was renting:

> The valley stretches from the sea four-and-a-half miles inland until lost in the interior's 3,000-foot peaks. At 6:00 A.M. on a November Sunday morning, the bay is already a scene of relaxed activity. As a light rain develops, old men move into the fishermen's bamboo shelter. One curses another about his chickens. At the mouth of the river, men, women, and children gather to catch tree-tree (fish no longer than one's fingernail) by weighting burlap sacks on the river bottom with stone and then covering the sacks with "bush" (branches of trees and shrubs). The small fish seek the shelter of the leaves but are caught when the fabric is suddenly lifted from the water. On down the black sand beach, young women and children sit where the water meets the shore. Young men swim to a fishing boat anchored farther out, climb aboard, and talk as the boat gently rocks with the rising and falling sea. A rainbow stretches from beyond a "board house" (house made of wood) on a point of land bathed in yellow light to the middle of the sea. In the other direction lies the valley, green and pastoral, with rugged hills covered in clouds.
>
> A lane lined by sprouting fence posts leads into the valley. Cattle, horses, and sheep intermingle on the lush, river-mouth land. Thorny, palmlike trees stand out on the nearby cliffs. They soon give way to coconut palm, mangoes, breadfruit, and citrus trees. A mile into the valley, where most of the villages are, one forgets the immensity and varied moods of the nearby sea and is only aware of the enfolding mountains, often misty with rain. Villages sprinkle the two miles of arterial road which, after the last village, winds on up into the mountains a short distance before becoming a track for walking and climbing to land terraced and planted primarily in eddoes or bananas. The fields continue as the land slopes steeply, but then give way to natural vegetation.

These descriptive notes were intended to portray the context in which more focused observations and conversations took place. They set the scene for discussion of the life of young people within that valley. They do not analyze or try to explain what was going on; they only describe.

In addition to setting the scene, good descriptive notes capture specific interactions among research participants. For example, Yvette was studying how adult learners perceive, create meaning, and support one another in long-term or intensive learning groups. Through multiple observations of core courses, she focused on the interactions of adult learners in two different cohorts:

> 3/3/97, 4:00 P.M., DOCTORAL COHORT OBSERVATIONS
>
> Students are arriving, they are sharing ideas about their projects with peers in the same project group. Most are sitting in the same seats as last week. *Will students sit in the same seats throughout the semester?*
>
> Prof (professor) tapes the multicolored handprinted (newsprint paper) agenda onto the classroom's right cinder block wall.
>
> K (s—student) passes out a photocopied bibliography from the 1997 NAWE Conference as a resource for books on the writing process.

C (s) shares information about a local conference students could attend.

K (s) passes a flier around the student circle (more of a square made up of long black lunch tables placed end to end, surrounded by molded black plastic chairs, the table square fills the room) on Women's History Month. All look at it with varying degrees of interest and then pass it on to the next student.

C (s) Asks the group to tell her which group she is now in from last month.

D (s) Asks group about information she never received because she wasn't at the fall retreat. She is told to call the program administrative assistant. She doesn't understand why she didn't get the information.

L (s) Shares the title of a book on the future millennium. The group listens but is slowly breaking into whispered conversations.

Whole group begins to engage in (full volume) side conversations with people with whom they are sitting.

Several handouts are passed around the circle for everyone. Some are for upcoming student presentations.

Photocopied material appears to be an artifact of the group, a resource for their learning process, work process, class act—activity. Higher education culture—and the meaning of photocopied materials? Everyone knows the passing routine.

Although Yvette's observation notes are primarily descriptive, she did not hesitate to insert a thought or question as it occurred to her. Some of her questions became part of formal interviews; others, she inquired into more informally. Yet other questions helped to guide her subsequent observations. Her noting "the passing routine" is an example of making the familiar strange, as she observed and posed reflective questions of everyday activities that went on around her.

Some qualitative researchers approach observations as just something to do to set the scene or to add a little texture to data obtained through conversations and interviews. Observations, however, work best in a back-and-forth process with interviews and conversations. They set the stage for things to discuss, for moving you out of your own assumptions of how things work, and for understanding what you are told. As narrative researchers Jaber Gubrium and James Holstein (2009, viii) state,

> Narratives reduced to transcripts are flat, without practical depth or detail. . . . The issue of what is not uttered or storied as opposed to what is communicated encourages us to consider the surrounding conditions of storytelling. Such information can only be discerned from direct consideration of the storying process within the circumstances in which it unfolds.

Analytical notes are part of the process of delving beneath the surface descriptions of what is seen and heard.

Analytic Notes.   Bateson (1984) says of her mother, Margaret Mead,

> Margaret always emphasized the importance of recording first impressions and saving those first few pages of notes instead of discarding them in the scorn of later sophistication, for the informed eye has its own blindness as it begins to take for granted things that were initially bizarre. When something occurs to you, *write it down,* she said. (165)

Analytic notes—those recordings of things that occur to you—are some-times called *observer comments*, but they should be more than comments. After each day of participant observation, the qualitative researcher should take time for reflective and analytic noting. This is the time to write down feelings, work out problems, jot down ideas and impressions, clarify earlier interpretations, speculate about what is going on, and make flexible short- and long-term plans for the days to come. Of course, reflective and analytic thoughts may come to you during participant observation and at other times as well. It is important to make note of these thoughts too—to write *memos* to yourself (Glaser and Strauss 1967), as Yvette did in the example above. Otherwise, the thoughts are apt to slip away. Mark these memos in some way to identify them easily as your own thoughts and wonderings. Analytic noting is a type of data analysis conducted throughout the research process; its contributions range from problem identifi-cation, to question development, to understanding the patterns and themes in your work.

As an example, I draw again from Yvette's field notes, this time from her reflective analytic notes after an observation session:

3/25/97, FIELD REFLECTIONS
There is a marked difference between the participation and interaction patterns of the whole group and small groups. In large group the dialogue often is constructed by the same people who offer statements that often act to support the group's dia-logue in the same way each time. There are those who speak openly and more often than others (Martin, Alexis and Dee). Some (Travis and Mel) speak at the end of dialogue segments to confirm or wisely summarize (rarely taking chances). Becky contributes statements that ask for clarification of tasks and ideas, Suzanne's state-ments seem riskier in that she experiments with articulating what she is learning to the group for verification. Beth questions authority.

There are those who rarely speak, they watch and respond when it is safe, after others have structured the dialogue direction. In addition to the large group dialogue, there are often whispered dialogues taking place simultane-ously (Katrina and Beth). What are the whispered dialogues about? Will I see changes in the dialogue patterns as time passes and topics change? When and why?

So what is happening?

1. Are adults negotiating the public/private duality of speaking and acting in the larger group where instructors are present? Is there a feeling of fear and uneasi-ness with the readings and project task that reduces iteration? No one wishes to appear unprepared, unintelligent. No risk taking?
2. Women are quiet except for a few who are used to public speaking. Some males dominate and have to comment on what just about everyone says. Some males are quiet.
3. Lack of time, and an over-ambitious project is taking away the time for corridor talk. The report is that students are becoming bitchy with each other. Could it be stress, pressure to perform, no time to thoughtfully communicate, reflect, engage in praxis . . .

Yvette's analytic notes moved beyond her initial descriptions of details in cohort members' interactions to reflecting on the patterns within those interactions and to raising questions about their meaning.

Research Diary.   More than observer comments or memos to yourself regarding thoughts about what you are observing and hearing, your research diary is a place for autobiographical notes that create a record of your behavior and emotions throughout the research. The research diary does not have to be a separate journal; rather, it is your intentions that matter. You take time to write thoughts that situate you within the research process. You might, for example, consider ways in which you are an insider and an outsider and what advantages and disadvantages each position provides (Hay 2005). Sunstein and Chiseri-Strater (2002, 95-96) suggest that you periodically ask yourself and write about the following:

1. What surprised you? (helps track assumptions)
2. What intrigues you? (helps track personal interests and positions)
3. What disturbs you? (helps track tensions and possibly stereotypes and prejudices)

Writing in your research diary becomes a means for thinking about how the research is co-created among you and research participants; how actions and inter-actions shape what follows, and where power dynamics lie. It is a location for reflecting on ethical issues that trouble you. And, the research diary often becomes a place to vent or express frustration and then, through continued writing, to bet-ter understand those emotions and derive more questions or devise new strate-gies. These notes also may become part of the final text, the researcher's story woven into the stories of others.

The following example is from the research diary I kept while in Oaxaca, Mexico. The notes were written after six weeks in the country. Through writing them, I figured out that I was dealing with a level of culture shock even though I had traveled and lived in many places before. I realized through writing that I didn't understand the rules by which many things worked. I felt too much an observer and outsider and unsure about how to be part of life in Oaxaca:

> 6:00 A.M. I'm not sleeping. I open the big window to the street to let in some fresh cool air. The air is heavy with smoke of burning garbage. I close the window and try to sleep, but I can't. I'm thinking about the people I saw begging on the street yesterday. It seems that more people beg on Sundays and I wonder if that is true or if they are just more noticeable because the streets are comparatively empty. It would be more comfortable to be on the streets on Sunday, I think. Do people give more easily on Sunday too? I am haunted by a woman and small boy I passed with-out stopping to unzip my backpack to find my purse and then unzip it to find some money. The woman had no legs and only stubs for arms. She was in a small red wagon, the kind a child might have in the U.S. Squatting next to her was a small boy, maybe seven years old. He had his head in his arms and was crying. Did he pull the woman (his mother?) to the sidewalk near the square? Does he have to care for her or is there someone else? How do they live? I think, how I could have said to

the boy (and I wonder why so much of my sympathy lies with him?), "Come, there is a woman three blocks down and around the corner who makes tacos. Let's get one for you and your mother."

Why am I so taken with them and not the woman I see every day chanting for assistance near the bakery or the man with the shakes who makes the rounds of the open-air cafes or the old man who is so stooped he walks bent over? I usually give to the two men (one blind) playing beautiful music outside the museum because they are "doing" something and it is lovely. But what can the woman with no legs and arms do? I try to figure out how I can more easily (why aren't pockets put in women's clothes?) always have several pesos available to give away. Several pesos? Why shouldn't I be giving more? What does giving do?

Suddenly I hear a heavy thud, followed by the screams of a woman and, somewhere, the barking of a dog. My immediate thought is of the dog I saw hit and left on the road to die near the market on Saturday. But the dog did not bark on Saturday. The screams continue and I reopen the heavy wooden shutters. I wonder if it is some sort of confrontation, but also I know somehow someone has been hit by a car. Maybe a bus. I can see a young woman on the steps to her building across from me. She is looking on down the road. I go into the other room and pull back the curtains. A man is lying on the road and two women are kneeling over him, smoothing his hair and crying. Several people have gathered and are standing around. One motions to me to call an ambulance. The police? I don't know. Who would I call? But I cannot call. I don't have a phone. One of the women stands and takes off her white sweater and lays it on top of the man. I feel helpless and useless. I am feeling very out of place.

These notes did not focus on anything related to my research. Although the notes are full of questions, none of them were ones that I wanted to shape into interviews. Rather, they were questions of me and of how to act and interact in a place I didn't know. Feeling insecure with my research project, with not knowing people well, and with the language, I was longing to connect. Then, I was bombarded with situations begging literally for my humanity and I felt frozen and distraught. To continue living in Oaxaca, I had to figure out how I was going to deal with both begging and traffic, interactions that became for me, symbolic of learning how to move in the culture as a whole. (Autobiographical notes and their use receive more attention in Chapter 5.)

Noting Advice.   The following guidelines are, in a sense, tricks of the participant observer's trade, gained through experience. They are lore about the process of *noting* as a participant observer:

1. Leave ample margins on either side of your notes for afterthoughts and for preliminary coding.
2. Make sure to include the date, time, and place of each observation.
3. Create your own form of shorthand to assist in note taking. For instance, in the Christian school study *Christian* soon became Xn, *student* S, *knowledge* K, *teacher* T, and *school* sch. I also use the same shortened forms for similar

prepositions and other commonly used words, relying on the context to differentiate them. Thus, *became* and *because* are both noted as b/c, *with* as w/, and *without* as w/o. If you know shorthand, then you may see this made-up shorthand as inefficient; if not, then my advice is to develop your own system.

4. When taking jotted notes, do not discuss your observations with someone else before writing up full field notes. Such talk not only dissipates the need to get your observations and thoughts down on paper but also can modify your original perceptions. This does not mean that you should not compare your interpretations with others, but you should first record your own observations and reflections.

5. Even if you have been taking full running notes throughout the day, your work is not done when the school bell rings or the sun sets. Read through the day's notes. Fill in remembered descriptions, clarify and expand briefly-noted events or actions, and reflect on the day in general.

6. Invariably, unplanned occasions provide data relevant to your research question. Include these casual encounters in your fieldnotes. Qualitative research is not delimited by time or space, even though when focusing on an institution such as a school, data collection generally occurs within set hours in a set location.

7. Plan to read and ponder your field notes frequently. If you are fortunate enough to be able to immerse yourself in the field, read through your field notes weekly and write memos of thoughts that arise from your notes. This is part of the ongoing analysis. You are starting to see themes and connections.

Do not worry if at first you feel either overwhelmed with all the activity in your site and unable to focus, or disappointed in that nothing special is happening. Lorna felt both when she set out to observe a child with special needs who had been mainstreamed into a regular classroom:

> My first observation left me feeling quite overwhelmed. I immediately was swept into a land of little, cute beings, who seemed to be swarming all over the place, chaotic, yet with some vague sense of order. Noisy, chattering, munching at snacks, getting up, sitting down, yawning, whining, working, listening, leaving, moving. At first, I couldn't even find the identified special needs child. With all that activity, I discovered how difficult it was to take notes. What should be written down? How do I stay focused? How do I deal with the little boy who asks me to help him with his spelling? And though I was specifically looking for interactions with the special needs child, at first, I found nothing out of the ordinary interactions, or almost none. At first glance, except for the "shadow," the aide, I couldn't see any impact of his being in the room. Dismayed, I decided, prematurely, that this data analysis will be boring, if not simple. I was wrong, of course.

Lorna had to stick with her observations over time before she began to see "the extent of and interaction of compassion, affection, and challenge involved in including these children in regular classes."

Finally, be reassured that variety in observations does not mean that someone got it wrong. Journalist Joan Didion (1988) describes how both she and her husband wrote very different books about El Salvador despite being together all of the time that they were there. Differentiating between "institutional" and "cultural" studies of pupils, Ball states, "The landscape looks different depending on the particular hill you happen to choose to stand on" (Ball 1985, 28). Subjective dispositions direct people to a variety of different things. This variety reveals the multiple realities of any social phenomenon, which together provide a fuller picture of the people, the times, and the place. Mary Catherine Bateson (1984) observes,

> You record carefully what your attention has allowed you to see, knowing that you will not see everything and that others will see differently, but recording whatever you can so it will be part of the cumulative picture. (164)

FIELDWORK ALLIES: VISUAL DATA, DOCUMENTS, AND ARTIFACTS

Visual Data: Photography, Video, Maps, and Diagrams

Until the rise of digital photography, extensive use of photographs and video was costly. Video cameras were large and intrusive; today you can get a video camera the size of a deck of cards. Technological advances drastically expand the possibilities of using photographs and video in research projects. Ethnographers and other researchers have used maps and diagrams in their work for some time, but these tools are employed in new ways in participant-oriented research. Banks (2007, 6–7) identifies three general ways in which visual data is used in research:

1. The researcher creates photographs, film, or drawings to document aspects of social interactions or of material culture;
2. The researcher gathers, analyzes, or makes use of images created or used by research participants, such as personal photograph albums, magazines, or television programs; and
3. The researcher and research participant collaborate in the creation and/or study of images.

These uses receive attention in the following sections.

Researcher-Created Visual Data.   Anthropology and psychology researchers began to use photography in the nineteenth century, viewing the camera as a scientific tool that would allow them to classify and demonstrate differences between individuals or groups of people. For example, facial expressions of inmates in insane asylums were taken to identify characteristics that could distinguish the "mad and the stupid." Researchers today clearly use photography and video in other ways, generally to extend observations. Grimshaw (in Bottorff 1994) describes the primary advantages of photographic/video use as that of *density* and *permanence*. The density of data collected through film is greater than that of human observation or audio

Photographing inside the seed bank at the International Rice Research Institute in the Philippines.

recording, and the nature of the record is permanent, in that it is possible to return to the observation repeatedly.

In *Visual Anthropology,* Collier and Collier (1986) describe photography as "an abstracting process of observation but very different from the fieldworker's inscribed notebook" in that photography gathers *specific* information "with qualifying and contextual relationships that are usually missing from codified written notes" (10). This was certainly true for Munoz (1995), who studied work, love, and identity in youths living in Puerto Rico. She reflected upon how photography contributed to her work:

> Photographs still what is moving so I can see it without blur: time, place, a glance, posture, details (What does her face express? What do his eyes say? What color is the dress she's wearing? The shirt he's wearing? What kind of material? Does she have earrings on? Do they have wedding rings? What is their hair like? What are their hands like?) All these combine to give a portrait, in black and white of a person caught at a particular moment in time.... Photographs provide another approach to knowledge that literally brings me face to face with my questions and their answers. (60–61)

Videotaping has been invaluable in qualitative research approaches such as ethnomethodology, event analysis, and microanalysis. Videotapes may be played and replayed, analyzed frame by frame, as a means for close observation aimed at uncovering the practices by which people perform some aspect of their everyday lives. For example, Pat wanted to understand how low-income mothers help their children to learn. She had access to videotapes of such mothers and their children in laboratory-play situations, and she observed the tapes over and over. Then she interviewed the mothers, using her observations as a guide for question development. Through her observations and interviews, Pat developed a detailed coding manual that incorporated both behavioral and cognitive information for analyzing the videotapes. Bottorff (1994) warns, however, that the limitations of this type of data collection include the lack of contextual data beyond the recording and the missed opportunity to be an active participant who is able to test emerging theories as they develop. By relying too heavily on this type of data collection, you can lose the value of being a *participant* in participant observation.

Maps and diagrams can be generated throughout your work. Mind maps, for example, are diagrams in which ideas, tasks, or other items are linked to and radiate out around a key word or idea. They are tools you can use to prompt, group, and classify thoughts. You might use mind maps or some kind of diagram to help focus your topic or to tease apart beginning theories about what's going on within the research site. You might use them to help produce questions and analytical thoughts while doing your research, and you might include them in your final presentation to demonstrate succinctly select aspects of the research. Just as outlining works better for some than for others, so does the process of mapping, but it is worth a try. It's a visual way to work with observations, thoughts, and their relationships. In addition to mind maps, consider creating representational maps. Researchers often sketch features of the research site to indicate how, for example, a teacher sets up her classroom or where plots of land are located in relation to people's homes. See Figure 3.1 for a map of agricultural intercropping on a small-holding in St. Vincent.

Researcher-generated visual data can be used in positivist, interpretivist, and emancipatory ways. It can be used to count, for example, kinds of interactions a teacher might have with different kinds of students in certain situations. It can also be used to stimulate research participants' reflections on their lives in relationship to issues of power or struggles in local and larger contexts.

Participant-Created or -Used Visual Data.   Researchers in the disciplines of communication and media studies frequently conduct content analysis of visual data (movies, television shows, magazines) used by research participants. Analytical procedures tend to rely on quantitative techniques and positivist traditions of objectivity, reliability, and so on (Banks 2007). A more qualitative kind of analysis can be done of participants' stored photos to provide historical and cultural context for a study. Peshkin (1978), for example, asked residents of his rural school-community study to show him their family albums, which contained pictures dating back as far as 70 years. Such pictures not only captured the past in a special way but also served as the basis for interviewing, suggesting topics that Peshkin would not have considered if he had not seen the photographs.

The term *photo-elicitation* refers to "using photographs to invoke comments, memory and discussion in the course of a semi-structured interview" (Banks, 2007, 65). Photos can help to put shy or reticent interviewees at ease by giving them something to turn to rather than have to make eye contact with the interviewer. This technique is particularly valuable for work with children. Although photos or images with which respondents are unfamiliar are sometimes used, qualitative researchers are more likely to use participant-generated photos, as Peshkin did, because the research intent is to learn from participants about their

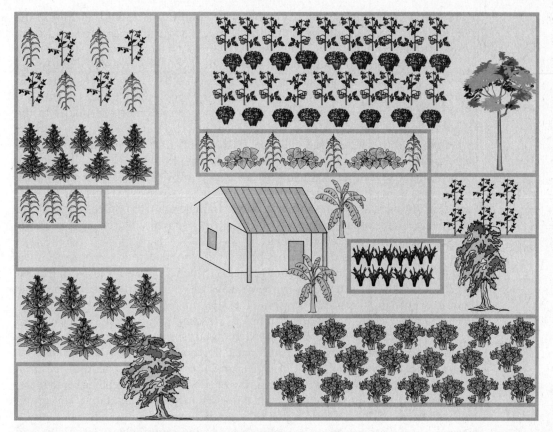

FIGURE 3.1   Map of Smallholding Intercropping

From Glesne, C. 1985. *Strugglin', but no slavin': Agriculture, education, and rural young Vincentians* (p. 71) Unpublished doctoral dissertation, University of Illinois, Urbana.

lives, not to study their responses to particular images, as in a psychological laboratory experiment. You might want to think about participant-created photos or videos as objects with "biographies" (Kopytoff 1986), whose stories can be told by the participants in your study.

Collaboratively Created and/or Studied Visual Data   With the advent of disposable cameras, some researchers started giving participants cameras to document aspects of their own lives (Mitchell and Allnutt 2008). Sometimes the resulting photos are used to learn more about perspectives of participants, as with the participant-generated photos discussed above. For example, special educator Bruce was interested in families' perceptions of their children with disabilities. He gave a camera to each family and asked them to take pictures of the child and family members in everyday activities. A member of his research support group suggested that he give each family another camera and ask family members to take five pictures each that for them symbolize the child but without the child in the picture. He could then interview family members about their pictures and learn about items that otherwise he would not have seen or asked about.

Sometimes, visual data are created or studied collaboratively to identify and address particular problems and struggles. Banks (2007, 78) describes a study in which two researchers (Schratz and Steiner-Loffler) gave small groups of primary school children cameras and asked them to take photographs of places in the school that made them feel good and of places that did not make them feel good. In teams of four self-selected children, each group first discussed "good" and "bad" places as well as how they wanted to take the photos. For example, did they want students, or teachers, or no one to be in the photos? Each team then took photos and created a poster showing the pictures and the team's reasons for its selections. Finally, each team presented its poster to the class. This process provided a great deal of information about ways to make the school a better place from the perspectives of the children attending.

When participants choose what photographs to take and which ones to use, participants gain voice in the research process (Mitchell and Allnutt 2008; Prosser and Burke 2008). If participants perceive ways in which visual media can assist them in expressing themselves to some intended audience, then researchers may have a part in making this expression heard. For example, Terence Turner worked with the Kayapó in Brazil to create a video that documented their resistance to a proposed government dam that would partially flood their land (Banks 2007).

Participatory mapping (also called *community mapping* and, recently, *ethnocartography*) refers to a group of people mapping or diagramming together some material aspect of their lives, usually with the assistance of a facilitator. The group walks through an area, mapping as they go, for example, agricultural use of a watershed or distribution of households by socioeconomic class, ethnicity, and access to resources. As they map, the group members discuss what works well and where problems lie. In *participatory diagramming,* people, again usually assisted by a facilitator, collectively produce a visual representation (e.g., drawing, diagram, chart, mind map) to convey relationships among key stakeholders, institutions, resources, or some contested issue in their community or group (Hay 2005, 289).

Although not always used in emancipatory ways, participatory processes can be powerful tools in action and postcolonial research. Anthropologist Mac Chapin, for example, worked with indigenous groups in Panama to create maps of their territories that included traditional boundaries as well as geographical and human-constructed places of local significance. Through the maps, the groups are increasingly able to gain legal claim to their homelands that are disappearing through governmental and outside encroachment: "Long-time victims of map-wielding outsiders, they are now learning about cartography so they can do battle on more-even terms" (Chapin and Threlkeld 2001, 21).

The use of photographs and videos raises specific ethical questions. Ethics boards require researchers to receive written permission if they plan to reproduce and make public (including publication in theses and dissertations) an image that makes a person identifiable. If you plan to take photos or videos, you will need to first get participants' consent to be photographed and, second, work out the issue of confidentiality. Will the photos or video be something only you (and, perhaps, participants) have access to? Are participants willing to forgo confidentiality and let the photos or film become public record? If so, what might be possible political, social, or economic consequences of using the images? Would participants be willing for you to reproduce the photos of settings in which they appear if you used technological means to blur their faces?

You need to carefully consider how visual data might be used in ways that are detrimental to people in them, and you also need to consider how visual data can reciprocate or assist participants. Schaeffer (1995), for example, got permission to take videos of people doing everyday things in Jamaica. He set up viewing sessions for participants and, if requested, their families and friends. These viewings were popular and became a vehicle for discussion and comment on the activities taking place. Banks (2007, 10) contrasts the gift of a researcher's words to that of photographs or videos:

> I suspect that there are few people who have been the subject of an academic research project who would be delighted to receive a copy of a professional peer-reviewed academic paper, still less actively request a copy from the author. Conversely, most people who have been filmed, photographed or videotaped as part of a visual research project are very pleased to receive copies, and some do indeed actively demand them.

More than the researcher's words (usually), the pictures are personal and meaningful.

Documents and Artifacts

Archaeologists reconstruct life in past times by examining the material culture left behind. *Material culture* refers to objects or artifacts bestowed with meaning and history by the people in that context. These artifacts provide archaeologists with the basis for hypotheses about how people fed, clothed, and housed themselves; with whom they communicated; and how they thought about gods and an afterlife. Archaeologists cannot observe and participate in the everyday life of those who once lived in the setting; they cannot interview men, women, and children. Yet, from the records people leave behind in the form of objects, archaeologists can re-create their probable lives.

You have it easier than archaeologists because you can both observe people in their normal interactions and ask them about the meanings of their actions. You also can access written documents. Documents can raise questions about your hunches and thereby shape new directions for observations and interviews. They also provide you with historical, demographic, and sometimes personal information that is unavailable from other sources. The following sections briefly address accessing historical materials as well as current documents and artifacts.

Archival Materials and Historical Research.   To understand a phenomenon, you need to know its history. Thinking historically, you will seek documents (minutes, letters, memoirs, wills, etc.) and photos or other artifacts that you might not access otherwise. Thinking historically, you might look for different respondents or ask different questions to get at oral histories. And having gathered historical data, you might see differently the patterns of behavior that were evident from current data and you might perceive a relationship of ideas or events previously assumed unconnected.

Historical documents give context to your study. Reviewing a town's newspapers and institutional newsletters is one way to get started. A town's or university's library archives are also a good place to begin, as are archives in museums, churches, and schools. Make use, as well, of electronic archives and Web searches for potentially useful contact information on organizations with relevant historical records. You will most likely get access to even more useful historical documents by letting it be known that you are interested in old letters, scrapbooks, photographs, and minutes of meetings. Such matters often work in a network fashion; once you find someone delighted by your historical interests, that source will lead you to someone else.

Historical research can be a qualitative research project in itself, particularly when you can talk with people who participated in some historical event and get their oral histories. Yet, even when the historical occurrence is too distant for oral histories, you can approach archival material and other documents in the same way you would interview transcripts and observation notes. First, you must figure out the focus of your historical search. Is it to provide a history of some social issue, such as immigration and subsequent changes in public schooling policies? Is it to provide a history of specific persons, institutions, or movements? Are you trying to show some relationship between ideas or events previously assumed to be unconnected? Or do you want to provide a re-interpretation of past events through a different theoretical lens—for example, as scholars have critiqued "Western" international development policies in the light of cultural and economic hegemony?

After figuring out your focus, you need to delineate the scope. Depending upon the amount of archival materials available, you may need to increase or decrease any or all of the following: geographical area, persons included, time span, and human activity category. For example, in my search to document historically women's participation in agriculture, I expanded the geographical area from the Midwest to include the West, and I expanded the category of *farming* to include what was often termed *gardening*, or growing vegetable and fruit crops for the farm family.

Look for secondary sources or books and articles already published related to your topic. As in any other literature search, secondary sources help determine whether you should continue to pursue your topic or whether it has already been written about in the same way you wanted to approach it. The sources that you need to spend ample time searching for, however, are primary documents—documents such as letters, memoirs, wills, and financial records. Remember to also look for photos, films, paintings, and other artifacts related to your topic.

Because you may not know exactly what to look for when you first encounter your boxes and files of archival material, you need to immerse yourself in it, just as you do when entering a new site for participant observation. Patience, determination, and time are needed to work your way through archives, but eventually you begin to form a story out of the materials. Read, note, and reflect and you will figure out how you want to focus in on the material and what categories of information and perspectives you want to develop.

Current Documents and Artifacts.   As a society that venerates the written word, we have many types of written documents. Diaries, letters, memoranda, graffiti, notes, memorials on tombstones, scrapbooks, membership lists, newsletters, newspapers, and computer-accessed bulletin boards are all potentially useful documents. A comparison of graffiti on the bathroom doors in the fundamentalist Christian school (only two statements observed all year, both witty but tame) with graffiti found in the community's public school (many and of various natures) reinforced the image of the Christian school students that our observations and interviews had provided us.

Students in the Christian school, as with students elsewhere, passed notes to one another during classes, then crumpled them and left them behind. These notes became artifacts in Peshkin's (1986) research—consistent with his other findings. Compare, for example, the substance of the message from a Christian school student (in the first letter below) with that from a public high school student (in the second letter below):

Joe

I'm not the kind of girl who lets a guy boss me around. I don't like any guy doing that to any girl. . . .
If you save me a seat at lunch, I'll sit with you. . . .
I'm not going to meet you anywhere on my bike 'cause Mom will somehow find out and I'd be in big trouble.
Plus, I'd feel very bad 'cause I'd have to lie about where I was going and what I was doing. . . . Talk to you later.

Rachel
(Peshkin 1986, 155)

Fran,

I'm gonna kick this girl Nicky's ass in 3rd period. She has a smart ass mouth! I'm 'bout to hit her in it.
Are you going to the class meeting today? I might. I'm going to the junior prom, my mom's going to get a dress for pregs but in style.
Bell just rang finish later.

Lisa
(Peshkin, unpublished letter, 1986 fieldwork)

Notwithstanding your comfort with the written word, do not forget other potentially useful artifacts. Artifacts are the material objects that, for your work, represent the culture of the people and setting you are studying. When you "read" an artifact, you try to get at the stories that surround it and which it embodies. Think about considering objects in terms of form, function, and symbol—how are they made, how are they used, and what do they mean to people? An object may have both a traditional or usual function and meaning, but also digress from tradition and take on creative new meanings, as is often the case within counter-culture movements. Consider, for example, how the VW bus got associated with hippies in the 1960s or how the meaning of having a tattoo changed in the United States when appropriated by pop culture in the past decade.

Artifacts of one culture or group may appear to an outsider as just "stuff," albeit artistic and attractive. To the insider, however, these artifacts tell stories that the insider can "read." For example, throughout the world, many indigenous groups continue to weave their own clothing, using intricate designs and color combinations. Outsiders often collect these weavings, appreciating the skill and beauty, but without necessarily knowing what the weavings "say." An insider would know at a glance, for example, what community the person wearing the woven garment comes from, if she is married or single, and the spiritual beliefs or ancestral tales linked to specific designs.

In addition to observed or "found" artifacts and documents, you can ask research participants to produce documents for you: to keep diaries, journals, or other kinds of records. If working in a school, you may be able to collaborate with teachers so that assignments simultaneously meet the needs of students, teachers, and researcher. For instance, if you are interested in children's self-concepts, you may be able to persuade English teachers to ask their students to write self-portraits and then let you read them.

In this mural in Oventik, Chiapas, marginalized and oppressed sectors of society are coming together and uniting under the auspices of the Zapatista movement. The mural includes many symbols with deep cultural connotations, including the clothing of the man on the left and the conch shell, or caracol, that he is blowing.

While in Saint Vincent, I asked the children who found my home an entertaining hangout to draw themselves as they imagined they would be when grown. From these drawings I pulled out themes for comparison with the themes that emerged from interviewing young adults. I also analyzed the reggae and calypso music played in Saint Vincent (particularly that composed by Vincentians for Carnival) for its agricultural and educational messages; my findings were consistent with hunches gleaned from participant observation and interviews. Graffiti, murals, drawings, notes, and songs are all *measures of accretion,* or things people have created. You can be on the outlook for *measures of erosion* as well, things people have worn away such as the paths across the grass on college campuses or the shine on handrails in front of popular museum exhibits. And as Stoller (1989) urges, think about using all your senses, not only sight.

Visual data, documents, artifacts, and other unobtrusive measures provide both historical and contextual dimensions to your observations and interviews. They enrich what you see and hear by supporting, expanding, and challenging your portrayals and perceptions. Your understanding of the phenomenon in question grows as you make use of the documents and artifacts that are a part of people's lives.

Table 3.1 summarizes various kinds of observational data that might become part of your research. It suggests ways in which the data might be documented and their possible uses in your overall research project.

THE PARTICIPANT OBSERVER'S ROLE

While living in Oaxaca, I periodically visited with members of a nongovernmental women's organization. They included me in their meeting with two female lawyers from the United States who were part of a large study focused on children's rights in Uganda, Mexico, and the United States. Because child mortality rates in Mexico were highest among indigenous groups, they had come to Oaxaca to learn more of the situations affecting children. The conversation went approximately as follows.

The director of the women's organization told about the group's work: "We find that the most important thing is to work for the economic independence of women. So we are working to help mobilize women to find resources, employment, and economic security. We also help them get information about health and education."

"But what about the children?" asked one of the lawyers.

The organizer replied, "We understand the relationship between women and children. We work to help the conditions of the whole family; we do not focus only on the child. The woman needs access to basic information on situations affecting health so that the whole family can be healthy."

The lawyers tried to keep the focus on children, asking what the group thought was the leading cause of death among children. One of the Oaxacan women answered, focusing again on women and the family as a whole, "Women

TABLE 3.1   Description, Documentation, and Use of Different Kinds of Observational Data

DATA	DESCRIPTION	DOCUMENTATION	TYPICAL RESEARCH USE
Setting Appearance	How a setting and/or people look	Observation notes, field journal, drawings, diagrams, photographs, video	Introducing setting and/or people in final report
Acts	Everyday behavior; what a person does	Observation notes, field journal, photographs, video	Raises questions for interviews; supports or challenges interview data; thick description; pattern analysis; generates hunches or hypotheses;
Events	Series of acts or behaviors, generally involving more than one person and bounded by time, planned or unplanned (e.g., a meeting or an argument)	Observation notes, field journal, photographs, video	Raises questions for interviews; supports or challenges interview data; thick description; pattern analysis; generates hunches or hypotheses
Processes	Explicit and implicit rules, regulations, and rituals that describe how a program, institution, or group works	Observation notes, field journal, diagrams, institutional documents	Raises questions for interviews; supports or challenges interview data; thick description; pattern analysis; generates hunches or hypotheses
Talk	What people say to each other.	Observation notes, video, audio recorder	Raises questions for interviews; supports or challenges interview data; thick description
Documents	Minutes of meetings, diaries, letters, notes, wills, financial records, photographs, drawings, etc., that come from research site(s)	Archival research, library research, document created by and/or shared by participants, found documents, etc. All can by photocopied	Raises questions for interviews; supports or challenges interview data; thick description; pattern analysis; content analysis; generates hunches or hypotheses
Artifacts	Graffiti, murals and other items created by participants as well as evidence of accretion (e.g., number of empty beer cans in weekend trash near different kinds of student housing)	Observation notes, photographs, video	Raises questions for interviews; supports or challenges interview data; thick description; generates hunches or hypotheses

Note: Table is an adaptation and expansion of a table in Holliday, A. 2002. *Doing and Writing Qualitative Research.* Thousand Oaks, CA: Sage (pp. 71–72).

work 13 to 15 hours a day. They, themselves, have many health problems. And they must deal with violence in the family. Alcohol is the principle factor of death for men in Oaxaca, directly or indirectly. But alcohol affects the whole family—not only in the level of violence, but in that the man drinks up money for the family."

As the researchers continued to probe about how children's rights could be supported, the Oaxacan women kept saying things like, "We focus on the whole family—we don't separate out the children." Coming from a culture that empha-sizes the individual over the collective, the women from the United States did not seem to recognize that their way of thinking was not prevalent in southern Mexico. They also never asked about Oaxacan perspectives on human rights, living, and dying. I found ironic that the targets for their global application of individual children's rights were indigenous people, the very groups that were struggling in Oaxaca and Chiapas for greater recognition of their communal rights to determine local issues.

These researchers, like so many other well-meaning professionals from "out-side," had a funded research project and were taking several weeks to talk with various people in Mexico. Realizing the vastness of what I did not begin to know or understand about Oaxaca after living there for half a year at the time, and yet filling my notebook with critiques of the dialogue as I listened, I couldn't help but think how different the conversation might have been if the two women had done a period of immersed participant observation in Oaxaca.

The participant observer's role entails a way of being present in everyday settings that enhances your awareness and curiosity about the interactions taking place around you. You become immersed in the setting, its people, and the research questions. One way to test if you are being there appropriately is whether you find within yourself a growing determination to understand the issues at hand from the participant's perspective. This indicates that you have been able to suspend your personal judgment and concerns. In the words of Sigmund Freud: "I [Freud] learnt to restrain speculative tendencies and to . . . look at the same things again and again until they themselves begin to speak" (Malcolm 1987, 95). Another test is whether or not you are seeing things you have never noticed before. After Andrea began her study of a community, she wrote the following in her field log:

> I went to a local restaurant for breakfast, caught myself watching the gathering of men at the breakfast bar, and found myself wondering for the first time: Who are those men? Why do they come here? How come I never noticed them before? Should I find out who they are—perhaps they represent some potential research rock yet unturned? I enjoy this newly honed sense of seeing.

Another gift of immersion is that everything you read and hear can be con-nected, or at least considered for connection, to your phenomenon. Ideas are gen-erated and notes pile up. It is a time of transformation, when a research persona emerges with a life of its own.

Anxiety: A Companion

Immersion in and connection to others' lives do not occur without tensions and problems. After finding a place to live in the Vincentian village, I wrote the following in my field log:

> I am moved into the house—complete with bats that fly out of the sink drain, a cockroach apartment complex in the kitchen cabinets, a strange smell of something dead under the kitchen floor, bat races in the ceiling every morning at four A.M., no refrigeration so that even bread does not last the night without molding, and a toilet which leaks.
>
> Moving in is easy, though, compared with moving out into the community to begin observation and informal interviews. I finally forced myself outside around nine A.M., although I was ready to go at 7:30—I just couldn't make my feet walk out the door. I felt out of place, naïve, unsure . . .

Although my work took place in another culture with its attendant novelty and strangeness, immersion into an unfamiliar setting within your own country can be as anxiety-producing. Expect to feel like a somewhat awkward newcomer, as people rightfully wonder who you are, why you have come, what you will do, and what sort of nuisance you might prove to be.

New participant observers often feel timid, sensing that as invaders of someone else's territory, they are unwanted and unnecessary. It is true that, unless engaged in collaborative research, you are neither invited nor necessary. If, however, you retain that timidity, then you will compromise your work because you will be too restrained about where you go, who you see, what you ask, or how much time you take. With a little effort and time, plus some skill, this awkwardness passes, and you begin to feel at ease. You need not become essential to the community to feel at ease and be welcomed; you just have to fit in with the local behavioral norms, and be agreeable, interested, and respectful.

Once accepted into the research setting, your companion anxiety latches onto new worries: Are you talking to the right people, observing the right events, and asking the right research questions? Soon after beginning his ethnicity study in Riverview, California, Peshkin (1991) noted the following in his field log:

> Titles keep popping into mind. This process begins earlier in each study. It is more than just a game. I really don't know what I can, should, or want to do. What stories does the place support? Today I got the first of my sinking feelings that I'm lost. The place is too big for me, and I won't be able to handle it. (personal communication)

He was able to "handle" it, and he did learn at least some Riverview stories. Anxiety of varying degrees is our constant companion: We need to acknowledge its presence, take account of its messages, and then continue our work.

In addition to courting anxiety, researchers face mental and physical fatigue from overdoing, especially from "overbeing," which is a sense of always being on stage and therefore on best behavior. Fatigue generally finds researchers after they have been in the field for an extended time; burnout becomes a possibility. When feeling overwhelmed with fatigue, it is clearly time to consider interspersing work with breaks of various sorts taken both inside and outside the field.

Participating

As discussed earlier, how much of a participant you can or should be in a study varies. Horowitz (1986) takes issue with the implication that the researcher is essentially free to choose the degree and form of participation:

> I will argue that fieldwork roles are not matters dictated solely, or even largely, by the stance of the fieldworker, but are instead better viewed as interactional matters based on processes of continuing negotiation between the researcher and the researched. Together, the qualities and attributes of the fieldworker interact with those of the setting and its members to shape, if not create, an emergent role for the researcher. (410)

Despite your interest, your own personal attributes may cause you to be denied access to some research topics or from participating in some events. Research participants often assign the researcher a role in keeping with their own conceptual frameworks. Horowitz was identified as a "lady" (which meant she was sexually unavailable) and as a "reporter" by the young male gang members she studied. The roles allowed her access to considerable information, but kept her from some areas of discussion and observation. In Saint Vincent, I became the "agriculture lady" who relayed messages between participants and governmental and non-governmental agricultural organizations with which I had contact.

Balance the costs and benefits of your participation. If, for example, a teacher asks you what you see from the back of her classroom, and you respond with advice or reinforcement, then you assume an expert role and risk losing your credibility as a nonjudgmental researcher. If you are enlisted as a free substitute teacher and do well with a class, then you make teachers aware of your teaching assets and, possibly, their teaching liabilities. If a class needs a driver for a field trip and you volunteer, then you may be overdoing the good-person role because of the resultant time drain on your work. Being the field trip driver, however, may provide an opportunity to observe students and teachers in a different context from the usual one. Unless you are choosing to do more action- or participant-oriented research, you will have to negotiate with others and with yourself on how much of a participant to be.

Marginal or Apprentice?

In conventional ethnography, researchers are sometimes called "marginal natives" (Freilich 1977) because, although they grow close to research participants, they generally remain sojourners who are physically and psychologically at the margin of life in the research setting. In physical terms, the researcher attends events but stays on the fringes, at the back of classrooms and meetings.

Although researchers and participants interact freely, the interaction usually is within a frame of guarded intimacy. The researcher does not take charge or play the role of change agent or judge, but stays also at the psychological margins of interactions. Remaining marginal "allows one to continue to spend time with groups when they are no longer friendly" (Horowitz 1986, 426) with each other. The point of the margin is that it offers the vantage of seeing without being the focus of attention, of being present without being fully participant, so that you are free to be fully attuned to what occurs before you.

Realize, however, that in some situations you may alienate your research participants by choosing to remain marginal. They may see you as aloof and even as exploitative. In *Death Without Weeping: The Violence of Everyday Life in Brazil*, Nancy Scheper-Hughes (1992) describes how, as a Peace Corps volunteer, she had spent time in an economically poor community in Brazil. She was active immunizing babies, administering penicillin injections, and working as a community organizer to create a community center and cooperative day nursery. Fifteen years later, she returned to the same community as an anthropologist to study "mother love and child death." Old neighbors and friends welcomed her back, but grew weary and disillusioned with her proclaimed role. They wanted her to help them as she had before:

> But each time the women approached me with their requests, I backed away saying, "this work is cut out for you. My work is different now. I cannot be an anthropologist and a *companheira* [comrade, friend 'in the struggle'] at the same time." I shared my new reservations about the propriety of an outsider taking an active role in the life of a Brazilian community. But my argument fell on deaf ears. (Scheper-Hughes 1992, 17)

Scheper-Hughes continued to conduct interviews and to remain somewhat marginal to the community until confronted by the women:

> Why had I refused to work with them when they had been so willing to work with me? Didn't I care about them personally anymore, their lives, their suffering, their struggle? Why was I so passive, so indifferent, so resigned . . . the women gave me an ultimatum: the next time I came back to The Alto I would have to "be" with them—"accompany them" was the expression they used—in their *luta*, and not just "sit idly by" taking fieldnotes. "What is this anthropology anyway to us?" they taunted. (18)

Scheper-Hughes returned five years later and assumed the combined role of anthropologist-*companheira*. Although she found this role difficult to balance and "rarely free of conflict" (18), it also served to enrich her understandings of the community as she demonstrates in her moving ethnography.

As participation increases, marginality decreases, and you begin to experience what others see, think, and feel. This can be absolutely worthwhile for yourself and research participants; no amount of advantageous marginality can replace the sense of things that participation offers. How you combine participation and observation will be dictated by what you hope to understand, your theoretical stance, and your research participants.

Ethnographers often develop a close working relationship with one or more members of the researched group or *local facilitators* (sometimes referred to as *local consultants* or *collaborators*). Previously they were labeled *informants,* a term with colonial connotations. Local facilitators assist in a variety of ways from making introductions to suggesting sources of data to responding to the researcher's analytical questions and thoughts. Some local facilitators are *co-researchers* in that they are partners in all or most aspects of the research process. In efforts to address power imbalances, some ethnographers "apprentice" themselves to someone in the community or group where they want to work (Tedlock 2000). They usually do so with someone with whom a relationship has already developed. Together the outsider and insider negotiate the terms for working together. The local facilitator may have ultimate control over everything from what is studied to what gets published. My perspective of *volunteer researcher* fits this model in that the researcher offers his or her services to the group and together they negotiate what the focus will be, how the research will be undertaken, and what can be put into a publication.

Gaining and Losing Self

Participant observation often places researchers in the lives of others in a self-consciously instrumental way. Participant observers are not merely visiting with the hope to see the sights, have a good time, and, in passing, learn a little about how locals live. Researchers have ends-in-view, purposes—however incipient—that underlie their presence in particular settings and direct their behavior while there. The inescapable truth is that researchers are not merely present as they would be in other ordinary circumstances of their lives. They shape their behavior throughout the study in a way that optimizes data collection.

You have control over your words and actions, but less control over other aspects of yourself—sex, age, religion, and ethnicity. But even with seemingly unchangeable characteristics such as gender or ethnicity, you do have some choice in how you present yourself. For example, Daniels (1967) elaborates on her "learned responses" to behave "appropriately" when working as a woman sociologist among Army officers in the 1960s:

> Certain behavior was considered inappropriate or even insulting from women: a firm handclasp, a direct eye-to-eye confrontation, a brisk, businesslike air, an assured manner of joking or kidding with equals were all antagonizing. Most galling of all was my naïve assumption that, of *course,* I was equal. It was important to wait until equality was *given* me. When I learned to smile sweetly, keep my eyes cast down, ask helplessly for favors, and exhibit explicitly feminine mannerisms, my ability to work harmoniously and efficiently increased. (275)

Most research situations do not call for such extreme impression management. In Saint Vincent, I always wore a skirt because shorts and slacks were not considered appropriate dress. In the Christian school, Peshkin shaved his beard, and we both carefully removed any minced oaths from our speech, such as "gosh," "darn," or "gee." Researchers often have to work for their acceptance, and this frequently entails a nonaggressive style or, as Lofland puts it, becoming "a socially acceptable incompetent" (Lofland 1971, 101). The extent to which you should modify behavior for research purposes is difficult to define: Where are the boundaries of integrity? When does adaptation go too far? In everyday life, you present yourself differently in different situations. Research is one more occasion for fashioning a presence, albeit more self-consciously than is ordinarily the case. At some point, however, does this impression management become a lie and transgress the boundaries of ethical warrant?

A number of people have collected research data through covert participant observation and, in so doing, monitored carefully their presented self (covert research is not currently supported). Dalton (1959) worked covertly as a firm manager to investigate management; Homan (Homan and Bulmer 1982) studied a Pentecostal sect as if he were a novitiate; Sullivan (Sullivan, Queen, and Patrick 1958) lost weight, altered age, and adopted a "new personality" in order to study Air Force recruits; and Humphreys (1970) studied homosexuals by taking on the role of "watch queen" in public restrooms. Researchers who study the powerful, the illegal, and the marginal often have used covert means of gathering data.

Covert research is fraught with questions and problems, discussed to some extent in the ethics chapter (Chapter 6). On one hand, some argue that covert observation is harmful to subjects, researcher, and the discipline. On the other hand, some believe that a measure of deception is acceptable in some areas when the benefits of knowledge outweigh the harm, and when the harm has been minimized by following conventions of confidentiality and anonymity.

Prepared and Flexible

Learning to be an effective participant observer takes some effort. Begin by asking what there is about your identity—such as gender, age, ethnicity, or country of origin—that might affect your access and data collection. Are there ways in which you can present yourself so that you will be welcomed? Second, do your homework and talk with "insiders" to discover normal attire and acceptable behaviors before entering the setting. You will make mistakes in your research interactions, but being prepared lessens the probability of major mistakes. Third, as you begin your role as a participant observer, be on the lookout for ways to better "fit in." This may mean brushing up on the latest music when working with teens, or keeping up with football scores when working in a male-dominated education department in the Midwest. Fourth, as participant observation continues, be aware of the different groups in the setting and carefully consider whether or not to become aligned with any one group. Unless your focus narrows so that you are concerned with only one group, such as the athlete student group, then it is probably best to remain unaligned. Fifth, a natural disposition is to share what you learn with others whom you know would be interested. Don't. Learning to be judiciously silent is critical, so that everyone who talks to you knows that he or she can safely tell you anything. Finally, stay flexible and open to changing your research plans in beneficial ways as you learn through participating and observing.

Bittersweet Times: Disengaging

> Everyone in anthro knows it, it's an open secret, but coming home from the field is as tough as going out. Maybe even tougher.
>
> (Berlinski 2007, 273)

Leaving the field may be a bittersweet time. You are glad to be done and have your life return to normal; you can finally get to the neglected tasks in other aspects of your life; and you can once again spend time with family and friends. Still, you are sad because something you have invested in highly is over. You may be leaving good relationships and good times. Even if you never personally accepted others' ideologies, most likely you came to empathize and enjoy interacting with them. It may be that you will never return to the setting under the same circumstances.

You may feel dislocated when you return full time to pre-fieldwork life. After all, you have adjusted to living properly in someone else's life. You may also feel different about yourself; long-time immersion in someone else's life enhances your general self-awareness. You feel relief at not always having to be watchful, yet you find yourself reevaluating your "normal" life through comparisons with the lifestyle of your research participants. You miss people, places, and ways of doing things. Of course, leaving a Caribbean village is different from leaving a secondary school in the city in which you normally live, but departure from both places tends to be bittersweet.

CONSIDERATIONS

Efrain and Enrique were informal leaders of a youth group in Oaxaca. After we decided to work together as co-researchers, we began discussing how the research would look. We created a kind of action research statement, describing our intent as one of documenting the ways in which groups of youth were shaping their life options in rural Oaxacan communities and inquiring into possible roles in this process for Efrain and Enrique's group. I, of course, suggested we gather data through interviews and participant observation. My co-researchers were clear in their response—they did not think highly of either interviews or observations.

From their experiences people had come to study them, not "with" them and they did not want to repeat that pattern. They described how a young woman from the United States, who was studying in Oaxaca for a semester, asked if she could spend time with them to learn more about their organization. In their hospitable way, they welcomed her. She arrived with a notebook and proceeded to move from the outside picnic tables to the office space to the meeting/dining area, taking notes. They suggested she put down her notebook and engage in conversation with them, but she resisted saying they should ignore her, that she was just there as a participant observer.

As this chapter has suggested, the woman's decision to set herself apart is not the only way to be a participant observer, but discussions with my co-researchers made me more aware of possible responses to the term and how alienating it can feel to be the recipient of another's gaze. Efrain and Enrique emphasized that we must work to not set ourselves apart from the youth we would be visiting. They suggested that instead of participant observation, we learn through *accompanying* the youth in their work, to engage in reflective dialogue with them, and to interact with other community members as well because the youth could not be separated from the communities of which they were part. The purpose was not, as my co-researchers put it, to observe someone as distant and different from them, but to learn through doing and moving with friends.

Depending upon your research purposes and degree of ideological compatibility, you may not be able to fully accompany others in their lives or even to be welcomed in the pursuit of doing so. Whether or not you hold the desire and are able to accompany those with whom you want to do research is, however, increasingly a key question for many in choosing a research direction.

RECOMMENDED READINGS

Bogdan, R., and S. Biklen. 2007. *Qualitative Research for Education: An Introduction to Theories and Methods,* 5th ed. Boston: Pearson/Allyn & Bacon.

Emerson, R. M, R. Fretz, and L. Shaw. 1995. *Writing Ethnographic Fieldnotes*. Chicago: University of Chicago Press.

EXERCISES

Observation Activities

1. With at least two classmates, attend a public event where you can take field notes. Write descriptive details as well as personal thoughts and questions. Afterward, share field notes with your classmates, noting differences and commonalities. What did you learn from each other? In what ways do you want to take field notes differently the next time?

2. To activate your reflective mind as you take field notes, draw a line vertically down the middle of pages in your observations notebook. Now choose something to observe which you can watch daily, over a week's time, how something changes, such as city workers reconstructing sidewalks on your block or evening use of the university library. Sunstein and Chiseri-Strater (2002, 93), from whom I borrowed this activity, write of a student who observed the state of the bathtub in the apartment he shared with several other guys. Figure out a topic and set aside time to observe daily. Record your observations on the left side of the line. On the right, reflect on the meaning of the changes. What questions arise for you? At the end of the week, write a short reflection on what you learned by keeping these notes.

3. Part of your observational tasks is to hone descriptive skills. Go to your research setting with your field notebook. Concentrate on observing the context only. Describe how things look, smell, sound, and feel. Write up your observations into a vignette, with the intention of having readers feel as though they are in the school, nursing home, physical therapy clinic, or whatever may be your research setting.

Share with a classmate and ask what else is needed to make the setting as vivid as possible.

4. Analysis and writing should be ongoing with the process of noting observations. To work on analysis and writing, do several more sessions of observation in your research site. Then read through your field notes and think about patterns. Can you identify the beginning of some pattern of activity? This is an analytical process. What are the events within the activity? Who tends to participate and what are the patterns of interaction? You most likely won't have all the answers at this point, but raising questions is part of your analytical work. Now, look at the descriptors you've used. Pick out those that best evoke the scene and activity. Thinking of both description and pattern, write up a vignette that would convey a snapshot to an outsider. Try to use some "insider" language that represents insider perspectives. Share the vignette with a classmate and together raise more questions for future observations and conversations at your site.

5. After several more observation sessions at your research site, create another vignette from your field notes. Bring both this vignette and your field notes to class and share with a partner. (This exercise is adapted from Sunstein and Chiseri-Strater 2002, 83–84.)

   ■ First, look at each other's field notes. Are observation pages numbered consecutively (if not in a bound notebook), and is each page dated, with time and location noted?
   ■ Do field notes show evidence of elaboration and reflections after observation periods?
   ■ Now, look at the vignette. What background or contextual information is needed so that someone not familiar with the setting can understand the research focus?
   ■ What other details are needed so that the reader can become immersed in the routines or rituals of the place?
   ■ What do you want to read more about?
   ■ What kinds of things make the piece trustworthy? What would help make it more trustworthy?
   ■ Do you learn anything about the observer and his/her feelings as well? What else do you want to know about the observer?

Document and Archival Activities

1. Brainstorm ways to gather data on your topic other than by taking notes or interviewing (e.g., collecting diaries, student papers, scrapbooks kept by research participants; taking photographs or asking participants to take photographs on some topic; drawing or asking participants to draw). Discuss ideas with classmates and then pilot test them with a research participant. Reflect upon what you learn and what new questions arise.

2. Immersed in observations and interviews, novice researchers often forget about seeking out the historical context and antecedents in their research arena. Think about what kinds of historical documents (e.g., policy papers, minutes, letters, newspaper articles, photos) you could access that would help to situate the historical context. Do not forget library archives, which often have collections of people's personal papers (e.g., journals, letters, expense logs) that might be useful for your

work. Check out at least two of these possible sources and enter in your field log your reflections on what each might contribute to your work.

3. The World Wide Web can be useful for your project in various ways. It can help you find the following:
   - Potentially useful books and journal articles,
   - Contact information of potentially relevant organizations or individuals,
   - Other perspectives on your ideas or theories via relevant chat rooms, blogs, or newsgroups,
   - Documents and other artifacts created by members in your area of research.

   Choose two of these items and seek out information related to your topic. Where does the information take you? How does it influence your research direction?

Visual Data Activity

1. Banks (2007, 55) suggests that researchers "try to imagine what their chosen area of study would 'look' like if all visual forms were removed. This should then help a researcher to identify what, if anything, the visual imagery is adding." Take Banks's suggestion. Write about your research setting with the sense of sight removed. What do you know about it through your other senses? In what ways do you need to better attend to these other senses during the next observation period? What, in particular, does the visual imagery add to your research focus?

CHAPTER 4

Making Words Fly: Developing Understanding through Interviewing

Memory
Spinning up dust and cornshucks
as it crossed the chalky, exhausted fields,
it sucked up into its heart
hot work, cold work, lunch buckets,
good horses, bad horses, their names
and the names of mules that were
better or worse than the horses,
then rattled the dented tin sides
of the threshing machine, shook
the manure spreader, cranked
the tractor's crank that broke
the uncle's arm, then swept on
through the windbreak, taking
the treehouse and dirty magazines,
turning its fury on the barn
where cows kicked over buckets
and the gray cat sat for a squirt
of thick milk in its whiskers, crossed
the chicken pen, undid the hook,
plucked a warm brown egg
from the meanest hen, then turned
toward the house, where threshers
were having dinner, peeled back
the roof and the kitchen ceiling,
reached down and snatched up
uncles and cousins, grandma, grandpa,
parents and children one by one,
held them like dolls, looked
long and longingly into their faces,
then set them back in their chairs
with blue and white platters of chicken
and ham and mashed potatoes
still steaming before them, with

boats of gravy and bowls of peas
and three kinds of pie, and suddenly,
with a sound like a sigh, drew up
its crowded, roaring, dusty funnel,
and there at its tip was the nib of a pen.

Think of interviewing as the process of getting words to fly. Unlike a baseball pitcher whose joy derives from throwing balls that batters never touch, you toss questions that you want your respondents to "hit" and hit well in every corner of your data park, if not clear out of it—a swatted home run of words. As a researcher, you want your "pitches"—your questions—to stimulate verbal flights from the important respondents who know what you do not. You want to tap into memories of "good horse, bad horse, their names" as described in Ted Kooser's poem. From these flights come the information that you transmute through the "nib of your pen" into data—the stuff of dissertations, articles, and books.

Getting words to fly is the subject of this chapter. It is a simple matter to express: Develop a clearly defined topic; design interview questions that fit the topic; ask the questions with consummate skill; and have ample time to "pitch" the questions to forthcoming and knowledgeable respondents. As with pitching balls, however, the process of creating good interviews takes practice.

INTERVIEWING: AN INTERACTION

What type of interaction is an interview? An interview is between at least two persons, but other possibilities include one or more interviewers and one or more interviewees. Interviewing more than one person at a time sometimes proves very useful: Children often need company to be emboldened to talk and some topics are better discussed by a small group of people or a *focus group* as discussed later in this chapter.

In conventional approaches, researchers ask questions in the context of purposes often important primarily to themselves. Respondents answer questions in the context of dispositions (motives, values, concerns, needs) that researchers need to unravel in order to make sense out of the words that their questions generate. The questions, typically created by the researchers, may be fully established before interviewing begins and remain unchanged throughout the interview (*structured interviews*). Questions may emerge in the course of interviewing and may add to or replace pre-established ones (*semistructured interviews*). Questions may develop on the spot through dialogue and interactions with only the research focus leading the way (*unstructured* or *conversational interviews*). Generally, qualitative researchers begin with some interview questions and remain open to reforming and adding to them throughout the research process—the scenario for advice in this chapter.

The questions you bring to your interview are not set within a binding contract; they are your best effort before you have had the chance to use them with a number of respondents. However much you have done to create useful questions, you should think of them tentatively, so that you are disposed to modify or abandon them, replace them with others, or add new ones to your list or *interview schedule*. The more fundamentally you change your interview schedule, however, the more frequently you may have to return to people whom you thought you had finished interviewing in order to ask them questions that emerged in interviews with others. In general, it is not advisable to say final good-byes to respondents; leave the door open to return.

Interviews can figure into a research project in different ways. In the positivist tradition, they can be the basis for later data collection, as in the form of a questionnaire. Not knowing enough about the phenomenon of interest, researchers interview a sample of respondents in the hope of transforming what they have learned into the necessary items and scales. Also in a positivist vein, interviews are sometimes used as a validity check of the responses given to questionnaire items. For example, what do respondents mean when they select "strongly agree" or "strongly disagree" as their response to some item? Probing in depth with a small sample of respondents who account for what they meant when they disagreed or agreed can indicate whether different respondents perceived the question in reasonably similar terms, as well as what underpins their reactions to it. In the interpretivist tradition, the interview can be the sole basis of a study, or it can be used in conjunction with data from other methods such as participant observation and document collection.

Given the face-to-face nature of ethnographic research, you may ask questions on the many occasions when something is happening that you wonder about. You inquire right then and there without formally arranging a time to ask your questions. Semistructured interviewing, in contrast, is a more formal, orderly process that you direct to a range of intentions. You may want to learn about events or experiences that you cannot see or can no longer see as is done through oral and life history interviews. Jan Myrdal (1965), in *Report from a Chinese Village*, reconstructed—through oral history interviews with many people—the transition in rural China between the passing of Chiang Kai-Shek's regime and the ascendancy of Mao Zedong. In a more recent example, Alan Wieder (2004) elicited testimonies of teachers in South Africa who fought apartheid. *Oral history interviews* focus on historical events, skills, ways of life, or cultural patterns that may be changing (Rubin and Rubin 1995). *Life history interviews* focus more on the life experiences of one or several individuals. Mary F. Smith (1954), in *Baba of Karo*, recreates—through life history interviews—the life of a Nigerian woman of the Hausa tribe.

Both oral history and life history interviews are examples of focusing on concepts of culture. "In cultural interviewing, researchers learn the rules, norms, values, and understandings that are passed from one generation of group members to the next" (Rubin and Rubin 1995, 168). Questions in cultural interviews ask people about their memories, experiences, and understandings of events in their lives.

Oral and life history interviews can also be a kind of witnessing that challenges and counters the "official story" as they document voices silenced or ignored by mainstream culture (Wieder 2004). Observation puts you on the trail of understandings that you infer from what you see, but you cannot, except through interviewing, get the actor's experiences and explanations.

Instead of interviewing about past experiences and events in people's lives, you might want to interview in search of opinions, perceptions, and attitudes toward some topic, for example, asking teachers their opinion about state-mandated changes in the middle school science curriculum. How do they perceive the impact of the changes on their work as teachers? What is their attitude about this impact? Concerned about the utility of the state's curricular mandate, you might conduct interviews to obtain data that will be instrumental for understanding teacher conceptions of science and obstacles to implementing proposals for reform. This would be a form of *topical interviewing* that focuses more on a program, issue, or process than on people's lives.

The opportunity to learn about what you cannot see and to explore alternative explanations of what you do see is the special strength of interviewing in qualitative inquiry. To this opportunity add the serendipitous learnings that emerge from the unexpected turns in discourse that your questions evoke. In the process of listening to your respondents, you learn what questions to ask.

DEVELOPING QUESTIONS

Question Content

What is the origin of the interview question? In ethnographic research, the experience of learning as participant observer often precedes interviewing and is the basis for forming questions. The things you see and hear about the people and circumstances of interest to you therefore become the nuggets around which you construct your questions. Of course, participant observation does not and cannot always precede question making. What then? Turn to your topic and ask, in effect: If this is what I intend to understand, what questions must I direct to which respondents?

Novice researchers sometimes confuse their research questions with their interview questions, thinking that they can modify their research questions to produce their interview schedule. "Your research questions formulate what you want to understand; your *interview* questions are what you ask people in order to gain that understanding" (Maxwell 1996, 74). Although there should be a relationship between research and interview questions, interview questions tend to be more contextual and specific than research questions. And their development "requires creativity and insight, rather than a mechanical translation of the research questions into an interview guide" (74).

The questions you ask in ethnographic inquiry should be anchored in the cultural reality of your respondents: the questions should be drawn from the respondents' lives. When Sarah interviewed student teachers about their class-room practices, she knew what to ask because she had both sat in their prepractice teaching methods class and later watched them perform in their own classrooms. But she also could have known what to ask by having taught a teaching methods class and supervised student teachers. In both cases, she could enhance the experiential foundation from which she generated questions by talking with others in the know, such as former student teachers and supervisors of student teachers, as well as by reading the relevant literature and acquainting herself with theories in the field.

The theory, implicit or explicit, underlying some behavior is an important source of questions. Daren, for example, planned to investigate what he called "the returning dropout," young people who dropped out of high school but later returned to study in an adult education program. Daren's questions originated from his knowledge of the literature and from his reasoning. Over time, they were modified by pilot testing and through consultation with other researchers and informants. They reflected theoretical considerations regarding his topic. He asked, for example,

1. For what reasons did returnees leave school in the first place? (suggests a connection between leaving and returning to school)
2. How did parents react to their decision to drop out? (suggests the likelihood of a parental role in leaving and returning)
3. Did they have friends who also dropped out? (suggests that peer influence could motivate leaving and returning)
4. How did they learn about the adult education program? (suggests the possible influence of the source of knowledge about the program)
5. In what ways were treatment of students and contents of instruction different in the adult program than in the high school program? (suggests the appeal of some particular features of the adult program compared with the high school program)

These discrete questions do not amount to a theory; they do, however, point toward an understanding of the complex phenomenon of returning to school, which is a precursor to theory. In short, with the answers Daren received from each of his returning dropouts, he advanced his ability to explain why dropouts return to school.

Theoretical assumptions of your methodological approach also shape the questions you ask. A theoretical assumption of ethnography, for example, is that, although highly variable and context specific, social behavior reflects patterns of a culture and that it is possible to discern and interpret these patterns. This assumption guides the ethnographer in asking interview questions about the ways in which people do things and the kinds of experiences and attitudes people have as well as of the meaning they make of some behavior or perspective. In comparison, a theoretical assumption of narrative inquiry is that people's narratives or stories about something "is a natural, obvious, and authentic window into how people structure experience and construct meaning in their lives" (Schram 2006, 105). This and other theoretical perspectives of narrative inquiry lead the researcher to focus on eliciting complete stories through interviews or to record the stories in the setting where they occur naturally. A poststructuralist theoretical assumption about interviewing is that if interviewers take a neutral stance, "they create a hierarchical, asymmetrical (and patriarchal) relationship in which the interviewee is treated as a research 'object'" (Rapley 2007, 19). This perspective suggests that the researcher engage with participants in cooperative projects that focus on dialogue, collaboration, and mutual self-disclosure. To sum up, the questions you ask say much more about you, the interviewer, and your theoretical perspectives than might be obvious at first glance. This chapter focuses on ethnographic interviews.

The Mechanics of Question Development

Todd, interviewing parents about their perceptions of portfolio use as a means of assessing their child's performance in school, stated, "I found I spent 45 seconds explaining each question, so I had to work to simplify them." Researchers often begin with questions that make perfect sense to them, but are less clear to their research participants. Michael Patton (2002), in his chapter on interviewing in the text *Qualitative Research and Evaluation Methods,* has some of the best advice around concerning the development of good interview questions. He talks about kinds of questions, urging the researcher to ask questions from a variety of angles.

Kinds of questions that Patton (2002) describes include experience/behavior questions, opinion/values questions, feeling questions, knowledge questions, sensory questions, and background/demographics questions. Experience/behavior questions are generally the easiest ones for a respondent to answer and are good places to begin to get the interviewee talking comfortably. Knowledge questions, in contrast, can give the impression of being tested. Respondents can readily feel embarrassed or at least uneasy when they have to say "I don't know" to a question that you assumed they would know. If a knowledge question is information that can be obtained from documents or from one person in the know, such as the department chair, get the information there and drop the question from your interview list for all respondents.

Patton (2002) also reminds us that we can ask our questions of the present, past, and future. Questions that ask for hypothetical musings about the future, however, tend to provide data that is neither "thick" in description, nor very useful during data analysis. The question, "How would you like the sports medicine clinic to be in 10 years' time?" generates little other than a wish list. Exceptions exist, of course, but the past and present tend to be richer ground for stories, descriptions, and interviewer probes.

"How a question is worded and asked affects how the interviewee responds" (Patton 2002, 353). Not only must you think about different kinds of interview questions, but also you need to work carefully with shaping the question as Todd discovered in his portfolio interviews with parents. Look through your questions and rework any that are dichotomous yes/no questions ("Do you participate in volunteer activities?") because such questions guide your respondent to give short answers. Rethink multiple questions ("Tell me about the last time you volunteered, how long you worked at the activity, and how you felt about doing so") because your respondent will most likely talk more fully about one of your several questions and forget the others. "Why" questions ("Why do you do volunteer work?") can also be problematic because each respondent might answer from a different perspective, even though he or she could speak to several (Patton 2002). As researcher, you want to investigate the primary categories or perspectives with all respondents. For example, one interviewee might answer why she does volunteer work with a discussion of childhood experiences. Another might talk about his need to give something back to the community. Yet another might report how volunteer work puts her in contact with people she would not be with otherwise. As a result of your "why" question, you will generate a list of reasons for participation in volunteer activities, but your understanding of volunteer work might grow even deeper if you asked each respondent about the role of family socialization, moral beliefs, and perceived rewards in his or her participation in volunteer work.

One kind of question to think about using is the *presupposition question*, a question in which the interviewer presupposes "that the respondent has something to say" (Patton 2002, 369). Novice interviewers often perceive the need to begin with a short-answer question such as, "Are you satisfied with your volunteer work?" followed by the more open-ended questions: "In what ways are you satisfied?" and "In what ways are you not satisfied?" You can often presuppose that satisfaction (or some other attribute) is a part of the work and begin with a statement such as "I'm going to ask you now about your satisfaction and dissatisfaction with your volunteer work. Let's begin with the ways in which it is satisfying for you."

Presupposition questions are useful. Leading questions are not. It is sometimes easy to confuse the two. In leading questions, the interviewer makes obvious the direction in which he or she would like the answer to go. Imagine if you began a question with the following, "It often seems that many people are focused on themselves, never thinking about environmental problems, homelessness, or poverty except as they, individually or possibly as a family, are affected. What does volunteer work mean to you?" If the question was asked in this way, could a respondent easily tell you that he spent spring break with Habitat for Humanity because his girlfriend had signed up to go? A presupposition question might, in contrast, presuppose that there are ways in which volunteer work is and is not meaningful (satisfactory, useful, etc.) to the respondent, but it does not lead the interviewee to answer in any specific way.

The following discussion is drawn from a study that Kelly Clark (1999) conducted with women academics who were among the first generation in their working class families to attend college. Her questions are examples of types of questions that can be raised for qualitative inquiry. They also demonstrate the importance of planning a series of interviews with the same person over time so that rapport can be established and time can be sufficient for learning from respondents.

Clark began with a question asking each woman what she does for work and to describe a typical day. Spradley (1979) refers to this type of question as a *grand tour* question, a request for the respondent to verbally take the interviewer through a place, a time period, a sequence of events or activities, or some group of people or objects. Grand tour questions are good starting points because they ask the interviewee for experiential detail that he or she can easily and readily answer.

A common mistake in interviewing is to ask questions about a topic before promoting a level of trust that allows respondents to be open and expansive. Therefore, Clark followed up her first question with another easy-to-answer question about the women's work: "How is it that you became involved in the work that you do?" The answers to this question allowed her to gently transition into the area she was particularly interested in learning about during the first interview session—the language used and feelings expressed regarding what it had meant and continued to mean to be a first-generation female academic. Clark planned to hold a minimum of three interviewing sessions with each woman. For the first session, she created questions that would reveal what the process of going to college had been like for each woman as well as reflective self-perceptions of why each had pursued the path she had. Questions for the second session were built on these interviews and probed into areas painful for some: the opportunities, choices, and systems of support that influenced each participant's individual and educational development. The final session was deeply reflective with questions designed to generate a detailed story of how each participant had gone about aligning a sense of self with higher education. By the second and third sessions, Clark could ask questions that would have been more difficult to ask in the first session because both rapport and the foundation for asking more complex, reflective questions had now been developed.

It's easy to pose questions that are too vague to elicit comprehensive responses. Asking "What was attending college like for you?" is so broad that a respondent might be tempted to either give a short-answer "okay" or launch into experiential stories that don't necessarily pertain to your interests. You can make such questions less vague by asking the respondent to recapture something by imagining it. Clark posed the following, "I'd like to have you go back to a time in your personal life that you've probably not thought about for some time. Remember when you were first introduced to the idea of going to college? There were likely many things you had to consider as the time drew nearer for you to spend your first day on campus. What did you imagine college to be like?" The idea is to provide mood and props for interviewees to recall something likely to be long unthought about. You want to ask questions that will cause them to recapture time, place, feeling, and meaning of a past event. Clark's next question continued to prompt for reflection upon events in the past as she asked, "Suppose I were present with you during one of your visits home. What would I see happening? What would be going on? Describe to me what one of those visits would be like."

Interviewees readily participated in answering Clark's questions because doing so caused them to reflect upon their actions and perhaps to put pieces of their lives together in ways that they hadn't done before. Because Clark had been a first generation college student herself, by the third session, the interview became more conversational in tone with back and forth sharing of each other's lives. By the third session, she could also ask directly about each interviewee's life epiphanies—occurrences or realizations that "cut to the inner core of the person's life and leave indelible marks on them" (Denzin 2008, 120). It is these kind of personal experience stories that are often most meaningful for both interviewer and interviewee.

With some topics (e.g., controversial or very sensitive issues), it may not be as easy to get a respondent's personal opinion. In asking questions, you have a choice of voices, and thus of degrees of directness and generality. You can ask "do you," "do nurses like you," "do nurses at your hospital," or "do nurses in general." The scope of the voice increases with each example as, accordingly, the degree of personal disclosure decreases. Whenever you sense your questions to be too personal to be asked directly, you can expand the generality, and assume that the longer the respondent talks, the more likely he or she is speaking in a personal voice.

That some questions are designated as warm-up questions suggests that others are best asked at the end. When you are reasonably comfortable with the form and substance of your questions, give attention to their order. Which belong at the beginning because they are easy to answer and answering them will reassure respondents that your questions are manageable? Which belong at the beginning because they are foundational to what you will ask later, or because they will give you the time needed to promote rapport? Which questions should be asked in special sequence? Which should be kept as far apart as possible because you want to minimize how the answer to one question might affect the answer to another? Which should be asked at the end because they are of a summary, culminating, or reflective nature? For example, Cynthia Stuhlmiller (2001, 75–76) conducted interviews with rescuers in the 1989 earthquake in San Francisco, California, an emotional topic. Toward the end of each interview, she asked questions like "What did you learn about yourself from your encounter?" or "What advice would you have for others?" As she states, "this directed narrators to consider the positive or growth-promoting aspects of the experience and enabled such thoughts to linger after the interview." Of course, we all know what happens to the best-laid plans of researchers. Your logical order may be sundered by the psychological order that emerges from your respondents' answers. Not needing to keep things straight, as you see it, they may talk in streams of language that connect to various parts of your questions, but in no way resemble your planned order. You then learn new ways that your questions connect.

Revising and Piloting

View the pre-interview process of question construction as a continuing interaction between your topic and questions and collaborators whom you enlist to play several facilitative roles in this process.

First, think of the pre-pilot-testing period as a three-way interaction among the researcher, the tentatively formed topic, and interview questions—tentative because in so thinking you are optimally open to what is known to be most realistic: that interview questions will change. Write questions, check them against your topic, possibly revise your research statement, and reconsider the questions.

Then, think of pre-pilot testing as a four-way interaction when the collaborators enter the picture. These collaborators or facilitators are your agreeable peers, who will read drafts of your questions in light of what you communicate as the point of your study. They bring their logic, uninvested in your study, to the assessment of your questions, and give you the basis for returning to your computer to create still one more draft. Such facilitators tell you about grammar, clarity, and question-topic fit. In addition, some facilitators may be informed by experience with the people and phenomena of your research topic and thus can ascertain if your questions are anchored in the respondents' cultural reality. No doubt, the most effective collaborators are the persons for whom your questions are meant. Your greatest challenge is to create questions that your respondents find valuable to consider, and questions whose answers provide you with pictures of the unseen, expand your understanding, offer insight, and upset any well-entrenched ignorance.

Finally, pilot your questions. Ideally, your pilot respondents are drawn from the actual group that you mean to study. Urge your pilot respondents to be in a critical frame of mind so that they do not just answer your questions but, more important, that they reflect critically on the usability of your questions. Since formal pilot studies are not always feasible, you might design a period of piloting that encompasses the early days of interviews with your actual respondents, rather than a set-aside period with specially designated pilot respondents. Such a period, if conducted in the right frame of mind—the deep commitment to revise—should suffice for pilot purposes. Sean, in reflecting on developing interview questions about the experiences of first-generation college students, observed.

> It was the actual pilot interview phase that most clearly informed my interview questions. Which questions resonated with my interviewee, and which ones fell to the ground (both figuratively during the interview and literally during the coding of the interview)? It is also the point at which the experience of the first generation student leaves the crisp pages of research documents and becomes a responsive, interactive experience . . . one which says, "Huh?" at the end of a poorly worded question, or continues at length in response to a good one.

Be prepared to let some questions fall to the ground.

The example shown in Exhibit 4.1 is taken from the work Kristina did on her questions for interviews with African women about their perceptions of their legal rights as women. Presented here are only a few of her questions from each of her subsequent drafts, so you can get an idea of how her questions evolved through her dedication to making them good questions and through feedback from her professor, peers, and eventually several pilot interviews.

DRAFTS OF KRISTINA'S QUESTIONS	BRIEF COMMENTS ON EACH DRAFT
Draft 1, October 2	*Draft 1*
1. How would you describe the position of women in your country, both economically and socially?	Notice how broad and general the first question is. Because it is such a large question, it would be difficult to know where to start in answering it.
2. I want to talk to you about any experiences you or your mother, or other women that you know have had, about owning property. How did you or the women you know gain property?	Again, where does one start and with whom—you, your mother, or other women? And what is meant by "gain"? What is meant by "property"?
3. How did you come to understand what rights a married woman has compared to her husband?	Question 3 is less broad than the others, but it still feels vague. How would you answer it?
Draft 2, October 9	*Draft 2*
In many countries around the world, women have inferior social and economic positions compared to men. This inferior position sometimes makes it difficult for women to exercise their rights in issues of marriage and property. I want you to describe first the rights women in your country face when it comes to marriage issues, and then we'll come back to the rights of women relating to property.	These preliminary words, an attempt to be more conversational in her approach, clearly state Kristina's position and could silence or lead women to answer in certain ways.
1. What kinds of rights do women have in your country around the issue of marriage?	Question 1 remains quite broad and vague and asked at a general level rather than engaging the women in discussing their own experiences.
Now I want to talk to you about issues relating to marriage. I'm going to divide this issue into two topics. First I want to talk about what rights a woman has when she is married, the kinds of things she can and cannot do, and rules or laws which may apply to a married woman. Then I want to talk about the same issues only concerning divorce.	Kristina's preliminary to the next questions is a worthwhile attempt to be more conversational and to alert the women to what kinds of questions are to come, but the words "I want to talk to you about . . ." or "I want to talk about . . ." do not work to bring the interviewee into the interview. It is also difficult to follow all the information presented.
2. What kinds of rules or laws apply to married women?	Question 2, like 1, is too broad, vague, and general.

(continued)

(continued)

3. What experiences have you had which helped you to understand what rules or laws apply to married women?

Question 3 finally gets at the woman's experience. Look at how this question seems more engaging than Question 3 of Draft 1.

Draft 3, November 11

Draft 3

1. If you had to generalize and describe how women in your country live, what would you say?

Nice beginning, but again very broad and difficult to answer.

Now I want to talk to you about issues relating to marriage. I'm interested in the sorts of rights a married woman has, the kinds of things she can and cannot do, what kinds of rules or laws apply to married women. These rights don't necessarily have to be actual laws but can be what is expected of a married woman.

Kristina might say "Now I would like to hear about . . ." which situates her as the learner in the interview process. What she goes on to say is useful and clarifying information for the interviewee.

2. What kinds of laws or rules apply to a married woman?

Question 2 continues to be asked at a general level, but the introduction makes it easier to think about an answer. Being a "knowledge" question, it could be regarded as an uncomfortable kind of test question by interviewees.

3. What do you think about these kinds of rules or rights?

Question 3 is a nice follow-up, and, I suspect, where the interviewee information will become more interesting.

Draft 4, November 18

Draft 4

I want to talk to you about your understanding of how women perceive marriage, divorce, and property rights in your country. I'm mostly interested in your perceptions of these issues, regardless of your knowledge about specific laws that apply to women. I'm going to break this interview into three sections beginning with marriage, then we'll talk about divorce, and finally we'll talk about women's property and inheritance rights.

Nice, clear introduction that sets out the scope of the interview and specifies that Kristina wants to understand the women's perceptions, not their knowledge of their country's laws.

1. I'd like you to tell me about the laws or customs concerning women and marriage in your country. How would you describe them? (probe for role of women, role of men, how roles have changed)

Question 1 is at a general level, but clear and direct with good prompts for areas in which to probe.

2. How were you raised to think about marriage? (probe for role of mother, father, friends, school, government programs)

Question 2 gets at the interviewee's socialization. It would prompt reflective, and, most likely, engaging answers.

3. What would you teach your children about women and marriage? (probe for differences between teaching sons and daughters)

Question 3 is an excellent question to get at the interviewee's values and opinions.

EXHIBIT 4.1   Example of Developing Interview Questions.

How a question is worded matters. Gubrium and Holstein (2009, 46) give examples of ways in which similar, but differently worded questions prompted different kinds of stories. "As you look back over your life, what are some of the milestones that stand out?" led interviewees to focus on various professional milestones. The question, "If you were writing a story of your life, what chapters would you have in your book," however, generated narratives drawn from the interviewees' overall life stories. On Kristina's part, the process of drafting and redrafting interview questions required time, thought, and effort. Her research benefited, however, with her later questions eliciting interesting and engaging information. The data you get are only as good as the questions you ask.

SETTING UP TO INTERVIEW

Where will you conduct your interviews? You need to find convenient, available, appropriate locations. Select quiet, physically comfortable, and private locations when you can. Defer to your respondents' needs, however, because their willingness is primary, limited only by your capacity to conduct an interview in the place that they suggest. If, for example, a location's lack of privacy dampens, if not defeats open discussion, or if its noise level precludes hearing, then the available site is not workable. If meeting where radios or televisions blare, your gentle request will generally suffice to get the sets turned off or at least down. An office set aside for the researcher on a regular basis is ideal for interviews with students conducted at school. Otherwise, you may have to use your creativity and move around, depending on the time of day—the lunchroom, auditorium, backstage, campus picnic table, and gymnasium are possible places. Teachers, counselors, and administrators are easier to meet because they have classrooms and offices.

When will you meet? "Convenient, available, and appropriate" apply also to the time of the interview. By *appropriate*, I mean a time when both researcher and respondent feel like talking. Again, however, you take what you can get and defer to the preferences of the respondent. School-based interviews usually follow a teacher's free-period schedule and a student's study-hall period. Barring these class-time opportunities, before and after school and lunchtimes are other possibilities. Meeting counselors and administrators requires fitting into their schedules when free of appointments.

How long will your interview last? An hour of steady talk is generally an appropriate length before diminishing returns set in for both parties. There are exceptions, for example, when less time is available to the respondent. Take what you can get, while trying to promote regularity—of location, time, and length of interview—so that you can say to your respondent at the interview's end, "Same time and place next week?"

How often will you meet? This is a variable, depending upon the purpose of the interview. A life history interview, for example, could not be completed in an hour interview. Some have taken dozens of hours (Atkinson 2002). Even most topical interviews require multi-session interviews to obtain trustworthy results. Just how many will depend on the length of the interview schedule and interview sessions, the interest and verbal fluency of the respondent, and the probing skills of the researcher. You might say to your respondents, "I would like to meet with you at least two times, and maybe more, certainly no more than is comfortable for you. And you may—without any explanation—stop any particular session or all further sessions." Then, it is your challenge to make the interview experience so rewarding that having more than two sessions, if needed, is unproblematic to the respondents.

How many interviews should you schedule for any one day? Stan, a working graduate student, was interested in perceived effects by students and teachers of an innovative bilingual program. He negotiated release time from his work for one day a week for two months. During this time, he planned to collect his data. When he began interviewing, he set up back-to-back interviews, trying to schedule five or more people to interview on the day he was at the school. He came to me, frustrated with delays and last-minute changes made to his plans, but determined to complete twenty interviews on the four Fridays during that month. I empathized with his personal time-constraints, but suggested that he revise his data collection plans, somehow extending the period. The limited time spent at the site, no matter how hard he worked when he was there, would not do justice to his inquiry. By scheduling interviews back to back, he did not have time to reflect upon and journal about each interview after its occurrence and thereby learn from it before the next interview. With such a tight schedule, he was probably more focused on getting through his questions than on listening, probing, and learning new questions that he, perhaps, should be asking. In addition, his anxiety over time was likely to be noted by his participants and they might give him shorter answers to speed up the process. Although I have scheduled three interviews in a day, I tend to agree with Karen O'Reilly (2005, 143) when she says, "I doubt anyone could manage more than two in-depth interviews in one day, and even less than that if the interview is very long or intense."

Stan might, for example, consider the phone or email as a way to follow up on, or even conduct some of his interviews. If he and respondents have access to computers with cameras, they could also hold the interview online, through programs such as iChat or Skype. Although conventionally perceived as not as ideal as face-to-face interviews, Internet-based interviews have some advantages (Meho 2006). They tend to be less costly than phone or face-to-face interviews, and they allow the researcher to access people from many different geographic areas and in politically sensitive or dangerous locations. Email interviewing has the additional benefit of decreasing the cost or time involved in transcription. It can also enable conversations with some groups that might not be as willing or able to participate in face-to-face interviews such as people with special characteristics (stroke survivors or those with speech impediments), the difficult to reach (executives), second-language speakers, or those who are particularly shy. If choosing to do interviews through email, you need to plan on multiple email exchanges over an extended period of time so that you can probe into responses, ask for clarifications, and follow new lines of thought.

RECORDING AND TRANSCRIBING

How will you note your face-to-face interviews? Whether by hand, audiotape, or videotape is a matter of your needs and the respondents' consent. It is not quite a toss-up as to whether you note by hand or tape recorder. With handwritten notes (or notes typed into your laptop computer), you are closer to being done writing when your interview is done; this is their distinct advantage. Also noting by hand is less obtrusive and less intimidating to some persons. But be aware of the message your respondent may deduce whenever you stop taking notes: the risky, "I no longer am noteworthy." You will also feel less in control of the interview when, as you handwrite notes, your attention is focused on the struggle to keep up with the respondent's talk (even knowing that this generally cannot be done), and you can only intermittently maintain eye contact and attend to all of the verbal and non-verbal cues that have bearing on your procedure. Interviewees may generally be patient and slow down, even wait for you to catch up if you explain your desire to note their words as fully as possible. Recording devices, however, provide a nearly complete record of what has been said and permit easy attention to the course of the interview.

Many persons will agree to the use of a tape recorder. Depending on the sensitivity of your topic and the unease of your respondents, you may want to wait until the end of the first session before you ask for permission to record. Recording devices require an electrical outlet; using batteries is acceptable but somewhat risky. Give due attention to the quality of your equipment. You don't need the added frustration of trying to decipher the words on the recording after your interview. Digital recorders have advantages over the older analog recorders in that they store data in a digital format that you can download as a sound file directly into your computer, making it easier to manage, store, and transcribe your interviews than when dealing with boxes of cassettes. Most recorders have built-in microphones, which are less effective than an external microphone; best of all are lapel microphones that can be attached to both researcher and respondent, particularly if there is sound around your interview site or you are interviewing persons who are soft-voiced.

If you are recording a lot of interviews and using an analog recorder, you might want to borrow or rent a transcribing machine with headphones and a foot pedal for reversing and advancing the tape, so that your hands are free to transcribe. Also, the machine rewinds the tape a little when you stop it, so you don't miss the first word or two when you begin the tape again. Doing this by hand is frustrating. Lorna reflected upon her transcription process without a transcribing machine:

> The worst problem was in transcribing the interviews verbatim. My initial attempts at home left me somewhat crazed; it took me about one hour to transcribe about ten minutes of conversation. In desperation, I hired someone to do this. However, the expensive transcriptions contained numerous "???," where the words were obscured. . . . I then had to go over the entire tapes to fill in missing parts of the interaction.

With technological advances, however, the transcription machine may soon be relegated to museums, next to mimeograph machines. If you have a digital voice recorder, you can download the interview recording to your computer. Free software helps you transcribe by allowing you to pause and restart the recording as you type the words into a text box (Gibbs 2007, 16). Although many qualitative researchers anxiously await the day when speech recognition software can transform all recordings into text, currently speech recognition software must be "trained" to recognize the voice of one person. What some researchers are doing, however, is a kind of simultaneous translation in which they use earphones to listen to the recording of an interview, pause it, and then speak the same words into their computer equipped with speech recognition software trained to their voice (Gibbs 2007; Mears 2009). Although such a system requires good equipment (and at least 1 GB of free space on the hard drive), repeating aloud each word of the interview could evoke thoughts and possible insights that simply typing the words would not. Carolyn Mears (2009) describes herself as a convert to voice recognition software, using it not only to transcribe, but also to "take notes" on texts she is reading. When she comes upon a paragraph that she might want to quote, she reads it out loud and the software types it into her document file. Some speech recognition programs to explore include Dragon NaturallySpeaking (for Windows), IBM ViaVoice (for Linux), and MacSpeech Dictate (for Mac).

When transcribing, it can be helpful in the long run to type (or state) the first name of the interviewee in ALL UPPERCASE, followed by a colon, every time she or he begins speaking. Not only can you see the name easily this way, but also you can search forward for parts of a specific interview (Gibbs 2007). If doing sensitive research (learning about drug use), then you need to make your references to participants anonymous from the beginning. If your research involves something less sensitive (principals' attitudes toward tenure for teachers), then it might be easier to use the interviewee's real first name until all data are collected. Then a pseudonym list can be compiled and you can search forward and replace real names with their pseudonyms. Some researchers use initials or even a number for names of interviewees, but, for me, this creates more distance between the interviewer, interviewees, and readers than pseudonyms.

How much you transcribe varies with research approaches and goals. If doing traditional ethnography, focused on cultural patterns and understandings, you can leave out most of the um's and somewhat ignore pauses and overlaps in conversations. If doing narrative ethnography or conversational analysis, however, you will want to transcribe in a way that shows pauses, overlaps, silence and the details of struggling for the right word (Gubrium and Holstein 2009). Also particularly important for narrative ethnography and conversational analysis is inclusion in the transcription of the interviewer's questions and prompts.

Whatever means can be afforded to minimize the agony of transcribing tapes—for analog transcribing, estimate five-plus hours per ninety-minute tape done by an experienced transcriber—should be seized. The good times of data collection can quickly pall if the transcribing doldrums set in. Reflect carefully on your needs. Replay your tapes on the way home from interviews. Browse through tapes and judge, given your purposes, how and how much you need transcribed.

Regardless of the means you select to record your interview, keep an account for every interviewee that includes the following: questions covered; old questions requiring elaboration; where to begin next time; special circumstances that you feel affected the quality of the interview; reminders about anything that might prepare you for subsequent interviews; and identification data that at a glance give characteristics (e.g., age, gender, ethnicity, socioeconomic status, experience, occupation) that have bearing on your respondent selection. These identification data allow you to monitor the respondents you have seen, so you can be mindful of whom else to see. Review your notes, listen to the tapes, and transcribe as soon after the interview as possible. In these ways, you also gain some idea of how you are doing as an interviewer, what you need to improve, what you have learned, and what points you need to explore further. If you wait until you have completed all of your interviews before hearing your tapes (or reviewing your notes), then you have waited too long to learn what they can teach you.

After you have transcribed about three interviews and have entered enough fieldnotes into a computer file (each with date, time, and place, of course), a peculiar phenomena occurs. Paranoia sets in that something will happen to your data. Someone will steal your computer. Your apartment or house will burn down. Or you'll just wake up one morning and it's not there. All have most likely happened. It's best to back up your files. Rather than disks, invest in a compact Flash drive or memory stick or a removable hard drive. These are more secure and easy to use. What you need to remember, however, is that each time you back up your files, you need to add the date to the file name. This prevents confusion later on if you need to use your backup. You might want to keep the compact Flash drive with you (I use a zippered pocket in my purse) so that, if something happens to your computer, your Flash drive doesn't disappear as well.

THE NATURE OF INTERVIEWING

Conducting interviews is well within the capacity of most researchers, although it is clearly true that some people take to it naturally and readily get better and more proficient. Others take longer to become adequate interviewers, particularly in learning how to probe and how to wait with silence.

Interviewing is not quite the same process for all its practitioners, any more than teaching, nursing, or counseling is. Its variability derives from who is conducting the interview with whom, on what topic, and at what time and place. Interviewing, in short, brings together different persons and personalities. Gender, race, nationality, sexual orientation, age, and all their possible combinations, can make for very different interview exchanges. Depending on the topic discussed, the location of the interview, and the temper of the times, the nature of the interaction will change as well. If you are a European American researcher interviewing a Mexican American official of the Mexican American Political League on the subject of farm workers, in the League's business office, during the heated times of a strike, you will conduct an interview that is imaginably different from one you would conduct if you are a Mexican American researcher, interviewing the same officer, on the same subject, in your office, at a time when labor peace prevails.

But even if all variables were the same and just the researcher of the same gender, race, etc. changed, the interview process could be expected to be observably different—albeit possibly equally good, for there is no one person who is exactly the right interviewer, any more than there is a "right" practitioner in the case of teachers, nurses, or social workers. Each researcher has personal strengths and weaknesses that form the basis of his or her interview style. Just as in non-research life, some persons engender nearly instant trust; they can safely ask direct, probing questions on hot topics early in an interview relationship. Some can make blunders and get excused over and over because they are eminently forgivable. Some create such an atmosphere of reflection and nurturance that respondents line up to be interviewed by them. Learn who you are, how you operate, and make the best of it. Do not expect the same reception from all respondents. They will take to you as variably as people do in general. This means that you will conduct some wonderful interviews, and others may not be helpful at all. Of course, your unsuccessful interview encounters should not always occur with the same type of person.

Interviewing is a complex act. In the early days of interviewing it might be easier to conclude, "This is not for me" than to exult, "I have found my niche!" Because there are so many acts to orchestrate, effective interviewing should be viewed the way that good teaching is: You should look for improvement over time—for continuing growth—rather than for mastery or perfection.

A number of things occur simultaneously in interviewing. First and foremost is your listening. Interviewers are listeners incarnate; machines can record, but only you can listen. At no time do you stop listening, because without the data your listening furnishes, you cannot make any of the decisions inherent in interviewing: Are you listening with your research purposes and eventual write-up fully in mind, so that you are attuned to whether your questions are delivering on your intentions for them? If they are not, is the problem in the question, in the respondent, or in the way you are listening? Has your question been answered and is it time to move on? If so, move on to what question? Should you probe now or later? What form should your probe take? Do you need to probe further the results produced by your probe? Have your questions been eliciting shorter and shorter if not monosyllabic returns, suggesting irritation with the topic or tiredness? The spontaneity and unpredictability of the interview exchange precludes planning most probes ahead of time; you must, accordingly, think and talk on your feet, one of those many interview-related skills that improves with practice.

You listen and you look, aware that feedback can be both nonverbal and verbal. You observe the respondent's body language to determine what effects your questions, probes, and comments are having. Do you see indicators of discomfort, and is the source of that discomfort in the physical conditions of your interview site or in the topic to which you are stimulating a response? Do you see signs of boredom, annoyance, bewilderment? What might be their source and their remedy, and is it within your means to find a remedy? Dick wrote in his log of causes that were beyond his control:

> I arrive at school on a day when classes have been called off because of a power outage at 7:30 A.M. on a cold winter day. The principal is afraid because it came back on some time afterward, but not before she had made the decision to call off school. Parents will be angry because they had to make alternative arrangements for childcare when the child could have been in school.

Dick needed to decide whether to proceed as planned with his interview.

Although listening and looking are critical, you forgo their gains unless you remember. You want to remember your questions so you won't constantly look down at your list, and so you won't be taken off guard when your questions are being taken out of order. You want to remember what has been said—by you and your respondent—in this session and in previous ones. You want to recall what you have heard, so that you can pick up on past points in order to make connections, see gaps and inconsistencies, avoid asking some questions, or rephrase other questions when you know that your first attempt at questioning fell short of your expectations and needs. You must of course remember to bear in mind your research purpose so that what you are listening to is being assessed in respect to your research needs.

You must also remember your responsibility for the quality of the respondent's experience. Are you attending to aspects of the interview that make it not just agreeable but interesting for the respondent? Your respondents' contentment derives from the satisfaction of talking with you, even if the topic stirs difficult memories. How satisfied respondents are can affect their willingness to continue to talk to you, the effort they put into their talk, and what they may tell other interview candidates about being your interviewee. Narrative research has brought attention to how stories are always told in collaboration, even during interviews:

> No matter how minimal, collaboration should not be discounted. Indeed, sometimes declining to participate in conversational give-and-take can put an end to a storyline; an apparent lack of attention or interest can put a damper on any

story. Conversely, measured participation may also facilitate storytelling, essentially allowing the narrator to command the floor in order to produce the extended turn at talk needed to formulate a story. (Gubrium and Holstein, 2009, 97)

When you are an interviewer, try thinking of your role as that of a conversational partner or collaborator whose conversational actions facilitate others in the telling of their stories.

Related to the quality of the respondent's experience is remembering to monitor your negative emotions. Unless involved in collaborative research projects that focus on learning through dialogue, you usually need to keep in check your disagreement with "disagreeable" views you may hear. When Bonnie learned through interviewing a nurse that her interviewee was seriously uninformed about the care and treatment of older, confused patients, she could not vent her irritation to the nurse and still maintain access. The venting may be acceptable and consistent with Bonnie's role as a nurse, but not with her role as a researcher. Keeping roles separate is hard but sometimes essential if you mean to collect data from people whose experiences and perspectives differ from yours. Moreover, you may be disappointed with the quality of your respondent's answer; nonetheless, you don't express this disappointment and rather look for positive means to improve the quality of your respondent's answer.

Finally, remember to keep track of time when interviewing in time-conscious cultures. Then, time remains for you to make some usefully culminating statements, such as, "Here's the ground we covered today. I was pleased to learn about

Interviews do not have to take place in sterile, formal settings. Make use of opportunities that allow you to learn from and with others in multiple places.

such and such. Would it be okay for next time if we went back to this and that point before we turn to the next subject?" In this way, you review and pave the way for your next interview session. You keep track of time so you can keep your promise to talk only for an hour and avoid overstaying your welcome or causing interviewees to be late for their next commitment. Take the time to negotiate and verify details of your next meeting, and be punctual for each appointment.

Listening, looking, and remembering in the comprehensive terms suggested here require developing your concentration. This means shutting off the myriad other aspects of your life so that you can fully attend to the needs of your interview. Achieving the appropriate level of concentration can be physically and emotionally draining, particularly in your early days as an interviewer. It is not excessively far-fetched to say that if you are not tired at the end of an interview session, then you might wonder about the quality of the session.

INTERVIEWER ATTRIBUTES

The following attributes do not ensure high-quality interviews; they are simply useful attributes to consider as you embark on research involving interviews. To what extent you must master these attributes, which ones have primacy, or which others may be substituted depends on you and the interview situation. Each attribute completes the sentence "The good interviewer is . . ."

ANTICIPATORY

As a good interviewer, you look ahead and ask, "What does the situation call for?" Some of the specifics about what to anticipate already have been mentioned. Your research summary is an example, in which you consider both what you must say in order to present yourself and your project cogently, and how what you say may vary from situation (pediatricians) to situation (the parents of children diagnosed with autism). What materials and equipment do you need to assemble for your interview session? If meeting a person for the first time, what do you already know and how might you learn more about the person before the interview? Who should you see next, in light of what you have been learning and not learning, and what arrangements need to be made to set up the next interviews? Anticipation feeds off the results of taking stock, an activity that might well be included at the end of the day in the daily task of field journal writing. Reflecting on each day is preparatory to anticipating what is next, both broadly in terms of your inquiry, and narrowly in terms of your next day's activities.

A LEARNER

Naïve characterizes the researcher's special learner role. It entails a frame of mind by which you set aside your assumptions (pretensions, in some cases) that you know what your respondents mean when they tell you something, rather than seek explanations about what they mean. Often, the hazard is that your research is on a topic about which you may know a great deal through study and personal experience. What you know is the basis for the assumptions that preclude you from seeking explanations and that shut down your depth-probe inclinations. If you second-guess your respondents, then you forego the chance to say, "Tell me more." The difficulty of being a learner is that assumptions generally are useful for simplifying relations with others. In your research capacity, you need not be relentless in asking "What do you mean?" but you must be alert to taking on the mindset of a learner, not an expert.

Pat reflected upon her role as interviewer and learner:

> I found that I enjoyed the interviewing process, but I had to be careful not to make it into a performance where I was the "star interviewer." Instead, I had to be aware that I was just the "seeker of knowledge." This became an important distinction for me when I first started because I had been concerned with how I would do as the interviewer—I had to shift my attention from me to the topic at hand and when I did this successfully, I found the interview to be enjoyable and meaningful.

Casting yourself as learner correspondingly casts the respondent as teacher. For many, this is a flattering role that enhances the respondent's satisfaction with being interviewed. And when you are a learner, you get taught.

ANALYTIC

Analysis does not refer to a stage in the research process. Rather, it is a continuing process that should begin as soon as your research begins. It follows, then, that interviewing is not simply devoted to data recording. It is also a time to consider relationships, salience, meanings, and explanations— analytic acts that not only lead to new questions, but also prepare you for the more concentrated period of analysis that follows the completion of data collection.

Gloria interviewed women who had left and then returned to the university. All had children. One woman told her that being away from home so much required that her husband change his participation in family life. Hearing this should have set bells ringing in Gloria's mind, but bells did not ring. She was not listening analytically at the time. The respondent's husband had to redefine his roles as spouse and father. Gloria needed to focus on the husband's behavior: include questions about it, probe it, and consider its meaning for other respondents. By not listening analytically, she could not make further use of what she was hearing.

As much as you might try to give your interviews the character of a good conversation, remember that research talk generally differs from other talk because it is driven by research purposes. When your data collection is complete and you enter a period of extended data analysis, you will find the analysis easier if all along you have been listening analytically and converting the results of ongoing analysis into further questions and notes that highlight thoughts and ideas.

THERAPEUTIC

You most likely have an opinion on the topic into which you are inquiring. As an ethnographic researcher, you want to learn the respondents' beliefs, experiences, and views rather than to persuade them of your perspective. This does not mean that you maintain zombie-like neutrality, nor that you never share your perspectives with participants. In some cases, knowing where the researcher stands on an issue is a precursor to access. In other situations (such as a study involving cancer survivors), you would not want to keep hidden your own cancer-related experiences and emotions. Some situations lend themselves to and, indeed, call for more self-disclosure and sharing during the interview. Whatever the situation, you work to set the tone and to build relationships so that your respondents can be as protective of spotted owls or as supportive of loggers' rights as they really are.

The specifically therapeutic aspect about the interview process is the unburdening effect of the respondents' saying safely whatever it is they feel. This effect is enhanced by the Rogerian "How did you feel about that?" "Would you tell me more about that?" The therapeutic dimension of good interviewing is part of what you can return to your respondents. It will not be uncommon for you to receive words of gratitude from respondents who are pleased with the opportunity for the profound, prolonged expression of personal views that your multisession interviews afford.

PATIENTLY PROBING

For qualitative inquiry, the interview is rightly conceived as an occasion for depth probes—for getting to the bottom of things. By so doing you do justice to the complexity of your topic. Qualitative researchers operate from the assumption that they cannot exhaust what there is to know about their topic. They may stop their investigation because they have run out of time or satisfied their particular research conceptualization. While the research remains in process, interviewing is a "what-else" and "tell-me-more" endeavor. The next question on your interview schedule should get its turn only when you have stopped learning from the previous one and its spinoffs. This is where patience comes in.

You need to concentrate on being patient in order to give due, unrushed attention and deliberation to the responses you elicit from each question you ask. Rush and the world rushes with you: If you communicate your satisfaction with your respondents' short-shrift replies, then you teach them how minimal your expectations are. Say, "Tell me more," and your interviewees will learn how to respond accordingly. You will find that the better you probe, the longer your interview time becomes. Short and few interview sessions are generally the mark of inexperienced or poor interviewers. With experience, the number of sessions increases.

Your probes are requests for more: more explanation, clarification, description, and evaluation, depending on your assessment of what best follows what your respondent has said. Probes may take numerous forms; they range from silence, to sounds, to a single word, to complete sentences. Learn which forms work best for you. Silence is easy to use, if you can tolerate it. Too little silence, and you may fail to have made clear that you were inviting more respondent talk; too much silence, and you may make your respondent squirm. The magical right amount of silence indicates, "Go on. Take some more time to think about your reasons for getting involved in grassroots organizing. I'm not in a hurry."

Silence leaves more time for thought. Silence is better than a menu of choices, as is rephrasing the question if it elicits no answer, or saying, "We can come back to that later if nothing comes to mind." Used judiciously, silence is a useful and easy probe—as is the bunched utterance, "uh huh, uh huh," sometimes combined with a nodding head.

Longer, more directive probes take various forms. A couple of examples of the many possibilities are, "I'm not sure I got that straight. Would you please run that by me again?" and (accompanied by a summary of what you thought you heard), "Did I understand you correctly?" Both types invite a rethinking by the respondent, and with rethinking may come elaboration. The summary alternative can also be used to preface, "Is there anything more you'd like to add to this?" Probes also can be simple questions: "How did that happen?" "What made you feel that way?" And more complex conditional questions: "If you had returned to graduate school 15 years ago, how might your life look different now?"

Exhibit 4.2 is a portion of Terry's interview with David, a child in her elementary classroom. Terry was interested in learning styles and in how children described their own learning processes. She talked to her class about theories of learning before interviewing some of the children. In this example, Terry used probes to open up and more fully understand David's perspective on his learning. The left column presents a portion of the interview while the right column contains comments on the probes.

As Terry demonstrates, it is clearly not the form of your probe that is most critical. It is your intent to probe, supported by your patience to linger and inquire rather than get on with completing the interview. The more nervous you are, the less patient you will be to probe and the less you will find occasion to do so. Missed opportunities for probing, however, plague us all. You will read your interview transcripts and find many occasions to groan over opportunities forgone. You were too tired, too satiated with ideas, or just didn't grasp what was being said. Given the intent to probe, the requisite habit and skill will develop—although you will always probe less than you could (as you learn in the ex post facto replaying of your tape or reading of your transcript).

NONTHREATENING

Among other qualities that could be used to describe a good interviewer is the quality of being nonthreatening. Tardif comments on its corollary—the

INTERVIEW TRANSCRIPT	COMMENTS
T: I'd like you to go back to when you were in kindergarten, a time you probably haven't thought about too much.	Good preliminary introduction to a question that eases the interviewee back to a past time.
D: Oh yeah, I can sort of remember some parts of it.	
T: Can you remember something that you learned back then?	Yes/No question, "Tell me about . . ." might have worked better.
D: Here's something that I can remember. I learned that when you are studying castles—I learned that they have arrow holes in the walls.	**D** gives a short answer about one item.
T: How did you learn that?	**T** opens up the interview with this probe.
D: The teacher said it. We were having a rug discussion, I think. The teacher was telling us some facts about castles. And I also remember how to divide stuff up equally. That's why I'm okay at dividing. . . . And I learned a trick in spelling "said." The teacher said, "it's sa-id instead of sed." I remember every single morning or almost every single morning we would play bingo on the rug until we could memorize our letters. I remember the first day I ever read a book. It's *Alligator in the Elevator.* It was my first book. I remember that after that I read all the books they had in the kindergarten. And then just kept on reading higher and higher levels. And by first grade I was reading adult books. I read the first book in the Tarzan series.	**D** can suddenly remember lots of things. He is not, however, really answering the "how" question except for learning specific things from his teacher.
T: Do you remember when you first learned to read?	Although a yes/no question, **T** is picking up on reading as an area to probe for the "how."
	And **D** addresses the "how."
D: This is what I always do. I can remember I did this when I learned to walk. I don't really do it, I just kind of stand back and practice ways of doing it for a while. I'm usually late at doing things. For instance, I was never really a toddler. . . . The first day I took a step, I just walked around. I never fell either, unless I tripped or slipped. In reading, I kind of looked at signs and I read little things at first and then I just tried reading a book after a while and I could read it.	

EXHIBIT 4.2   Examples of Using Probes in an Interview.

sense of safety she felt in talking to Young, a sense that Young could convey by being outside Tardif's personal and professional world:

> I found it easier to discuss my thoughts and feelings regarding some of my professional decisions with Beth [Young] than I did with many of my colleagues. There was a freedom of expression afforded me in these sessions that was not present in my everyday contacts. Beth was not a threat to me in any professional sense—she did not have a stake in any of the issues that had been discussed. (Young and Tardif 1988, 8)

Young's advantage as a nonthreatening outsider is a part of the case against doing research in your own workplace or with people with whom you already have a relationship.

A good interviewer never does anything to make respondents look or feel ignorant. Be attuned to the respondent's anxiety at the prospect of being interviewed. When trying to make interview arrangements, you will discover that respondents often try to excuse themselves on the grounds that they have not had enough schooling or they don't know enough. Even otherwise sophisticated respondents will be diffident about their performance, saying, "I don't know if that's what you're looking for or not."

Respondents may perceive your questions as testing, in the way they thought of questions as students at school. You may inadvertently present your questions and respond to answers in tones that suggest you are testing. Accordingly, you need to reassure, not only when you present yourself at the outset of interview arrangements, but also in the course of the interviews when respondents understandably want to know if they are being helpful to you. You need to reassure that it is perfectly permissible to say "I don't know," "I have no idea," or "I never even thought about that before."

AWARE OF POWER AND HIERARCHY

Particularly through the work of feminist and poststructuralists, the hierarchical nature of the interview process has been challenged. Fontana and Frey (1994) state,

> . . . the emphasis is shifting to allow the development of a closer relation between interviewer and respondent, attempting to minimize status differences and doing away with the traditional hierarchical situation in interviewing. Interviewers can show their human side and answer questions and express feelings. (370)

Yet, how to minimize status differences is difficult when research roles are different from everyday interactions. In discussing interviews to gather information on the lives of women, Davies (1996) notes how, even though you may work to structure an interview so that "it is the woman's own logic and ideas that steer the conversation" (584), the interview is still different from a conversation: "it is not a discussion where mutual information is shared, but one where the interviewee's experience is placed at the centre" (584).

How much you work to make relationship less hierarchical depends on your philosophical and theoretical positions and on the research purpose, topic, and desires of research participants. Since action, critical, and post-structural inquiries are more likely to involve research participants as co-researchers to some extent, the dialogical process is inherently valuable to learning about each other's perspectives, often as part of research goals. In conventional ethnographic research, some topics easily lend themselves (and call for) more dialogical sharing than others. In Busier's (1997) case studies of women in recovery from anorexia, the sharing of her own experience with anorexia allowed her access to women who would not have talked about their own experiences with someone who had not "been there." Yet, in the Christian School study, expression of our beliefs and opinions may have denied us access to the school.

Qualitative researchers are neither always emotionally removed and controlling of the research process, nor are they always openly sharing of their own opinions and seeking collaboration. All need to be mindful, however, of status differences inherent in research interactions and work to mini-mize them. Think about ways research participants could become more involved in and benefit more from the research. Finally, if you remain uncomfortable with the decidedly hierarchical nature of conventional inquiry, choose topics that allow or require more sharing of self, work only on projects requested by research participants, or explore further the possi-bilities of action, critical, and poststructural research.

CARING AND GRATEFUL

When you consider the time, effort, cooperation, and flying words that respondents give you, you need to be able to communicate at the end your appreciation. Leave time after your interviews for the expression of your gratitude and for other informal talk. In fact, during such informal time (with tape recorder off) you may occasionally learn more than when you were plugged in.

Your gratitude to interviewees for their participation in your research project is readily within your power to provide. Another type of return is not necessarily within your grasp, though it is a common by-product of the interview process. A young man told me in the course of an interview, "I tell you things I've never told myself." Given the amount of time qualitative researchers spend with their respondents, the research experience can affect respondents' thoughts and behavior. Questions raise consciousness. Respon-dents learn about themselves, you, and research.

Researchers speak of the exhilaration of conducting interviews as did Glen, who interviewed people involved in an alternative educational program: "Every interview provided another angle, and more capacity than the last. I began to realize that the interviewing was becoming slightly addictive, like endorphins after a good run." And researchers tell of the rewards of meeting new people and of coming to understand some they thought they might not want to meet. Andrea commented,

> One of the most enjoyable surprises was finding common ground with those respondents I was least inclined to interview. I would be struck, upon leaving, at how pleasant a time we had together. . . . I wrote in my journal: "Up close, these people don't seem as extreme to me as they appeared before I met them."

If your interview sessions are pleasant and sometimes exhilarating for you, then they most likely are for your respondents as well. Communicate your thanks.

SOME TYPICAL PROBLEMS

Fortunately, it is only once that you can do something for the first time (or do we believe that because it is consoling?). Helen reflected in somber tones about the beginning of her interviews:

> Things don't always work the way you plan. It took me a month to get access. Then when I got there I learned the interview guides had not been passed out. I had asked the principal to identify teachers who knew a lot, and found he had simply told various people that they would meet with me. About a third of the way through the first interview I realized that the pause button was still on my tape recorder.

Making the best of bad times may be all that you can manage as you try to salvage something from an interview, at least chalking it up as an occasion to get to know your respondent.

Remembering to check your tape recorder comes easier after your initiation. Beyond problems most commonly associated with the novice's early days are others that can occur to anyone at any time. For example, your respondents do not answer the question you ask. What is going on? The reason may simply be that the respondent has innocently (without a hidden agenda) taken a fancy to discussing something else. If you can listen as gracefully to their off-target (in your terms) as you do to their on-target talk, then the time that you lose may be more than offset by the enhanced quality of your respondent's answers. With the serendipity that abounds in qualitative research, the perceived off-target talk may even lead you into a relevant and related territory of which you were not aware, opening up a whole new path for understanding. Or it may simply be that your question was not clear or the respondent was too nervous to concentrate. Look for other suitable words in which to recast your question. If restating does not help, go on to other questions rather than risk the respondent developing feelings of inadequacy.

The reason for not answering a particular question, or for respondents' turning the focus of talk to topics of their own, may be more complex. Jennifer had a respondent who brought the talk around to safety in the nursery school, when Jennifer had the virtues of outdoor play on her mind. In time, Jennifer realized that her respondent gave very little time in her program to outdoor play and was saving herself from embarrassment in an interview that was directed exclusively toward outdoor play. In still more time, Jennifer realized that she needed to preface her interviews with the clearest possible statement that her inquiry on outdoor play was free of advocacy, so that respondents could continue to feel good about themselves—whether they did or did not include play in their nursery school program.

Such prefacing is critical to effective interviewing because respondents logically conclude that if you ask a lot about something, you must think it is important. This may be true, but it does not necessarily make you an advocate. To the extent that you appear as an advocate, your respondents may become defensive or tell you what they think you want to hear. Try explaining to them that you believe there are both successful and unsuccessful teachers who emphasize outdoor play; that you are not making judgments about success; that you want only to understand the place of outdoor play, or lack of it, in their nursery school curriculum. If it is there, what are the reasons? If it is not, then, again, for what reasons?

When respondents show a pattern of turning away from your questions, they may be saying obliquely what they won't say directly: "I don't want to continue this interview." Other forms of resistance to being interviewed are missed appointments and monosyllabic replies. The resistance may be apparent or real. Apparent resistance may result from respondents' being preoccupied with personal matters that preclude concentrating on your matters. If they want to talk about their personal problems, your listening may clear the deck for them to return to your questions. Cutting short your current session or postponing further sessions for a few weeks may suffice to return to normalcy. Do not prematurely conclude that respondent resistance is tantamount to their wish to terminate all further interviews. It may be that your questions are treading on matters too sensitive for them to discuss with you. Be gently direct. If you observe resistance, ask about it: "It seems to me that you have not been comfortable. . . . Are there areas you'd rather not talk about?" You might even ask, "Do you think we ought to stop the interviews?" If you do not hear yes, then you can continue interviewing and judge the quality of what you're hearing. If it is poor, shorten your list of questions and end the sessions as soon as you can manage to do so.

Far removed from the problem of resistance is the problem of the nonstop talker. Respondent fluency is wonderful if it is on your topic, but if not, then you need to learn to redirect the flow of talk. Making a wordless sound or a physical sign, such as a slightly upraised hand, may stop the stream of words so you can apologize for your interruption and pick up on something the respondent has said that you can probe. Or summarize what the respondent has said and then bridge to where next you wish to go. The idea is to avoid making an abrupt shift to a topic distant from where the respondent's talk had been.

In interviews, as in ordinary conversations, people make contradictory statements. Consider the possibilities that contradictions connote: the evolution of the respondent's thinking about the topic; the respondent's confusion about the topic; the respondent's being comfortably of two minds about the topic. Is the topic generating the contradictions worthy of clarification? If so, then you need to probe further into the respondent's most recent statement, right then and there. In addition, you can raise the topic again at your next session, inviting more thought on it. You could also take the two seemingly contradictory positions and put them into a question like the following: "I've heard some people say . . . I've heard other people say . . . What's your thinking about these two positions?" When the respondent has replied, you can continue: "Is it possible that both are right?" The point is, when you ask questions, especially about complex matters, you cannot reasonably expect complete, carefully considered responses to be ready at hand. If you allow respondents time to think, then you will get more reflective replies. It may also be that, when explained, the responses that at first appeared contradictory to you, are not at all.

Though not a problem in the same sense as those just stated, you may find it problematic to decide whether or not the interviews—a particular session or the entire series with one person—went well. In one sense, "going well" means getting answers that fit the questions you ask and that you can visualize as part of your forthcoming text; careful listening will indicate whether this criterion is met. In another, more serious sense, going well means creating connection and trust so that the talk delves below the surface of things. Trustworthiness of both researcher and respondent is likely to increase with time. Clearly, the more one deems a person trustworthy, the more he or she will speak fully and frankly to that person. Thus, judging how the interviews are going may be tentative at first—you feel good about the interview because the flow of talk was easy, smooth, uninhibited, and on target—and confirmed or challenged later as your relationships develop (or don't) and as you acquire data from other sources.

FOCUS GROUP INTERVIEWS

Facilitating a discussion on a particular topic among a selected set of people, or *focus group* interviewing, has gained popularity in recent years. Gathering a group together to answer questions on a topic is not, however, a new data-gathering technique. During World War II, for example, focus group research was used to develop effective training material for the troops (Morgan 1997). After the war, focus groups were primarily used for market research until the 1980s, when health researchers, in particular, began using group interviews to develop better means of education related to health issues like contraception and AIDS prevention. Increasingly, other disciplines have embraced focus group research. Group interviews are particularly useful in action and evaluation research where participants can express multiple perspectives on a similar experience such as the implementation of a particular policy or curriculum. A focus group can also be valuable in a pilot study. If participants are selected from the research site and know that part of their purpose is to assist in creating the research design, they can help you learn about aspects of the research site—language, norms, customs—in addition to helping you figure out overall research questions, participant selection and data collection strategies, and, perhaps, ways in which the research can better involve and contribute to the community or group being researched.

I tend to use *focus group* interchangeably with *group interview*, although some distinguish differences. For example, Bloor and Wood (2006, 99) state, "group interviews tend to proceed as a question-and-answer session with the researcher posing the questions, whereas focus groups will be characterized by more debate among the participants themselves perhaps facilitated by focusing exercises." Using these definitions, a researcher might set up a group interview to save time and travel by being able to interview more than one person over the same time period. Each participant would be expected to answer the same question in turn. In contrast, the researcher would use a focus group to better understand how a group would discuss some issue and elicit multiple perspectives in the process. My perspective is that group interviews, defined in this way, are not an ideal way to do interviews and do not allow for confidentiality and ease in the conversational and probing aspects possible in one on one interviews. Although group interviews, in this light, might be the only means for data collection in some situations, they set the scene for neither the depth nor intensity that can be reached through both one on one and focus group interviews.

Morgan's 1997 text *Focus Groups as Qualitative Research* provides a comprehensive discussion of focus group research. He suggests that "the simplest test of whether focus groups are appropriate for a research project is to ask how actively and easily the participants would discuss the topic of interest" (17). Planning focus group research requires some different design decisions than that needed for one-on-one interviews: Where can you meet as a group? Who should you invite to participate in each group? How many people should be in each group? How many groups should you include? Morgan gives sound advice on each of these issues as summarized in Exhibit 4.3 on designing focus group interviews. If you are planning to include focus groups in your research, read his book.

Focus group interviewing relies heavily on facilitation or moderator skills. As in one-on-one interviews, the researcher designs questions aimed at getting words to fly. Unlike one-on-one interviews, however, discussion does not rely on turn-taking between interviewer and participants. Instead, it depends on interaction within the group, stimulated by the researcher's question(s). The researcher becomes the moderator or discussion facilitator who helps the group set up ground rules at the beginning (only one person talking at a time, allowing others to have their say, etc.) and then may only have to pose or redirect a question from time to time, keeping track of the clock so that the various items are addressed. As in individual interviews, the focus group facilitator often begins the session with an experiential question that each participant answers in turn; and thus the facilitator works to get not only base-line experiential data, but also everyone comfortable in talking. Sometimes, at the end, each person is again asked to speak,

Where?	Focus group interviews often take place in some sort of community office space, a university seminar room, or, occasionally, in someone's living room. In the "two-thirds" world, focus groups generally take place in a public space, frequently outdoors.
Who?	Depending upon the topic, homogeneous groups in terms of gender, age, race, or sexual orientation, etc., can allow for a more free-flowing, relaxed conversation as well as facilitate the development of analytical concepts based upon data gathered in different kinds of groups. As Morgan (1997) warns, you want homogeneity in potentially influential background variables, but not in attitudes toward the topic. Focus groups are generally made up of strangers, but in some cases, such as in most action and evaluation research projects, participants may be coworkers, classmates, or otherwise known to each other.
How many in a group?	Small groups of six to ten participants generally work best. If the groups are larger, they tend to break into subgroup discussions that are difficult to facilitate and record.
How many groups?	Projects generally plan for three to five focus groups, but as Morgan (1997, 44) states, "The safest advice is to determine a target number of groups in the planning stage but to have a flexible alternative available if more groups are needed."
How long should a focus group last?	Generally, focus group gatherings are scheduled for one to two hours. Morgan (1997, 47) suggests setting the length at ninety minutes, but telling the participants to plan on two hours. This allows for longer discussions if the conversation is intense and also helps control for either a late start or early leavers.
How many questions are needed?	Four or five good questions should suffice for a somewhat structured focus group session. In a more unstructured session, you may need to pose only one or two broadly stated topics or questions.

EXHIBIT 4.3   Designing Focus Group Interviews.

summarizing his or her position on the topic. Morgan (1997) provides a good list of techniques for moderating groups with varying levels of facilitator involvement. He notes that if your focus group is comprised of teachers or organizational personnel who are used to managing groups, with a little instruction, they will run the groups for you.

Recording focus group discussions can be challenging. Except in sessions where participants run discussions themselves, trying to both moderate and note discussion is difficult. Tape recording the discussion is generally necessary (perhaps with two tape recorders in different locations to pick up soft voices as well as to have one recorder act as a backup). Sometimes the researcher brings along someone to assist with notation, jotting down who is speaking along with several spoken words so that this information can be entered into the transcription.

Internet technology has simplified recording issues for some focus group researchers who conduct "real time" focus groups online. In discussion groups or chat groups, all participants are online at the same time. The researcher poses a question and participants type responses that are transmitted to the whole group. People can reply to any one message at any time. Advantages include having a recorded script of the discussion with each respondent identified and the ability to have a virtual meeting space in which geographically separated people can participate. These virtual gatherings also tend to be less expensive and easier to schedule than face-to-face focus groups. Disadvantages include the inability to easily facilitate the discussion because it tends to move so rapidly with people responding simultaneously to different messages. Sometimes the person who types the fastest dominates the discussion or determines the direction it takes (Mann and Stewart 2000).

Virtual reality sites are another possibility for online focus groups and address some of the disadvantages of chat groups. Each participant logs on to a virtual world, chooses an avatar, sometimes uploading a photo of themselves for their head. A room with a large seminar table and chairs (or campfire with logs for sitting) could be the setting. As each participant joins the virtual world, their avatar appears and the real-time interaction complete with actions and talk can begin.

Non-real-time focus groups can also be conducted. This process is more like email in that questions go out to all participants and each can respond to the group when convenient. Advantages include the ability to include people from diverse time zones, to generate long, reflective comments, and to involve a large number of people (Mann and Stewart 2000). A disadvantage is that you tend to lose the group interactive nature, the strength of most focus group research. Setting up a blog can also serve as a kind of non-real-time focus group that "allows researchers to establish virtual communities with those sharing their specialization . . ." (Runte 2008, 314). Alternatively, pre-established blogs can also be a source of varying perspectives on a topic. For example, a nurse pursuing a doctorate with a specialization in Elder Care found a wealth of material at the New York Times blog site for "The New Old Age" (http://newoldage.blogs.nytimes.com/2008/). Semiprivate blogs can be used to publish early drafts of material and to get feedback from a select group of readers—a semiprivate blog could be used also as a kind of member check as you analyze and begin writing.

In summary, focus group interviewing can be an efficient use of time in that it allows access to the perspectives of a number of people during the same time period. In addition to learning about the research topic itself, focus group interviews can be useful as exploratory research to help determine the line of questioning you want to pursue in individual interviews or to figure out what sites might be most productive for participant observation. And, it can be a useful way to gather further insight into issues that developed through analysis of individual interviews or to member check your developing understandings with your participants. Focus group research can also have emancipatory qualities if the topic is such that the discussion gives voice to silenced experiences or augments personal reflection, growth, and knowledge development.

Focus group research is not without drawbacks. In particular, ethical problems related to confidentiality can arise and the researcher may decide accordingly to not bring up certain topics. With focus groups, the researcher should expect to not get as in-depth information from any one person as with individual interviews, although this may not be the case if multiple sessions are held with the same group. And, although the discussion may generate new ideas as people explore their experiences and perspectives, it may also silence some people whose ideas are quite different from the majority of those speaking. Contrarily, some might pose a more extreme perspective than they would ordinarily simply to counterbalance an opposing viewpoint. Finally, setting up the focus group event takes work and moderating the discussion can be exhausting as one tries to balance allowing the discussion to flow versus guiding its direction.

CONSIDERATIONS

The type of interviewing emphasized in this chapter is *semistructured*—you have specified questions you know you want to ask; *open*—you are prepared to develop new questions to follow unexpected leads that arise in the course of your interviewing; and *depth-probing*—you pursue all points of interest with variant expressions that mean "tell me more" and "explain." The intent of such interviewing is to capture the unseen that was, is, will be, or should be; how respondents think or feel about something; and how they explain or account for something. Such a broad-scale approach is directed to understanding phenomena in their fullest possible complexity. The elaborated responses you hear provide the affective and cognitive underpinnings of your respondents' perceptions.

Interviewing is an occasion for close researcher-participant interaction. Qualitative research provides many opportunities to engage feelings because it is a distance-reducing experience. The feelings in question are those that are involved in researchers' relationships with others—the matter of rapport—and those that are involved in researchers' reactions to and reflections on what they are learning—the matters of subjectivity and reflexivity (the issues in Chapter 5). Before turning to the next chapter, however, I conclude with a few considerations regarding the interviewing process.

A group of students, several other faculty members, and I had just entered a Warli village in India, where we were going to stay for several days. The Warli people, like other indigenous groups in India, have been struggling for land rights in the forested hill areas where they have traditionally lived. Our group of thirty-four dropped sleeping bags and packs in the community building, a large wattle and daub structure with an earth floor covered by a veneer of cow dung that binds the dirt and keeps down the dust. After being fed a meal of rice, dhal, and greens, our translator-guides said that the village women would meet with the female students inside the room where we had put our belongings and that the village men would meet with the male students outside under a tree.

As part of an international education program focusing on culture, ecology, and justice, we were living and studying in five different countries over an eight-month period. In addition to other assignments, each student was responsible for doing comparative research on a topic of his or her choice such as women's roles in agriculture or forces for and impacts of migration. Students, therefore, were not at a loss for questions when the opportunity presented itself. Although not always adept in forming good questions that elicited on-target answers, students were beginning to feel uneasy about a larger issue. In our thirst to have questions answered, were we missing out on authentic exchanges, if that were possible in the short time periods (one night to one week) we stayed in most villages? How were our questions limiting what we were learning and how were the questions setting the stage for a specific type of interaction, more or less controlled by ourselves, the outsiders? What would happen if we had no questions, no agenda?

We proceeded with our questions. After a while, the students gave the floor to Jo, whose research project focused on reproductive health. She asked, "What kinds of problems do women have during childbearing?" Our interpreter, who had worked as an advocate and activist among the villagers, suggested that she change the question so it asked each woman to state how many children she had born and, of those, how many were living. One by one the women answered, "I have born seven children, three are living." "Five, two are alive." "Nine, four are still with me." These simple answers by each woman, often holding a child in her lap in our circle on the dirt floor, were stunning in revealing the complexity of the women's physical and emotional lives, and, in contrasting their lives to our own. Previously formulated questions disappeared as students urgently wanted to know more of these women's lives—why had their children died? What happens when a child dies? What role do their husbands play in child rearing? What are all the daily tasks required of the woman? Now that so many men have to migrate to other areas to make some money, how has that affected the women's lives? The women smiled over our questions, and always politely answered. When one laughed as she said, "Well, I'm glad the men are gone often—they aren't here to beat us as much," we were again bewildered, not only by her statement but that she had laughed as she said it. We didn't know how to begin to interpret. We had little context for understanding.

Equally, they wanted to know about us and seemed amazed with our answers when they turned our question around and asked us, at least twenty women of childbearing age, how many children we have had and how many had died. None of us had children. They then wanted to know how many of us were married since we were all beyond the age at which they marry (generally by age 13). None of us were married. They wanted to know what kinds of crops we raised. None of us were from farm families, although some of us liked to garden and grew a few summer vegetables when we were in one place long enough. They asked questions of us that we hadn't considered asking of them—what songs did we sing in the evenings, what dances did we dance together? The only dance we could come up with that we all knew was the hokey-pokey. As the exchange continued, we, the outsiders, despite our vast economic privileges, began to feel somewhat bankrupt in terms of cultural practices and community connections. I do not know what the Warli women thought of us overall, but some expressed sincere sympathy for me, a woman with graying hair, who had neither husband nor children.

That researchers would even consider asking strangers questions about their lives is a practice developed over the last century, a practice reflecting, in part, the democratization of knowledge or the belief that everyone has a perspective to contribute. According to Gubrium and Holstein (2002), the growth and acceptance of interview research is part of modernization. Those of us from Westernized countries are used to surveys and interviews as a way of gathering information. We fill them out or take the time to answer questions without giving it much thought. Interviewing is not only an accepted research method in Western cultures, but also a main source of entertainment whether listening to Terry Gross on public radio or watching Oprah Winfrey on television.

In order for this democratization of knowledge (as well as commodification of *self*) to occur, another change took place first: the individualization of the *self*. "The notion of the bounded, unique self, more or less integrated as the center of awareness, emotion, judgment, and action, is a very recent version of the subject" (Gubrium and Holstein 2002, 6). In many other societies, a collective self made up of family or community or tribe is the seat of authority, not the individual. The collective self is a concept that's difficult to grasp for many raised in individual-focused societies.

The interview process, despite being the mainstay data gathering technique in qualitative research and despite its role in documenting the voices of many perspectives, can also be seen as having its roots in a kind of colonizing approach to research. Typically, the researcher is "in control," developing the questions and thereby determining the direction of the interaction. Typically, the interviewer tries to remain open and to not influence what the respondent will say through body language or verbally. The respondent is thereby treated somewhat passively, as a receptacle of knowledge, which the researcher is "mining." And, the researcher, although managing the interaction, is somewhat passive as well in that, other than the questions, he or she contributes as little as possible to what is being said.

As poststructuralist scholars challenge conventional research practices, the interview process, itself, is under scrutiny. How can we co-construct interviews? How do we learn from each other and create a dynamic in which no one person is pitching the questions while the other is sending words flying? In other words, how do we co-construct knowledge? Whose story are we telling when we do interview research and for what purposes? Do different situations call for different kinds of interview practices? When? How do we decide?

Bringing these "considerations" up here, at the end of the chapter, is not meant to imply that you should disregard previous sections with its advice steeped in the interpretive paradigm of research. All disciplines go through "moments" (Lincoln and Denzin 2000) (and sometimes fads), in which scholars embrace new ideas, reassemble them, incorporate some aspects, discard others. Qualitative research is not a static procedure, and those of us who practice it hope it never becomes so. Current challenges make the process more personally interesting and morally vital as we struggle to determine the kind of researchers we each want to be and how our choices reflect, challenge, and contribute to differing perspectives.

Through these considerations, I also want to remind you that what we come to know, whether "gathered" or "co-constructed," is always partial, always fragmented. I mentioned that while we were inside the community center with the Warli women, the male students and faculty were outside with the Warli men. While our group of women grew increasingly depressed with what we were learning, the male students were feeling elated. They and the Warli men had discussed intensely the struggles for community and for communal autonomy. They had shared philosophical perspectives and found common ground in their needs for connection, friendship, and brotherhood. In the same village, on the same evening, we regrouped from our conversations with two very different understandings of Warli life.

RECOMMENDED READINGS

Gubrium, J., and J. A. Holstein. 2009. *Analyzing Narrative Reality.* Thousand Oaks, CA: Sage.

Gubrium, J. F., and J. A. Holstein (eds). 2002. *Handbook of Interview Research: Context and Method.* Thousand Oaks, CA: Sage.

Holstein J., and J. Gubrium (eds.). 2003. *Inside Interviewing: New Lenses, New Concerns.* Thousand Oaks, CA: Sage.

Morgan, D. 1997. *Focus Groups as Qualitative Research.* Thousand Oaks, CA: Sage.

Patton, M. 2002. *Qualitative Research and Evaluation Methods,* 3rd ed. Thousand Oaks, CA: Sage.

EXERCISES

Class Exercises

1. The following activity is adapted from Berg (1995, 63). Turn to a classmate and decide who will be the speaker and who, the listener. The instructor assigns a topic that students know about, but are not particularly invested in, such as their opinions on the tenure and promotion process for university professors. The speaker talks for 30 seconds on the topic and then the listener repeats what he or she has heard, using the speaker's words ("I" statements). Then students change roles and repeat the exercise. The instructor then assigns a more personal topic such as "first conscious awareness of racism" and increases time allotment to a minute. Students follow the same procedure as above. At the end of the exercise, discuss nonverbal aspects of the two scenarios: What were differences in body language? In the level of sound? In the tone of what was being said? Which kind of topic would make for a better interview? What kinds of things should the interviewer observe, in addition to listening to the words being spoken?

2. Return to your class's practice research statement developed at the end of Chapter 2. As a class, create five interview questions that would help one understand the chosen topic. Pilot the questions by interviewing each other. Each student should have time to be both interviewer and interviewee. As interviewers, students take full, running notes of the interview. As interviewees, students reflect on the questions and make suggestions to reword, extend, or delete. After the interviews, reflect as a group both on the questions and the interviewing process. As homework, type up your interview transcript, filling in details where remembered. Hold on to these transcripts for a later exercise.

Individual Exercises

1. This exercise is adapted from one of Roorbach's (1998) writing exercises. With your topic firmly in mind, imagine that you are the interviewee and that you are sitting across from Barbara Walters (or Terry Gross). Without any notes in front of you, turn on a tape recorder and enact the interview, playing both the interviewer and interviewee. What kinds of questions does Barbara ask? What are the tough questions? Where will the heartwarming moments be? Where are the shockers? What will everyone be talking about tomorrow? Continue through the interview until it comes to a satisfactory close. Play the interview back and transcribe all the questions. Seriously consider how each might work for your research project.

2. After your interview with yourself, create five to ten open-ended interview questions for your research project. Pilot the questions with a classmate, asking your partner to pretend that she or he is one of your participants. Work together to reshape the questions. Then pilot the questions with someone who has had experiences similar to your research population or ask the questions of a research participant who is willing to collaborate with you on developing your questions. Reshape the questions again after reflecting upon what worked, what did not, and what new questions arose.

CHAPTER 5

Personal Dimensions: Field Relations and Reflexivity

When I stayed away too long, they scolded and snubbed me. When I was not comple-
tely fair (and sometimes even when I was) in the distribution of attention, I paid dearly
for it.

(Myerhoff 1979, 27)

Recent decades have seen a drastic change in scholarly thinking regarding how qualitative researchers should be in relationship to research participants and how and why they should inquire into those relationships. Once interpretivist and more recent theoretical perspectives began to reshape the conception and enactment of field relations, the positivist concern with objectivity and bias no longer made sense. In positivist work, researchers were urged to take a "fly on the wall" approach, remaining neutral and impartial in dealings with participants so that they would not influence actions and responses. With a primary goal of research that of contributing to knowledge in the scientific community, the interests and desires of research participants were often not considered. The researcher and researched were seen as separate entities with one being the seeker or inquirer and the other being the receptacles of particular bodies of knowledge. The inquirer's role was to uncover/excavate (note the mining metaphors) that knowledge and to process the "raw" data into something usable by the communities of which the researcher was a part.

No wonder that such approaches to research are perceived by many as exploitative and colonial. Poststructuralists, feminists, and indigenous scholars have been at the forefront of challenging previous perspectives on study purposes, field relationships, and roles of power and reflections in the research process. This chapter introduces you to some of these debates that continue both in the field and in research institutions.

FIELD RELATIONS

> Our informants tell and show us what they do because they are in a research situation with us as individuals; this encounter and the knowledge produced through it can never be objective. Therefore it is essential that we attempt to understand the subjectivities through which our research materials are produced.
>
> (Pink 2007, 367)

Qualitative research is often used interchangeably with the term *fieldwork*. As a researcher, your work occurs in a place or places (including virtual reality places) rather than in a laboratory setting. In those places, you develop relationships with others who live and interact there. You gain access, create rapport, develop trust, interact, conduct yourself ethically, and finally you leave and do something with what you've learned. You do none of this alone, but rather in relationship with others in the research site(s). The nature of these relationships is the topic of the first half of this chapter.

Before the past several decades, as mentioned above, much fieldwork remained influenced by positivist thought while, at the same time, challenging aspects of that paradigm. In reference to field relations, fieldworkers were particularly conscious of trying to remove bias from observations and interactions. In another often-used metaphor, this included entering the field with the mind as a "clean slate." Researchers worked to not convey their own perspectives on the issues into which they inquired. In other words, "objectivity" and a kind of scientific detachment remained constructs that many researchers worked to achieve. Some researchers today not only challenge whether objectivity in fieldwork is possible, but also ask questions such as "whose interests does the objective stance serve?" For example, Russell Bishop (2008), writing from an indigenous Kaupapa Maori perspective, argues that scientific communities' emphases on validity, reliability, and objectivity have "dismissed, marginalized, or maintained control over the voice of others" (171). He goes on to say that choosing to do qualitative research does not automatically mean that this changes. When researchers do not make explicit their interests and concerns, but rather work to appear neutral and to monitor all subjectivity in the sake of objectivity then this continues a "colonizing discourse of the 'other'" (171). Savyasaachi (1998, 90), a scholar and activist in India, argues that such neutrality "discourages dialogues and discourses across differences, prevents exchange of ideas and becomes a means to accumulate and monopolise symbolic capital." The research participant continues to be viewed as an object to be studied rather than as a person with whom to engage in conversation.

In this chapter, the process of establishing and maintaining field relationships and the complexities of doing so receives attention before discussion of reflexivity and the process of critically reflecting upon self and relationships in the context of research procedures.

Establishing and Maintaining Field Relations

Rapport. Rapport and trust are two concepts that have been used to describe ideal field relations in qualitative inquiry. The dictionary defines *rapport* as the "relation characterized by harmony, conformity, accord, or affinity" and notes that it refers to the "confidence of a subject in the operator as in hypnotism, psychotherapy, or mental testing with willingness to cooperate" (*Webster's* 1986). Rapport is an attribute that is instrumental to a variety of professionals, from used-car salespersons to marriage counselors. Its function, however, varies. For example, counselors establish rapport so that clients can feel sufficiently comfortable to disclose information; their intent is to attain ends shaped by the clients' needs, as they and the clients ascertain them. Researchers traditionally established rapport to attain ends shaped primarily by their own needs. As Freilich (1977, 257) states, "The researcher . . . 'engineers' people and situations to get the type of data required by the study." Feminists, poststructuralists, and others challenge this instrumental use of rapport in which researchers paradoxically seek to engender cooperation while maintaining distance through benign neutrality, suppressing their own perspectives on the issues at hand.

Rapport is often used interchangeably with trust, although some are careful to distinguish differences. Wieder (2004, 25) sees "rapport as a research tool and trust as a living relationship," stating that it is trust, not rapport that facilitates people to tell their stories. *Trust*, according to the dictionary, is "firm belief or confidence in the honesty, integrity, reliability, justice, etc. of another person or thing" (*Webster's* 1986). For many, qualitative research should move in a direction in which trust is needed for working together on the issue under inquiry. Rapport, however, is often a precursor to building trust and part of gaining access and "fitting in."

Fitting In. Malinowski's emphasis on fieldwork sent generations of anthropologists, sociologists, and later healthcare workers, educators, and others into various natural settings attempting to ascertain the "insider's" point of view. The literature and lore of fieldwork portray consummate researchers as sensitive, patient, friendly, and inoffensive. They have a sense of humor and a high tolerance for ambiguity; and they learn the other's language, wear appropriate dress, and maintain confidentiality. Such factors help the researcher fit in.

Measor (1985) discussed the role of appearance and shared interests in her data collection in a British school. She found that how she looked mattered to both students and teachers and that this in itself caused a problem because each group had a different notion of appropriateness. As a result, Measor sought a compromise that showed she was fashion conscious, but not too much so. Figuring out how to best manage appearance or behavior is not always easy. Davis (2001) was interested in nurses' use of computers and arranged to do ethnographic work in a hospital. For her, openly taking notes on her observations was easily done because hospitals are "paper-oriented" cultures. Her identity as researcher, however, was complicated by the ease with which she "fit" the setting. Patients mistook her for a receptionist when she sat in the office area and became annoyed when she continued with her note taking, rather than assisting patients. When she sat taking notes in the reception rooms, confusion still surfaced: "One patient who had suffered a heart attack asked me if I wanted to see the doctor before him" (43).

If doing research with strangers, chances are that to fit in, at least in some situations, you will have to act in certain ways that you might not otherwise if you did not have the researcher role. This could mean "getting mad" or "causing a disturbance," as Pettigrew (1981) discovered while working among Sikhs in the Punjab. When someone made a derogatory remark, she could not ignore it with a tolerant, indifferent attitude. In keeping with cultural rules, she had to display her opposition in order to maintain respect and rapport. Conversely, when Pettigrew witnessed the blatant sexist treatment of women, she could not object, or she would not have been allowed to stay. Whitehead and Conaway's (1986) book *Self, Sex, and Gender in Cross-Cultural Fieldwork* contains many examples of ways in which researchers managed their behavior and appearance to build and maintain rapport. For Regina and Leon Oboler (1986), working with the Nandi in Kenya, developing rapport meant that they could not openly display affection for each other, a condition they met:

> It pleased us when people would comment to us, with approval, that we acted just like Nandis because this implied that they viewed us as unlike the Europeans they had previously encountered. (43)

You consciously reflect upon your behavior so that people who are unaccustomed to the presence of researchers in their lives will be at ease in your presence.

That your appearance, speech, and behavior is acceptable to research participants does not have to imply stifling your own personality into a bland, removed researcher. Rather it means learning and being respectful of the customs and expectations within the culture of the group with whom you are working. Of course, this requires more consideration in some studies than in others. Teachers in the Christian day school that Peshkin (1986) and I studied were actively involved in rallies protesting the Equal Rights Amendment. As researchers concerned not only with rapport, but also with maintaining access to the school, we could not be seen endorsing what was antithetical to core fundamental Christian belief. Thus, rapport can place limitations on the researcher's ordinary interactions and expressions.

Yet, you do not have to always agree with your research participants in order to fit in. Sometimes when researchers question participants' viewpoints, they receive information they would not obtain otherwise and are even more accepted into a group as a result of open dialogue. "Fieldworkers worry," state Kleinman and Copp (1993), "that participants will interpret disagreement as unfair criticism or rejection, and thus it will drive a wedge between them. But...saying what one thinks can be an *engaging* experience and thus constitute closeness rather than distance" (40). When to disagree and when to keep opinions to yourself is one of those issues that depends upon other factors such as your mode of inquiry, the nature of your topic, and the kind of relationships you have developed.

Developing and maintaining rapport obviously involves more than consideration of one individual at a time; it calls for awareness of social interactions among participants. Researchers enter into social systems in ways that demonstrate that participants are valued—that is, that the worth of their time and attention and association is appreciated. Thus, if you are not equitable in the time you allot to participants, you may risk bruising feelings or eroding relationships, as Myerhoff (1979) observed in the opening quotation to this chapter.

You may remain uninvolved in the politics of your site, but this does not free you from needing to understand the political landscape and the pitfalls into which you might tumble. Maintaining rapport is associated with becoming informed about your setting's social and political structure. It is no small matter to be aware of the formal and informal loci of power, of the issues that irritate, and of the history that continues to shape current behavior. All of this is part of rapport—both developing it and keeping it.

Juefei Wang (1995), an educational researcher from China who has been living in Vermont, reflected on the role of time in the development of rapport in the United States and China. He indicates that rapport building may look very different in diverse cultures. After a short introduction to his study, most Vermont respondents were willing to talk openly with Wang. Most Vermonters were also willing to participate in his research, but some would simply decline with a "No thank you, I'm not interested," or refuse to answer certain questions saying, "I don't know." He contrasts the U.S. response to that in China:

> Among the people I have interviewed in China, probably over a hundred altogether, I have never had the case of fast-paced trust building. Even with young, open people, it takes me longer to build the trust. I have to find a way to make the interviewees believe that I am one of them. They talk about their families; I ask questions about their parents, wives, husbands, and children, and tell them about mine. They complain about their low pay; I tell them my pay is not high either. This is the process to build trust. It takes much longer, yet it can be long-lasting.
>
> In China, I have never had any refusal for cooperation. The frank American way of saying "I don't know" would not be acceptable by most Chinese. . . . They would always try to save face for me by not refusing me, yet they can always find a way not to give me anything valuable or anything at all. (2)

Wang describes how it took him over a week in China to get personal information from a school principal that, in the United States, he would have received in less time. He states:

> Modesty is still a virtue of the nation. This fact makes it very difficult when a researcher tries to find out about the interviewee's roles in an organization. The interviewee talks about other's contributions without talking about him or herself. (3)

Part of your role as researcher is to learn the culturally appropriate ways to develop and maintain rapport and to make the necessary cultural bridges in your own expectations and behavior.

Building Trust.   Rapport does not always lead to trusted relationships, but building trust tends to begin with establishing rapport. When asked, "How do you know when you have rapport," students in my qualitative research course replied:

- The way the interview goes shows rapport. When the interviewee keeps looking at her watch, you know you have not achieved good rapport.
- Rapport comes when the interviewee gets something out of the interview. One person told me, "No one has asked me this before." In good interview situations, people get to think about things that they have not put together before. They learn about themselves in the process. Another person told me, "I think I got more out of this than you did." You feel good then.

The first student describes how being attuned to the nonverbal language of participants can inform you about your research relationship, although people do check the time for reasons other than boredom. The second student introduces the concept of reciprocity into the relationship. Rapport and trust is more easily achieved if both parties get something out of the interaction. Research participants often find being part of a study interesting and will welcome the opportunity to reflect on matters of importance to them.

This willingness can be found where least expected. Andrea received a letter from one of her interviewees after their first meeting. The interviewee expressed sincere desire to get together again, sent information relevant to their discussion, apologized for being too enthusiastic, and complimented Andrea on the approach she was taking to investigating change in a small rural community. The interviewee was a developer with whom Andrea had postponed talking because she doubted her ability to keep an open, interested, learner perspective. Ironically, she found herself fascinated both by what he had to say and by his clear, logical, sensitive way of expressing his point of view. Rapport, obviously, had been achieved.

Generally, people will talk more willingly about personal or sensitive issues once they know you, once rapport has morphed into trust. In most cases, this means giving the participant time to learn that you are the sort of person who is reliable, honest, and willing to carefully listen and engage with another. Dick tells of doing an interview with a teacher aspiring to be a principal. Dick had a single, one-and-one-half hour interview scheduled and felt dismayed going into it. "These people," he said beforehand, "will never tell a stranger all this information." But the interviewee was someone who talked easily, and Dick responded appropriately. After forty-five minutes, during which Dick thought he was getting good information, the interviewee asked, "Now that I know you, can we go back to one of the earlier questions?" Dick was delighted that he had been able to develop rapport sufficient for the interviewee to reveal deeper layers of information comfortably. He also learned that many layers of data existed and that, even though his single-session interviews might give him enough data for his purposes, he was getting "thinner" data than he could through multiple interviews.

Feldman, Bell, and Berger (2003, 36–38) discuss how what they term *commitment acts* can foster trust. Commitment acts are those activities in which you, as researcher, offer time or energy to the community you are researching. What you do can range from the mundane (chaperoning a school fieldtrip) to the global (creating a video to share previously silenced perspectives of a group). The acts "provide an opportunity to create a stronger web of trust, openness, and rapport between researcher and informants" (37). Through commitment acts, you demonstrate that you value time and interactions with participants and you create the opportunities to get to know each other as people. Although contact over a long period of time does not assure the development of trust, time may prove to be a determining condition. Time allows you to substantiate that you will keep the promises you made when you were negotiating access and time allows you and participants to grow in relationship to each other.

Developing and maintaining rapport and trust with children and adolescents adds extra dimensions to the research process. The role (supervisor, leader, observer, friend) the researcher takes in relationship to children affects the kind of information gathered and the development of rapport and trust. Fine and Sandstrom (1988) distinguish researcher relationships with children on the dimensions of extent of positive contact between child and adult and extent to which the adult has direct authority over the child (14). In particular, they explore what it means for an adult to be a "friend" with a child.

Rebecca, in her dissertation research with adolescent girls and the role of friendship in their lives, found herself in a "friendly" role with the girls. The contact with them was highly positive. She arrived at their homes with art supplies, drove them to ice cream shops, and engaged them in talk that led to their requests for personal advice from her. Although responsible for the girls when with them, Rebecca did not have authority over them. Her evolving connection to the girls led

Research relationships often involve doing things together that do not focus on the research topic.

her to realize that she could not simply say "goodbye" when her data collection was through. Rebecca maintained contact after the study.

Taking Breaks. "Once we feel connected to the people we study, we think we must consistently feel good about them" (Kleinman and Copp 1993, 28). Always feeling good about your participants, however, may not be the case. Given the stress of fieldwork, maintaining relationships sometimes requires taking breaks. Immersed in a life that is not your normal one, you may periodically need to get away to be with people you know or to talk to those who have similar beliefs and ideas if not shared in the research site. You may need to blow off steam or simply disappear for a few days so that you do not destroy the rapport that has been developed.

Fieldwork accounts do not always address this need, but field notes or journals do. Malinowski's (1967) diary while among the Trobriand Islanders is a well-known example. It became the place for him to vent his feelings and make statements that would not have endeared him to his host community. Immersion is valued, but it can be overdone. Taking breaks promotes your ability to mindfully make the multitude of daily decisions needed in your work. Gaining distance by whatever means—trips, reading, personal journals—is sometimes necessary. Remember, as well, that you do not need to like or be liked by all research participants, although your work is apt to be more rewarding for all parties if mutual liking occurs. As Wax (1971, 373) states, "One can learn a great deal from people one dislikes or from people who dislike one."

Complicating and Enriching Dynamics in Field Relations

Friendship, connection, and issues of power are aspects of field relations that can complicate and enrich research interactions and interpretations. The following sections address problems and possibilities associated with research friendships and power relationships.

Friendship in the Field

> It is not indifference, but care, concern and involvement that sustains a continuous discourse with people and prepares the ground for the legitimacy of an inquiry.
>
> (Savyasaachi 1998, 110)

When a distinction between rapport and friendship was made in qualitative literature, the overwhelming tendency in the past was to warn against forming friendships because of the hazards of sample bias and loss of objectivity. These hazards were linked to overidentification, also called *over-rapport* and *going native* (Gold 1969; Miller 1952; Shaffir, Stebbins, and Turowetz 1980; Van Maanen 1983). As Tedlock (2000, 457) writes, researchers were "to cultivate rapport, not friendship; compassion, not sympathy; respect, not belief; understanding, not identification; admiration, not love."

Friendship was linked to biased data selection and decreased objectivity in three different ways (Gans 1982; Hammersley and Atkinson 1983; Pelto and Pelto 1978; Zigarmi and Zigarmi 1978). First, data bias could result from a somewhat unconscious subjective selection process. Researchers might be tempted to talk primarily with people they liked or found politically sympathetic. If they followed such impulses, "the pleasure of participant observation [would] increase significantly, but the sampling of people and situations . . . may become badly distorted" (Gans 1982, 52). Or it could be that researchers would talk to a variety of people, but overidentify with one group. They then would hear what this group had to tell them, but less fully what other groups told them. Therefore, they might censor their own questioning process to avoid alienating those with whom they were overidentifying.

In the second situation, researchers could be consciously aware of their best data sources but denied access to some of them because of their friendship with others. "Every firm social relationship with a particular individual or group carries with it the possibility of closed doors and social rebuffs from competing segments of the community" (Pelto and Pelto 1978, 184). In the Caribbean, I attempted to maintain access simultaneously to alienated young adults, to unalienated young adults, to government officials, and to estate owners. I found myself frequently explaining to those of the unalienated group my time with the more alienated.

In the third situation, research participants overidentify with the researchers. In doing so, they act in ways that they perceive the researchers want them to act or in ways that impress them. Van Maanen (1983) cites the example of police he studied who used overly aggressive patrol tactics in an effort to increase their worth in the eyes of the observer. In sum, friendship was perceived as something that could affect the behavior of researchers or research participants, with consequences for data collection and analysis. It appeared, therefore, that researchers should avoid friendships in the research setting or, at least, with research participants.

With the conventional concern for detachment and objectivity made problematic, friendship is now seen, by some, as a research ideal. Tedlock (2000, 458) suggests that the prescription against friendship was more than Western science's obsession with objectivity. She locates it in a colonial context where crossing from rapport to friendship and love was viewed as a kind of cultural and racial "degeneration," referred to as "going native." Throughout history, some researchers have formed friendships, fallen in love, and become "complete members" of a new society. They just didn't write about it as freely as they can now.

Feminist researchers have been at the forefront of advocating research relationships that include reciprocity, empathy, equality, and friendship if possible. Nonetheless, most recognize that a truly nonhierarchical relationship is difficult to create unless engaged in collaborative work. As Behar (1993) states,

> Feminist ethnographers have found themselves caught inside webs of betrayal they themselves have spun; with stark clarity, they realize that they are seeking out intimacy and friendship with subjects on whose backs, ultimately, the books will be written upon which their productivity as scholars in the academic marketplace will be assessed. (297)

Wincup (2001, 28) reflects upon her research with women awaiting trial and how she had different kinds of relationships with different people in her research site:

> Although I established rapport and empathy with some women and formed close research relationships with others, I also had negative feelings toward some during the fieldwork. Most women who appeared in courts were charged with minor property offences, however, I met women charged with crimes of violence, child abuse, and murder. I also saw women bullying and victimizing other women.

Henry (1992) discusses what happened to an eighteen-year friendship when she hired her Japanese friend as her research assistant. She traces her confusion as the friendship became strained due to competing demands of friendship and the research. Although she felt that the situation ultimately contributed to a deeper understanding of the people studied, she lost a good relationship in the process.

Friendship and intimacy is messy, emotional, and vital. No matter how much you try to practice "relational ethics" (Flinders 1992) with research participants, no matter how much your friendships go beyond the inquiry, feelings of exploitation or betrayal may erupt from time to time in either researcher or participant. Yet, friendships in themselves are not always without pain, nor do they always last forever.

Field Relations and Power.

We are most likely to abuse our power when we least feel we have it.

(Kendall 2009, 115)

Power poses different challenges in conventional approaches to qualitative inquiry than in collaborative research. This section first addresses power in researcher or institutional driven projects and then in more collaborative approaches.

Conventional qualitative researchers are not always in positions of authority, particularly if studying "up," inquiring into the lives and behavior of the elite or politically powerful. Generally speaking, however, if researchers are making most of the research decisions regarding with whom they talk, what they observe, and how and for whom they analyze and write up the data, they are in a position of power relative to research participants. One of the ways in which researchers address the power imbalance is through various modes of reciprocity. If interviews are meaningful to research participants and conducted well, they may assist interviewees in better understanding aspects of their own lives. Some repeat and group interviews can support not only individual reflection, but also empowerment. Researchers can also help out in a variety of ways, giving of their time or labor.

Leslie Bloom (1998, 35) notes that power is not necessarily something that you have or don't have, but rather "power is situated and contextualized within particular intersubjective relationships." She goes on to make the useful observation that some of the controversies that derive from discussing researcher power results from conflating power with researcher responsibility and then from conflating researcher responsibility with researcher exploitation: "It suggests that having the authority to collect data, interpret it, and produce a text is inherently an act of exploitation or even violence done by the researcher to the almost victimized respondent" (Bloom 1998, 36). The point she makes is that a difference exists between the researcher's power to use the research for academic gains and the researcher's power to be responsible and responsive to the research participant and to the researcher–participant relationship.

Collaborative approaches to fieldwork often involve both community insiders and outsiders. In collaborative inquiry, the issue of power shifts, and power is often shared more equitably or sometimes lies more in the hands of the community that is the focus of study. Research purposes and questions are identified by and focused to assist, in some way, those participating in the research. As people work together toward a common goal or purpose, particularly when addressing issues of injustice or inequities which marginalize, co-researchers from various cultural and racial backgrounds become partners in a research struggle that can take their relationship beyond that of insider/outsider. Alan Wieder (2004, 25) reflects upon the oral history work in which he participated with teachers in South Africa:

> While my position as an American academic, an outsider, appeared to help facilitate interviews initially, my relationships with South African colleagues, the teachers I interviewed, and living in Cape Town, moved me on an unwritten continuum towards insider status because we connected as educators and human beings. . . .

He recognizes that cultural, political, and personal factors help to create insider and outsider differences, but urges researchers to

> be open to the possibility of the insider/outsider binary breaking down as the witness/oral historian relationship becomes closer and the oral historian facilitates the witnesses' voice by producing testimony that combines experience and a deeper meaning and becomes part of the counter narrative. (Wieder 2004, 25).

Connecting.   Similar to Weider's reflections on connecting as human beings with South African teachers, Marleen Pugach (personal correspondence, 1995) writes of a research relationship that reminds us that connection and care in our relationships is often of great importance:

> Last March first I drove north, ate my last green chile cheeseburger at the Owl Bar, and headed east, away from the mountains and toward my other home in Wisconsin. Today, my former landlady called to tell me, a year to the day after I left, that a good friend of mine had died. . . . The shock is enormous—I am not ready for Carmen to be gone. She was the one who would not let me tape record our conversations, but she shared the most phenomenal stories about the old "Hispanic" community from up on the river. . . .
>
> She told me that living "out of town" would be fine for the kids, that she had raised one in the city and one in the country. That comment gave me the confidence to rent our house amidst the yucca, mesquite, roadrunners and rattlesnakes. I don't think she knew that. We used to meet for breakfast or lunch at my favorite hole-in-the-wall Mexican restaurant. . . . I'm sure I never was able to get down

enough of her real words; our meetings crossed the line between research and friendship. . . .

We talked last in November, just before her son's wedding. I sent a Christmas card, I never found out if she read the copy of *Animal Dreams* I sent as a thank-you gift for having us all there in August. This is not a research relationship. I went to Havens to learn enough to tell a story, but the real story is that you can't separate yourself from the people who welcomed you for all those months. What do I say about Lisa, who called to tell me that Carmen had died? This is not a research obligation, born out of my need to know about life on the border. . . . I am left with the uncomfortable feeling that spending time in a place you want to study is a real liability if you're inclined to build relationships. It's not a case of collaborative research for the purpose of action. . . . It's a case of friendship, not cultivated over long years, but with depth because you recognize that you were meant to be friends even if the study had never happened; it was simply the occasion for a friendship that already should have been.

Bringing qualitative research into what is already your home territory releases you from this potential liability; you keep your friends, your social context, and you tiptoe only a little distance from where you always have been. Intensive fieldwork in a new location pushes the question. It is not an issue of power relationships that I'm trying to understand here. Instead, it echoes the things I've been wondering about for months: can you do ethnography without making wonderful, lifelong friends? Would you want to? . . . Carmen helped me, to be sure, and it is only if I write well that I can properly acknowledge her contributions. But what I really wish is that she would still be there, on the ranch, telling me that whenever I return to Havens, my room there is ready. No one told me about this part of it.

Marleen's reflections demonstrate how research relationships can transcend the public realm into the private. Her story moves us to consider how we want to experience the multiple kinds of relationships that might enter into research. She suggests that we interact with openness, honesty, and respect; not with the masks that rapport can provide or with the walls of professional distancing. In effect, Marleen urges us to be authentic in interactions and to honor the consequences of acting with genuineness.

Postmodern arguments work to complicate the notion of authenticity, however, raising questions about the possibility of transparency or genuineness in a world where fluid, partial, and unstable subjectivities of researcher and participant interact. This is part of the discussion on reflexivity in the next section.

REFLEXIVITY

Critical subjectivity involves a self-reflexive attention to the ground on which one is standing.

(Reason 1994, 327)

Reflexivity is an awareness of the self in the situation of action and of the role of the self in constructing that situation.

(Bloor and Wood 2006, 145)

Reflexivity grew in importance in the 1980s, through challenges to conventional research by feminist scholars and others who work out of emancipatory theories as well as some poststructuralists who raised questions about the authority of textual representations (Bloor and Wood 2006). Although used in multiple ways for differing reasons in qualitative writing (see Pillow, 2003), reflexivity generally involves critical reflection on how researcher, research participants, setting, and research procedures interact and influence each other. This includes "examining one's personal and theoretical commitments to see how they serve as resources for generating particular data, for behaving in particular ways . . . and for developing particular interpretations" (Schwandt 1997, 136). You ask questions of your research interactions all along the way, from embarking on an inquiry project to sharing the "findings." You ask these questions of yourself and record your reflections in your field log. You ask questions of others about the research process and listen carefully to what they say, noting their answers, and perhaps changing the course of inquiry. You listen to the questions asked of you by research participants and consider how the questions may indicate certain concerns or expectations. You answer as fully as you can and then examine why you answered in the way you did. You ask questions of the sociocultural-political context in which you ask your questions. In a sense, you conduct two research projects at the same time: one into your topic and the other into your "self" and, paraphrasing Reason (1994), the ground on which you stand.

Researchers tend to discuss reflexivity by inquiring into either their own biases, subjectivity, and value-laden perspectives or into the appropriateness of their research methodology and methods, including concerns regarding data collected, interpretations made, and representations produced (Madison 2005, 124–125; Potter 1996, 188). They frequently do so with the goal of making their research more accurate, legitimate, or valid, although this purpose is a matter of contention in postmodern thought. Even though reflexivity is not a "cure" and even though one can never know oneself well enough to critique oneself, the work of reflexivity is useful. This chapter addresses reflexivity with a discussion of the personal dimensions of subjectivity, emotion work, positions, and positionality.

Subjectivity

> Any study of "an other" is also a study of "a self."
> (Sunstein and Chiseri-Strater 2002, xiii)

> We cross borders, but we don't erase them; we take our borders with us.
> (Behar 1993, 320)

In the positivist paradigm, objectivity is a goal and subjectivity, an undesired state of affairs. *Subjectivity,* in this sense, is equated with bias and seen as something to control against and to mitigate its influence in research. The term has long held negative connotations. In more recent times, many, especially poststructural scholars, have explained that the binary opposition, objective/subjective, is no longer useful because no person can get rid of the subjective and thereby achieve objectivity. Objectivity is viewed as neither possible, nor desirable. Further, feminists have long pointed out that it is usually women who are defined as subjective against the more objective "man of reason."

In the 1980s and early 1990s, researchers based in the interpretivist paradigm began to dispute the notion of subjectivity as something negative (Denzin and Lincoln 2000; Oleson 2000; Peshkin 1988b; Wolcott 1995). These researchers recognized subjectivity as an integral part of interpretivist research from deciding on the research topic to selecting frames of analysis. Rather than bias, they saw subjectivity as the personal selves created historically and began to claim the term. Peshkin (1988a, 1988b), for example, titled one article "Virtuous Subjectivity: In the Participant–Observer's I's," and another "In Search of Subjectivity—One's Own." The perspective among qualitative researchers at that point in time was that subjectivity, in terms of bias, should be monitored for more trustworthy research, and also that subjectivity, in terms of personal history and passions, could contribute to research. It was perceived as impossible for qualitative researchers to escape themselves, nor would they want to. Peshkin was one of the first qualitative researchers to try to make explicit the different ways in which he was present in his research.

Peshkin[1] viewed subjectivity as autobiographical, emotional states that were engaged by different research situations. He began to reflect upon his various research projects and the various subjective lenses they elicited. When he did his study in Mansfield, a small Midwestern rural town, he became entranced by the sense of community there. He liked Mansfield and its people, and he did not want them to lose their community feeling. His next school-community study was in the fundamentalist Christian setting of Bethany Baptist Church and Bethany Baptist Academy. While there, he did not feel moved to admire their sense of community because other emotions were on high alert. He wrote,

> I knew that I was annoyed by my personal (as opposed to research) experience at BBA. I soon became sharply aware that my annoyance was pervasively present, that I was writing out of pique and vexation. Accordingly, I was not celebrating community at Bethany, and community prevailed there no less robustly than it had at Mansfield. Why not? I was more than annoyed in Bethany; my ox had been gored. The consequence was that the story I was feeling drawn to tell had its origins in my personal sense of threat. I was not at Bethany as a cool, dispassionate observer (are there any?); I was there as a Jew whose otherness was dramatized directly and indirectly during 18 months of fieldwork.

As Peshkin entered his next school-community study in urban Riverview, where he planned to learn how ethnicity operated in the lives of students and parents in the school and community, he resolved to look for instances of his own subjectivity, noting feeling and circumstances. He incorporated his reflections into what he described as a set of "Subjective I's." As in Mansfield, the "Community–Maintenance I" was present, but the Riverview research situation called forth emotional states that previous studies had not, such as what he termed his "Pedagogical–Meliorist I":

> This . . . is a defensive self. It is directed toward students, generally minorities, whom I observed getting nowhere in their classrooms. They were being taught by teachers who had not learned enough, often did not care enough, to make a difference in their students' lives. Class time for both students and teachers was an occasion for little more than marking time until the bell released both from their meaningless engagement. This circumstance, regrettably common, disturbed me more than I had ever been disturbed by the ineffective teachers I had observed at other schools. The difference at Riverview High School was that the students in such classes were usually minorities, those who came to school with two strikes against them. I found myself doing what I never before had done as I sat in the back of classrooms: hatching schemes that would alter the classrooms I was watching, schemes that were calculated to reorient instruction and make a difference in the lives of the students.

Tracing your subjective selves, as Peshkin described them, shows points on a map of yourself. These points do not create a complete map because no research evokes all of your strong emotions and positions. Some perspectives surely will appear again in other studies; just as surely, new ones will appear in other studies. And most likely, no two people doing the same study would have the same personal responses, although many educators and social service professionals have identified a "Justice I" and a "Caring I" when, using Peshkin's work, they reflected upon the emotional reactions triggered by their own research projects. Lorrie provides an example:

> I view my inquiry into how physical therapists work with elders with dementia through several lenses. First, and most connected to me, is the *personal lens*. The personal lens comes from my past, derived from the relationship I had with my maternal grandmother. Second, I view this topic through a *justice lens*. I have seen elders treated unfairly by healthcare providers; they don't receive the same quality of treatment as younger people, even when they have the same problems. Third, I am looking at this research through a *caring lens*. I have a strong interest in having the elders in our society treated with the respect and dignity they deserve. I want everyone in society to know what resources exist in our elderly community members.
>
> To address the *personal lens*, I must return to my experience as a child. My parents were older when I was born—the age of my peers' grandparents. Essentially, I skipped a generation. Consequently, I found myself surrounded by elderly people on both sides of the family. The most influential person was my grandmother. My grandmother had multi-infarct dementia. She was treated very poorly by an underqualified and undereducated staff in one of the local facilities. After she died, I knew that I had to work specifically with elders; it was something that I could not ignore, a calling.
>
> The basis of my personal interest in geriatrics stems from my relationship with my grandmother and my observations of the care she received at the most vulnerable point in her life. However, I also see the personal lens linked with the

justice lens. I have always been sensitive to people who are oppressed or underprivileged. I believe that the elderly, especially those without financial resources and without advocates, are the most vulnerable members of our society. In many ways they are more vulnerable than children because most children have strong advocates, parents. Elders have multiple needs; far too often, they are neglected or taken advantage of.

Finally, I see my *caring lens* connected to both the personal lens and justice lens. Having spent many hours with elderly individuals, I am well aware of what they have to offer. I value elders. I see them as wise, interesting people with rich experiences. Elders deserve to be treated with a special dignity.

Keeping track of your subjective selves and then inquiring into their origins, as Laurie did, can make you aware not only of your own perspectives, but also how those perspectives might lead you to ask certain questions (and not others) and to make certain interpretations (and not others) of interactions within the research setting. Poststructural scholars and others, since Peshkin's early work, have complicated his understanding of the work of subjectivity in qualitative research. They assert that subjectivity is not composed of "lenses" that you can put on and take off but rather that each of us live at the complex and shifting intersections of identity categories such as race, class, gender, sexual orientation, age, wellness, nationality, and so on. In some research situations, a person's gender, for example, may seem more significant; in others, one's age. In any case, neither the researcher's nor participants' subjectivities are stable.

Emotion Work

Part of being attuned to your personal views and perspectives is being attuned to your emotions. Instead of trying to suppress your feelings, you use them to inquire into your assumptions and to shape new questions through re-examining previous perspectives. "Ignoring or suppressing feelings are emotion work strategies that divert our attention from the cues that ultimately help us understand those we study" (Kleinman and Copp 1993, 33). For example, Tsing (1993, 68) reports how she learned from her emotions, which flared when a research participant suggested that she did not work:

> Once Ma Salam's mother tried to flatter me by saying that I didn't work (*bagawi*) but only "traveled" (*bajalan*). My first thought was to take offense and argue for my industriousness; in the United States, to do no work is to be worthless. But I soon realized my mistake: for Meratus to "work" is to do repetitive caretaking activity, while to "travel" is a process of personal and material enrichment.

It is when you feel angry, irritable, gleeful, excited, or sad that you can be sure that your personal views are at work. The goal is to explore such feelings to become aware of what they are telling you about who you are in relationship to your actions, reactions, and interactions with research participants and to what you are learning and what you may be keeping yourself from learning or perceiving.

Wincup (2001, 29) described how, during analysis and writing, she made use of emotions evoked in her research with women awaiting trial:

> Gradually, I began to realize that my own emotions could be used constructively to enhance the research without compromising the ability to step back and offer analysis and interpretation. Reliving my fieldwork experiences brought my data alive. My emotional awareness encouraged me to listen more closely to the accounts of the women I interviewed, and to think carefully about the ways I could do justice to the women's stories as I created my ethnographic account.

By taking notes, you can become aware of how your personal history is being engaged in your research. You can get hints about which perspectives might be called into play during your research by reflecting on how your research is autobiographical. When I ask students to do this, I stress that I don't want their life story, but I want to know how their research topic intersects with their life. What does their approach to research say about them and why is their research statement, of all the research statements they could pose, of interest to them?

Kristina, whose interview questions were discussed in Chapter 4, planned to interview women from Africa about their perspectives on women's legal rights related to marriage, divorce, and property. At first, she thought she had chosen her topic because she was preparing to move with her husband to East Africa for several years and wanted to use her thesis requirement as an opportunity to learn something about the lives of African women. As she considered how her topic was autobiographical, however, she realized that her choice had deeper roots:

> My interest in women's rights began in ninth grade with a talk by a women's rights activist that I attended with my mother. The activist told her life story of being raised in the Mormon Church and her struggle to support the Equal Rights Amendment which eventually resulted in her excommunication from the Church of Latter Day Saints and her divorce. Until that evening, I had believed that discrimination against women was part of the past. I distinctly remember my mother saying to me, "You think that there aren't any more barriers for women, but you'll see." Her statement caught me off guard. I was a successful student; I was planning on going to a competitive college and pursuing a career in law or business. But I began to pay more attention to women's issues, especially those which highlighted inequalities between men and women.
>
> My parents' divorce a year after this event dramatically shaped my ideas about women and marriage forever. They had been married for 20 years and while both of my parents struggled after the divorce, my father recovered much more quickly, both financially and emotionally. My mother had somehow "invested" more of herself in the marriage and at the end found herself "bankrupt" with fewer resources to help her start her life over. I think the unequal responsibilities between my parents (Mom being primarily responsible for me, my brother, and the house), as well as her limited work experience, made it more difficult for her to create a new life. Since this time I have been acutely aware of the increased burdens women generally carry in many family situations and I think this awareness has helped me to focus my interests on African women's legal rights around marriage, divorce, and property.

By understanding the ways in which her topic was autobiographical, Kristina could become more aware of her own attitudes toward and emotional investment in issues of marriage, divorce, property, and women's rights as she began her interviews with African women.

Noting and reflecting upon your emotional reactions and the way in which they connect to who you are, your history, and experiences is important. Monitoring these subjective feelings is not the same as controlling for them. When you track your emotions, you learn more about your own values, attitudes, beliefs, interests, and needs. You learn that your history and experiences are the basis for your behaviors and interpretations in interactions and thus, for the story that you are able to tell. They are the strengths on which you build. They make you who you are as a person and as a researcher, equipping you with the perspectives and insights that shape all that you do as a researcher, from the selection of topic clear through to the emphases you make in your writing.

Mark describes how tracking his emotions helped him to see in new ways. He was researching attitudes of officers in corrective facilities toward the schooling of their wards:

> The most unexpected event during the research process was that I changed my mind. Several field log entries identify my concern over my judgmental stance regarding officers. I recognized that I must be cognizant of this and had to be careful to place "no prior constraints on what the outcomes of the research will be" (Patton 1990, 41). In the field log, I reminded myself "that during this research I am not a reformer." What surprises me now is that I have come to respect more what the officers do in their day-to-day routines in the cellblocks. By their sharing their thoughts and experiences with me, I have been informed, and consequently reformed. In their own way, they are also involved in helping a rather difficult clientele overcome massive barriers and become better people. I am delighted.

To the best of your ability, try to acknowledge your theoretical and personal attachments during the course of your research. Although it is not possible to be complete in documenting your values, emotions, and perspectives, you can become tuned to the selves generated in particular research situations. You can reflect upon, inquire into, and responsibly convey those "selves" to the readers of your work. You can do this in direct or indirect ways. For example, you may clearly state the theories you used to interpret data and the kinds of relationships in which you engaged, or, more indirectly, you may write in any number of creative analytical ways (see Chapter 9) that indicate to the reader your personal persuasions and turmoils.

In recent times, the language of subjectivity has become subsumed into discussions of reflexivity, with an emphasis on tracking, questioning, and sharing ways in which we shape and are shaped by the research process. For example, Guba and Lincoln (2008, 278) state that "Reflexivity forces us to come to terms not only with our choice of research problem and with those with whom we engage in the research process, but with our selves and with the multiple identities that represent the fluid self in the research setting." They refer here to the different kinds of research-related selves identified by Shulamit Reinharz (cited in Guba and Lincoln 2008, 279): "research-based selves, brought selves (the selves that historically, socially, and personally create our standpoints), and situationally created selves." They go on to say that reflexivity "demands that we interrogate each of our selves regarding the ways in which research efforts are shaped and staged around the binaries, contradictions, and paradoxes that form our own lives" (279).

Embodiment, Positions, and Positionality

Each of us has fixed attributes that affect, in conjunction with the socio-cultural-historical context, how we act in the world and how others respond. These fixed personal factors that are either impossible or difficult to change are referred to as *identity categories* or as *embodiment* and include attributes such as skin color, gender, age, size, and physical disability (Sunstein and Chiseri-Strater 2002). These identity categories should not be viewed as having an essential meaning, as being true everywhere for all people, or as being solely responsible for particular actions or reactions. Rather, they interact in complex ways with other attributes, histories, and contexts—the *positions* we inhabit.

Positions tends to refer to aspects of one's person that are not necessarily embodied in the person and include both ascribed characteristics (nationality, ancestry) and achieved characteristics (educational level, economic level, institutional affiliation, etc.). By simply looking at a person, you cannot necessarily determine the person's educational level, for example. *Subjective positions* include aspects of your life history and personal experiences that help to form your values (Sunstein and Chiseri-Strater 2002). Coming of age during the Civil Rights Movement could be a subjective position that is an important part of how you see the world no matter what your skin color. Yet, most likely, this subjective position would interact with skin color in different ways. Thus, embodiment and positions interact, as they do with *positionality*, or to the researcher's "social, locational, and ideological placement relative to the research project or to other participants in it" (Hay 2005, 290).

Researchers have little control over embodied factors and limited control over their positions (some, such as nationality or educational level could be—unethically—misrepresented or not disclosed). Researchers cannot control positionality in that it is determined in relation with others, but they can make certain choices that affect those relationships. For example, entering into research with a mindset of openness, curiosity, and desire and willingness to interact in collaborative ways is likely to result in a different positionality than one in which the researcher maintains a mindset of entitlement, self-centeredness, and control. Madison (2005, 9) states, "positionality requires that we direct our attention beyond our individual or subjective selves. Instead, we attend to how our subjectivity in relation to the Other informs and is informed by our engagement and representation of the Other." Positionality is not fixed and, perhaps, should be plural, since relationships vary between and among people and change over time.

Being attuned to positionality is being attuned to intersubjectivity, how the subjectivites of all involved guide the research process, content, and, ideally, the interpretations. As Myerhoff (1979, 26–27) indicates in the following quote, her observations and interviews with Jewish elders activated emotions within her participants that, in turn, shaped their behavior:

> The old people were genuinely proud of me, generous, and affectionate, but at times their resentment spilled over. My presence was a continual reminder of many painful facts: that it should have been their own children there listening to their stories; that I had combined family and a career, opportunities that the women had longed for and never been allowed.

In another example, Lather and Smithies (1997) observed HIV/AIDS support groups and conducted interviews with women in the groups. Their work, which spanned several years, became important to many of the participants, as the following quotations indicate:

> I'm really excited about you guys writing this book and I want you to get it published right away. . . . Going through the interviews and hearing everyone's story, a lot of this stuff, we don't talk about in group, we don't talk about like how do you really feel about that stuff. (xxvii)
>   When are you guys going to publish? Some of us are on deadline, you know. (169)

Lather, Smithies, and the women living with HIV/AIDS formed relationships, laughed, cried, and re-examined their lives through the project. And the women's urgency to get their story told pushed Lather and Smithies to desktop publish an early version of their book, *Troubling the Angels.*

As research relationships develop, the negotiation of subjectivities is ongoing, with the potential for values, attitudes, and understandings of both researcher and participants to be changed through the research process. Reflecting upon the interplay between researcher and researched is essential for understanding how research relationships influence fieldwork and interpretation. As Welch (1994, 41) states, "We create our own stories, but only as coauthors."

Thinking about the interplay of subjectivity, embodiment, and positioning of yourself with that of research participants assists in data interpretation and representation. In fact, how you position yourself within the text is yet another positioning, a "textual positioning" (Madison 2005). Ask yourself how those in the research site would react to your interpretations, to your words. Is your interpretation paternalistic at times? Are participants coming across as one-dimensional, perhaps as oppressed, powerless victims? Or, does it romanticize, leading to the possibility that you have overlooked "deep-seated contradictions, detailed symbolic meanings and troubling questions" (Madison 2005, 126)? How is the representation missing the complexity of the lives studied? Try to take on the position of a research participant and read your words thinking about their impact and meaning to you as someone who has been "researched." Rather than the voice of the expert who authoritatively presents "results," the reflexive stance involves honestly and openly locating your positions and positionalities in the research, reflecting upon how they interacted with your observations and interpretations.

CONCLUSIONS

Why is so much attention focused on field relations and reflexivity? What if you just want to get on with the business of doing research? Why engage in what some have described as potentially devolving into "navel gazing?" Sultana (2007, 376), a Bangladeshi researcher, states of her fieldwork on water resources management, "I do not believe that being reflexive about one's own positionality is to self-indulge but to reflect on how one is inserted in grids of power relations and how that influences methods, interpretations, and knowledge production. . . ." Ultimately, this thoughtfulness about and critical engagement with the personal dimensions of research can lead to more ethical work, the topic of the next chapter. Reflexive thought assists in understanding ways in which your personal characteristics, values, and positions interact with others in the research situation to influence the methodological approach you take, the methods you use, and the interpretations you make. It forces you to think more about how you want to be in relation to research participants. It can help you make use of personal passions and strengths while better understanding the ways in which the knowledge you produce is co-constructed and only partial. Pillow (2003) argues for "reflexivities of discomfort" (188) that "do not seek a comfortable, transcendent end-point but leave us in the uncomfortable realities of doing engaged qualitative research" (193).

Michael Patton (2002, 66) provides a diagram titled *Reflexive Questions: Triangulated Inquiry*. It suggests kinds of reflexive questions one could ask of oneself, of research participants, and of the audience. The diagram illustrates that each person is situated in a sociocultural context of embodiment and positions ("culture, age, gender, class, social status, education, family, political praxis, language, values") that interact and provide "screens" for differing perspectives. Using Patton's categories, the following questions draw from and expand upon his questions:

Inquirer
- What are my theoretical and philosophical beliefs about doing research, and how do they guide me to do this kind of research?
- What in my autobiography led me to this topic?
- Why did I select each particular person who is in the study?
- Why did I form the particular interview questions I use?
- Why do I observe where I observe?
- What kind of relationships have I developed with research participants and why?

- What kind of relationships do I desire and for what purposes?
- What do I think I know and how did I come to know it?
- What values and experiences shape my perspectives and my research decisions?
- As I analyze and interpret the data, what do I choose to include and what do I choose to omit and why?
- What became the important analytical themes and why was I able to think of those themes?
- With what voice do I share my perspectives?
- How much do I inscribe myself into the text and how do I present myself when I do?
- What do I do with what I have found?
- What are the consequences of my choices?

Participants
- How do they know what they know?
- What shapes and has shaped their worldview?
- How do they perceive me? Why? How do I know?
- What stories do they tell about me?
- What stories do they tell others of the research process?
- How do/would they respond to what I am writing?

Audience
- How do they make sense of what I give them?
- What perspectives do they bring to my presentations?
- How do they perceive me?
- How do I perceive them?
- How do these perceptions affect what I say and how I say it?

The previous questions are guides for questions you may want to address in your field notebook. Most likely, neither you (nor your readers) would want to dwell upon answers to each question in a final report. At the least, however, you need to provide background to the decisions you make so that the reader can better understand (and question) the interpretations you make. Ideally, you also demonstrate clearly your own belief systems (social, political, ideological, theoretical) and how they link to the actions you take. Interpretivists often claim "understanding others' perspectives" as a research purpose. Reflexivity challenges your ability to ever "know" the other. Perhaps a more attainable goal is to understand the self in relationship to those with whom you interact.

Reading here about research relations and reflexivity is like reading about other aspects of the research process: It may represent the beginning of understanding the place of each in your research. For you to make your positionality explicit, however, you have to engage in personal encounters with self and others throughout the research process. Aware that there is something to seek, to uncover, and to question, you are ready to be informed through the research experience.

RECOMMENDED READINGS

Pillow, W. 2003. Confession, catharsis, or cure? Rethinking the uses of reflexivity as methodological power in qualitative research. *International Journal of Qualitative Studies in Education,* 16(2), 175–196.

EXERCISES

1. Reflect upon the nature of the optimal research relationships in your study. What implications do such relationships have for developing and maintaining rapport? For developing and maintaining trust?

2. Write a few pages in your field journal about the ways in which your research topic is autobiographical. Think deeply about this—why did you choose the research questions, of all possible questions, that you did? What do those questions say about you?

3. Reading ethnographies is a good way to expand your thinking about doing and writing-up fieldwork. In this activity, divide into groups of four or five, with each group taking a different ethnography to read. Plan to meet several times as you read the book to discuss specific aspects of the book (you could also do periodic in-class reports). You might, for example, focus one discussion group on how the author incorporates observations and interviews into the text and another discussion group on the organization of the ethnography. Accompanying this chapter's topics, reflect upon how the researchers position themselves in the work. What do you learn about the author? What do you learn about field relations? What other things would you like to know? Why?

ENDNOTE

1. Peshkin's reflections on subjectivity that are presented here are taken from the first edition of *Becoming Qualitative Researchers* and drawn from Peshkin 1982b, 1988a, and 1988b.

CHAPTER 6

But Is It Ethical?
Considering What's "Right"

Neutrality is not pluralistic but imperialistic . . . reinscribing the agenda in its own terms.

(Christians 2000, 142)

Research in itself is a powerful intervention . . . which has traditionally benefited the researcher, and the knowledge base of the dominant group in society.

(Tuhiwai Smith 1999, 176)

As a group of students entered their second semester together in a qualitative research methods class, they reflected on the role trial and error had played in their best-learned lessons. Ernie wondered, "Can you even consider the possibility of learning research ethics through trial and error?" With increased awareness of ethical issues, they deliberated over perceived ethical dilemmas and wondered about unintended consequences of their work.

This group of students realized that ethical considerations should accompany plans, thoughts, and discussions about each aspect of qualitative research. Ethics is not something that you can forget once you satisfy the demands of university ethics committees and other gatekeepers of research conduct. Nor is it "merely a matter of isolated choices in crucial situations" (Cassell and Jacobs 1987, 1). Rather, ethical considerations are inseparable from your everyday interactions with research participants and with your data.

Ethical decisions are not peculiar to qualitative inquiry. Guidelines for ethical conduct grew out of medical and other types of intrusive research and led to emphases on informed consent, avoidance of harm, and confidentiality. Different epistemological systems give rise to different ethical concerns (Lincoln 1990; Scott 1996). Positivist inquiry emphasizes separation between researcher and researched while, in most interpretivist research, researcher-researched interaction is common. The distance between researcher and participants does not make a study more conducive to meeting ethical standards. Indeed, a neutral stance, in itself, is construed as an ethical issue because it can mean objectification of others.

Much ethical discussion and consideration in qualitative research, therefore, concerns the nature of relationships with research participants.

Many feminist, critical, and indigenous researchers argue that research purposes, themselves, are an ethical issue and that intentions must go beyond bestowing "hope" for future contributions, and glossing over "abuses of power and human need in the present" (Christians 2000, 144). Such perspectives require that the research purposes and processes be constantly negotiated with research participants. What constitutes ethicality then becomes determined through dialog and is heavily contextual. It follows that choosing your topic and designing your methods can be perceived as an ethical issue because what you choose to research and how you design the inquiry relates to your philosophical and ethical stance on the purpose and nature of research.

Generally, this chapter focuses on ethical issues that arise out of the researcher-researched relationship in qualitative research approaches. It does not discuss those ethical issues generic to all types of research, such as falsifying results or publishing without crediting co-researchers. As in previous chapters, unequivocal advice on "right" or "wrong" ways to behave is difficult to provide. Rather, the issues raised here are meant to alert you to areas that need consideration and forethought, so that you can possibly avoid learning ethical lessons through trial and error.

ETHICAL CODES

Nazi concentration camps and the atomic bomb served to undermine the image of science as value-free and automatically contributing to human welfare (Diener and Crandall 1978). Medical research in the United States that resulted in physical harm to subjects (such as the Tuskegee Syphilis Study) and social science research that caused, at the least, psychological pain (such as the Milgram shock experiment) led to the formation of codes of ethics by different professional organizations and academic institutions. By 1974, the federal government had mandated the establishment of Institutional Review Boards (IRBs) at all universities that accepted federal funding for research involving human subjects. Other countries established similar groups (e.g., the University Ethics Committees in Britain, the Human Research Ethics Committees in Australia). Five basic principles guide the decisions of IRBs when reviewing applicants' proposals:

1. Research subjects must have sufficient information to make informed decisions about participating in a study.
2. Research subjects must be able to withdraw, without penalty, from a study at any point.
3. All unnecessary risks to a research subject must be eliminated.
4. Benefits to the subject or society, preferably both, must outweigh all potential risks.
5. Experiments should be conducted only by qualified investigators.

Various professional groups created their own codes of ethics tailored for research in their disciplines. The ethical guidelines adopted by the American Anthropological Association (AAA) address issues that ethnographic researchers in particular face. The AAA Code of Ethics has evolved through several iterations, most recently amended and adopted by the AAA membership in 1998. The following portion is taken from their five-page statement (see http://www.aaanet.org/committees/ethics/ethcode.htm) and focuses upon researchers' responsibilities to people and animals with whom they work and whose lives and cultures they study.

1. Anthropological researchers have primary ethical obligations to the people, species, and materials they study and to the people with whom they work. These obligations can supersede the goal of seeking new knowledge, and can lead to decisions not to undertake or to discontinue a research project when the primary obligation conflicts with other responsibilities, such as those owed to sponsors or clients. . . .

2. Anthropological researchers must do everything in their power to ensure that their research does not harm the safety, dignity, or privacy of the people with whom they work, conduct research, or perform other professional activities . . .

3. Anthropological researchers must determine in advance whether their hosts/providers of information wish to remain anonymous or receive recognition, and make every effort to comply with those wishes. Researchers must present to their research participants the possible impacts of the choices, and make clear that despite their best efforts, anonymity may be compromised or recognition fail to materialize.

4. Anthropological researchers should obtain in advance the informed consent of persons being studied, providing information, owning or controlling access to material being studied, or otherwise identified as having interests which might be impacted by the research. It is understood that the degree and breadth of informed consent required will depend on the nature of the project and may be affected by requirements of other codes, laws, and ethics of the country or community in which the research is pursued. Further, it is understood that the informed consent process is dynamic and continuous; the process should be initiated in the project design and continue through implementation by way of dialogue and negotiation with those studied. . . . Informed consent, for the purpose of this code, does not necessarily imply or require a particular written or signed form. It is the quality of the consent, not the format, that is relevant.

5. Anthropological researchers who have developed close and enduring relationships . . . with either individual persons providing information or with hosts must adhere to the obligations of openness and informed consent, while carefully and respectfully negotiating the limits of the relationship.

6. While anthropologists may gain personally from their work, they must not exploit individuals, groups, animals, or cultural or biological materials. They should recognize their debt to the societies in which they work and their obligation to reciprocate with people studied in appropriate ways. (American Anthropological Association 1998, 2–3)

The AAA Code of Ethics includes directives on the researcher's responsibilities to scholarship and science, the public, students and trainees, and applied work.

Many of the principles are general and open to interpretation; nonetheless, they provide a framework for reflection on fieldwork, sensitizing you to areas that require thoughtful decisions.

In light of today's codes of ethics, a number of studies from the 1950s and 1960s would never be approved. Generally, subjects were drawn from low-power groups; in some cases, they gave information only to have the findings used against their own interests by people in positions of power (Punch 1986). Ethical codes help to mitigate this occurrence. Nonetheless, as some researchers observe, ethical codes can also protect the powerful. For example, Wilkins (1979, 109) notes that prisoners' rights are rarely a matter of concern for authorities until someone wants to do research in prisons. In effect, authorities can protect themselves under the guise of protecting subjects. Institutions that require explicit consent often have elaborate screening devices to deflect research on sensitive issues. Galliher asks, "Is not the failure of sociology to uncover corrupt, illegitimate covert practices of government or industry because of the supposed prohibitions of professional ethics tantamount to supporting such practices?" (Galliher 1982, 160).

In addition, aspects of ethical research codes are culturally based. Lipson (1994) points out how Western codes of ethics focus on respect for the individual and for individual rights, while "in many other cultures, 'personhood' is defined in terms of one's tribe, social group, or village" (341). She uses examples from her work with Afghan refugees to demonstrate how "Afghans do not think of themselves as individuals who have their own rights or autonomy, but as members of families" (342). Because people in many parts of the world think and act in terms of community, rather than the individual, Howitt and Stevens (2005, 38) suggest that the non-local researcher has the ethical obligation to obtain formal or informal community-based research agreements that may go far beyond IRB guidelines in that the community may become involved in "identifying appropriate research goals and questions, appropriate ways to seek knowledge (culturally specific, appropriate methodologies), and appropriate ways for research findings and knowledge to be shared."

With cross-cultural research dilemmas in mind, a commission raised the issue of whether or not the AAA had the moral authority to create a code of ethics if it also espoused *cultural relativism*. That is, they asked if moral codes of different cultures can be considered as morally equal, how was it that the AAA could develop a code of ethics for conducting research? In their discussion, the commission concluded that although cultural relativism is an important intellectual stance for understanding practices within a culture, it does not mean that the researcher has to agree with any or all of the practices of a people being studied. For example, although slavery is generally considered wrong, the practice continues to exist in some places and is worthy of study. The commission eventually agreed that the development of an ethical code was important as a guide for people doing field research. That ethical codes may preclude certain kinds of research or that they may be culturally based are not grounds for dismissal, but rather indicate how, in qualitative research, standards of ethicality may evolve as your research perspectives grow and your participation increases.

INFORMED CONSENT

Though informed consent neither precludes the abuse of research findings, nor creates a symmetrical relationship between researcher and researched, it can contribute to the empowering of research participants. The appropriateness of informed consent, particularly written consent forms, however, is a debated issue that accompanies discussions of codes of ethics by qualitative inquirers. Through informed consent, potential study participants are made aware (1) that participation is voluntary, (2) of any aspects of the research that might affect their well-being, and (3) that they may freely choose to stop participation at any point in the study. Originally developed for biomedical research, informed consent is now applicable when participants may be exposed to physical or emotional risk.

Sometimes the requirement of written consent is readily accepted, as in the case of obtaining parental consent before studying young children. In other cases, as recognized by IRBs, the very record left by consent papers could put some individuals' safety at risk if discussing sensitive topics (i.e., crime, sexual behavior, drug use). In some cross-cultural situations, consent forms can be seen as part of Western bureaucratic tracking systems. With a heritage of loss through signing names, many in postcolonial countries are understandably mistrustful of forms, especially those requiring signatures. Another quandary is that qualitative research plans often change, particularly in long-term studies, rendering the standard one-time consent at the beginning of the project potentially problematic.

Margaret Mead stated, "anthropological research does not have subjects. We work with informants in an atmosphere of mutual respect" (in Diener and Crandall 1978, 52). Field relationships continually undergo informal renegotiation as respect, interest, and acceptance grow or wane for both researcher and participant. As the relationship develops, the researcher may be invited to participate in ways he or she hoped for, but could not have sought access to in the beginning (from secret ceremonies to executive golfing rounds). When research becomes collaborative, cooperation, active assistance, and collegiality may exceed the demands of informed consent (Diener and Crandall 1978; Wax 1982). Indeed, cooperation and partnership may be more relevant to the ethical assessment of qualitative fieldwork than whether or not informed consent forms were signed.

RESEARCHER ROLES AND ETHICAL DILEMMAS

In the beginning stages of interpretivist research projects, novices tend to see their research role as one of data gathering. As they become more involved in fieldwork, they find themselves functioning in a variety of roles depending upon research purposes and procedures, their own characteristics, and personal attributes of research participants. Some of the roles may worry the researcher while others may be attractive but perplexing in relationship to their data-gathering goal. This section addresses several roles that qualitative researchers easily assume: exploiter, reformer, advocate, and friend. Different ethical dilemmas accompany each role.

Exploiter

> Esperanza has given me her story to smuggle across the border. Just as rural Mexican laborers export their bodies for labor on American soil, Esperanza has given me her story for export only. . . . The question will be whether I can act as her literary broker without becoming the worst kind of coyote, getting her across, but only by exploiting her lack of power to make it to *el otro lado* any other way.
>
> (Behar 1993, 234)

Questions of exploitation, or "using" your others, tend to arise as you become immersed in your research and begin to rejoice in the richness of what you are learning. You are thankful, but you may begin to feel guilty for how much you are receiving and how little you seem to be giving in return. Take this concern seriously. Many researchers, as uninvited outsiders, have entered a new community, mined the raw data of words and behaviors, and then withdrawn to process those data into a product that served themselves and, perhaps, their professional colleagues. Research participants usually remain anonymous. In contrast, researchers may get status, prestige, and royalties from publications (Plummer 1983). Researchers sometimes justify their actions with trickle-down promises such as, "Through getting the word out to other professionals (special educators, nurses, social workers), we will be able to help other people like you." Today, some refer to this type of research as *colonial research*.

Exploitation involves questions of power and control. If you are not engaged in collaborative research projects, then how do you decide if you are "using" your participants? Mitzi began to interview homeless mothers about the schooling of their children. She agonized over questions of exploitation:

> What am I giving back to these homeless mothers that I interview? It seems so unfair that this middle class privileged person is "using" this needy population . . . Can someone in a shelter tell me they don't have time? Privilege allows my response [of no time] to others to be OK. For them, that response would be suspect.

Dick, in his study of first-year principals, felt he "used" his relationships, his contacts, and his friends all over the state to get data.

Mitzi and Dick ask difficult questions. They were both working on dissertation studies and feeling as though they were receiving more than they were giving. They most likely were. One could ask, however, in what ways were they giving back to the communities? Mitzi and Dick treated interviewees with respect and dignity. That was ethical. They listened carefully, making sure they understood what was told to them. That was ethical. Mitzi worked in social services and Dick in public education. Both planned to incorporate what they were learning in the work they did and to share it with others. That was ethical. Neither made promises to participants to solve their problems; rather they listened to their stories and resolved to make their voices heard. That was ethical.

If the standard of ethicality is resolving the difficulties of people from whom you collect data, and resolving them right away, then much research is doomed never to begin. Nonetheless, the question of exploitation needs serious attention; a question that has led many researchers to make the choice of more collaborative-based research. Try answering the following questions posed by Linda Tuhiwai Smith (1999, 173):

- Who defined the research problem?
- For whom is this study worthy and relevant? Who says so?
- What knowledge will the community gain from this study?
- What knowledge will the researcher gain from this study?
- What are some likely positive outcomes from this study?
- What are some possible negative outcomes?
- To whom is the researcher accountable?

If your answers clearly show that you do all the decision-making and acquire the most, think seriously about modifying your research design.

Intervener/Reformer

Unlike the exploiter role, which researchers wander into but want to avoid, the intervener or reformer role is one researchers may consciously decide to assume. As a result of conducting research, researchers may attempt to right what they judge to be wrong, to change what they condemn as unjust. Through observations at a zoo, Nancy grew increasingly concerned over what she considered to be inhumane treatment of certain animals and agonized over what to do with her information.

In the process of doing research, researchers often acquire information that is potentially dangerous to some people. Don was interested in the history of an educational research organization. As he interviewed, he lamented, "I'm hearing stuff that I neither need nor wish to know about attitudes and relationships." The process was complicated for Don because he was investigating an organization in which he himself was involved.

As I interviewed young Caribbean farmers about their practices, I unexpectedly learned about the illegal cultivation and marketing of marijuana. And as Peshkin interviewed students in his ethnicity study, he became privy to information like the following:

> You know about the corner store, right? No? Gosh. They sell alcohol to anyone. Anyone. My friend and I went there to buy some chips and the guy who was standing behind the counter said, "You guys drink? I'll sell you some wine coolers. I won't tell your parents. Don't worry about it. Want some wine cooler?"

When research participants trust you, you invariably receive the privilege and burden of learning things that are problematic at best and dangerous at worst.

Your ethical dilemma concerns what to do with dangerous knowledge. To what extent should you continue to protect the confidentiality of research participants? If you learn about illegal behavior, should you expose it? If those of us in the above examples informed authorities of our knowledge, we would jeopardize not only our continued research in those sites, but also possible subsequent projects. None of us discussed our knowledge with other research participants, nor personally intervened. If what you learn relates to the point of your study, explore ways to communicate the dangerous knowledge so that you fully maintain the anonymity of your sources. Continual protection of confidentiality is generally the best policy (Ball 1985; Fine and Sandstrom 1988).

In their book *Knowing Children*, Fine and Sandstrom (1988) discuss how preadolescents "not only behave in ways that are unknowingly dangerous, but also knowingly and consciously behave in ways that are outside the rules set by adults" (55). As trust develops between the researcher and children, words and actions of the children may pose ethical dilemmas for the researcher. A child may, for example, act as a bully or make a sexist comment. Fine and Sandstrom conclude that "children must be permitted to engage in certain actions and speak certain words that the adult researcher finds distressing. Further, in some instances, the researcher must act in ways that are at least tacitly supportive of these distressing behaviors" (Fine and Sandstrom 1988, 55).

The question remains, however, of how "wrong" a situation must be before you should intervene on the basis of your unexpectedly acquired knowledge. If, for example, as a researcher you suspect ongoing emotional abuse of a child, do you react differently than if your work puts you in contact with students being offered alcohol at the corner store? Could not the latter also be construed as a case of child abuse? How do you decide where the lines are between a felt moral obligation to intervene and an obligation to continue as the data-collecting researcher?

No definitive answers can be provided for many questions and again, judgments are made on a mix of contextual elements and personal compulsions. Some preventative measures, however, will help avoid such dilemmas. Laurie, a nurse, conducted research in a hospital setting. She worried about what she should do if she observed malpractice while in her research role. Finally, she discussed her worries with her cohorts in a qualitative research methods class. By taking the worry seriously and putting it through a variety of configurations, the class urged Laurie to meet with her gatekeepers and with the nursing staff she was observing and interviewing to get their advice on how she should proceed if she observed malpractice.

Developing some sort of support group to discuss worries and dilemmas is a valuable part of the research process. Some researchers build a panel of experts into their research design. A student's dissertation committee can serve this function, but expert panels and dissertation committees do not necessarily know how to deal with ethical questions that arise in qualitative research. Ideally, the researcher has a support group made up of others who, although perhaps involved in substantively different topics, are all struggling with similar methodological questions.

Advocate

Advocates are like interventionists in that they decide to take a position on some issue that they become aware of through their research. Unlike interveners or reformers who try to change something within the research site, the advocate champions a cause. As Lynne interviewed university custodians, she was tempted to become an advocate:

> I keep asking myself to what extent the research should improve the situation for custodians. This is magnified somewhat by my feeling that I have been a participant in the process, raising issues with custodians that many by now have come to terms with or raising expectations that some good will result. Even though my research was for the purpose of understanding and not "fixing," how can one come so close to what is judged to be a very bad situation and walk away? I keep asking myself, "Do I own them solutions or at least some relief?" My answer is always "no," but then I keep asking myself the same question, probably because I just don't like my answer.

Lynne's research heightened her concern for the well-being of the custodians she studied, and the "take-the-data-and-run" approach left her uncomfortable. In the interpretivist tradition, advocacy can take a variety of forms—presentations and publications among the most readily available. Lynne needs to decide whether such formats will serve her concern, or if there are others that are within her competency that would be acceptable to the custodians. She expresses well a motivation of some qualitative researchers who seek out more collaborative or participatory action research.

Finch (1984) experienced a quandary over publishing data she collected through her study of playgroups. She found that child-care standards differed among working- and middle-class women.

> This evidence, I feared, could be used to reinforce the view that working-class women are inadequate and incompetent childrearers. Again, I felt that I was not willing to heap further insults upon women whose circumstances were far less privileged than my own, and indeed for a while, I felt quite unable to write *anything* about this aspect of the playground study. Finch (1984)

Finch resolved her dilemma by distinguishing between the structural position in which the women were placed and their own experience with that position. This enabled Finch to "see that evidence of women successfully accommodating to various structural features of their lives in no way alters the essentially exploitative character of the structures in which they are located" (Finch 1984, 84). Thus, she described the child-care practices of the working-class women in a way that would support them in an unfair and unequal society. Finch did not alter her data; she did not explain away the differences she uncovered. Her ethical sensitivity led her to contextualize her findings, so that the behavior of the two groups of women was framed within the differential realities of their lives. Confronting the ethical dilemma resulted in more effective interpretation.

Friend

Researchers often have friendly relations with research participants; in some cases, the relationship is one of friendship. Whether friendship or friendliness is the case, ethical dilemmas can result. You may gain access to intimate information given to you in the context of friendship rather than in your researcher role. Should you use such data? Both Hansen's (1976) exploration of Danish life and Daniels' (1967) investigation within a military setting relied on personal friendships as channels for information. Hansen (1976) expressed her discomfort with her role as researcher and her role as friend: "The confidential information I received was given to me in my role as friend. Yet, I was also an anthropologist and everything I heard or observed was potentially relevant to my understanding of the dynamics of Danish interaction" (Hansen 1976, 127). Hansen refers to a particular confidential story told to her by one woman:

> Later that day I would record this conversation, alone, without her knowledge, in my role as anthropologist. In my role as investigator the conversation became "data." Would she have spoken so frankly about this and other more intimate subjects had she understood that I listened in *both* roles, not only as friend? (129)

As she continued to gather data, Hansen grew concerned over how she would protect the anonymity of her interviewees and struggled with thoughts on whether public description of behaviors violates an individual's right to privacy. She and Daniels both experienced ethical dilemmas over publishing findings that would possibly discomfort their friends, if not betray their friendship relationships.

Both Hansen and Daniels need to ask whether their narrative truly needs to include all that their friends tell them. Will the narrative hold up if the troublesome bits are excluded? Can these troublesome bits be presented in less troublesome ways? In the end, should we not let our friends be judges, by submitting to them what we have written, and taking our lead from their decisions?

In Busier et al.'s (1997) article "Intimacy in Research," the authors argue that intimacy can be a "route to understanding" (165) but that it carries with it responsibilities and considerations, including reflexivity on the nature and influence of the relationship, analysis of the role of power in the relationship, and attunement to relational ethics. In relational ethics "the derivation and authority of moral behavior [is located] not in rules and obligations as such, but in our attachments and regard for others . . ." (Flinders 1992, 106). Predicated on trust, care, and a sense of collaboration, relational ethics is at the core of research in which friendship relationships are welcomed.

THE RESEARCHER–RESEARCHED RELATIONSHIP

No matter how qualitative researchers view their roles, they develop relationships with research participants. Unlike the friendship relationships described previously, conventional research relationships are generally asymmetrical, with power disproportionately located on the side of the researcher. Thus, codes of ethics instruct researchers to consciously consider and protect the rights of participants to privacy, to reflect on and mitigate deceptive aspects of research, and to consider issues of reciprocity.

The Right to Privacy

In discussions of the rights of research participants, privacy is generally the foremost concern. Participants have a right to expect that when they give you permission to observe and interview, you will protect their confidences and preserve their anonymity. Respect confidentiality by not discussing with anyone the specifics of what you see and hear. When a principal asks you what you are learning from the teachers, you respond with something like the following:

> I am really enjoying talking with your teachers. They seem to take both their jobs and my research seriously and are therefore helping me tremendously. It's too early yet to know what I can make of all the information I'm receiving, but a couple of themes have been emerging and I'd like the opportunity to discuss them with you. Do you have the time?

Such a response leads away from particular individuals and toward the discussion of general concepts, which respects the principal's interest in your findings without violating any of your commitments to teachers. Such discussions must balance your unqualified obligation to the teachers with your appreciation of the principal's natural interest in your findings. It also makes use of an opportunity for participant feedback or a "member check" (Lincoln and Guba 1985) on your analytical categories.

Researchers sometimes argue over whether unobtrusive methods, even in public places, invade rights of privacy. This discussion usually includes debates on the use of covert observation (to be discussed in the next section, "Deception"). One position is that covert observation in public places is permissible because people ordinarily watch and are watched by others in public places. Accordingly, social scientists should be able to observe as well. A counterpoint is that when such observations are systematic, recorded, and analyzed, they no longer are ordinary and thereby violate rights of privacy.

Similar arguments develop around less discussed means of unobtrusive data collection. Diener and Crandall (1978) describe a study in which researchers used both surveys and the contents of garbage bags to discover what people bought, discarded, and wasted in different sectors of Tucson, Arizona. The findings concluded that poor people waste less food than higher-income people, and that there is a marked discrepancy between self-reports on alcohol consumption and evidence from bottles and cans in the garbage. Although garbage content was not linked to particular households, the examined bags often included envelopes with names on them. Do such studies violate privacy rights?

The issue of privacy arises again during the writing-up phase of the qualitative inquiry process. To protect the anonymity of research participants, researchers use fictitious names and sometimes change descriptive characteristics such as age or hair color. Fictitious names, however, do not necessarily protect participants as demonstrated by two frequently cited cases: West's (1945) *Plainville, U.S.A.* and Vidich and Bensman's (1968) *Small Town in Mass Society.* Despite made-up names, the towns were easily identified by descriptions of their characteristics and locations, and people in the towns easily recognized themselves in the descriptions of individuals. In both cases, research participants were upset by the portrayals of the towns and their inhabitants. Critics (see Johnson 1982, 76) point out that West, for example, focused on the negative, that he looked with an urban perspective, and that he used offensive and judgmental words such as "hillbilly" or "people who lived like animals."

Plummer (1983) states that although "confidentiality may appear to be a prerequisite of life history research, it frequently becomes an impossibility" (142). He cites several examples: Fifty years after the original study, Shaw's (1930/1966) Jack Roller was located for reinterview, and after a month of detective work, a reporter tracked down Oscar Lewis's (1963) *Children of Sanchez.* In addition to breaches of privacy, these examples also illustrate potential difficulty in observing the ethical principle of "doing no harm." Although "no harm" may be done during the research process, harm may result from making research findings public. In publishing findings, the researcher needs to consider how the manuscript could potentially affect both the individual and the community. If specific information about an individual were released, would it cause him or her pain? If collective information about a community were published, does it harm its reputation or social standing? If the researcher's analysis is different from that of participants, should one, both, or neither be published? Even if respondents tend to agree that some aspect of their community is unflattering, should the researcher make this information public? In sum, what obligations does the researcher have to research participants when publishing findings?

Scott (1996) distinguishes between *open autocratic research* and *open democratic research.* In the open autocratic case, the researcher is open with research participants about all aspects of the research and invites their feedback on research interpretations, but does not give the respondents the rights of veto. In open democratic research, participants have the right to control not only which data are collected but also which data are included in the research report, through a series of negotiations between researcher and project participants. In the first situation, power resides with the researcher; in the second situation, community power and politics affect what gets researched and reported. Both positions can be problematic.

Despite justified worry about protecting anonymity, researchers may also have to deal with anonymity declined. Jacobs (1987) tells of an anthropologist who wrote about a community in Melanesia; she disguised villagers and their location through use of pseudonyms. Three years later, she returned to the field to distribute copies of her manuscript to those who had been most helpful and to ask permission to conduct further study. People liked the book and felt the accounts were correct, but told her that she had gotten the name of the village wrong and the names of the individuals wrong. She was told to be more accurate in the next book.

When her second book was completed, she sent a copy to the village and asked for comments as well as whether they still wanted actual names used. When she did not get a direct reply to her question, she used the same pseudonyms in her second monograph.

In another case of anonymity declined, an applied medical anthropologist worked for three years in an urban African American community. Before she published her articles, she asked community members to read, comment on, and criticize them. They complimented her on her accuracy, but questioned her use of pseudonyms for the town, the health center, and the individuals who "struggle to improve the healthcare for our people" (in Jacobs 1987, 26). The anthropologist explained the reasons for privacy conventions and how disclosing names could result in possible harm. In the end, she omitted the actual name of the center and its location, but she acknowledged the names of staff members in footnotes. This decision was made collaboratively.

The emphasis on confidentiality may, in itself, reflect a Western bias. In some countries, such as Tanzania, the prevailing expectation for research projects is that names of interviewees will be published in an appendix, and "to deviate from this procedure may be perceived as either confusing or arrogant" (Ryen 2007, 221). Yet, as indicated above, publishing names of all participants can be problematic, particularly if the research is dealing with sensitive issues in which statements by participants conflict with perspectives of people in positions of power.

Privacy and the Internet

The use of Internet communications as a forum for data gathering raises new ethical challenges to the right to privacy (Mann and Stewart 2000; Robson and Robson, 2002). The use of such technology makes it relatively easy to gather data from a widespread population and removes the time and money-consuming task of transcription. Also, a researcher can easily share and receive feedback on research findings with participants. No clear ethical guidelines pave the way, however, for researchers using computer-mediated communications. One problem is that contexts are neither private nor public, but rather on a kind of continuum between private and public (Elm 2009). For example, some investigators have observed online communities or conducted interviews in chat rooms. Are such places public venues? Should consent be obtained from all participants in chat rooms, newsgroups, or mailing lists? If researchers are using information from such sources and want to gain consent, they must consider how they will do so since participation can be sporadic and change frequently. It is also more difficult to promise confidentiality in Internet communications, particularly to users of chat groups. You can use pseudonyms in your published text, but if you include quotations, it is easy to track down the source by conducting a search for the quote.

Robson and Robson (2002, 95) advise researchers to pay attention to not only ethical codes for doing social science research but also to codes of conduct, or *netiquette*, developed by online communities. For example, the Computer

Professionals for Social Responsibility (CPSR) has produced a set of privacy guidelines that include the need for individuals to be made aware of any collection of personal information and of how the information will be used. In 2000, the Association of Internet Researchers appointed a working group with the task of creating ethical guidelines for Internet research (see www.aoir.org/reports/ethics.pdf). This is a useful guide, but technology changes quickly, and the Internet context is so varied that many questions regarding its use remain.

More computer-related privacy and consent issues arise with the increased possibilities of archiving and making widely available all aspects of research—from interview transcripts to videotapes. Consent may be released for current use of research data, but can consent be given for some unknowable future use by someone the participant has never met? These kinds of quandaries posed by technology and Internet research make it imperative that researchers carefully consider not only ethical guidelines but also the ethical treatment of participants in light of the context of their particular studies (Baym and Markham 2009).

Deception

> It is interesting, and even ironic, that social scientists espouse some of the techniques normally associated with morally polluted professions, such as policing and spying, and enjoy some of the moral ambivalence surrounding those occupations.
>
> (Punch 1994, 91)

Chris was interested in researching the gay community on a university campus. He attended a meeting of the Gay/Lesbian Alliance as a participant observer, jotting notes unobtrusively. Because the meetings were open to the public, he originally saw no reason to proclaim his role as researcher. As that first meeting continued, however, he struggled with feelings of deception and guilt. Finally, he quit taking notes and decided to meet with the organization's officers and obtain permission to attend meetings in the role of researcher.

Conventionally, we regard deception as wrong. Nonetheless, its role in research has been debated over time. Deception easily enters various aspects of research, and it can take the form of either deliberate commission or omission. For example, in covert studies, participants never know that they are part of a research project. Some researchers have misrepresented their identities and pretended to be people they were not; others have presented themselves as researchers but have not fully explained what it was that they were researching. This latter practice is called omission, or *shallow cover* (Fine 1980). The decision to deceive generally rests on a concern to ensure the most natural behavior among research participants.

Punch (1986, 39) raises two questions concerning the role of deception in research: (1) Are there areas in which some measure of deception is justified in gaining data? and (2) Are devious means legitimate in institutions that deserve exposure? These questions summarize the debate over the use of deliberate deception in research.

Covert research gets its strongest support from those who advocate research of the powerful. As in investigative journalism, access to the workings of some groups or institutions with power would be impossible without deception. Van den Berge says of his research in South Africa, "From the outset, I decided that I should have no scruples in deceiving the government" (in Punch 1986, 39). If you, like Van den Berge, view an institution as "essentially dishonorable, morally outrageous and destructive," do you ignore it and study something more publicly acceptable in order to avoid being deceptive? Jack Douglas, a strong supporter of the *utilitarian* or "ends justify the means" approach, states,

> The social researcher is . . . entitled and indeed compelled to adopt covert methods. Social actors employ lies, fraud, deceit, deception, and blackmail in dealings with each other. Therefore the social scientist is justified in using them where necessary in order to achieve the higher objective of scientific truth. (in Punch 1986, 39)

From the utilitarian perspective, deception in research has been justified by potential benefits to the larger society. Ethical decisions are made on the basis that moral action is that which results in the greatest good for the greatest number. This perspective went hand in hand with the positivistic belief that value-neutral science was possible and that rational thought and science could solve the world's problems. Critics of this position argue that although costs and benefits may be estimated, both are impossible to predict and to measure. Furthermore, who is to set the standards that determine when something is for the greater good of society? Who defines what is "good?" This approach overlooks the power and ideology of institutions (from pharmaceutical labs to the U.S. Congress) that support much of the research that is done and therefore get to decide what is "good" (Christians 2000).

For most interpretivists, the utilitarian position—that one does what is necessary for the greater good—is overshadowed by the *deontological* ethical stance, which posits that moral conduct can be judged independently of its consequences. The deontological framework holds up some standard, such as justice or respect or honesty, by which to evaluate actions. This position changes the nature of the researcher-researched relationship and readily makes it unethical for researchers to misrepresent their identity to gain entry into settings otherwise denied to them or to deliberately misrepresent the purpose of their research. Bulmer (1982), for example, argues that covert research is not ethically justified, practically necessary, or in the best interest of social scientists. He views the rights of subjects as overriding the rights of science, thereby limiting areas of research that can be pursued. Bulmer suggests that the need for covert methods is exaggerated and that open entry may more often be negotiated than is commonly supposed (Bulmer 1982, 250).

Even when you are as honest and open as possible about the nature of your research, you will continue to develop ethical questions concerning your fieldwork. Many of the questions will be context-bound, arising out of specific instances in each study. For example, informed consent regulations indicate that you should disclose to potential participants all information necessary for them to make intelligent decisions about participation. Yet doing so is difficult in qualitative research because often you are not fully aware of what you are looking for, among whom, or with what possible risks. "The researcher is in a perplexing situation," states Erickson. "He or she needs to have done an ethnography of the setting in order to anticipate the range of risks and other burdens that will be involved for those studied" (Erickson 1986, 141). Although the partial nature of your knowledge does not obviate the propriety of informed consent, it does make implementing it problematic.

Reciprocity

In some kinds of research, reciprocity is assumed to be a matter of monetarily rewarding research subjects for their time. Although participants in qualitative research sometimes receive payment, the issue of reciprocity becomes more difficult because of the time involved and the nature of relationships developed. The degree of indebtedness varies considerably from study to study and from participant to participant, depending upon the topic, the amount and type of time researchers spend with participants, and the degree of collaboration.

Glazer (1982, 50) defines *reciprocity* as "the exchange of favors and commitments, the building of a sense of mutual identification and feeling of community." As research participants open up their lives to researchers—giving time, sharing intimate stories, and frequently including them in both public and private events and activities—researchers become ambivalent, alternately overjoyed with the data they are producing, but worried by their perceived inability to adequately reciprocate. As I wrote up my Caribbean work, I reflected:

> Cultural thieving is what ethnographers do if their written product is limited in its benefits to the gatherer and, perhaps, his or her community. Also known as "data exportation" or "academic imperialism" (Hamnett and Porter 1983, 65), the process is reminiscent of past archaeologists carrying stone, pottery, and golden artifacts away from "exotic" places of origin to the archaeologists' homeland for analysis and display. What is owed to the people observed is the question. Are the terms of trade more than glass beads? (Glesne 1985, 55–60)

Researchers do not want to view people as means to ends of their choosing. Nonetheless, in non-collaborative qualitative work, they invariably cultivate relationships in order to gather data to meet their own ends. In the process, researchers can reciprocate in a variety of ways, but whether what they give equals what they get is difficult, if not impossible, to determine.

Equivalency may be the wrong standard to use in judging the adequacy of your reciprocity. What can you do for those teachers who let you spend hours at the back of their classroom, or for those nurses who come to your interview sessions week after week? Literally, their time is invaluable to you. Is there anything within your means to deliver that your research participants would perceive as invaluable to them? Probably not. Often they do not have a relationship with you that puts you in a position to have something that, typically, is of such consequence to them. What you do have that they value is the means to be grateful, by acknowledging how important their time, cooperation, and words are; by expressing your dependence upon what they have to offer; and by elaborating your pleasure with their company. When you keep duty teachers company, assist participants in weeding their gardens, or speak to the local rotary club, you demonstrate that you have not cast yourself as an aloof outsider.

The interviewing process particularly provides an occasion for reciprocity. By listening to participants carefully and seriously, you give them a sense of importance and specialness. By providing the opportunity to reflect on and voice answers to your questions, you assist them to better understand some aspect of themselves. If your questions identify issues of importance to interviewees, then interviewees will invariably both enjoy and find useful their roles as information providers. By the quality of your listening, you provide context for personal exploration by your interviewees.

Although researchers do not wittingly assume the role of therapist, they nonetheless fashion an interview process that can be strikingly therapeutic. Obligations accompany the therapeutic nature of the interview. Self-reflections can produce pain where least expected, and interviewers may suddenly find themselves face to face with a crying interviewee. Tears do not necessarily mean that you have asked a bad or a good question, but they do obligate you to deal sensitively and constructively with the unresolved feelings, without taking on the role of analyst. If appropriate, you might suggest people, organizations, or resources that may be of help. Follow up through letters or conversations to assist such interviewees in feeling comfortable with their degree of personal disclosure. When Dick interviewed

Reciprocity can take many forms. Here a student is helping members of the National Trust of Great Britain clear non-native vegetation out of a coastal area. Consider ways in which you could reciprocate in your work.

first-year principals, one began to cry as he expressed his stress and frustration with the job. When Eileen interviewed students of color about their experiences on a predominantly white campus, a young man began to cry as he talked about leaving his home community. At first, both Dick and Eileen were stunned, but they sympathetically listened. Finally, they suggested people and organizations that might be of interest and assistance to the interviewees.

The closer the relationship between researcher and research participants, the more special obligations and expectations emerge. For example, Cassell (1987) tells of an anthropologist who, during her initial fieldwork and successive summers, was accepted as granddaughter of an elderly Southwestern Native-American couple. Their children and spouses treated her as a sister. One summer, when the anthropologist returned to the reservation, she learned that her "grandfather" showed signs of senility, was drinking heavily, and was hallucinating. His children and their spouses left soon after her arrival saying that they had cared for him all year and that it was now her turn. Although his care took full time and her planned research work did not get done, the anthropologist felt she had no choice but to honor her "occasional kin" status. She also felt, however, even more a part of the family and free to bring with her an emotionally and educationally challenged nephew the next summer. Her "kin" helped tremendously in dealing with him. In another example, biographer Rosengarten wrote about his work with Ned Cobb and the form of his reciprocity: "There was one special reason why Ned Cobb's family agreed to busy itself with me, apart from the feelings between us. My work with Ned revived his will to live" (Rosengarten 1985, 113).

Interviews and other means of data collection can contribute to raised expectations in less intimate relationships as well. When researchers spend days and months asking people about their problems and aspirations, they elicit voices of dissatisfaction and dreams. In the process, they may encourage people to expect that someone will work to alleviate their plight. If, as a researcher, you plan only to publish your findings, then you must find a way to make that clear to research participants throughout the data-gathering process. Through written reports, however, qualitative researchers frequently convey reciprocity by their tales of injustice, struggle, and pain. Reciprocity may also include making explicit arrangements to share royalties from publications.

Cultural Considerations

Patricia Martin and I met in Oaxaca, Mexico. As we shared research stories, we found ourselves independently focusing on three concepts important to Oaxacan society—community, communal autonomy, and hospitality. We had observed ways in which these cultural values guided people's actions and interactions in Oaxaca and as we talked, we began reflecting upon how these concepts could serve as ethical frameworks for our research processes specifically and qualitative research generally (see Martin and Glesne, 2002). I'll use "hospitality" as an example.

Patricia and I began by discussing how we had responded to the hospitality offered to us by the communities that served as our research sites. Conscientiously incorporating greater reciprocity (sharing food and time, in particular) within the daily process of fieldwork was undoubtedly one step for us to better respond to hospitality. As we tried to imagine hospitality as an ethical framework for doing research, we began seeing differently our previous emphases on the role of power in research relationships. Rather than focus on trying to equalize power in relationships, a lens of hospitality would compel us to attend to exchanges of care, compassion, and generosity. Hospitality asks us to see aspects of relationship that include and then go beyond inequities in power. It also demands that we, as researchers, act in culturally hospitable ways. A code of ethics for research in New Zealand's Maori communities (Tuhiwai Smith 1999, 120) supports this notion. It includes culturally specific ideas that relate to being hospitable:

- Show "respect for people."
- "Present yourself to people face to face."
- "Look, listen . . . speak."
- "Share and host people, be generous."
- "Be cautious."
- "Do not trample over the *mana* [fundamental duties and rights] of people."
- "Don't flaunt your knowledge."

The lens of hospitality also suggests that, as Western researchers, we need to go beyond the terrain of individual research to the academic communities within which our work is enmeshed. How do we transform our own communities to make them more hospitable? If hospitality were an ethic for Western academia, in which the foreigner, the stranger, the "other" is given a place within the "we" (Esteva and Prakash 1998, 87), then other knowledge standpoints would have to be more fully welcomed within academic communities.

ETHICS OF REPRESENTATION

As researchers write up and make public their work, they need to take into account ethical aspects that have already been mentioned such as promises of privacy and anonymity, as well as ways in which to reciprocate and possibly collaborate. This section addresses representing research in artful ways (e.g., drama, short stories, poems, videos) which can have particular ethical implications for research participants, audiences, and presenters (Sinding, Gray, and Nisker 2008). In arts-based representations, participants' words and images are more likely—than in academic publications—to be seen by the public, including those who live in the same communities as research participants. A general ethical guideline is that research participants should be able to read, observe, or somehow engage with the art and to discuss its representation before it goes to a wider public. Researchers need to "anticipate ways that their representations may harm people witnessing them, especially people most affected by the subject matter" (Sinding, Gray, and Nisker 2008, 462). For example, a dramatic portrayal of people who have lost a family member to cancer could be quite distressful to not only the respondent whose story provided the impetus for the depiction, but also for others in the audience with similar experiences. Researchers in these situations could consider providing opportunities for audiences to participate in postperformance discussions or other forms of engaging with the material. Performers themselves can be affected by the process of representation: "There is, it seems, something about the process of representing things artistically—of undoing the familiar language, of reaching for new words, of distilling the experience into an image, of embodying it—that is especially powerful, and especially disruptive" (Sinding, Gray, and Nisker 2008, 460). Presenters can be particularly vulnerable if they identify personally with the issue at hand. Arts-based research encourages us to delve further into issues of ethics than items specified by IRBs.

NO EASY SOLUTIONS

By their nature, ethical dilemmas defy easy solutions. Researchers continue to debate whether or not some people or areas should be researched and, if so, how. They question whether or not fieldwork is inevitably deceitful. They argue over the role of conscious deception or omission in fieldwork. They raise ethical questions about the use of power in relationships, particularly with economically poor and "deviant" groups. And they question whether codes and regulations can successfully shape research ethics. Concern for ethics and research relationships have, in fact, led many qualitative researchers to include in their research procedures processes that surpass those of IRB regulations. Conscious, ongoing reflections on intentions, the researcher's role, relationships, and political implications are all part of this.

Plummer (1983) identifies two ethical positionings: the ethical absolutist and the situational relativist positionings. The absolutist relies heavily on professional codes of ethics and seeks to establish firm principles to guide all social science research. The relativist believes that solutions to ethical dilemmas cannot be prescribed by absolute guidelines but have to be "produced creatively in the concrete situation at hand" (141). Pointing out weaknesses in both positions, Plummer suggests a combination: broad ethical guidelines with room for personal ethical choice by the researcher. Ethical codes certainly guide your behavior, but the degree to which your research is ethical depends on your continual communication and interaction with research participants throughout the study. Researchers alone must not be the arbiters of this critical research issue.

The tradition of ethics that set the standards for IRBs and committees is undergoing challenge by a new social ethics, sometimes referred to as "feminist communitarianism." Described as "communitarian, egalitarian, democratic, critical, caring, engaged, performative, social justice oriented" (Lincoln and Denzin 2008, 542), this new ethic creates a community characterized by "moral obligation on the part of qualitative researchers, responsibility and obligation to participants, to respondents, to consumers of research, and to themselves as qualitative field-workers. . . . [and mandates] a stance that is democratic, reciprocal, and reciprocating rather than objective and objectifying" (Lincoln and Denzin 2008, 543). Rather than strive to create neutral principles for moral judgments, as utilitarian ethics has done, this new perspective calls for an ethics rooted in human relations, care, and socio-historical context: "What is worth preserving as a good cannot be self-determined in isolation, but can be ascertained only within specific social situations where human identity is nurtured" (Christians 2008, 201). From this perspective, "the mission of social science research is enabling community life to prosper" (Christians 2008, 201), and purpose and methods become collaborative and participatory.

This new ethic and the accompanying trend for researchers to take moral activist stances on issues involving power and injustice, raise new questions for research ethics. In particular, we must ask on what basis can activist stances be taken and to whom and how is the researcher accountable? Such discussions take us into terrain that is more complicated than meeting the requirements of IRBs. As we, in the social sciences, embrace multiple ways of critiquing, researching, and knowing, we have to forge new ways of constructing ethics, focusing on specific contexts, participants, and relationships among all involved.

RECOMMENDED READINGS

Christians, C. 2008. Ethics and politics in qualitative research. In N. Denzin and Y. Lincoln (Eds.). *The Landscape of Qualitative Research,* 3rd ed. (pp. 185–220). Thousand Oaks, CA: Sage.

Flinders, D. 1992. In search of ethical guidance: Constructing a basis for dialogue. *Qualitative Studies in Education,* 5(2), 101–115.

Howitt, R., and S. Stevens. 2005. Cross-cultural research: Ethics, Methods, and relationships. In I. Hay (Ed.), *Qualitative Research Methods in Human Geography,* 2nd ed. (pp. 30–50). New York: Oxford University Press.

EXERCISES

1. Choose one of the following ethical dilemmas (either individually or as a group in class) and reflect upon what you would do if you were the researcher.

   a. You are interviewing college women who are anorexic, but whose anorexia is no longer active, about their schooling experiences. You have arranged to interview each of your participants at least five times over two consecutive semesters. During the third interview with one participant, just after the winter holidays, you begin to suspect that her anorexia is active again because of her obvious weight loss and a few of her comments. When you ask her how her health is, she replies that she is feeling great. What do you do?

   b. You are working on an intellectual biography of a well-respected university president. Most of your interviews are with the president who has obviously consented to your request to compose an intellectual biography, including some attention to his formative years. You are reading all of his published works and interviewing some family members as well as significant colleagues. In the process, you uncover some potentially damaging or, at the least, unflattering information about his private life. What do you do?

c. You are inquiring into a refugee resettlement program in a small southern city, with particular interest in educational aspects and community involvement. Through development of rapport and time spent volunteering with the program, you begin to learn how an early immigrant is seemingly taking financial advantage of recent refugees. He is charging for information and services that should be provided through the settlement program and people are going to him, rather than trying to get their needs met through the program. You want to protect the new refugees from exploitation and to report the behavior of the earlier immigrant, yet you also worry that perhaps you don't fully understand what is happening culturally. What do you do?

2. In small groups, look up the code of ethics for a particular discipline or organization (with each group taking a different association). Think about different philosophical orientations for approaching research (e.g., positivism, interpretivism, critical). How do the codes reflect various orientations? As a large group, discuss similarities and differences among the codes.

Following are some sites you might want to check:
- American Anthropology Association: www.aaanet.org/committees/ethics/ethcode.htm
- American Psychological Association: www.apa.org/ethics
- American Sociological Association: www2.asanet.org/members/ecoderev.html
- American Folklore Society: www.afsnet.org/aboutAFS/ethics.cfm
- Association of Internet Researchers: www.aoir.org/reports/ethics.pdf
- British Educational Research Association: www.bera.ac.uk/files/guidelines/ethical.pdf
- British Sociological Association: www.socresonline.org.uk/info/ethguide.html
- Society of Professional Journalists: www.spj.org/ethics.asp

3. Reflect in your field log on potential ethical issues that might arise during your study. What can you do to minimize their potential? What would you do if faced with your ethical concerns? Discuss with at least one classmate.

CHAPTER 7

Finding Your Story: Data Analysis

I can no longer put off the inevitable. I've been home about three weeks now, and I've found as many distractions as I could to avoid coding. I've organized my files, I've set up the study and done a major reorganization so I can spread out the stacks that will soon pile up. I'm reading, I'm thinking, and as a way of really beginning, I took out the book prospectus I wrote in November. During the last months at my site, I put a few Post-it notes into the prospectus file with other BIG looming ideas, ones that showed me I would have to tinker with the planned structure. Today I thought I'd just print out a sheet of the tentative chapter structure to put up on the wall (and delay coding once again?). I began typing it, and what did I find? It's all wrong, it doesn't capture the way I've been thinking at all. The power of the shift hit me head on. I tried to reorganize the chapters, but I found that wouldn't work either. So instead I wrote out the big themes I have been thinking about in my sleep, while I drive, when I cook Passover food . . . and that's where I'll have to start.

(Pugach, Correspondence, 31 March 1994)

Qualitative researchers approach data analysis in different ways. Linguistic traditions, for example, focus upon words and conversations, treating "text as an object of analysis itself" and may use formal narrative analysis, discourse analysis, and/or linguistic analysis as tools for making sense of data (Ryan and Bernard 2000, 769). Researchers from more sociological traditions tend to treat "text as a window into human experience" (Ryan and Bernard 2000, 769) and widely use thematic analysis as a means of data analysis. Thematic analysis involves coding and segregating data for further analysis and description. This approach receives primary attention in this chapter, although several other forms of analysis are introduced in the following section.

VARYING FORMS OF ANALYSIS

Data analysis involves organizing what you have seen, heard, and read so that you can figure out what you have learned and make sense of what you have experienced. Working with the data, you describe, compare, create explanations, link your story to other stories, and possibly pose hypotheses or develop theories. How you go about doing so, however, can vary quite widely. This section introduces you to a few of the ways you might work to make sense of your data. The form of analysis you choose is linked to other methodological decisions, including theoretical orientation, research questions, and data collection. These varying forms are presented here in an effort to stimulate your interest in ways of making sense of qualitative data and to encourage you to read widely on modes that may resonate with you. This section begins with conversation analysis from linguistic traditions, moves next to a form of narrative analysis that combines linguistic and sociological traditions, followed by semiotics from sociological traditions, and finally by thematic analysis, which receives further discussion throughout the remaining sections of this chapter.

Conversation Analysis

Originating as a kind of ethnomethodological research,

> Conversation analysis studies the various practices adopted by conversational participants during ordinary everyday talk. This may include how participants negotiate overlaps and interruptions, how various failures (such as hearing and understanding problems) are dealt with during the interaction and how conversations are opened and terminated. (Bloor and Wood, 2006, 39)

Generally, data for conversation analysis studies are talk in everyday occurrences; thus these data are not obtained through interviews but through tape or video recording of conversations, such as in the classroom. With a focus on details of conversation, from time intervals between utterances to stress on certain words, the conversation analyst employs a system of transcription that uses various symbols to indicate nonverbal aspects of a conversation. Conversation analysis might be used, for example, in a study of a hospital implementing interprofessional communication and teamwork to improve patient safety. Through conversation analysis, the researcher would examine how roles of doctors, nurses, technicians, and aids are created by participants' talk.

Narrative Analysis

Researchers across the social science disciplines use narrative analysis but often for different purposes. As Bloor and Wood (2006, 119) state, "linguists might examine the internal structure of narratives, psychologists might focus on the process of recalling and summarizing stories, and anthropologists might look at the function of stories cross-culturally." Narratives may be collected in situ by tape recorder or video or through interviews. If obtained through interviews, the process is generally one of asking broad, open-ended questions such as "Tell me about . . . " and then letting the interviewee tell his or her story with as little interruption as possible. Rather than dissect these stories into themes and patterns, the analysis process is often concerned with both the story itself and the telling of the story.

Focusing on the story that is told is one way to approach transcripts in which interviewees talk substantially from their lives. For example, if you have conducted interviews with women who have suffered the loss of a child, hearing how they have made sense of and have healed (or not) from that loss, you might read and re-read transcripts of each narrative and make note of the events included in each story; the feelings and reactions expressed; the meanings each woman made of her story; and any explanations (Gibbs 2007, 63).

You could also focus on the linguistic and rhetorical forms of telling the stories. Often stories are analyzed in terms of beginning, middle, and end, but the telling also tends to fit one or more particular dramatic styles—tragedy, satire, romance, comedy (Gibbs, 2007, 67). If all the stories of your interviewees were told in more or less the same way, then you would reflect upon why that might be so for the particular group of women interviewed. If the stories had very different structures, you would reflect upon that and try to figure out why. Gubrium and Holstein (2009, 69) make the point that people's narratives often bear "diverse plot structures and themes," that go unnoticed "unless the researcher is aware of compositional options at the start." The narrative analyst looks at how the storyteller links experiences and circumstances together to make meaning but also realizes that circumstances do not determine how the story will be told or the meaning that is made of it.

Drawing from sociological traditions, Gubrium and Holstein (2009, xvii) emphasize the need in narrative work to go beyond the transcript: "The sense of story and story-teller under consideration centers on the social organization of narrativity." In other words, the context in which the narrator tells the story influences what is told and how it is told. Who asks the questions that invite a story? How are some stories discouraged or silenced? For example, stories my father told me about his participation in World War II through interviews I conducted for the Library of Congress Veteran Project are likely to be different tellings than when he gathered with other WWII vets in Washington, DC, on Veteran's Day in 2008. Gubrium and Holstein call their work "narrative ethnography" and describe it as "a method of procedure and analysis involving the close scrutiny of circumstances, their actors, and actions in the process of formulating and communicating accounts. This requires direct observation, with decided attention to story formation" (2009, 22).

Semiotics

Semiotics focuses on signs and symbols, basically anything that possesses information. Written and oral texts obviously make use of signs that convey information, but a sign could also be a red hat, a pierced tongue, or a bag of tamales in contexts where each conveys some meaning. For something to be a sign, there has to be a *signifier* (red hat) or something that carries the message and the *signified* or the concept that is conveyed (member of a Red Hat Society of older women). In semiotic analysis, the focus is on how signs create or evoke meaning in certain contexts. An integrated system of signs produces a *social code*. "Semiotics aims to uncover the dynamics beyond surface meanings or shallow descriptions and to articulate underlying implications" (Madison 2005, 63). For example, Silvia, an undergraduate student at Warren Wilson College, undertook a semiotic analysis of the kinds of student groups on campus. She did a series of interviews to get student perspectives on the kinds of groups, but much of her work consisted of observations of what people wore, their ornamentations, and interactional behavior. She became particularly intrigued with distinct ways in which different groups of students used particular signs and symbols to distinguish themselves from other groups and to communicate issues of identity with other students. Semiotics, therefore, is concerned not only with what a sign denotes or represents, but also with what the sign connotes or "means" in particular cultural contexts.

In looking at how signs interrelate to construct meaning, Roland Barthes and others have inquired into ideologies and systems of power in order to suggest ways in which certain signs get taken as "natural"—as the way things are or should be. For example, many from the United States assume that people in other parts of the world aspire to the American way of life. They perceive people in the "two-thirds world" as "poor" and sometimes as "lazy." These perceptions could be based, at least in part, on the ideology that economic growth is "progress" and "natural" if you work hard. Critics point out how colonial and neo-colonial histories have robbed many countries of their wealth and maintained patterns of inequity. Many of these critics, however, continue to focus on how to make others more like the US, as though it is the standard to emulate. The semiotic researcher might analyze the symbols and signs of a "good life" in various parts of the world, and relate them to ideologies within those cultural contexts.

Thematic Analysis

In thematic analysis, the researcher focuses analytical techniques on searching through the data for themes and patterns. One of the important aspects of this work is data coding. With data coded, you read through all the pieces of data coded in the same way and first try to figure out what is at the core of that code. Then you might look at all the data scraps coded the same way for one case and see how it changes or varies in relationship to other factors, for example across events or times. Finally, "you can explore how categorizations or thematic ideas represented by the codes vary from case to case, from setting to setting or from incident to incident" (Gibbs 2007, 48).

Grounded theory research uses a search for themes and patterns to build theory. This form of research has specific rules for coding with which you need to be familiar if undertaking grounded theory inquiry. Researchers who do not call their work "grounded theory," however, find many of the concepts and practices used by grounded theorists useful for their own work in thematic analysis. *Constant case comparison* is one such concept borrowed from grounded theory. If you practice constant case comparison, you take on the mindset of looking for how each of your cases vary in terms of such things as events, participants, settings, or word use. You might select and compare extreme cases, looking for aspects that stand out that you might not have noticed otherwise, or you might look for subtle differences in similar cases.

One way to help you make comparisons is to create tables in which you put cases—for example, in rows down the page and selected aspects you have coded across the top. In each corresponding cell, you would summarize the coded material, sometimes using parts of quotations, but keeping it short, at this point, focusing only on the main ideas. Comparing cells can begin to trigger questions about relationships of the aspects you have selected and send you back to your data or to making other kinds of comparison charts. Creating these charts is part of the analytical process; they are not meant to be included in your final paper although some version of them might be used if appropriate and particularly telling.

Making comparisons is an analytical step in identifying patterns within some theme. Looking for patterns tends to focus attention on unifying aspects of the culture or setting, on what people usually do, with whom they usually interact, etc. Thematic analysis should go beyond identifying the general or the norm. A strength of qualitative research is that it can help reveal underlying complexities. One of your tasks, therefore, is to be aware of the tensions that exist and where and why people differ from the norm. Sometimes your participants make this easy for you as they readily express their dissimilarities or argue with other participants. Other tensions or distinctions are less evident or even hidden to you because of your own assumptions, values, and perspectives. When doing fieldwork in the rural Caribbean, I assumed all was fine in the female-headed households that predominated until a teen-age research participant came to my house distraught because his father, whom he hadn't seen in years, appeared on his doorstep wanting financial assistance. Note in your reflexive journal when you feel jarred, confronted, or contradicted in the research process. Write about your perspectives and then write about others' perspectives. Once you note specific patterns, look through your data for contradictions. How do they get expressed? By whom? When? The remainder of this chapter describes more fully procedures for thematic analysis.

EARLY DATA ANALYSIS

Data analysis done simultaneously with data collection enables you to focus and shape the study as it proceeds. If you consistently reflect on your data, work to organize them, and try to discover what they have to tell you, your study will be more relevant and possibly more profound than if you view data analysis as a discrete step to be done after data collection. O'Reilly (2005, 187) gives an example of how she involved ongoing data analysis with data collection in her research on British migration to Spain:

> I noticed that when two British people meet there they tend to kiss each other on both cheeks, as the Spanish traditionally do. This had never been written in my field notes because I hadn't thought it important until I realised I had seen it happen a lot. I started to watch more closely and note down similar things. I became aware that it is just the British migrants who do this and not the tourists, and that

the migrants are more likely to do it when they are in the company of tourists. I then began to notice that in the company of tourists migrants would use the occasional Spanish word when talking to each other. This led me to thinking about the relationship between migrants and tourists, whereas until then I had focused more on the relationship between British and Spanish people. I thus began, during fieldwork, a closer analysis of migrants and tourists and their behaviour and attitudes towards each other that I would not have been able to do once I had left the field. I started to sort through the notes and data I had collected, assigning things to a new heading of "tourist/migrant relations," and discovered many new occurrences I had not noticed before.

Observations and connections such as those described by O'Reilly need to be made while still in the field. Writing memos to yourself, developing analytic files, applying rudimentary coding schemes, and writing monthly reports will help you begin to learn from, create new hunches or new questions, and manage the information you are receiving.

Memo Writing

By writing memos to yourself or keeping a reflective field log, you develop your thoughts; by getting your thoughts down as they occur, no matter how preliminary or in what form, you begin the analysis process. Memo writing also frees your mind for new thoughts and perspectives. "When I think of something," said graduate student Jackie, "I put it on a card. I might forget about the thought, but I won't lose it. It's there later on to help me think." Even as you become intimately familiar with your data, you can never be sure of what they will tell you until analysis and writing are complete. As you work with data, you must remain open to new perspectives, new thoughts. Gordon, another graduate student, stated,

> I have found that my analysis goes on even if I am not actually working with the data. Insights and new ways to look at the data arise while I am at work at other things. Probably the most productive places for these insights are on the long drive to class and during long, boring meetings when my mind is not actively engaged.

It is particularly important to capture these analytic thoughts when they occur. Keeping a recorder in the car can help, as can jotting down your thoughts wherever you happen to be, day or night. If you wait until the end to write, your work will not be as rich, thorough, and complex as it would have been otherwise. Recording only observations and interview notes in your field journal is not enough. As often and as soon as possible, reflect on your field notes so you can clarify and add to them. If you do not reflect on your fieldwork, what was clear to you in September will not necessarily be so in December. Writing helps you think about your work, and about new questions and connections. In addition, all this writing adds up—you will have a lot of thoughts already on paper when you begin working on the first draft of your manuscript. These comments and thoughts recorded as field journal entries or as memos are links across your data that find their way into analytic files.

Analytic Files

Analytic files (see Lofland and Lofland 1995) build as you collect data. You may begin with files organized by generic categories such as interview questions, people, and places. These files provide a way to keep track of useful information and thoughts. As your data and experience grow, you will create relevant specific files on the social processes under investigation, as well as on several other categories such as reflexivity, titles, thoughts for introductory and concluding chapters, and quotations from the literature.

Each of these specific files serves a distinct purpose. The reflexivity file, for example, is a place for you to record your observations, thoughts, and questions on how you, as researcher, and your research procedures interact with and influence research participants and vice versa. Given the bearing of your subjectivity and the nature of your interactions on the way you perceive your data, you cannot meaningfully separate the two (although you can forget their relationship). But by keeping track of your perspectives, feelings, and interactions, you will become attuned to the outlook that shapes your data analysis.

The title file contains your efforts to capture what your narrative may be about (Peshkin 1985). Although your research project has a stated central focus (per your research proposal), you do not really know what particular story, of the several possibilities, you will tell. Conjuring up titles as the data are being collected is a way of trying out different emphases, all of which are candidates for ultimately giving form to your data. The titles become a way of getting your mind clear about what you are doing, in an overall sense, although the immediate application may be to concentrate your data collecting as you pursue the implications of a particular focus. In short, your search for a title is an act of interpretation. Titles capture what you see as germane to your study; but as your awareness of the promise of your study changes, so do your titles.

Files related to introductions and conclusions direct you to two obvious aspects of every study—its beginning and its ending. Regardless of the particular name that you give to your introductory and concluding chapters, you frame your study in the former—providing necessary context, background, and conceptualization. You effect closure in the concluding chapter by summarizing, at the very least, and by explicating the meaning that you draw from your data as befits the points of your study even if this means raising more questions or illuminating multiple perspectives rather than providing answers. It is never too early to reflect on the beginning and ending of your work, much as the formal preparation of these chapters may seem a distant dream when you are caught up in collecting data. Ideally, the existence of these files alerts you to what you might otherwise miss in the course of your study; they stimulate you to notions that, like your titles, are candidates for inclusion in your forthcoming text. Until the writing is actually done, however, you will not know which will be the surviving notions.

The quotation file contains quotations from your reading that appear useful for one of the several roles that the relevant literature can play. Eventually, they will be sorted out among chapters, some as epigraphs: quotations placed at the heads of chapters because they provide the reader with a useful key to what the chapter contains. Other quotations will be the authoritative sprinklings that your elders provide as you find your way through the novel ground of your own data. Through resourceful use of quotations, you acknowledge that the world has not been born anew on your terrain. The quotation file, like other files, is meant to be a reminder that reading should always inspire the question: What, if anything, do these words say about my study?

Analytic files help you to store and organize your own thoughts and those of others. Data analysis is the process of organizing and storing data in light of your increasingly sophisticated judgments, that is, of the meaning-finding interpretations that you are learning to make about the shape of your study. Understanding that you are in a learning mode is most important; it tells you that you need not be all at once as accomplished as eventually you need to be to meet the challenges of data analysis. It reminds you that by each effort of data analysis, you enhance your capacity to further analyze.

Rudimentary Coding Schemes

> This experience lends entirely new meaning to the term "fat data." I can't even imagine reading everything I have, but I know I need to. And coding it? And all the while you're writing, events are still evolving in the community and you really can't ignore that, either. . . . So you really don't stop collecting data, do you? You just start coding and writing.
>
> (Pugach, Correspondence)

Marleen Pugach was still at her research site when she wrote this note, realizing her need to begin to organize the data she was acquiring. Sorting your data into analytic files is a place to start. Through doing so, you develop a rudimentary coding scheme.

As the process of naming and locating your data bits proceeds, your categories divide and subdivide. Learn to be content, however, with your early, simple coding schemes, knowing that with use they will become appropriately complex. In the early days of data collection, coding can help you to develop a more specific focus or more relevant questions. For example, interested in the role of school boards in small, rural communities, Cindy began a pilot study by observing meetings of one rural school board and interviewing its members. After fifteen hours of data collection, she reread and began to code all of the data she had gathered. In the process, she reconceptualized her problem statement:

> My initial problem statement was so broad it was difficult to work with. The process of coding and organizing my codes has helped to determine an approach to solidify a new problem statement that will lead me in a focused exploration of two major areas of school board control—financial and quality education.

Unlike a squirrel hoarding acorns for the winter, you should not keep collecting data for devouring later. Rather, examine your data periodically to insure that your acorns represent the variety or varieties desired, and that they are meaty nuggets, worthy of your effort.

Establishing the boundaries for your research may be continuously difficult. Social interaction does not occur in neat, isolated units. Gordon reflected on his work:

> I have felt right along that it is questionable whether I am really in control of this research. As I immerse myself in the analysis of my data, I begin to be sure that I am not. I constantly find myself heading off in new directions and it is an act of will to stick to my original (but revised) problem statement.

In order to complete any project, you must establish boundaries, but these boundary decisions are also an interpretive judgment based on your awareness of your data and their possibilities. Posting your problem statement or most recent working title above your workspace may help to remind you about the task ahead. Cindy used a computer banner program to print out her working title, which she taped to the wall over her desk. The banner guided her work whenever she lifted her head to ponder and reflect.

Monthly Reports

Throughout the data collection process, writing monthly field reports for yourself, for committee members, or for the funding agency is a way to examine systematically where you are and where you should consider going. Keep them short and to the point, so that they don't become a burden for you to write or for your readers to read. Headings such as those I call "The Three P's: Progress, Problems, and Plans," help you to review your work succinctly and plan realistically. In reflecting on both the research process and the data collected, you develop new questions, new hunches, and, sometimes, new ways of approaching the research. The reports also provide a way to communicate research progress to interested others, keeping them informed of the whats and hows and giving them a chance for input along the way.

Maintaining Some Semblance of Control

> When anthropologists, sociologists and others talk about the "richness" of field data, this can be another way of expressing the sheer volume and complexity of information they collect and store.
>
> (Dicks et al. 2005, 2)

By the time you're finished collecting data, expect to be overwhelmed with the sheer volume—notebooks, note cards, computer files, manila files, and documents—of data that has accumulated. You truly have acquired "fat data"; their sheer bulk is intimidating. Invariably, you will collect more data than you need.

The physical presence of so much data can lead you to procrastinate, rather than to face the task of focused analysis.

It may help to think of the amount of film that goes into a good half-hour documentary. Similar to documentary filmmaking, the methods of qualitative data collecting naturally lend themselves to excess. You collect more than you can use because you cannot define your study so precisely as to pursue a trim, narrowly defined line of inquiry. The open nature of qualitative inquiry means that you acquire even more data than you originally envisioned. You are left with the large task of selecting and sorting—a partly mechanical but mostly interpretative undertaking, because every time you decide to omit a data bit as irrelevant to your study or locate it somewhere you are making a judgment. Gordon reflects on his experience with sorting data:

> Sorting the data is actually less difficult than I feared, and it certainly is not worthy of the apprehension I suffered before getting started or the procrastination growing out of the apprehension, which has left me behind schedule. Before I began, the job seemed immense and endless. Once started, I found that it is not really one large task but more a series of small, discrete tasks. These tasks seem to be equal parts drudgery and intuition.

Dealing with fat data requires methodical organization. Keeping up with data organization during the collection process makes the bulk less intimidating and easier to manage, as Gordon further observes:

> Transcribe notes onto the computer after each interview and observation. This admonition has been prompted by my discovery that a fairly substantial part of my data is not in readily usable form. I have had to go back after three months and type my notes because I find it hard to use data that I cannot read easily. Drudgery. . . .

Keeping up with data involves transcribing interviews and observation notes to computer files, making analytic files, writing memos to yourself, and developing preliminary coding schemes.

At some point, you stop collecting data, or at least stop focusing on data collection. Knowing when to end this phase is difficult. It may be that you have exhausted all sources on the topic—that there are no new situations to observe, no new people to interview, no new documents to read. Such situations are rare. Perhaps you stop collecting data because you have reached theoretical saturation (Glaser and Strauss 1967). This means that successive examination of sources yields redundancy and that the data you have seem complete and integrated. Recognizing theoretical saturation can be tricky, however. It may be, for example, that you hear the same thing from all of your informants because your selection of interviewees is too limited or too small to get discrepant views. Often, data collection ends through less than ideal conditions—the money runs out or deadlines loom large. Try to make research plans that do not completely exhaust your money, time, or energy, so that you can obtain a sense of complete and integrated data.

LATER DATA ANALYSIS: ENTERING THE CODE MINES

In the early days of data collection, stories abound. Struck by the stories, you tell them and repeat them. You may sometimes even allow them to assume an importance beyond their worth to the purposes of the project. Making sense of the stories as a whole comes harder. You do not have to stop telling stories, but in thematic analysis you must make connections among the stories: What is being illuminated? How do the stories connect? What themes and patterns give shape to your data? Coding helps answer these questions.

When most of the data are collected, the time has come to devote attention to analytic coding. Although you may have already developed a coding scheme of sorts, you must now focus on classifying and categorizing. You are ready to enter "the code mines." The work is part tedium and part exhilaration as it renders form and possible meaning to the piles of words before you.

Marleen's words (Correspondence, 3 May 1994) portray the somewhat ambivalent psychological ambience that accompanies entering the code mines:

> I'm about to finish the first set of teacher transcripts and begin with the students. This will probably mean several new codes . . . since it is a new group. I hope the codebook can stand the pressure. One of the hardest things is accepting that doing the coding is a months-long proposition. When my mother asks me if I'm done yet, I know she doesn't have a clue . . .

"Coding is how you define what the data you are analyzing are about" (Gibbs 2007, 38). It is a progressive process of sorting and defining and defining and sorting those scraps of collected data (i.e., observation notes, interview transcripts, memos, documents, and notes from relevant literature) that are applicable to your research purpose. By putting pieces that exemplify the same theoretical or descriptive idea together into data clumps, you begin to create a thematic organizational framework.

The word *coding* is confusing to some, often because they first became familiar with the term and its use in quantitative research, where open-ended responses tend to be categorized with the purpose of counting. As a result, for example, the quantitative researcher can claim, "Sixty-three percent of the parents worried about issues of safety, but only 12 percent believed that higher taxes should be part of the solution." Counting is not a primary goal of qualitative researchers. Qualitative researchers code to discern themes, patterns, processes, and to make comparisons and build theoretical explanations.

Some qualitative researchers prefer the terms *index* or *categorize* rather than *coding*. In a sense, qualitative researchers are "indexing" all their notes and transcripts, similarly to the way publishers index books. I'm not sure it matters which word to use, as long as you realize that coding in qualitative research is for different purposes than in quantitative work.

Begin by trying to code (or index) a transcript or field observation line by line. As much as you try to set aside the theoretical frameworks that guide your research, those perspectives tend to find their way into the codes you choose. That is to be expected. What you want to avoid is imposing an a priori set of codes on your data. Line-by-line coding helps to immerse you in the data and discover what concepts they have to offer. As you read line by line, jotting possible codes in the margin, try to abstract your code words, removing them slightly from the data. For example, a line in your field notes that reads, "Ms. Wilson asked the students to sit in their seats and to stop talking. She then took her seat and sat there quietly for at least three minutes before the room quieted," could be coded as "controlling students" or a number of other codes depending upon research purposes. The point is that your code is a category of activity of which the piece coded is an example.

In qualitative research coding, you eventually want to show relationships between things. To help you figure out what to code and how, ask yourself questions about your data that would lead to categorizing relationships among data (Gibbs 2007, 75): Are there different types of, causes of, consequences of, attitudes toward, strategies for, and so forth. In the example above, Ms. Wilson's request and waiting was construed as a strategy for controlling students. Coding this line would then lead you to look for other strategies used as well. While you are reading and coding, also look for particular words used by participants to talk about their world. Some of these words become useful codes as well, referred to as "in vivo" codes.

Arranging your codes in hierarchies is part of the analysis process, so play with your codes. Can you arrange them into categories and subcategories? Do you see places where several codes can be combined? Are there places where other codes should be pulled apart into two or more codes? Try out your new coding scheme on the same document and see how it works, then try it on another transcript and some observation notes. What new codes are added? Go back and forth like this until you are no longer adding substantially more codes, realizing that as you continue to code, you will most likely add more—sending you back to look for other expressions of that code in previous parts of your text.

As a result of coding your data, you are creating a framework of relational categories for your data. For example, you begin to see differing perceived consequences of a required reading program on teachers' interactions with students. You may begin to see patterns, noticing, for example that more recent teachers reacted to the reading program differently than teachers who had been at the school for a number of years. As you work with clumping the codes, you begin to see ways in which things that you hadn't put together before may fit together.

In addition to working to analyze relationships among all your coded data, you also need to be cognizant of what was not said or demonstrated in some way. What kinds of things appeared taken for granted or were not discussed? Using differing theoretical arguments, can you raise questions about why some topics or perspectives (e.g., race, gender, class) might be ignored? As Gibbs (2007, 145) states:

> There are many examples of poor student work—and published work—that . . . are simply organized as a description or summary of each of the main themes found in the data. . . . You need to go beyond this. Re-examine the data and find phenomena that are not necessarily immediately obvious from what is being said or done.

Coding and organizing data is an analytical step, but not the end-all to data analysis. Your codes are the starting point from which you go on to "look for patterns, make comparisons, produce explanations and build models" (Gibbs 2007, 78).

Diane is a graduate student who has been interviewing blind men and women who have graduated from a post-secondary residential program that provides rehabilitation training as well as academic remediation for transition into independent adult living, including employment and/or higher education. Diane, also blind, is particularly interested in the role of hope in the experiences of blind students and in the ways in which hope gets fostered, expressed, and used. Her literature review led her to a theory on hope and its application to rehabilitation along with a scale that lists factors and dispositions associated with hope. Diane considered using this theory as a framework for analyzing her data, but then decided to do a thematic analysis of the interview transcripts as a first step and to then augment her discussion with aspects of the hope theory as it fit the story that grew out of her data.

Her preliminary coding, shown in Exhibit 7.1, led her to identify five major themes or codes, each with a number of subthemes or subcodes. As Diane works

---

Evolving Codes and Subcodes in a Study of Hope in Students Who Are Blind

1. Navigating Change and Challenges
   a. Developing self concept
   b. Finding and exploring options
   c. Challenging external expectations (attitudes of family, peers, society)

2. Communicating Needs
   a. Asking questions
   b. Negotiating relationships
   c. Filtering input (figuring out what is and is not needed)

3. Self-Directing
   a. Making decisions
   b. Initiating opportunities
   c. Educating others about one's abilities and needs (self-advocating)

4. Establishing Independence
   a. Cultivating skills
   b. Finding employment
   c. Managing time

5. Gaining Confidence
   a. Accessing resources
   b. Influence of others
   c. Contributing to others

EXHIBIT 7.1   Evolving Codes and Subcodes

through each major clump of data, she will, most likely, relocate some data scraps under other major headings. Writing is a continuation of the coding process as codes get merged, more finely divided, or relocated to other places. Neither the assignment of a code nor the code name itself is inviolable; rather you rename and reassign data as you see fit to help you organize and make sense of the data. After all, except when working with a team of researchers, the codes are personal inventions in the interest of facilitating understanding.

To facilitate developing and working with a coding scheme, make a codebook. Assign each major code its own number and page. Below the major code, list the number assigned to the subcode, the subcode name, and an explanation of the subcode. Writing the explanation will help to keep you from what Gibbs (2007) refers to as "definitional drift," in which the material you code earlier on is slightly different in meaning from the material you code at a different time. For example, in my work with young people in Oaxaca, "resisting" was one of my codes. Early on, I defined "resisting" as forms of speech or actions that demonstrate disagreement with governmental rules. As my work progressed, "resistance" became more complex and I began to see it tightly linked with a category I called "maintaining indigenous autonomy."

Start the codebook soon after beginning to collect data so that it will reflect the emerging, evolving structure of your manuscript. It is highly personal, meant to fit you; it need not be useful or clear to anyone else. Although there may be common features and a common intent to everyone's data analysis process, it remains, in the end, an idiosyncratic enterprise. The proof of your coding scheme is, literally, in the pudding of your manuscript. The sense your manuscript makes, how well it reads, depends, in large part, on your analytic framework. Because coding is an evolving process, it is advisable in the early stages to use a pencil to mark both data scraps and the codebook. Be overgenerous in judging what is important; you do not want to foreclose any opportunity to learn from the field by prematurely settling on what is or is not relevant to you. In marking sections and giving them a name, you make judgments about which items are related and therefore belong under the same major code. The same subcode (such as anxiety, or theory, or ethics, in the codebook for this book, for example) may appear under several major codes. This indication of themes that may run throughout the work alerts you to look for their presence or absence under other major headings.

When you have collected and coded all of your data scraps, keep your codebook in front of you and proceed to the next phase of data analysis: arranging your major code clumps into a "logical" order by asking yourself which clumps, or parts of clumps, belong together in the final code arrangement for your manuscript. Through such analysis, you sort out what you have learned so that you can concentrate on writing up your data.

The coding, categorizing, and theme-searching process is not as mechanical as the previous description may make it appear. Rather, it is a time when you think with your data, reflecting upon what you have learned, making new connections and gaining new insights, and imagining how the final write-up will appear. Let's hear from Marleen (Correspondence, 3 May 1994) again:

> I now have a regulation codebook complete with several major codes and sub-codes . . . and I see already, in the process of coding, how they stretch out and then collapse and then multiply again as you complete more and more of the analysis. I also realize that you never really are in a pure mode of coding. It's a very strange dynamic. You find yourself in the midst of what seems to be a very technical process—drawing brackets, locating the number for the subcode, moving through the pages, and then you find yourself needing to write down some narrative to anchor a set of thoughts you didn't have before, or to pin down a new way of thinking about something. A good example for me is how the teachers talk about their own language learning capacity . . . these dialogues suddenly seemed much more important than I ever would have imagined when I was in Havens (the now official pseudonym). And they have their own rhythm, a rhythm I didn't know was there before. This is when I know things are going well.

The art of data transformation is in combining the more mundane organizational tasks with insight and thoughtful interpretations.

After hours of fieldwork, Andrea undertook the coding/analysis process for the first time and reflected upon it here. In her descriptive portrayals, you may see your own struggles, achievements, and realizations.

> I approached my first attempt at coding with the vivid analogy of being in "the code mines" in mind. Beginning the process was indeed like preparing to descend into a mineshaft. The thought of dropping into the dark, cold abyss of interviews and countless reflections made me shrink from the task. Perhaps, in the lightless confusion of data, I would not be able to sort out any meaning to it all. Perhaps, after seven months of collection, I would find no gold nuggets of wisdom in the walls of my code mines. Perhaps, like the miner, I needed to better prepare myself for entering the bowels of my notebooks and field logs.
>
> Hence I consciously entered into a series of avoidance tactics that kept me in the light of day as yet another week flew by. I finished transcribing my last three tapes. I backed up my disk. I reorganized my files. I considered reflecting more on my previous reflections. I even flipped through my Word Perfect manual, on the pretense that I might find an ingenious way to manage my codes, someday. I kept a fire going in the wood stove to ward off the cold I constantly felt in my bones.
>
> Finally, the day came. I could put it off no longer; indeed, I was dreadfully remiss in waiting so long. I approached my first-semester notebook of interviews with images of Tolkien's Bilbo Baggins approaching the cave of Gollum. I must retrieve the precious ring, or never return to class and Professor Gandolf. I laid open my first interview next to my new, brightly colored coding notebook.
>
> Anticipation far exceeds the event in the exploration of the unknown. Three pages of codes flowed from my pen from the first interview. They were familiar words, words repeated on paper, on tape, and in my mind throughout my whole study. Like the Hobbit with his ring on, I disappeared into my interviews for hours.

After the initial showering of codes, each interview added fewer to my list. That was comforting. I had a sense that the list would be manageable. The second interview added only one page of new codes, the third a half page. After that, each interview produced one new code and usually elaboration or clarification on some previous codes. Before I was done, the maze of words began organizing themselves in my mind. I flipped to a clean page and began jotting down umbrella phrases to collect subcodes under.

I am no longer a Pennsylvania coal miner dreading my life's work. I am no longer the Hobbit with but one precious ring. Today I am Smog the dragon sitting upon a mountain of jewels, stolen from my interviews. They lay, however, disheveled beneath me and hard to account for. So today my task is to organize my treasures that I might know what I have before I go on. The task is a bit easier because I made some notes as I was coding. I began clumping my codes into broader categories. They fall into neat piles, with only a few exceptions. These I place temporarily until I can consult with my fellow researchers. So ends, for me, the dreaded imagery of life-threatening mine shafts. I have much real work ahead, but I have dealt with the anxiety of passing the test.

DISPLAYING DATA

Miles and Huberman (1994) created a comprehensive text on using data display in the analysis of qualitative work. They describe data display as "an organized assembly of information that permits conclusion drawing and action taking." Making an analogy to "you are what you eat," they claim, "you know what you display" (Miles and Huberman 1994, 11). Matrices, graphs, flowcharts, and other sorts of visual representations assist in making meaning of data, as well as in exposing the gaps or the areas where more data are needed. Data display can be, therefore, another on-going feature of qualitative inquiry. You may find visual representations useful in developing the research statement, in collecting and analyzing data, or in presenting aspects of the study.

As you begin to conceive your research by working on the research statement and plans for data collection, data displays help you to identify the elements of your study. Expect the displays to change as you learn more. After data collection has begun, urge Miles and Huberman (1994), create diagrams that reflect some, risk; that is, use one-directional arrows that indicate potential cause and effect. Doing so forces you to begin to theorize about the social phenomenon under study. Figure 7.1 is an example of a thematic data display by Penny Bishop (1998, 171). She created the diagram as a way to help her understand and present the major concepts evolving through her inquiry into effective partner team teaching in middle schools.

After becoming absorbed in using a computer graphics program to display her work, Andrea teased another student about her 61 pages of notes: "Want me to reduce it to one good graph?" Data display provides the skeleton of your work. Just as observing Earth from a satellite allows you to see the overall pattern of geologic structures and human adaptations to these structures, data displays help you to see the overall patterns in your research without getting lost in the details.

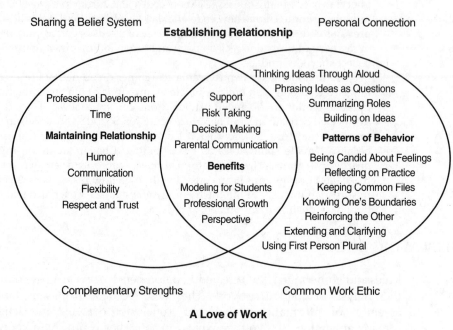

FIGURE 7.1   The Relational Work of Partner Teaming

Source: From Bishop, P. 1998. *Portraits of Partnership: The Relational Work of Effective Middle Level Partner Teachers.* Unpublished doctoral dissertation (p. 171), University of Vermont, Burlington.

When thinking about displaying your data, experiment with a variety of forms. Tables provide detail, but bar and line graphs often portray patterns more vividly. If you are comparing two or more groups over time, line graphs are particularly useful. Matrices that use symbols such as + and 0 rather than numbers can aid in uncovering patterns. For example, if investigating perceived constraints to effective education in six rural schools, you might, after a round of interviews, develop a table similar to Table 7.1.

With the table before you, you would look for patterns and begin to form some hunches about what was going on, using your knowledge of each rural town and school. For example, you would notice that schools 2, 3, and 5 all perceive their tax base as a problem, but not their communication between school and community. Schools 1, 4, and 6 are just the opposite. Returning to your data, you would try to figure out possible explanations. Although the communities are similar in size, you would note that the communities that host schools 1, 4, and 6 have a sizable proportion of nonnatives who have moved to the area in recent years. The communities that host schools 2, 3, and 5 do not. You might then hypothesize that the newcomers are bringing more money into the towns and, along with it, strife in school governance decisions. In reflecting on possible reasons for the pattern of

TABLE 7.1 A Matrix Example of Constraints to Effective Education in Six Rural Schools

SCHOOL	TAX BASE	COMMUNICATION WITH COMMUNITY	STATE POLICY	ACCESS TO INFORMATION	ACCESS TO EXPERTS
1	0	+	+	0	0
2	+	0	+	+	+
3	+	0	+	0	0
4	0	+	+	+	+
5	+	0	+	+	+
6	0	+	+	+	+

Key: + = perceived as a constraint by school personnel

0 = not perceived as a constraint by school personnel

responses in the categories of access to information and access to experts, you might wonder whether distance from the state's largest city makes a difference. Developing a new matrix, you would then map your hunches as demonstrated in Table 7.2. Such matrices-forming work serves to suggest both new questions and people or sites for investigation, as well as to make sense of the data collected.

Borrowing from the natural sciences, cognitive anthropologists use taxonomies to assist in displaying social phenomena. In this approach, the researcher seeks to understand how others classify "cognitive domains," or salient aspects of the world. Structured interviews are used to elicit individual classificatory schemes. Each category is probed for subcategories and sub-subcategories until the interviewee's categorization scheme is fully mapped. For example, Janet Davis (1988) investigated eighth graders for categories of the cognitive domain she called "things kids do at school." Through interviewing, she found that major categories included picking on other kids, sitting in classes, being nice to teachers, and acting up. Davis went on to investigate subcategories, such as all the ways that kids are "nice to teachers." She then probed for sub-subcategories such as how a

TABLE 7.2 A Matrix Example of Data Patterns and Researcher Hunches Regarding Constraints to Effective Education in Six Rural Schools

SCHOOL	TAX BASE	COMMUNICATION WITH COMMUNITY	ACCESS TO INFORMATION	ACCESS TO EXPERTS
native/near city (3)	+	0	0	0
native/not near city (2, 5)	+	0	+	+
mixed/near city (1)	0	+	0	0
mixed/not near city (4, 6)	0	+	+	+

Key: + = perceived as a constraint by school personnel

0 = not perceived as a constraint by school personnel

Take tests
Sit in classes
Be nice to teachers: Do what you're told
                               Turn in assignments
                               Talk nice, use good grammar
                               Don't talk out of turn
                               Don't talk during lectures
                               Try to become a pet (get in with teacher)
                               Do extra stuff
                                   Volunteer
                                   Sweep floor
                                   Kiss their butts

EXHIBIT 7.2   Partial Taxonomy of the Domain "Things Kids Do at School"

student becomes a teacher's pet. Exhibit 7.2 is extracted from Davis's taxonomic chart of the domain of "things kids do at school" (Davis 1988, 115–116). Taxonomic charts help researchers to see what they know and don't know about a particular cognitive domain.

A student at the University of Vermont investigated the types of undergraduates enrolled there as defined and categorized by undergraduates. Although categories were not necessarily mutually exclusive, the interviewer found that, according to interviewees, there were preps, punkers, out-of-staters, Vermonters, granolas, squids, nerds, smarts, intelligents, and jocks. Many of these categories had subcategories such as both normal and progressive granolas or positive and negative jocks. Such information lends itself to a taxonomic chart that can then be used as a type of guide for discussion of the cognitive domain.

Mathematics also can be useful in determining patterns. Regarding the use of mathematics in anthropology, Agar (1980, 132) comments:

> Anthropologists, more than other social scientists, have mathophobia. One of my favorite wisecracks is to define mathematical anthropology as what happens when anthropologists number their pages. . . . Most of the points I need to make are made with simple frequency distributions. If that is all you need, stop there. . . . If you choose not to use statistical procedures in your systematic testing, it should be because you know enough about them to know they are inappropriate, not because the very thought causes you to break out in a rash.

Simple frequency counts can help to identify patterns. For example, imagine that you have been inquiring into the attitudes of young people toward agriculture in the rural Caribbean. Through interviews with eighty-five persons, including twenty-five employed in town, fifty working in agriculture, and ten living in rural areas but not working in agriculture, you receive mixed answers to the question "How do young people feel about working land?" Your first frequency distribution

TABLE 7.3   Frequency Distribution of Perceived Attitudes Toward Working the Land

	POSITIVE ATTITUDES	NEGATIVE ATTITUDES
Town employees	4	21
Agricultural workers	21	29
Other rural people	0	10

(represented by Table 7.3) suggests that young people are not very interested in doing agricultural work. Yet, by listening to and rereading the interviews, you form the hunch that the attitudes are linked to land tenure. You go back to your interviews and rework the frequency counts, taking into account the relationship of each interviewee to the land. This time your frequency distribution demonstrates a definite pattern in the relationship between attitudes toward doing agricultural work and land tenure (see Table 7.4). The numbers assist in shaping a more specific hypothesis about attitudes toward farming.

USING COMPUTERS

Qualitative researchers have used computers primarily as a tool to assist in collecting, managing, sorting, and presenting data. Increasingly, however, they are realizing ways in which computers provide new sources of data as well as exciting and powerful ways to share studies. This section includes a brief overview of computer use in qualitative research and makes cursory introductions to some of the software that assist in working with qualitative data.

An Overview Of Computer Use

Computers revolutionized the handling of quantitative data. Because qualitative researchers work with words and without discreet variables, they initially found it difficult to use technology efficiently in applications other than word processing.

TABLE 7.4   Frequency Distribution of Perceived Attitudes Toward Working the Land by Dominant Land Tenure Situation of Interviewee

	POSITIVE ATTITUDES	NEGATIVE ATTITUDES
No land worked	0	25
Agricultural laborer	0	13
Works family land	5	5
Shares crop/rent	2	17
Works land rent-free	10	0
Works own land	8	0

As computers became more pervasive in our lives, and more usable through the development of software, more qualitative researchers regularly look to computers to assist in the research process.

Computers can play a role in almost every aspect of qualitative research, even at the initial, participant selection stage. Penny used electronic mail, or email, at the beginning of her work to consult a national panel of expert practitioners in order to develop a profile of effective middle-level partner teams. She went on to make initial contact with several of her research participants using email as well. The use of email not only facilitated the process, but also provided written documentation of the communication, something telephone use would not have done. Email can expedite communication between researcher and others throughout the research process.

Computers can assist in keeping a record of fieldwork activities. Forms can be developed for recording data collection dates, sites, times, and people interviewed or observed (see Table 7.5). In this way, an account is kept not only of progress in data collection, but also of gaps in data collection since one can easily see where and with whom time is spent. As with manual documentation, the researcher needs to take care in storing data and protecting the anonymity of participants. The computer makes it easy to change real names to pseudonyms wherever they occur within a file, and, through using password access protection on your computer, you can further assure confidentiality.

Computers can be used systematically to record field notes, interview transcripts, and observation notes. Some researchers carry their laptop or notebook computers into the field and eliminate taking observation and even interview notes by hand. The process of editing and expanding upon hastily typed notes or of transcribing interviews from tapes into the computer familiarizes researchers with the data and enables them to record new questions, thoughts, and hunches in files labeled as such. Because the computer forces the organization of data, it provides occasion for constant reflection. The data stored in computer files are easy to access for preliminary analysis that can further guide data collection. The concreteness and specificity necessary for computer use require researchers to be clear and explicit about their decisions, responding, in part to urgings by Miles and Huberman (1994) and others that qualitative researchers delineate their analytic

TABLE 7.5 Sample Form for Keeping Interview Records

DATE NUMBER	DATE INTERVIEWED	INTERVIEWEE	TRANSCRIBED	TIME	ROLE	SUBJECT	NOTE
18	4/8/09	C. Perez	4/10/09	1.5	teacher	Math	—
19	4/9/09	D. Brown	4/10/09	.5	admin.	—	late; not completed
20	4/9/09	M. Levine	4/20/09	1.0	teacher	history	—

methods. Computer use can therefore help to demystify qualitative analysis and contribute to its accountability.

Performing the tasks involved in data analysis is easier with data recorded on computer files than it is with data recorded through manual means. Computers can assist in sorting, referencing, counting, coding, and displaying data. Various types of programs, including word processors, database managers, graphics, spreadsheets, and qualitative software, can be used. Beginning researchers should use caution, however, in using the quantitative facilities of computers inappropriately because computers make it nearly effortless to count. For example, one could easily compare how many times a particular word appeared in the interviews of two separate groups. This might appear interesting, but it may not be particularly meaningful. Exceptions exist, of course. Word counts are sometimes useful in qualitative inquiry. For example, in a study where parents were asked to describe their children, the researchers counted the number of times various descriptors were used and sorted them by gender of the parent (Ryan and Weisner 1996, 777). Mothers were more likely than fathers to use words like friends, creative, or honest, while fathers were more likely to use words like good, lucky, student, or independent. This led the researchers to posit some tentative hypotheses regarding mother's and father's concerns for interpersonal versus individualistic or achievement-oriented attributes.

Without dispute, computers make the writing and rewriting process easier. Excerpts from files in which data have been recorded or analyzed can be inserted into the report without having to retype long sections. Computers are also allowing researchers to think about representation of their data through hypertext and hypermedia. With these technologies, "readers" are able to interact with text, data, and applicable literature, moving as they desire from narrative to field notes to audio reproduction of an interview to images to methodological notes. By the click of a button, the reader chooses a unique path through the research.

Computer Software

Generally referred to as CAQDAS, or computer-assisted qualitative data analysis software, programs were originally developed to help researchers code their data and then easily retrieve chunks of data by codes. Since these early CAQDAS programs, many others have been developed that moved beyond simple coding and retrieving procedures. Despite the powerful assistance that CAQDAS can be, the programs remain tools. Some people unfamiliar with CAQDAS programs think that the right software will be able to pull out major themes or develop and apply research codes to their data. This is not the case—the researcher remains the decision maker and interpreter. He or she needs to be intimate with the data in order to know what to ask the software to do.

What can CAQDAS programs help you do? They can provide assistance in "searching, marking up, linking, and reorganizing the data, and representing and storing your own reflections, ideas, and theorizing" (Weitzman 2000, 806). The computerized speed allows the researcher to play with data, sorting and trying out hunches to a much greater degree than manually possible. Analysis programs also provide clear audit trails that may be seen as contributing to the trustworthiness of the analyses. Some assert that analysis programs encourage greater rigor because they easily show negative cases that might be ignored otherwise (Seale 2002). As with conducting an interview or taking field notes, however, the effectiveness of computerized programs depends upon the skill of the human being in front of the machine.

Weitzman (2000) classifies programs that can assist in qualitative data analysis by their functions, as summarized below:

TEXT RETRIEVERS
These kinds of programs allow you to do a variety of things, but in particular, you can search for words or phrases or a combination of several words within some specified distance. You can then collate the various passages into files for further analysis. This categorization of data tends to be referred to as *coding* or as *indexing*.

TEXT-BASED MANAGERS
These are database programs that are "good at holding text, together with information about it, and allowing you to quickly organize and sort your data in a variety of ways and retrieve it according to different criteria" (Weitzman 2000, 808). Seale (2002, 655) provides the example of comparing statements made by men to those of women about satisfaction with the quality of health care for various symptoms. These programs make easy the development of matrices that can show statistical analyses. Text-based manager programs include askSam, Folio Views, Idealist, and others.

CODE AND RETRIEVE PROGRAMS
These programs tend to be developed by qualitative researchers particularly for qualitative data analysis. In general, they support the application of codes to text. Then the program will retrieve and compile data according to codes. Most programs allow for various kinds of Boolean searches ("and", "or", and "not"). For example, in a study on migration, a researcher may have applied codes such as "working in cities," "working in agriculture," "planning to stay in host community fewer than two years," "planning to stay in host community at least five years," and "possessing work visa." One could then search for all instances of the codes "working in a city" *and* "planning to stay fewer than two years," and *not* "possessing work visa" and then compare that data with other configurations, looking for similarities and differences. Some code and retrieve programs include HyperQual, QUALPRO, and Data Collector.

CODE-BASED THEORY BUILDERS
These programs are like the code and retrieve programs in that they do these functions, but they also support theory building. Generally, they are able to graphically represent coding structures and patterns, demonstrating relations

among codes and creating hierarchies of classifiers. Some have extensive hypertext link features. Examples of code-based theory building programs include AQUAD, Atlas/ti, HyperRESEARCH, and QSR NVivo.

CONCEPTUAL NETWORK BUILDERS
These programs assist in building theory through the development and representation of network displays that show relationships among concepts.

Because computers make it easy to store, sort, retrieve, and display data, some researchers have begun to investigate hypermedia technology that allows both researcher and "reader" to move between different kinds of media, different times in the research process, different voices, and different presentations (Dicks et al. 2005). Through hypermedia technology, you could, for example, provide access to interview transcripts, newspaper clippings, minutes of meetings, photographs, audiotapes and videos of interviews, etc. Although ethical issues of confidentiality abound, hypermedia allows the creation of a "text" that can be accessed and interpreted in multiple ways, producing a very different representation of research than the linear text. Obviously, as computer technology evolves, the possible uses in qualitative research expand.

Should you use CAQDAS in your research? "Of course, you don't have to use software at all," states Gibbs (2007, 40) in his useful text *Analyzing Qualitative Data*. He reminds us that, "For most of the last century, those undertaking qualitative analysis did not or could not use software. Most of the classic studies using qualitative research were undertaken without electronic assistance" (40). If you are doing a large project with lots of interviewees and want to analyze thematically, then CAQDAS would probably be useful. If doing oral history with a few respondents, or creatively representing data (see Chapter 9), a code and retrieve program would most likely not be useful at all. You need to decide what it is that you want a program to help you do and then figure out if it's worth the time learning how to use the program and the investment in procuring it. Articles and books will help you decide, as well as computer web searches. Exhibit 7.3 provides some starting places.

Some argue that the whole process of coding and fragmenting data, which CAQDAS assists researchers to do, reflects "an implicit assumption that data reduction and aggregation lie at the heart of the task" and leads to a "quasi-positivist version of qualitative data analysis" (Dicks et al. 2005, 13). The way you choose to analyze your data needs to fit with your research questions, sets of data, and theoretical predispositions. Seeking themes and patterns or developing theory, modes of analysis for which CAQDAS are often useful, are neither the only nor necessarily the appropriate approaches.

In summary, the computer is a tool that can help make the researcher's work less tedious, more accurate, faster, and more thorough. It does not, however, think for the researcher. The researcher decides what to enter into the computer, what to ask it to do, and how to use the results of the computer's mechanical manipulations. The products of computer-assisted analysis are only as good as the data, the thinking, and the level of care that went into them.

www.atlasti.com	ATLAS.ti	for texts, photographs, video, and audio data
www.qsrinternational.com	NVivo	for text-based data
www.qualisresearch.com	Ethnograph	for text-based data
www.researchware.com	HyperRESEARCH; HyperTRANSCRIBE	for texts, graphics, audio and video data for transcribing audio or video computer files
www.code-a-text.co.uk	C-I-SAID	for texts, audio, and video data

You can try out many programs by going to websites and downloading a demonstration file. This is by no means an exhaustive list, however. Scolari, a division of Sage Publications, makes available a range of research methods software. An easy way to find out about other programs and to figure out what program may best fit your needs is to go to a qualitative discussion group site and ask. Try QUALRS-L@LISTSERV.UGA.EDU, hosted by the University of Georgia, with more than 1,700 subscribers.

EXHIBIT 7.3   Qualitative Data Analysis Software Web Sites.

MAKING CONNECTIONS

> If you can't explain your theory to a bartender, it's probably no good.
> (Astrophysicist Ernest Rutherford quoted in Roorbach 1998, 53).

Qualitative researchers use many techniques (such as coding, data displays, and computer programs) to help organize, classify, and find themes in their data, but they still must find ways to make connections that are ultimately meaningful to themselves and the reader. Wolcott (1994) discusses *description, analysis,* and *interpretation* as three means of data transformation, or of moving from organization to meaning. Description involves staying close to data as originally recorded. You draw heavily on field notes and interview transcripts, allowing the data to somewhat "speak for themselves" (10). This approach answers the question, "What is going on here?" (12) and the narratives of descriptive analysis often "move in and out like zoom lenses" (17), selecting and portraying details that resonate with the study's purposes.

Furney (1997) researched the implementation of special education reform in several elementary public schools. She includes descriptions throughout her text as one means to convey the findings in her cross-case analysis. The following example is from observations of Instructional Support Team (IST) meetings (Furney 1997, 97):

> Balancing their lunch trays on their knees (somehow that cafeteria smell of hot dogs, applesauce, and lukewarm milk never changes in schools), Andy and Danielle describe the positive things that have happened for Kevin over the last week. They tell us about the points he's earned for using good language, his recent triumph over a classmate in a computer game, and how they and Kevin resolved an issue on the playground. Kevin describes his recent trip to the Woolworth store in town where he and his friend George perused the aisles looking for ways that Kevin could spend the money he has been earning restocking the soda machines in the teacher's room at school.

Furney's narrative includes carefully chosen details to place the reader in the context of an IST meeting in one of the schools.

Wolcott (1994) describes *analysis* as a second category of data transformation. Analysis, according to Wolcott, is the identification of key factors in the study and the relationships among them. This method typically extends description in a systematic manner. It entails identifying essential features and the ways in which the features interact. Detailed coding schemes, data displays, comparisons to a standard, and other means of identifying patterned regularities are all useful in analysis. Note that the use of the term *analysis* is a bit confusing here since researchers (myself included) often refer to description, finding patterns, and interpretation as data *analysis,* rather than data transformation. Nonetheless, Wolcott's (1994) discussion is useful, and I recommend his text *Transforming Qualitative Data: Description, Analysis, and Interpretation.*

Furney's (1997, 142) study provides many examples of analysis (as described by Wolcott) throughout the text:

> The evolution of the Instructional Support Teams (ISTs) in the three schools raises some interesting points. On the one hand, the three principals spoke during the original and follow-up interviews about the positive aspects of naturally occurring collaborative structures that appeared to lessen the need for the more formal IST structure. On the other hand, they viewed the somewhat more formalized versions of their ISTs that had evolved over time as being necessary and generally positive.

This consideration of the principals' views of instructional support teams moves away from description toward identification of patterns or trends in the data.

Interpretation is Wolcott's (1994) third means of data transformation. He notes that interpretation occurs when the researcher "transcends factual data and cautious analysis and begins to probe into what is to be made of them" (36). He discusses several strategies for data interpretation, including extending the analysis, using theory to provide structure, connecting with personal experience, and exploring alternative means of presenting data.

Once more, Furney's (1997, 174-175) research provides an example of this mode of data transformation:

> In brief then, the schools in this study of Act 230 have helped to confirm my belief that caring for students should constitute the central purpose of education and guide its efforts to change. . . . In placing students at the center of the agenda for school reform, a host of related changes become apparent. The challenge to care for students implies an agenda to promote social justice and deal with issues of diversity. . . . Placing care at the center of a school also seems to require the establishment of a form of leadership that is both visionary and participatory, and creates a sense of shared responsibility and an openness to change.

In this example, Furney moves beyond description and analysis to probe into the framework of caring. As she asserts the role of caring as the central purpose of education, she presents an interpretation of her findings.

Notice in the above examples that Furney kept her comments linked to the schools in her study. Much has been written about the inability of using qualitative research for generalizations beyond the group or settings studied. This includes your need to be careful to not generalize to others outside your study but of the same ethnic, age, gender, or sexual orientation group as those in your study. Perhaps your study included interviews and observations with ten white teachers and ten African American teachers and through data analysis, you uncovered different patterns in these teachers perceptions of their experiences that followed skin-color lines. As a result of your work, you can propose hypotheses about what might be happening for a larger population, but you may not claim that "White teachers tend to experience x, while African American teachers experience y." You can say, however, that such and such were the patterns in your study. Make clear, however, the population from which you are making your claims and be as specific as possible. To change "three out of ten" to "33 percent" is neither meaningful nor appropriate for qualitative work. Remember that your purpose is that of elucidating the range of possibilities and of transforming your data into a useful form that communicates the promise of your findings. These forms include (but are far from exhausted by) description, analysis, interpretation, evaluation, and theory.

Holliday (2002, 100) presents a descriptive diagram labeled "From Data to Text," demonstrating data transformation. In the diagram, data move from "rationalized sections of messy reality" to "thematic organization of data" to "text of data analysis section or chapter." The diagram traces the distancing of data from "reality." Distancing from "reality" is a problem for some who argue that data should be presented in as natural a state as possible. This perspective ranges from those who see it necessary to keep in every "umm" in interview transcripts; to those who aspire to use computer technology to provide public access to interviews, field journals, documents, and photos; to others who call for more holistic forms of data analysis that do not fragment data into artificially-constructed categories. No matter what type of (or how much) analysis you choose to do, you need to recognize that data, in any form, are already distanced from and different from the social reality from which they were taken. Ultimately, few readers are interested in wading through reams of raw data from a research project. Analysis, making data sensible and accessible, is an important part of the researcher's job. Data transformation, no matter what approach is taken, is the prelude to sensitive outcomes that describe, make connections, and contribute to greater understanding, or at the least, more informed questioning.

TRUSTWORTHINESS OF YOUR INTERPRETATIONS

Hollway and Jefferson (2000, 55) identify four core questions researchers should ask themselves as they work with their data. Each question is linked to the trustworthiness of analytical interpretations:

1. What do you notice?
2. Why do you notice what you notice?
3. How can you interpret what you notice?
4. How can you know that your interpretation is the "right" one?

What Do You Notice?

"What do you notice?" suggests that when you notice one thing, you do not notice something else. Ask yourself "Whom do I not see? Whom have I seen less often? Where do I not go? Where have I gone less often? With whom do I have special relationships, and in what light would they interpret phenomena? What data collecting means have I not used that could provide additional insight?" Using more than one method for data collection and more than one type of respondent can contribute to more complex perspectives on an issue. Consciously and continuously searching (during research planning, data collection, and data analysis) for negative cases can help to point out points of view you may be ignoring. "I didn't confirm all of my opinions, which was nice," said Andrea in the final report of her community study. "Maybe there is some validity to what I found."

Why Do You Notice What You Notice?

The question "Why do you notice what you notice?" indicates the need to reflect upon your subjectivity in terms of what you observe and hear, and to engage in reflexivity, critically thinking about the research process as a whole. Continual alertness to your own biases and theoretical predispositions (see Chapter 5) assists in producing more trustworthy interpretations. Reflect upon how your commitments lead you to behave and interpret in particular ways. Also reflect upon how what you notice is shaped by the research setting and participants in their reactions to you. What is it that research participants want you to see and why?

How Can You Interpret What You Notice?

To address the question, "How can you interpret what you notice," *time* is an important consideration. Lincoln and Guba (1985) describe *prolonged engagement* (spending sufficient time at your research site) and *persistent observation* (focusing in detail on those elements that are most relevant to your study) as critical in attending to credibility: "If prolonged engagement provides scope, persistent observation provides depth" (304). Time at your research site, time spent in interviewing, and time building sound relationships with participants all contribute to trustworthy data.

Continually asking and striving to answer reflexive questions like those posed in Chapter 5 also contribute to more trustworthy interpretations. When you constantly challenge your own process and assumptions, you are more likely to catch yourself reflecting your own cultural positions (e.g., male, European American, working class, heterosexual) onto others and neither asking nor hearing perspectives that differ. You are also less likely to generalize from one or several responses to everyone.

How Can You Know Your Interpretation Is The Right One?

The question "How can you know your interpretation is the right one?" suggests the enlistment of others to provide feedback. Share the interpretive process with research respondents as a form of member checking. Obtaining the reactions of research participants to your working drafts is time-consuming, but doing so may (1) verify that you have reflected their perspectives; (2) inform you of sections that, if published, could be problematic for either personal or political reasons; and (3) help you develop new ideas and interpretations. For example, when Penny compiled her participant-observation notes into a "day-in-the life" of an effective, middle-level partner team, she shared the initial draft with team members. They reflected on the accuracy of the depiction, as well as noted patterns of behavior of which they were previously unaware. In her field notes, Penny wrote:

> I'm glad I took the opportunity to share my writing with Liza and Hope. They really helped me feel confident that my perceptions of their relational work are an accurate representation by their standards as well. I think they got something out of it too, as they laughingly noticed their tendency to phrase ideas as questions, to unconsciously rotate the facilitation of class discussion, to be up front about concerns, and to finish one another's sentences.

By sharing working drafts, both researcher and researched may grow in their interpretations of the phenomena around them.

To assist in your interpretations, do not forget the invaluable assistance of friends and colleagues. Ask them to work with portions of your data—developing codes, applying your codes, or interpreting field notes to widen your perceptions. To promote trustworthiness, Lincoln and Guba (1985) suggest a procedure for enlisting an outsider to "audit" fieldwork notes and subsequent analysis and interpretations. For students working on theses and dissertations, your committee members are logical auditors of your work. I ask students to keep three-ringed notebooks, tabulated and with a detailed table of contents as described in Exhibit 7.4. Developing such inclusive notebooks not only make fieldwork audits easy, but also enforce a kind of organizational process that assists in dealing with "fat data."

This last question, "How can you know your interpretation is the right one?" asks you to consider the frameworks you use to interpret what you notice. Analyzing work from more than one framework (theoretical triangulation) can lend trustworthiness to your interpretations. This question, however, is also a kind of trick question. Is there any "right" interpretation? Any kind of social interaction can be examined from multiple frameworks, including frameworks for which you may have no developed conceptual understanding. Unraveling these multiple interpretations is what makes qualitative work particularly fascinating and potentially useful as you learn to think and see and help others to think and see in new ways.

Limitations

Part of demonstrating the trustworthiness of your data is to realize the limitations of your study. Your responsibility is to do the best that you can under certain circumstances. Detailing those circumstances helps readers to understand the nature of your data. Discuss what documents, people, or places were unavailable to you. Discuss what is peculiar about your site or respondent selection that could

Use three-ring notebooks in which you can label dividers for organizing data and research thoughts. What follows is an outline for the bare essentials of keeping track of your research data and process. You can organize it in a way that makes sense to you, but include ALL the pieces listed below.

1. Table of Contents (*clear and detailed*)
2. Fieldwork Plans (*all versions, dated, and chronologically arranged*)
   a. Purpose for fieldwork
   b. Concept map(s)
   c. Research statement and research questions
3. Interview Questions (*all versions, dated, and chronologically arranged*)
4. Participant-Observation Notes
   a. Note date, location, and the beginning and ending time of each.
   b. Record as fully as possible the interactions taking place.
   c. While in the process of observing, you may be struck by thoughts concerning the process. Jot them down, but mark them in some way as your opinions, judgments, or questions.
   d. After completing an observation, read through your notes. Make scribbled renditions legible and add remembered, but omitted descriptions. Do this as soon as possible, while your memory is fresh. Entering observation notes into computer files often helps with this remembering process.
5. Interview Notes
   a. Note date, location, and the beginning and ending time of each interview period.
   b. If not taping, record as close to verbatim as possible. After completing an untaped interview, read through your notes as soon as possible. Make your scribbled renditions legible and add remembered details. You may want to use a different color so that you can easily tell later which notes were taken on site and which were added. This can also be done on the computer.
   c. If taping the interviews, include any notes that were taken, along with transcriptions.
   d. After the interview, you may be struck by thoughts concerning the process or with better interview questions. Jot all this down.
6. The Reflexive Journal (*All thoughts and reactions should be recorded along the way and not at the end of your research. The main purpose is to reflect on what you are doing while you are doing it. Date all entries.*)
   a. Begin your reflexive journal when you start conceiving your research project. Develop thoughts about the purpose and significance of your research topic. Work out exactly what it is you want to learn and why.

(continued)

(*continued*)

> b. Keep a running record of all questions your fieldwork raises. This list may include questions you would like to ask other people, substantive questions, or methodological questions.
>
> c. Record thoughts about you as researcher and your assumptions about, interactions with, and feelings toward research participants. Think about what areas of subjectivity are roused by your fieldwork. How do you think you are affecting the data collected? What things should you perhaps do differently?
>
> d. Record any problems you may be having in the fieldwork process. Think about possible solutions to these problems.
>
> **7.** Analysis
>
> a. Organize and extend thoughts triggered by data collection. This is beginning the stages of analysis in that you are reflecting upon what you are seeing and creating hunches about what is happening.
>
> b. Codes (keep all versions, dated, and chronologically arranged)
>
> c. Show coded data (this may be done after it has been sorted)
>
> d. Keep a record of all versions of potential themes or patterns
>
> e. Include working diagrams, charts, matrices.

EXHIBIT 7.4   Instructions for Fieldwork Notebooks

illuminate the phenomena of interest in some lights but not in others. Approach the description of your study's limitations as part of setting the context. Limitations are consistent with the partial state of knowing in social research, and elucidating your limitations helps readers know how they should read and interpret your work.

The settings and scenes you describe and all the words you gather through your research are not inherently meaningful in themselves. Rather you make them meaningful through your analysis and interpretations. As Tomas Schram (2006, 13) states, "The communication of this meaning through your interpretation is always negotiable and incomplete. In the end, it is a matter of how plausible your ideas appear to others, and how persuasively you make your case for their significance." In an article on James Agee, author of *Let Us Now Praise Famous Men,* John Hersey concludes with a quotation from Mrs. Burroughs, a woman from one of the tenant families portrayed in Agee's book: "And I took it home and I read it plumb through. And when I read it plumb through I gave it back to her and I said, 'Well everything in there's true. What they wrote in there was true'" (Hersey 1988, 74). James Agee would have been pleased to learn that Mrs. Burroughs affirmed his interpretations of her life. You want your interpretations to be trustworthy, to be affirmed by the Mrs. Burroughses in your research lives and also by your colleagues who may use your work in the range of ways that trusted outcomes can be used—to describe, confirm, expand, and inform.

CONSIDERATIONS

> In Yaqui to be *kia polove* is to be without desire for "things." There is no concept of "poor" for a noncomparative, communal society. A Yaqui is only poor when he deals with the whites or the Mexicans.
>
> (Véa 1993, 31)

After eight hours on a bus traversing twisting roads that steadily climbed, my friend Patricia and I arrived in Hautla, a village spread out along a mountainous ridge in northern Oaxaca. We journeyed there as a break from our respective research projects, both of us visiting the area for the first time. The next day, we walked along mountainous roads and paths with vistas looking out over layers of the Sierra Norte. By the time we returned to town, it was almost dark and past the hour when cafés served the light meal normally eaten in the evenings in Oaxaca. We were hungry though and finally found an internet café where we could get Oaxacan hot chocolate, foamy and thick, and tortillas with cheese.

The café proprietor took our order, brought our food, and asked if he could sit with us. As we talked, we learned that he was also the principal of the local high school. Unable to leave my research behind, I began forming a question. Intrigued with how the young people with whom I was working were involved in some way with improving aspects of their community's environment, I asked him to describe the attitudes of young people in Hautla toward the environment. He paused and then replied, "We don't really talk of the environment here but rather of *harmony*." He went on to describe harmony as a connection among all things, including those not seen. Each field, tree, rock, and river had a *dueno* or guardian and traditionally people made offerings to the *duenos* before cutting a tree or removing a rock, aware of the possibilities of offending some entity and suffering consequences.

His sentence—"We don't really talk of the environment but rather of *harmony*"—shattered my assumed categories. Even though I had heard people talk about nature spirits before, even though I had read about the importance of *harmony* in Oaxaca, and even though a shaman had revealed to me my *naguals* or nature allies, I had kept assigning what I was reading and hearing and experiencing to my Western categories of people, animals, environment, religion/spirituality, etc. The principal's sentence finally fragmented my categories. They ran together, blending, mixing, and muddying my view. I know that I do not yet fully understand the concept of *harmony* the way many in Oaxaca do, but I know better some of my own myths of perception. And although I continue to fall back on my old categories, I know they are artificial. I've seen and felt something different.

The process of categorization is both a strength and problem of data analysis. We categorize to make sense of things, to help us see patterns in social interaction. We need categories to develop hunches, hypotheses, and theories. Even though we may look for "native language" and consciously try to get at the categories others hold in their heads, we can't fully escape the categories to which we have been socialized. I think that ethnographic work is particularly useful, however, when we can begin to reorder the world into categories that are not our own. As qualitative researchers, we often say we want to get at multiple perspectives, but less frequently do we challenge our frameworks for expressing these perspectives. Doing so widens the horizons for experiencing life around us while demonstrating more fully how knowledge is socially constructed and always partial in its power to describe or explain.

REFLECTIONS

This chapter concludes with an excerpt from a paper written by Gordon. He had completed his course-based research project and was reflecting on the analysis process, of which writing—the next topic for discussion—was a part:

The paper is written, the computer clicks softly to itself as it cools after its long ordeal, and my cards lie scattered over the floor and desk. The paper lies in my briefcase in its bright blue cover, ready to be read and reviewed. It is done! It is over! Now what?

After filling every waking moment with analysis and writing, leisure causes a kind of withdrawal. What does one say to one's wife and family? What does one do with all that time? I feel compelled to turn on the computer, to fill the blank screen with words once more. My mind is locked into the analysis mode, examining menus, cereal boxes, and junk mail and placing them in precise matrices. I compulsively buy and hoard 5 × 8 cards and glue sticks. I need to break the cycle, to fight my way back to the normal life of the nonresearcher. What to do?

What else can I do? I'll analyze the process.

My first thoughts concern the holistic nature of the process. There really is no way to separate the parts of research from one another. Data gathering includes parts of analysis, analysis leads to more data, writing leads to a greater understanding of both analysis and data. The process is totally holistic, each piece absolutely necessary to the whole. I am reminded of this as I stoop to pick up my cards, the various coding categories scribbled off, edges bent, and the writing illegible. How do you analyze information you can't read? One thing seems to be certain: Next time I begin the analysis as I do the data gathering. To separate the two processes by three months doesn't work. All the soft nuances are gone, the tones and the shades of meaning are missing.

Another interesting discovery is that the writing process actually is an important part of the analysis. A lot of my insights and much of the understanding I gained from my research data came through the writing process. For me, writing is the final organization of my thoughts. Next time I will begin writing sooner.

A final thought is that matrices really help. By organizing my data into matrices, I was able to see in two or three dimensions. I realized only at this point that my really profound data concerned peer pressure on children, not parental pressures. Next time I will use more matrices.

This is a small first step on my way back to reality. By this time next week, the hours of writing and preparation will only be a fond dream that fades ever into the dust of newer crises. And yet, if I could only rewrite page 7, I bet I could . . .

RECOMMENDED READINGS

Gibbs, G. 2007. *Analyzing Qualitative Data*. Thousand Oaks, CA: Sage.

Gubrium, J., and J. Holstein. 2009. *Analyzing Narrative Reality*. Thousand Oaks, CA: Sage.

Miles, M., and A. M. Huberman. 1994. *Qualitative Data Analysis: An Expanded Sourcebook*, 2nd ed. Thousand Oaks, CA: Sage.

Wolcott, H. 1994. *Transforming Qualitative Data: Description, Analysis, and Interpretation*. Thousand Oaks, CA: Sage.

EXERCISES

Class Exercises

1. Return to the class *research practice* exercise (Chapters 2 and 4). With interview transcripts in hand, create a codebook for the interviews. Begin in small groups, agreeing on major and minor codes. Then, as a whole class, look at the ways each small group coded the interviews. Discuss the different kinds of stories each coding scheme might tell. Eventually, come to an agreement on a class coding scheme. Then each student should code, with the class coding scheme, the interview that he or she conducted.

2. Take the coded interviews from the above practice exercise. Cut and sort by major codes. Divide the class into small groups, each group receiving the data from one or more major code(s). Groups then work with the data associated with their code(s): sorting by minor codes and looking for patterns, relationships, and further categorizations. Make note of analytical findings. Hold onto these clumps of coded data for a future exercise.

Individual Exercises

1. Now that you have an overall view of an interpretivist, ethnographic process for doing qualitative research with thematic analysis, consider designing a study on the same topic as you've chosen but using a different methodological theoretical framework (e.g., conversation analysis, narrative analysis, critical discourse analysis, or semiotics). Choose another approach, read up on it, and then reflect upon how each of the following might differ from your currently designed study: research question(s), study purposes, data collection procedures, researcher–researched relationships, and analysis framework.

2. Remember the research diagram you created when working on your research statement? Without looking at it, diagram your research now, incorporating the sense you are making of observations, interviews, and other data. Compare the diagrams. Reflect in your field log on what you have learned about your topic, making notes of particular gaps or questions that remain.

3. Most likely you have not yet collected all your pilot data (the process of accessing, scheduling, and collecting data is taking longer than you ever dreamed). Nonetheless, begin with what you have and try creating your own codebook.

CHAPTER 8

Crafting Your Story: Writing Up Qualitative Data

. . . one hopes that one's case will touch others. But how to connect? Not by calculation, I think, not by the assumption that in the pain of my toothache, or my father's, or Harry Crosby's, I have discovered a "universal condition of consciousness." One may merely know that no one is alone and hope that a singular story, as every true story is singular, will in the magic way of some things apply, connect, resonate, touch a major chord.

(Pachter 1981, 72)

Writing gives form to the researcher's clumps of carefully analyzed and organized data. It links together thoughts that have been developing throughout the research process and jotted in memos and journals. The act of writing also stimulates new thoughts, new connections. Writing is rewarding in that it creates the product, the housing for the meaning that you and others have made of your research endeavor. Writing is about constructing a text. As a writer, you engage in a sustained act of construction, which includes selecting a particular "story" to tell from the data you have analyzed, and creating the literary form that you believe best conveys your story. It perhaps matters to some—but needs no resolution—whether the researcher's construction is more like that of an architect, proceeding from a vision embodied in a plan, or like that of a painter, whose vision emerges over time from intuition, sense, and feeling. For many, constructing a text is quite possibly some combination of both plan and intuition. This chapter touches on intuition, but it focuses on strategies for writing, questions of form and style, and responsibilities of the writer.

ROLES OF THE WRITER

By the time we finish reading a good ethnography, adroit rationalization has made familiar what at first seemed strange, the other, and has estranged us from what we thought we knew, ourselves.

(Shweder 1986, 38)

A woman once asked me to review and provide feedback on her dissertation work, which she was completing at another university. She had developed her interview questions (both closed- and open-ended) and had scheduled her interviews with a number of administrators throughout the nation, but had not yet collected any data. Nonetheless, she had compiled a document of nearly 200 pages, divided into five chapters: introduction to the problem, review of literature, methods, findings, and summary with recommendations. She had completed the first three chapters and much of the last two, leaving blank spaces for percentages and applicable phrases once the data were available.

I do not know how many dissertations and research reports are written this way; not many, I hope. Those that are cannot do justice to the data in that they forfeit interpretation. They neither show respect for the time and input of the respondents nor call on the analytic and creative qualities of the writer. And they do not succeed in making the strange familiar or in estranging us from ourselves.

This section addresses three possible roles of the writer of qualitative inquiry: artist, translator/interpreter, and transformer. Although writers do not always play all three roles, they nonetheless should keep them in mind.

Artist

To make meaning of data, writers employ technical procedures that are to some extent routine and mechanical, but writers of good qualitative studies also are artists who create. In his edited book *Extraordinary Lives*, Zinsser (1986, 17–18) states:

> [Research] is only research. After all the facts have been marshaled, all the documents studied, all the locales visited, all the survivors interviewed, what then? What do the facts add up to? What did the life mean? This was the central question for the six biographers, and to hear them wrestling with it was to begin to see where the craft crosses over into art.

Craft involves the strategies and procedures authors use to write their story. The form and style of the presentation require artistic sensibilities, which seem to involve a mixture of discipline and creativity. As artists, qualitative researchers move into the murky terrain where others may regard them as journalists, fiction writers, or worse. As artists, they seek imaginative connections among events and people, imaginative renderings of these connections, and imaginative interpretations of what they have rendered. They do this not only in the worthy cause of making their work accessible, but also to do full justice to what they have endeavored to understand. The next chapter focuses on artistic renderings in qualitative research.

Translator/Interpreter

The ethnographer is sometimes described as a translator of culture. The researcher works to understand the others' world and then to translate the text of lived actions into a meaningful account. Although the translator metaphor suggests struggle with representing the nuances of meaning, it can also imply that the researcher is an objective middleperson, rather than someone whose perspectives and personality affect the portrayed account. To the contrary, qualitative researchers are interpreters who draw on their own experiences, knowledge, theoretical dispositions, and collected data to present their understanding of the other's world. As interpreters, they think of themselves not as authority figures who get the "facts" on a topic, but as meaning makers who make sense out of the interaction of their own lives with those of research participants. "An ethnography," explains Shweder (1986, 38),

> begins with an ethnographic experience: With your eyes open you have to go somewhere. Yet a culture is never reducible to what meets the eye, and you can't get to ethnographic reality by just looking. A culture is like a black hole, those compacted stars whose intense gravitational forces don't let their own light particles escape. You can never know it's there by simply squinting your eyes and staring very hard at it. If it is real at all, you can know it only by inference and conjecture.

Inference and conjecture are mainstays of the interpretive process. Inferences are made about the relationship of one thing to another, on the basis of carefully collected, carefully analyzed data.

Translations in this interpretive sense can help both researchers and readers to see differently, to know new things. In Anne Michaels's (1996) exquisitely written novel *Fugitive Pieces*, the main character, as a small boy, watched his family get killed in Nazi Germany. He could not talk of it until much later, after he moved to Canada and learned English. Translating the events out of their language of origin allowed him to explore what happened and what the events meant for his life and for others. Fiction writers and poets learn that when they are surprised by what their writing reveals to themselves, their effort is working. Like the character in Michaels's book, creative qualitative writers seek translations that will allow them to reveal and reorder in surprising and meaningful ways that which they have observed, heard, and experienced.

Transformer

It is to the role of transformer—not necessarily in the sense of reformer but rather of catalytic educator—that many writers of qualitative research aspire. As others read your story, you want them to identify with or be a witness to the problems, oppression, worries, joys, and dreams that are the collective human lot. By reflecting on other's lives in light of their own experiences, readers acquire new insights and perspectives on some aspect of human interaction, and, perhaps, are moved to action. This process of learning about self through understanding others is a gift of qualitative research done well. Shweder (1986, 38) states it well:

> Good ethnography is an intellectual exorcism in which, forced to take the perspective of the other, we are wrenched out of our self. We transcend ourselves, and for a brief moment we wonder who we are, whether we are animals, barbarians or angels, whether all things are really the same under the sun, whether it would be better if the other were us, or better if we were the other.

Writing up your work so that it contributes to transformative experiences requires the application of disciplined procedures and artistic creativity to meaningful data. We now turn to the disciplined procedures of writing.

STRATEGIES FOR WRITING

> Writing-up research is like making maple syrup. Forty gallons of sap boil down to one gallon of syrup. I have 40 gallons of data to reduce to a gallon of "Grade A" descriptions and interpretations. Right now, my syrup is a bit thin.
>
> (Sandi, Vermont student)

Getting Started

Most of us can find numerous excuses to postpone writing. We have to read more, see more, and talk more; we must recode and reanalyze; and, inevitably, we feel compelled to mop the floor, make a phone call, do anything to avoid sitting down and writing. That those who spend much of their life writing also experience anxiety over getting started may be of some comfort. Novelist Anne Lamott (1994, 6–7) describes the banshees that distract from writing:

> And you try to quiet your mind so you can hear . . . above the other voices in your mind. The other voices are banshees and drunken monkeys. They are the voices of anxiety, judgment, doom, guilt. . . . There may be a . . . listing of things that must be done right this moment: foods that must come out of the freezer, appointments that must be canceled or made, hairs that must be tweezed. . . . There is a vague pain at the base of your neck. It crosses your mind that you have meningitis. Then the phone rings and you look up at the ceiling with fury, summon every ounce of noblesse oblige, and answer the call politely, with maybe just the merest hint of irritation. The caller asks if you're working, and you say yeah, because you are.
>
> Yet somehow in the face of all this, you clear a space for the writing voice, hacking away at the others with machetes, and you begin to compose sentences. You begin to string words together like beads to tell a story. You are desperate to communicate, to edify or entertain, to preserve moments of grace or joy or transcendence, to make real or imagined events come alive. But you cannot will this to happen. It is a matter of persistence and faith and hard work. So you might as well just go ahead and get started.

So, while the novice procrastinates (and, in the process, prolongs the anxiety), those with more experience write. As the Portuguese proverb goes, "When there is no wind, row."

It helps to know that writing, like data analysis, is not a discrete step in the qualitative research process. Ideally, and not at all unrealistically, you should write throughout the time of data collection and analysis. Long before you begin a phase of work that you can call "write-up time," you should be writing. In fact, it is useful to be conscious at the outset of a research project that it will culminate in words, sentences, paragraphs, pages, and chapters. Distant though it may be, this culmination will arrive. Aware that it will, you should look and listen, analyze and interpret, and be attuned to the prospect that the results will be words to be read. Your efforts to collect data and make something of them should be in the spirit of a quest for what will appear in written form.

If you follow this advice, then you will have files of field notes and research memos, many containing well-developed thoughts in usable paragraph form. A time will come, however, when more of your effort will be put into writing than anything else. This time is often preceded by feelings of intense anxiety manifested in a variety of ways and labeled "writer morassity" by a student research support group in Vermont for whom metaphors of bogs, swamps, and slow drownings recurred. The writer gearing up for writing is often unsociable and ill-tempered while sorting and resorting data, trying to organize thoughts. Woods refers to the "pain threshold" of writing, asserting that researchers must be masochists who confront the pain barrier till it hurts as they rework ideas that seemed brilliant before exposed to paper. He likens the suffering that the writer feels to that of other artists, and urges them to view the anxiety as a rite of passage that "is as much a test of self as anything else" (Woods 1986, 171).

Writing is a lonely process. While writing about people and social processes, you paradoxically remove yourself from the world of human beings. This estrangement is functional in two ways: First, you need to be by yourself because you need time to concentrate on writing. Woods (1985, 88) observes that "research may benefit teaching, but the converse does not apply" because assisting others distracts you from focusing on your own work. Those who try to write dissertations or other research reports while "on the job" are likely to agree. Most writers do best with daily periods of extended time set aside for writing.

Second, estrangement is also functional in that it separates you from the research site. The distancing helps you to approach writing from a perspective that is more global than situation specific:

> If one does not distance oneself from them [research participants], then there is a danger of being unable to dismantle the data, select from them, and re-order the material. One is left in the position of someone who, when asked to comment on and criticize a film or novel, can do no more than rehearse the plot. The ethnographer who fails to achieve distance will easily fall into the trap of recounting "what happened" without imposing a coherent thematic or analytic framework. (Hammersley and Atkinson 1983, 212–213)

So writers withdraw, immersed in their data and thoughts about the research, intending to give form and meaning to that which they have observed and heard and read.

Several strategies can help you deal with the anxiety and alienation that accompany beginning to write:

1. Develop a long-term schedule with realistic deadlines. Expect to spend as much time, if not more, in focused data analysis and writing as you

spend in data collection. You need time to play with the data and your words, to share drafts with research participants and colleagues, and to rework drafts a number of times. You need time, as well, to do justice to the considerable investment you have made in planning your study and producing data.

2. Develop a short-term schedule. Figure out when you are most creative in your writing. If possible, make appointments with yourself to write for three to four hours, four to five days per week. Expand the hours when you can. Some authors, with more flexible schedules, set a number of pages to be written each day rather than an amount of time to work. Somewhere around five double-spaced typed pages a day is a reasonable amount, unless you have nothing else to do but write.

3. Set aside a place for writing where you will be as free as possible of interruptions and distractions. When you go there, do not make phone calls, or check e-mail, or read books. Write.

4. Be prepared to write at other times and places. Many days become fragmented, with numerous short periods of unproductive time. Keep a notebook (or note cards) with you and stay open to ideas concerning your project. Jot down your thoughts when they strike you, whether in the midst of a boring meeting, or riding the bus home, or working on something else. Murray (1986) suggests using fragments of time to make lists, notes, and diagrams; search out quotes; sketch outlines; and draft titles and key paragraphs.

5. Begin by editing yesterday's writing. Writers tend to need a gearing-up period before getting started. Many find that editing what they wrote the day before helps them get into the new day's work, keeps the flow consistent, and assists in producing a better draft. Beginning by editing yesterday's writing not only lets you know exactly where to start today, but also allows you to revise that which seemed perfectly clear as it was written but may appear obscure a very short time afterward.

6. When stuck, read your work aloud. Reading aloud reveals the rhythm, flow, and tone of the piece and often helps to form the thoughts and words that will follow.

7. When stuck, write. Write without concern for syntax, coherence, or logic. Write to work out ideas and thoughts; obsess over form and style later. It helps to acquire a "first-draft mentality," that is, the state of mind in which you give yourself permission to write without concern for appearances. You write this way knowing that you will revise later and clarify what may be very messy indeed. You write this way appreciating that it is best to produce a draft of any quality rather than be held back by premature concerns for form and style. A great obstacle to writing is holding inappropriately high standards for the quality of your early drafts, particularly your first draft. A standard that is too high will put you on the road to the paralysis of writer's block. Better to settle for a draft of *any* quality, trusting in revision to produce order, style, and worthy words.

Taking the attitude of conversing with your peers may facilitate the flow of words as suggested by Murray (1986, 147):

> No publication is the final theological word on a subject. Too many academics believe they have to write *the* article or book on their topic. That is impossible. Each publication is merely a contribution to a continuous professional conversation. I was paralyzed by the idea that I had to deliver the Truth—Moses-like; I began to write when I realized all I had to do was speculate, question, argue, create a model, take a position, define a problem, make an observation, propose a solution, illuminate a possibility to participate in a written conversation with my peers.

The written-conversation idea is easily extended by choosing a person that you know—a friend, relative, colleague, or research participant—and writing with that person in mind.

8. When the written-conversation idea fails, don't underestimate the power of engaging in dialogue. Getting together with another person and talking through the statement "What I am really trying to say in this section is . . . " will often enable you to move beyond your sticking point.

9. Establish or join a writing group. Not only does this kind of interaction provide ongoing feedback; it helps to establish regular deadlines. As well intentioned as you are in setting your own short- and long-term due dates, there is nothing like having to be accountable to others to help you meet those deadlines.

10. Finally, immerse yourself in exemplary ethnographies and qualitative studies, as well as in novels, poetry, and great works of literature (during non-writing hours). Your reading provides models and sources of inspiration. "Read widely as well as deeply," advises Murray (1986, 149).

Once you have started writing, keep at it. The clumps of notes carefully organized and segregated by either computer files or tangible paper clips and rubber bands are the makings for the qualitative researcher's text. As your "to do" clumps shrink in number and your "done" box fills, you have evidence of progress.

Keeping At It

In Beryl Markham's (1942/1983, 154) conception of progress,`

> A word grows to a thought—a thought to an idea—an idea to an act. The change is slow, and the Present is a sluggish traveler loafing in the path Tomorrow wants to take.

You should not wait until you know exactly what the thoughts, ideas, and words should be before beginning to write. Writing "helps people generate, develop, organize, modify, critique, and remember their ideas" (Fulwiler 1985, 23). British historian Sir Steven Runciman (in Plante 1986, 78) emphasizes the role of writing in forming ideas: "When I'm writing, I'm dealing with something being revealed

Student on a Maori Marai in New Zealand, forming her thoughts and gaining insight through the process of writing.

to me all the time. I get the insight when I'm actually having to try to put it into words." Writing helps to develop your thoughts and ideas and to discover what you know and how much more there is to know. Therefore, it is best to begin sooner rather than later.

Although you may begin writing with an overall organizational plan in the form of chapters, the act of writing is likely to reshape the plan, reorganize the pieces, subsume some sections, and add others. For example, the process of writing restructured Peshkin's (personal notes, May 24, 1988) outline for his book *The Color of Strangers, the Color of Friends: The Play of Ethnicity in School and Community* (1991):

> I think being immersed in writing is like being immersed in anything—you are never far from the work, you have continuity, thoughts get thought that might not get thought at all or not until much later. The latest appearance of a gain—break-through would be too strong—was the relegation of what was to be an entire chapter, Chapter 5, to a *part* of a chapter, Chapter 1. A chapter on the "town today" struck me as more fitting for the introductory stuff I have put in Chapter 1.
>
> So thinking, when I went to arrange the clump of notes, I was thinking small—part of a chapter, rather than big—an entire chapter. So thinking, I discarded lots of data that I'd originally put in the "town today" clump. Which is to say, I have a lot less to write and can look forward to soon getting on to real Chapter 5, which now looks to be "education today," having done "education history" in Chapter 4. What is becoming clear is that my chapter outline, made when I had finished all coding, holds up only until I prepare to write a new chapter. Then, in light of the previous chapters done, I know whether the new one will fit next as the chapter, fit elsewhere as a chapter, fit somewhere as a part of a chapter, or fit nowhere at all.

Writing up is a continual process of organizing and reorganizing your material as you work through what sense you are making of the data. Frequently, in interpretive inquiry, the researcher dissects interview transcripts and observations into themes and patterns, but this is not the only way to write up data. The final text can take many forms, drawing from your theoretical and methodological orientations in combination with your personal inclinations. For example, those working with narrative analysis often retell the stories they've heard as a whole and then focus on analyzing and describing how the narratives are told and on what is included and excluded in the telling. The use of creative writing techniques contributes other vehicles for thinking about and representing data and will be discussed in Chapter 9. Thematic analysis is commonly used in qualitative research reports, however, and receives attention here.

Thematic presentation of data is derived from analytic procedures involving coding and segregating data into categories and thinking about their relationships to each other and to guiding theories. Begin on a macro level: After coding all of your data (including your research journal, memos, and notes from books and articles), work with codes and theories to make an overall outline. The outline organizes the data and assigns data clumps (the coded bits of paper, note cards, computer printouts, and documents) to chapters or major sections. Somewhat like the Russian doll within a doll, these organizational steps are repeated within each chapter and then within each chapter subsection.

Once your writing begins, the date bits within each carefully sorted clump will look different. No longer homogeneous, they need to be sorted into subclumps that possibly make up subsections of the text. For example, suppose you have a major code on "resolving conflict" for a study of first-year principals. Under "resolving conflict," you further categorize the data by techniques used, such as "holding meetings," "using humor," "turning the matter over to others," and "ignoring the situation." Now suppose that within the subclump "turning the matter over to others," you realize through reading and thinking about the material there that first-year principals sometimes turn budget conflicts over to the school board, but personnel conflicts over to the superintendent. Your data scraps could be arranged accordingly. To write up your data, you continuously, progressively sort and consider relationships of one piece of data to another.

All data scraps do not necessarily end up where originally filed. As you work with the data, you may move individual pieces to a place that makes more sense now that you are writing; or you may relegate them to a miscellaneous pile that you scan at the beginning and end of each chapter or major section to see if something fits. Or you may file them in a discard file, concluding that they really are tangential to your story. Through this progressive sorting process, you increasingly impose order on your data. Yet, at the same time, the order is flexible; it continuously changes, shaped by the ideas that your writing generates.

Not only are you imposing order on your data at this stage, but also you are engaging in the analytical process of selecting which data of all the data you collected to use in the text. Wolcott (1990, 18) describes this as "the painful task" of letting go of data. "The trick," he states, "is to discover essences and then to reveal those essences with sufficient context, yet not become mired trying to include everything that might possibly be described" (35). Ask your committee members to describe the most wearisome qualitative research paper or dissertation they have read. Most likely they will depict reports where authors felt compelled to insert seemingly every quote collected in list-like fashion with little interpretation or analysis. Kvale (1996) provides eight guidelines for reporting interview quotes (266–267). I emphasize three: (1) Quotes should not make up more than half the text in any descriptive or analytical chapter; (2) quotes should be kept short, ordinarily no more than half a page; and (3) quotes should be interpreted with the researcher clearly stating what perspective they illuminate. These are not hard and fast rules. A whole chapter, for example, may be primarily the edited words of an interviewee. As guidelines, however, they may assist you to let go of some of your data.

Discussing the organizational procedures of your writing is relatively easier than discussing what makes it more than a linear report of what you did and what you learned. Your writing develops how you interpret what you saw and heard by carefully integrating themes that support a thesis and create or augment theoretical explanations. No mechanical procedure exists for doing so. Rather, you must be so immersed in your data that you are open to those flashes of insight that come when least expected. Such moments make connections and provide perspectives that allow the pieces to fall into place.

Drafts and Revisions

Expect your work to go through a number of drafts before it reflects the polish of a well-crafted manuscript. The first draft of your manuscript is like a roughly hewn form emerging from a block of wood as a sculptor works. To make the form a work of art, the sculptor carefully continues to shape the form, creating details, smoothing rough spots, and polishing the overall piece. Successive drafts do the same for the author's words. When your first draft is completed, read it for overall cohesion and then add, move, or eliminate sections as needed. In another reading, focus on the clarity of your theories and descriptions. With more readings, tighten, sharpen, and brighten (Trimble, in Jeske 1984) your work: Tighten by eliminating unnecessary words. Sharpen by reworking passive statements and employing precise and lively words. Brighten by simile and metaphor, by wit and lively description. Grammar, spelling, and punctuation should also get a turn. Aspiring novelist Stephen King, while in high school, sent a manuscript to an editor and received back a formula that King (2000, 222) says he continues to heed: "2nd Draft = 1st Draft − 10%." In the process of working to remove 10 percent of the manuscript, you tighten, sharpen, and brighten.

Do not overlook the contribution of a reading that attends to subheadings. Subheadings benefit both author and reader. Scan your subheadings to check the order of the parts within each chapter. Try listing all of your subheads on a separate page, then reconsider their most effective order. In addition, name any previously unnamed sections. Although unnamed sections may be easy for you to make order of—easy because the words are yours and you are familiar with them—that is not the case for the reader. With only two subheadings to structure thirty-eight typed pages, for example, too much of your chapter is left unstructured. Finally, reexamine the content and the order of paragraphs and pages within each section.

Artisans sometimes have assistants who help in certain stages of crafting a work. Qualitative researchers have colleagues or peers and research participants who play invaluable roles in polishing the final product. Enlist them to respond to your interpretations, ideas, and forms of expression, and allow time for such input in the shaping of your manuscript. Choose people who are comfortable enough with your relationship to be honest and direct with you. Stephen King (2000, 217), who gives copies of his work to six or seven friends before sending it to the publishers, gives the following advice: "If everyone who reads your book says you have a problem . . . you've got a problem and you better do something about it."

THE TEXT: QUESTIONS OF STYLE

Variety in Text Organization

Marleen Pugach spent a year doing her ethnography of a school in a town on the border between the United States and Mexico. In considering questions of text organization, Marleen (personal correspondence, 1994) pondered how, out of the many possible ways to tell her story, she was going to frame her data:

> The analogy, it seems to me, is the making a movie analogy . . . that you need miles and miles of film to edit it down to something respectable. And I need all of this "stuff," my transcripts, field notes, newspaper clippings, and documents so I can figure out how to use the best of it all wisely, and set it within a framework that makes sense . . . and that I create. This is the challenging and scary part . . . the framework. Of course the transcripts and the rest of the data tell the story, but in reality I tell the story and these data, while they are the guts of the story, are used in the service of the framework. I'm not suggesting that the framework comes out of nowhere, or is just a creation of my fertile imagination, but just that the great subjectivity of it all is very much on my mind. This balancing of the data and one's own view is really at the heart of the task, isn't it? We gloss it over by reminding people not to get "wedded" to their categories too quickly, to let the story "emerge" from the data. But in a way these are very glib attempts to describe what is a terrifically delicate process—writing a real story, a consistent story, a true-to-the-data story that makes sense both to the local population and to the readers who have never been there. As the researcher, you have been there. And you are in a very powerful position in terms of how you frame all of the data you are now in possession of. This is VERY hard work.

Creating the frame for your data is hard work and, as Marleen observes, it is not just a matter of what your data "say" but of what you *and* your data say. The researcher's frame, however organized, generally falls into one of several ethnographic conventions. Van Maanen (1988) discusses, in particular, the realist, confessional, and impressionist conventions in his book *Tales of the Field*. The next chapter expands upon these and other conventions of writing-up inquiry. To some extent, the type of tale determines the voice and style of writing. To a lesser extent, it shapes text organization, the focus of this section.

Authors use a variety of strategies to organize their presentation of qualitative research. Sometimes they apply one basic strategy to the whole text; sometimes each chapter or parts of chapters employ different strategies. This is yet one more decision for you to make in light of the story you feel compelled to construct. To help you make such decisions, read a variety of ethnographies, research reports, and journal articles, observing, as you do so, the techniques and formats other writers use to present their work. Following are some useful starting points for thinking about text organization:

- *Thematic approach.* Probably the most frequently used technique is organization by themes or topics. By analyzing the data, the researcher generates a typology of concepts, gives them names or uses "native" labels, and then discusses them one by one, illustrating with descriptive detail. For example, to organize a discussion of qualitative research and cultural ethics, Patricia Martin and I (2002) used the themes "community," "autonomy," and "hospitality." These themes came up constantly in our conversations with people in Oaxaca, as well as in literature we were reading. In our write-up, we applied the terms as headings, described the meanings and usage of the concepts among the people with whom we worked, provided examples from our separate research projects, and then considered how each concept could inform inquiry practices.
- *Natural history approach.* In the *natural history* approach, the text re-creates the fieldwork process and the researcher's perception of investigation, connections, and learning. Through this technique, the author can portray a sense of people and place and their interactions with the researcher (typical of impressionistic tales).
- *Chronology approach.* In the *chronology* technique, "the pattern follows some 'developmental cycle,' 'moral career,' or 'timetable' characteristic of the setting or actors under investigation" (Hammersley and Atkinson 1983, 217). If the passage of time is particularly critical to the study, then the chronology technique is appropriate. For example, Peshkin's (1982a) book *The Imperfect Union* chronicles the struggle between a village and a school board over the closing of the village's only remaining school.
- *Zoom lens approach.* Another technique involves narrowing and expanding the focus. The author moves from descriptive detail to theoretical abstraction or vice versa. Like a zoom lens, the text glides through various levels of generality. Spradley (1979) advocates this technique when he identifies six levels of statements that he believes should be a part of ethnographic writing. The levels range from universal statements about a cultural or environmental situation to incident-specific statements. The writer, says Spradley, moves back and forth through the various levels. Accounts written only at the more general levels will be dry and dull with no examples to ground theoretical

statements. In contrast, those written at the more specific levels may make for interesting reading, but fall short of analyzing the sociocultural and political significance of the data.

■ *Narrative approach.* In a blending and consolidation of interview transcripts, Teran (2002) organized and condensed into a narrative his hours of interviews with Mexican scholar and activist Gustavo Esteva. Teran periodically inserted his own explanatory or analytical comments, but, in essence, one chapter of his dissertation is an ordered rendition of Esteva's words. The following example begins with Esteva's words; then, in italics, Teran (2002, 59–60) sets up the organizational schema for the continuing narrative:

> Although I tried to suppress the memory of my grandmother for 40 years there is no doubt that she remained in my subconscious and influenced the direction of my work. It was her voice that called me to work in the *campo*, to concern myself with the *campesinos*, with the Indian people. But I did not see that for a very long time. When I say that I suppressed the memory of my grandmother, I don't mean to say that I had a bad memory of her. As I said before, I had a wonderful image of her and of my time with her in the market. What I suppressed during all these years was the possibility of living in her world. I denied that she was a Zapotec Indian because the indigenous world was seen as a world of misery, poverty and backwardness; a world that had to be left behind to make room for the modern world. What I suppressed was the possibility that my grandmother's world could serve as a path for my own life; as something in which I could gain inspiration for fashioning my life. It was 40 years later that I begin to see those memories with another set of eyes. They opened a window to a different world; to a world that ultimately seemed more mine. It was a world in which I re-encountered my roots; an encounter that came by way of memory.
>
> *Esteva's journey to the land of his grandmother, took him through a series of encounters that ultimately brought him to a way of life and set of priorities different from the Western mindset that his education imposed on him. In Spanish "encuentro" or encounter is opposed by the word "desencuentro," which literally means "disencounter" or the non-materialization of an expected meeting or occurrence. Desencuentro then can be thought of as a turning point where the expected fulfillment of a goal, of a dream, is shattered and a dramatic new direction is taken. Esteva's story reveals three key encounters and consequent disencounters: God, Marx, and indigenous roots.*

■ *Separation of narrative and interpretation.* Yet another organizational technique is to separate narration and theoretical interpretations, as in Willis's (1977) *Learning to Labor.* He first engages the reader with a narrative account of the research setting that is rich in description, dialogue, events, and interaction. Then the writing style changes dramatically as he applies theory and develops his own theories through detailed analysis of the data.

■ *Amalgamation approach.* Amalgamations are another organizing technique. Ashton and Webb (1986) analyzed interview and observation data from a number of people, created categories or types or respondents, and then developed descriptive portraits of each type through amalgamation of the

TABLE 8.1   Example of Theme Categories and Illustrative Responses

OCCUPATIONAL DESIRE CATEGORY AND ILLUSTRATIVE RESPONSE	NUMBER WHO AGREE
Something good (economically or in self-satisfaction)	10
"Any kind of occupation that gives them satisfaction and joy."	
It's up to them	10
"I would not choose for my children."	
Schooling first	6
"Right now they must first further their education."	
A life unlike mine	4
"I want to bring him up so he doesn't have to hustle as I do, and let him have an open mind so he can learn easily without having to lie or fool anybody."	

data. Researchers who have spent months "shadowing" a few people may amalgamate the observed activities into a "typical day" for each participant as Wolcott (1973) did in his book *The Man in the Principal's Office*.

■ *Data display.*   Data display in tables, charts, or graphs are not an overall organizational schema, but they can supplement text by introducing or summarizing categories or ideas discussed in detail in the text. Table 8.1, adapted from my work in the Caribbean, exemplifies one way of illustrating theme categories that grew out of interviewees discussing their occupational desires for their children. Some authors have used data displays as a kind of sidebar to their text, condensing material into a form that provides another way of interacting with the data.

The techniques mentioned here are not the only ways to organize your writing, but rather some of the strategies you might consider.

Integrating Data

As these various modes of organizing your data suggest, no rules or recipes exist for writing qualitative research articles or theses. Conventionally, ethnographers tend to integrate data from interviews, observations, and documents along with relevant quotations and information from published sources. The focus is on thinking with the data as a whole and constructing meaning, rather than compartmentalizing the information into sections or chapters called "review of literature," "data analysis," "findings," etc. Exhibit 8.1 provides an example of my integrating field notes, interview quotations, and literature sources in a section (edited down) from an article about my collaborative research in Oaxaca (Glesne 2003, 207–208). This section focuses on the autonomous nature of community.

TEXT	ORGANIZATIONAL APPROACH	DATA SOURCE
The previous examples suggest that as youth struggle to plan and develop a *proyecto de vida* [fulfilling vocation], they considered how the project would benefit the village as a whole. It took me a while to see this. At first, I wondered how their focus was different than a small-business approach in a U.S. community and wrote in my field-note reflections:	*Natural history*	
It struck me that all of the interviews had a capitalistic bent. Wasn't gaining an income a main concern of the youth? Wasn't a major problem that of obtaining capital to begin projects? . . . When I asked my coresearchers, they listened patiently and then replied that ultimately their work is about autonomy, . . . the issue was not so much that of making money, but of having a proyecto de vida *. . . that would support life within a community and allow life in that community to be lived autonomously.*		*Field notes*
After this discussion, I began noticing how frequently the word "autonomy" was part of conversations and interviews. Through probing, I came to understand more fully that autonomy implies a "we" rather than an "I," a "we" that includes family first of all and, then, community. The following statement by one of the youth highlights the sense of obligation that is part of the notion of communal autonomy, as well as the idea that autonomy is something people create or work to develop:		*Interviews and conversations*
There are young people who don't know about autonomy. They depend on their parents, and their parents work for the government and so they have no autonomy. For us, autonomy is doing something that you want to do which will be of benefit to you and your community and your country. . . .		*Interviews*
As I listened to the youths' expressions about the nature of their connections to each other and their work, I began to understand autonomy as a life quality of communities. . . . Bonfil Batalla (1996) described the history of Mexican nation-state building as one of "de-Indianization." Communal autonomy has provided a way to maintain and regenerate traditional customs and values, to resist the processes of de-Indianization. In today's world, this venture becomes one of not only maintaining the traditional but also imagining and constructing alternatives to pressures from both the nation-state and globalization.	*Zoom out*	*Literature*

EXHIBIT 8.1   Integrating Field Notes, Interviews, and Other Sources

BEGINNING AND ENDING

However the substantive sections of a work are organized, they conventionally include an introduction and an ending. The introduction usually states the purpose of the paper or book, presents the problem of inquiry, provides a general context to the problem, and foreshadows what is to come. Since many authors do not know with sufficient certainty what is to come until after they have written it, they often write the introduction last.

The ending should be a conclusion, which is quite different from a summary. "A summary is redundant and an affront to those readers who have actually read the paper, and a cop out for those who have not read it, however useful to them" (Glaser 1978, 132). Summaries reiterate what has been said; conclusions deal with the "so whats." They stimulate thought and transcend the substantive content presented earlier. Wolcott (1990, 56) also emphasizes the importance of the concluding section. He cautions the writer to "recognize and resist the temptation of dramatic but irrelevant endings or conclusions that raise issues never addressed in the research." And instead of trying to tie everything up into neat, understandable packages, Wolcott suggests that you leave yourself and readers "pondering the essential issues."

Often, the concluding chapter gets short shrift because the author is exhausted from all that precedes it and feels pressed for time. The writing well runs dry just when it should be at its fullest. When authors fail to deliver adequately on the promise of their data, they fail to do justice to their investment in their research project. The concluding chapter then becomes the weakest production rather than the transformative piece it could be.

Begin by appreciating the significance of your concluding chapter. Take care to schedule time for its completion—more time, in fact, than you may want to believe is necessary. Review all preceding chapters as preparation for writing the conclusion. Review your research questions so that you are certain to address all of them, and take note of what emerged as consequential that was not anticipated by your questions. Finally, worry yourself continually with the questions: Am I doing full justice to what I learned? Am I saying enough for readers to appreciate what I intend as *my* contribution to the matter under study?

When you have completed your concluding chapter, read it and your introductory chapter together. Have you done in the end what you announced in the beginning that you meant to do? Have you discussed all of the questions you raised? If not, why not? Your opening chapter presents readers with expectations that they anticipate will be met in the course of subsequent chapters, and that will culminate in the final chapter.

Finally, pay attention to how you end your report, to the last sentence the reader reads. Delamont (1992) analyzed examples from the endings of ethnographies and other qualitative works. She found that some had academic "essence" statements, others pointed forward to the next project, and yet others, often the ones most journalistic in style, left the last word with a research participant.

Pulling several favorite ethnographies from my shelves, I end this section with last sentences from Munoz, Tsing, and Myerhoff:

ACADEMIC ESSENCE EXAMPLE
Working together means taking on the risks and vulnerabilities of exploring the places where something catches: the unsettled and unsettling *fronteras* where the unfinished stories of identity are lived. (Munoz 1995, 257)

LOOKING FORWARD EXAMPLE
Uma Adang's poem speaks to both Indonesians and foreigners within shifting and limited frames of meaning. This—not timeless truth—is the power of all creative work. We reread and write today to draw from this heritage and move beyond it. (Tsing 1993, 301)

AN IMAGINARY CONVERSATION WITH AN INFORMANT WHO HAD DIED—MYERHOFF SPEAKING
I still don't know Hebrew or Aramaic or Yiddish or Torah or Talmud. Neither do I know the prayer, nor can I light the fire or find my way to the place in the forest. But now I have been told about these things and perhaps this will be sufficient. (Myerhoff 1979, 272)

Specifics Of Style

As with the overall form of your work, no absolutes govern the shaping of your style. The closest you can get is to apply what guides "good writing" in general to your writing of qualitative research. Brush up on grammar rules. Read *The Elements of Style* (Strunk and White 1979) again. Or curl up with *Eats, Shoots & Leaves* (Truss 2003).

The following guidelines for good writing seem specifically applicable to qualitative research writing. They are where I see most room for improvement in student papers and qualitative research articles:

1. *Make sentences active.* Give passive statements an actor and avoid "it is" and "there are" constructions. Instead of "data collection was carried out over a seven-month period in two different hospitals," state "I collected data over seven months in two hospitals." As Strunk and White (1979, 19) assert, "when a sentence is made stronger, it usually becomes shorter. Thus, brevity is a by-product of vigor."

2. *How are readers being addressed?* Make sure that "you," "one," or "people" are not used interchangeably, as in the following sentence, "When one is writing up research, people need to read and edit their work carefully or you might make reading your work so convoluted that one won't read it."

3. *Read through your manuscript making particular note of verb tenses.* Do you switch from present to past in the same paragraph? In general, whichever tense you choose should be used throughout your paper.

4. *If you begin a sentence with a participial phrase, make sure it refers to the subject of your sentence.* Strunk and White (1979, 14) provide wonderful examples violating this rule:
   - "Being in a dilapidated condition, I was able to buy the house very cheap."
   - "As a mother of five, with another on the way, my ironing board is always up."
5. *Think "parallel construction" when creating a sentence linking similar expressions.* In the following sentence, work to make each descriptive phrase parallel in structure: "The ADHD children in the study often sat detention at school, teachers gave them lower grades, siblings found them "annoying," and they were frequently knowledgeable about how things worked mechanically." (Often, the ADHD children in the study sat detention at school, experienced lower grades, knew how things worked mechanically, and were considered "annoying" by their siblings.)
6. *Make images concrete.* Use descriptive words. Turning again to Strunk and White (1979, 21), note the difference between the following sentences:
   - "He showed satisfaction as he took possession of his well-earned reward."
   - "He grinned as he pocketed the coin."
7. *Writers are fond of advising novice writers to "show, don't tell."* Instead of saying that something you learned was "interesting" or "important," write in a way that readers find the information "interesting" or "important" themselves.
8. *Avoid the jargon trap.* "It is a way to strike a pose as a smart, well-versed, current member of a hot and influential in-group. But more than one hot and influential in-group within ethnographic circles has become, over time, a cold and impotent out-group" (Van Maanen 1988, 28).
9. *Avoid wordiness.* For example, the sentence "There is some question as to whether he is the person who should be in charge of running the school owing to the fact that he rarely reads or utilizes educational research findings" is better written, "Because he rarely uses research findings, some people question his role as principal."

Try reading your draft with a mindset for "making sentences active" and edit appropriately. Then read it again, this time concentrating on clarity and concreteness of images and examples. Then read (and edit) for jargon, trite metaphors, and wordiness. With each reading, you shape your work, eventually forming a product that is worthy of your time and your reader's.

Schooled to write reports in a passive and authoritative manner with little, if any, of the researcher showing, some of you may experience some confusion as you let go of old habits. Even when students find some joy in their writing, as they work to write up qualitative research they are often overwhelmed by questions that they have not had to ask before. Following are some of the commonly asked questions. In response, I offer thoughts toward answers. In practice, a number of factors may influence the answers, including the demands of funding agencies, the expectations of supervising committees, the author's theoretical disposition or research tradition, and the degree of risk that the researcher is willing to take with creative forms of presentation.

1. *Question:* Is it ok to use "I"?

   Answer: Writing in the first person singular fits the nature of qualitative inquiry. The presence of "I" in your text reflects your presence in your research setting. Your "I" says that yours is not a disembodied account that presumes to be objective by virtue of omitting clear reference to the being who lived through a particular research experience and lived with other people in the course of that experience. Avoid the obtrusive "I" that says, "Look at me," because the story you tell is not, usually, foremost about yourself. Use "I" in the sense of saying that you were present; it is well for both writer and reader to remember this fact. Moreover, it would be foolish for you to hide behind veils of awkward sentence construction, particularly if your ideal is graceful, clear, and cogent writing.

2. *Question:* When I am describing and analyzing what I saw and heard, do I also evaluate what I experienced?

   Answer: In discussing her biographical work on Alice James, Strouse states, "Getting brave enough to venture my own views was really what writing the book was all about" (1988, 190). Your writing is interpretive; to pretend otherwise is to fool yourself but perhaps very few others. Nonetheless, the purpose of interpretivist research in general is to increase understanding, not to pass judgment. There may be a fine line between finding fault and finding meaning. Taking heed of this line is worthwhile. Tell the story from perspectives of your participants—most likely, you will have multiple versions to tell; do not use data to tell the story that a priori you want told.

3. *Question:* Can I tell a "story" in a thesis or dissertation, or do I have to follow the conventional format of problem statement, literature review, research methods, findings, and conclusion?

   Answer: The qualitative researching student has an advisor and committee whose judgments may set the guidelines and orthodoxy for the student's writing. In general, however, qualitative research has no conventional organizational format. Telling a story, or following any particular chapter arrangement, is likely to be a matter of negotiation with your committee, a negotiation that should be undertaken early. From my perspective, the conventional dissertation format is not congruent with the openness of qualitative inquiry and the variable forms that may best suit the stories to be told.

4. *Question:* Should I include a section titled "literature," or should I integrate the literature throughout the text?

   Answer: Depending on your study and audience, you may find both useful. Integrating the work of others with your own is accepted ethnographic practice. Since your work may build on and extend the theories of others, you should make due reference to these other works, but do not allow them to overshadow your own thoughts and ideas.

5. *Question:* What use should I make of historical and current documents pertaining to sites other than the one I am investigating? For example, in a study of a one-room schoolhouse, Jody collected numerous historical documents pertaining to both her site and similar sites, including diaries of one-room schoolteachers. Can she use the documents from the similar sites? If so, how?

   Answer: Use whatever materials, however collected, that enhance your case. The question is not where the material came from, but whether it will help.

6. *Question:* When quoting participants in the text, should I reference my interview notes? If so, how?

   Answer: I don't, but your committee may insist that you do. Other than for audit checks, it seems meaningless to provide such references when general readers do not have access to your notes. In addition, such referencing interrupts the flow of the text. If, however, you are working to document your study through hypertext or hypermedia, you will provide links in your text to transcripts and/or taped interviews.

7. *Question:* If in a quote the interviewee uses the name of a person or place, do I change the names to provide anonymity? If so, do I use brackets or some other means to demonstrate that the name has been changed?

   Answer: If by naming the person or place you will breach your commitment to anonymity, then the answer is clear: Use pseudonyms. A general footnote at the beginning of your work can clarify your intent to alter names and places as needed. Thereafter, I see no need to call attention to the changes you make in the interest of preserving anonymity.

8. *Question:* When quoting someone, should I leave in every "umm," "you know," and other unconscious patterns of speech?

   Answer: Let your methodological approaches and research purposes be your guide. If you are doing conversational analysis or some forms of narrative analysis, then such utterances could be an important part of your data and you will want to transcribe in a way that shows the person struggling for the right word, along with pauses and hesitations. If, however, you are interested in patterns and cultural understandings, these speech patterns contribute little. When quoting, you might want to leave in enough of such sounds and words to represent the person's speech, but not so many as to embarrass the speaker or to impose on a reader's patience.

9. *Question:* How do you assure confidentiality and anonymity to a person who plays a major role in a study and whose position is singular and central to the study (e.g., a school principal or superintendent)?

   Answer: "When total confidentiality or anonymity cannot be guaranteed, the issue becomes, in part, one of ongoing communication and agreement . . . between the investigator and research participants" (Johnson 1982, 85). This is a sensitive matter. You may feel particularly constrained in what you say because you cannot safely disguise the person's identity. My suggestion is to begin by saying all that you would like to say. Then reread what you have written as if you were that person and edit appropriately. Finally, send a copy of your prose to that person and take your cue from his or her reaction.

10. *Question:* How do you describe and report unfavorable attitudes toward a person, program, or site when that person, program, or site is identifiable by research participants and by others in nearby areas?

    Answer: Ask yourself if it is at all necessary to report anything negative about persons and places that are identifiable. A commitment to scholarship does not provide a license to injure those who allow you access to their words and deeds. If your research, however, has a clear evaluative component and that component is a negotiated aspect of your entry arrangements, then the matter of negative findings assumes another perspective.

11. *Question:* Should I use precise counts, or imprecise terms such as "a few," "almost all," or "a majority"? For example, if I interviewed twenty persons, how much do I count when analyzing and reporting the data?

    Answer: Although some reference to frequency may contribute to your presentation, keep in mind that numbers do not play the same role in qualitative research that they do in quantitative research. Qualitative research has the potential to make many useful contributions, but these do not include generalizations derived from sampling in the quantitative tradition. When to count and in what ways to count are judgments that you make linked to your research purposes. To rule out all counting is to shut down a possible way of presenting your data that is fully warranted by your intent. To count as a basic way of structuring your data is to insert the rationality of the positivist paradigm where, ordinarily, it does not belong. Nonetheless, counting not only may be useful, it also may be necessary, as in many ethnomethodological and conversational analysis studies.

12. *Question:* Should I end my written report with a list of recommendations? If I'm in an applied field of study, shouldn't I be prescriptive?

    Answer: The need to be useful is both understandable and desirable. Useful outcomes, however, do not always take the form of prescriptions. You must ask yourself: Have I designed my study for the purpose of being prescriptive? If so, then prescribe. If not, then the prescriptions, although interesting, are bootlegged onto a study designed to do other things. Do what you set out to do, and do it as well as you can. Attend to the matter of prescriptions when it is clearly suitable to do so. To focus on them when they are not integral to your design is to take effort away from where you planned it to be.

This set of questions and answers covers some of the practical considerations that arise in bringing a research process to fruition. They are important but secondary considerations, preceded in priority by commitments: to collect data the best ways you can; to have something to say—a matter of analysis, imagination, and boldness; to be enthusiastic about your topic; to intend to write well; and, not least, to revise and revise and revise.

RESPONSIBILITIES OF THE WRITER

Writing is a political act: Carefully think through both the intended and the unintended consequences of your words. Your first responsibility is to your research respondents, those persons whose cooperation is the basis of your research. Ask yourself whether your choice of words results in judgments rather than in descriptions and interpretations of a place and its people. Note the difference between saying the "community is backward" and "10 percent of the adult population can neither read nor write" (Johnson 1982, 87). Nagel, a biographer, gives good advice: "Writing about another person's life is an awesome task, so one must proceed with a gentleness born from knowing that the subject and the author share the frailties of human mortality" (1988, 115). As a researcher, strive to understand the complexity of social phenomena. In doing so, you will most likely discover that research participants are as human as you are—neither saint nor sinner. Portray that humanness, neither disguising it with a hidden agenda of your own, nor overlaying it with emphases and highlights that gild—or wound, damage, and denigrate.

Central to the responsibility to research participants is the following question:

> Are we placing research participants and their site(s) at undue risk because of our interactions with them? We should imagine a scenario in which the location(s) and their participants are revealed and ask ourselves what the possible consequences of that discovery would be. (Johnson 1982, 87)

How could what you write be used either positively or negatively? Would individuals be subjected to unwanted publicity? Would the disclosure of data about identifiable individuals or groups with little power be exploited by others who have power? Should you omit certain descriptions, discussions, or interpretations from the manuscript?

Another consideration is your responsibility to the larger community of social scientists. Ask yourself whether your portrayal will preclude another study at the same site, by you or by someone else. Will participants be reluctant, if not adamantly negative, about allowing another researcher in? If so, what harm have you done to research opportunities and fellow inquirers, in addition to research participants?

You must also be responsible to yourself. Your research discoveries can have political ramifications for your job and your interactions with "superiors," particularly if researching in your own backyard. Bonnie, for example, gave a copy of her final report to the nursing supervisor who was both the gatekeeper to her research participants and her "boss." The supervisor was unhappy with the report findings and told Bonnie that if she published them, she could not return to work in the hospital. Consider the consequences of your words on yourself as well as on others.

How do you avoid the research complications that may disrupt your own life as well as those of research participants? The surest way is to anticipate complications and to work them out along the way by collaborative arrangements with research supervisors and research participants. Anticipate to whom findings of any but the most obviously laudatory type could prove disagreeable and include those persons in the preparation of the "controversial" sections. That is, treat your findings as tentative; discuss them in very general terms, not as *the* results. Solicit reactions to your words from research supervisors and participants. In addition, look for colleagues who will read your manuscript for examples of judgment, criticism, and potential ethical and political problems. The idea is to avoid complications, rather than have to get out of them.

Research is a political act, involving resources, policy, power, and ethics. Throughout the research process, the political context is generally limited to the research site(s) and the researcher's relationships with participants and, sometimes, with their supervisors (as well as the researcher's supervisors). Writing extends the complexity of research politics because it invites in a third party—the reader—with all the ramifications that inclusion of this invisible but vital participant may generate for both researcher and researched. Chapter 9 delves more deeply into the politics of writing through examining the role of language in conveying meaning— particularly how language and form connote and transfer values.

RECOMMENDED READINGS

Huddle, D. 1991. *The Writing Habit*. Hanover, NH: University Press of New England.

King, S. 2000. *On Writing: A Memoir of the Craft*. New York: Pocket Books.

Lamott, A. 1994. *Bird by Bird: Some Instructions on Writing and Life*. New York: Pantheon Books.

Wolcott, H. 2001. *Writing Up Qualitative Research*, 2nd ed. Thousand Oaks, CA: Sage.

Zinsser, W. 1988. *Writing to Learn: How to Write and Think Clearly about Any Subject at All*. New York: Harper & Row.

EXERCISES

1. Return to the *research practice* exercise (last visited in Chapter 7). In the same small groups that worked on data analysis, begin to write up your section of a group report. The purpose of this exercise is to practice making decisions about how to express themes, patterns, and descriptions; what to use as supporting evidence; and which interviewee words to include and which to leave out. In your own individual research (or in an actual group project), you would want to be fully acquainted with all the data and the relationships among them as a whole. For this practice exercise, however, work only with the data for your section.

2. After each group has shaped a written report for its section, decide on a seemingly logical order for the combined report. Then, group by group, read the "class report." Discuss the ways in which different groups reported their data.

CHAPTER 9

Improvising a Song of the World: Language and Representation

Our knowledge is contextual and only contextual. Ordering and invention coincide: we call their collaboration "knowledge." The mind is a blue guitar on which we improvise the song of the world.

(Dillard 1982, 56)

Sandelowski (1994) locates qualitative research "at the meeting place between art and science" (55). In the past, most social scientists desired to be perceived as scientific, not artistic. Because science was associated with fact and objectivity, social scientists used language considered objective, precise, neutral, and nonmetaphoric (Richardson 1990; Stewart 1989). The song of the world could be reported but not sung. Some anthropologists wrote poetry or short stories for literary journals and others published field memoirs (often under pseudonyms), but usually they did not mix direct discussion of their field experiences, personal reflections, and poetic compositions with their ethnographic writing (Bruner 1993).

More recently, the contextual nature of knowledge along with the role of language in creating meaning has become a focal point of thought and discussion with scholars highlighting, in particular: (1) how the research tale cannot be separated from the teller, the researcher; (2) how the language the writer chooses carries with it certain values; and (3) how all textual presentations are "fashioned" and, thereby, in a sense, fictions. As discussed on the next pages, these ideas have influenced how I, and others, think about writing up qualitative inquiry. They have also helped to open a space for playing with form in research representation, a topic addressed in this chapter.

THE TALE AND THE TELLER

Researchers have always told stories to friends and colleagues of research relationships, dramatic field events, and day-to-day drudgery, but tended to omit such stories from written reports. They also left out discussion of subjective lenses through which they viewed their research. Rather, they presented their research with an authoritative "this is the way it is" stance (Van Maanen, 1988), often referred to as *literary realism*.

Qualitative researchers today ask how social science and self are "co-created" (Richardson 2000). From this perspective, what you know about your research—reflected in your interpretations—is intertwined with what you know about yourself. Therefore, authors increasingly write themselves into their texts, acknowledging that they have always been there, creating meaning. How authors reflect upon their work and inscribe themselves into their texts, however, varies in degree and style.

A text (all of it or a section) may take the form of what Van Maanen (1988) calls a "confessional tale." In confessional tales, the point of view is not that of "natives," but that of fieldworkers, reflecting upon themselves as researchers. Authors of confessional tales often portray themselves as human beings who make mistakes and blunders, but who eventually "learn the rules" and come to see things in new ways.

Rebecca wrote a confessional tale about her early stages in exploring adolescent girls' friendships. Passages within the tale convey her sense of insecurity and naïveté as she ventured into the "field":

> I move to a desk situated in front of the row the girls have claimed and set down my backpack. As I begin to unpack my materials I wonder how I should begin. "Hi, my name is Rebecca and I'm here to tell you a little bit about my study that you agreed to be a part of." All of the girls stare at me in silence, some with shadows of apprehension on their faces. I sit down on the desk behind me and adopt a stance and manner I hope minimizes my authority role.

After the introductory meeting with the girls, Rebecca felt relieved to have completed her first research "act." Despite her awkwardness, she encouraged the girls to talk, and she left excited by what was to come.

Linden (1993) states, "fieldwork confessions abound, yet reflexive accounts of how other cultures and cultural 'others' act on field workers are rare" (9). Reflexive accounts demand more than personal tales of research problems and accomplishments. They require thought about the researcher's position and how the researcher affects and is affected by the fieldwork and field relationships, as Linden (1993, 2) exemplifies in *Making Stories, Making Selves: Feminist Reflections on the Holocaust*:

> Writing this book has compelled me, repeatedly, to turn inward. Over and over again, I have examined the impress of the Holocaust on my Jewish consciousness. My self-reflections became an integral component of my research, inseparable from the book "about" Holocaust survivors I had initially planned to write. This process transformed my Jewish identity, and the book tells that story as well.

In the text, Linden presents her own memories, family stories, and evolving sense of identity along with the narratives of the Holocaust survivors.

In *Translated Woman,* Behar (1993) addresses socioeconomic class differences between herself and Esperanza, the Mexican woman with whom she conducted research for several years. Behar also reveals details of her family life as she was growing up that she perceived influential in her research interpretations. Ever reflexive, she later discusses the effects of having written about her family. Her mother, angry at Behar's exposure of the family's "dirty laundry," asks her, "If you had to ask Esperanza for permission to write about her, why don't you have to ask permission to write about us?" (Behar 1995, 72). Since we are relational beings, exposing lives of those around us is a potential hazard of reflexivity.

Another potential risk of reflexivity is to use research as a kind of self-therapy or to focus as much on self as on other. Cynically referred to as ethnonarcissism, some reflexive accounts appear to be ways for people to make more of themselves than of the world around them. As a researcher, you are inseparable from your findings. Just what to write about yourself in the text—and how much—remains, however, an issue worthy of consideration.

THE RESEARCHER'S LANGUAGE

> Whatever reality is, besides existent, our sense of it . . . comes inevitably out of the way we talk about it.
>
> (Geertz 1995, 18)

Meaning is more complex than the definition of words. The very choice of the language you use—whether clear and coherent, complex and disruptive, removed and formal, or personal and evocative—tells a story in addition to what you mean it to say. For example, consider researchers who pepper reports with *utilize, finalize,* and other *ize*-ending words instead of shorter terms such as *use* and *finish.* By their word choice, they take on the air of academic pretension, but not necessarily that of good writers, as Strunk and White (1979) remind us.

For another example, in crafting this book, I want to write in a style accessible to those of you who are novice researchers, to use clear, expressive language and examples that engage. But what meaning does my language choice produce? What messages do I reproduce? Certainly, I simplify much and simply ignore more. I gloss over historical catalysts and social philosophies. I do so not because they don't matter but because my primary intent is to welcome in those of you new to qualitative research. I trust that you will go on to read, discuss, and discover elsewhere variety and complexity in research perspectives and methodologies. In doing so, however, am I inviting you into a seemingly intriguing and engaging process without warning properly of all the hidden alleys and curves? Am I encouraging "bad science" (and art) if some of you read this text and think that you now know all about being qualitative researchers? I don't want to deceive, or provide a false sense of "knowing," but both may be possibilities because of the language I choose.

"Language does not 'reflect' social reality, but produces meaning, creates social reality" (Richardson 2000, 928). For example, passive, disembodied sentences ("The study was conducted . . .") convey a sense of objectivity where the researcher and his or her actions (excitement, worries) disappear. For another example, return to my discussion of writing this text and my intent to use clear, accessible language. Lather (1996) states that "plain speaking" can imply "a mirroring relationship between the word and the world" (527). She argues that sometimes we need to read and not easily understand in order to move our thinking beyond the taken-for-granted. Tsing (1993) takes a similar perspective, referring to her own ethnographic writing strategies as "guerrilla tactics of multiple, uneasily jostling theories and stories . . . in which curiosity is not overwhelmed by coherence" (32–33). In essence, Lather and Tsing push me to ask questions of language use in this text, and I urge you to do so as well, not only of this text but also of your own.

THE RESEARCHER'S REPRESENTATIONS

> A life as lived is what actually happened. . . . A life as told, a life history, is a narrative, influenced by the cultural conventions of telling, by the social context.
>
> (Bruner 1984, 7).

A life as told is a re-presentation of that life; the life and the telling are not the same. Rather, the narrative—the telling or the writing—is always an interpretation of other peoples' lives, an interpretation that qualitative researchers struggle with representing.

For many years, the realist tale (Van Maanen 1988) was the dominant form of ethnographic representation. Authors minutely documented details of the lives of people studied, using closely edited quotations to portray participants' points of view. The researcher, however, was absent from much, if not all, of the text, taking a position of "interpretive omnipotence" (Van Maanen 1988, 51) where the life was told, but in a way that assumed that the life and the telling were practically the same. In other words, the representation seemed to be *true* to life.

Liebow, in his 1967 book *Tally's Corner*, explored the lives of "streetcorner" men who hung out on Tally's Corner in inner-city Washington, DC, in the early 1960s. Liebow discusses, among other things, his own background and issues of class and race (he is white; the streetcorner men are black) in an appendix. In the text, however, Liebow (1967, 57) primarily presents descriptions of what he heard and saw, words of people with whom he spoke, and generalized interpretations such as the following:

> A crucial factor in the streetcorner man's lack of job commitment is the overall value he places on the job. *For his part, the streetcorner man puts no lower value on the job than does the larger society around him.* He knows the social value of the job by the amount of money the employer is willing to pay him for doing it. In a real sense, every pay day, he counts in dollars and cents the value placed on the job by society at large.

Liebow's writing is clear, descriptive, and engaging. In his portrait of a group of inner-city African American men and their relationships with work, women, children, and friends, Liebow provides the reader with a sense of "this is the way it really is."

How you represent others has consequences. Edward Said was influential in confronting the perceived neutrality of research writing in the late 1970s. He argued that cross-cultural researchers who portrayed others as "exotic" or "backward," for example, assumed positions of privilege as people who could classify another, rendering those described silent, objectified, and dominated (Dicks et al. 2005). The role language plays in assigning value continues as a focal point in the "crisis of representation" confronting qualitative researchers. This crisis demands, among other things, that you question whether you can ever fairly represent experiences of another.

Giving up an authoritative stance means that you no longer can profess to know everything, but, from my perspective, you can claim to *know something*. Your knowledge, however, is always partial, situated in a particular context with specific historical understandings (Richardson 2000). That your understanding is incomplete does not make it unimportant, nor does it mean that you scatter methodological discipline and rigor to the wind. You may, however, want to experiment with representational form, making even more explicit your role as cocreator of research tales, improvising order.

THE ART OF REPRESENTATION

> If we learn to "read" and "write" in a manner similar to the way the painter paints, we may well be able to sensualize prose which represents others so that our books become the study of human beings as well as human behavior.
>
> (Stoller 1989, 40)

Richardson (2000) refers to the variety of nontraditional ways in which qualitative researchers are representing their inquiry as *creative analytic practices*. Throughout much of the 1990s, these writing practices were called "experimental" or "alternative," labels that "reinscribed traditional ethnographic practices as the standard, the known, accepted, preferred, tried-and-true mode of doing and representing qualitative research" (Richardson 2000, 930). Using artistic forms of expression as guides, some researchers seek to combine the "strengths of science with the rewards of the humanities" (Stoller 1989, 9). To do so, they draw upon literary traditions such as drama, poetry, and narrative to represent their work; some use nonverbal forms such as photography, dance, and painting.

Eisner (1997, 8) suggests that using creative analytic practices can help to create a sense of empathy for research participants; generate insight and attention to complexity; increase the kinds of questions that researchers ask as they think within new mediums; and make better use of the variety in researchers' representational abilities. Ethnographies employing creative analytic practices such as

Lather and Smithies (1997) *Troubling the Angels: Women Living with HIV/AIDS* and Anna Lowenhaupt Tsing's (1993) *In the Realm of the Diamond Queen: Marginality in an Out-of-Way Place* are multigenre constructions, made up of many voices, and inclusive of emotional reactions as well as analytical descriptions.

Agar (1995) likens the "new ethnography" to creative nonfiction. Creative nonfiction writers want, he says, "to blend factual content and fiction form, to play the roles of both observer/reporter and textmaker, to commit equally to artistic and empirical truth, and to research fact not as an end in itself but as a means to art" (117). Agar (1995, 128–129) worries, however, that for some, this could lead to an emphasis on form over content:

> Textuality as a consciousness-raising concept is long over-due. But textuality as the primary focus for what ethnography is all about is, I think, a mistake . . . a move to new textual forms without more attention to the research processes that ground them would be a serious ethnomistake.

Similarly, Eisner (1997) warns, "We also need to be sure, if we can be, that we are not substituting novelty and cleverness for substance" (9). You need to take these cautions seriously, and yet, give yourself license to play with form, to expand your repertoire of expressive modes. As you become familiar with different forms of representation, you will be able to more critically reflect on the appropriateness of the form.

Experimenting with form is as much (or more) about the process as the product. After a semester course focused on data analysis and writing, including an emphasis on creative analytic practices, I asked students what they learned about their research and themselves through writing their work in more creative ways. Their answers suggested, in particular, that using creative analytic practices is a *freeing* experience that accesses feelings and encourages broader perspectives:

- It allowed me to get at feelings, and my relationship with others, in ways that I could not possibly have done in another form. It also allowed me—*freed* me—to think about what might have been, what might be now.
- It magnified the learning which happens during the writing process. It *freed* up my perspective to envision and construct meanings that go beyond my usual monophonic world.

In terms of what students learned about themselves, they usually mentioned something about the process of writing as in this response from Glen who worked hard with drafts and redrafts all semester: "I learned that my writing could be more interesting for me to write and for others to read."

Writing in different modes helps you to think about data in new ways. When creating drama or reader's theater, for example, you tend to focus on dialogue and how people's words support and challenge each other. When developing a short story, you are more likely to focus on observations, writing descriptively of the setting and actions as well as using words of research participants. Exploring ways of representing data, therefore, "forces [you] to think about the meanings and under-standings, voices, and experiences present in the data. . . . Analytical ideas are developed and tried out in the process of writing and representing" (Coffey and Atkinson 1996, 109). When writing up data as a play, poetry, or narrative, you still read, reread, analyze, and interpret your data, but how you think about them and how you order them will vary with form, stressing, in the process, different issues. The same data tell slightly different stories, depending upon the form you choose—a somewhat disconcerting, but fascinating realization in itself. Playing with language and form is also an avenue for encouraging a spirit of discovery and creativity within you as you work.

The following sections highlight autoethnography, poetic transcription, drama, and short story as creative forms of representation. Examples are pre-sented to encourage you to try out different forms. Some research experiences may be best expressed in a particular form, but this presupposes that you are familiar with and versed in a wide range of expressive styles. As you try out various forms, continually reflect upon what the mode of representation allows you and the reader to know about research participants, you as researcher, and the meaning you are making.

AUTOETHNOGRAPHY

> Each time I have attempted to do theoretical work it has been on the basis of elements from my experience. . . .
> (Foucault, cited in Rajchman 1988, 108)

The term *autoethnography* is used in a variety of ways: to describe narratives of a culture or ethnic group produced by members of that culture or ethnic group; to describe ethnographies of the "other," but one where the writer interjects personal experience into the text as in the confessional tale; and, more akin to autobiography, to investigate self within a social context, whether it be your own or that of another culture (Reed-Danahay 1997). Here, I am using *autoethnography* to refer to the kind of writing that inquires into the self as part of a sociocul-tural context.

Autoethnography begins with the self, the personal biography. Using narra-tives of the self, the researcher goes on to say something about the larger cultural setting and scholarly discourse, taking a sociological rather than a psychological perspective. Carolyn Ellis and Arthur Bochner (1996, 2000) have been at the fore-front of autoethnography, creating texts individually and together and encourag-ing others to delve into their own lives to explore sociocultural milieus. In autoethnography, researchers often use literary techniques to portray dramatically their experience. Ellis (2004) even wrote an autoethnography methods book in the form of a "methodological novel."

In autoethnographic texts, readers are often asked to "'relive' the events emotionally, with the writers" (Richardson 2000, 931). Yvette Pigeon (1998) does this as she takes the reader through her first exposure to her doctoral program. She presents her account as a way to introduce concepts of adult education, particularly the role of a cohort of peers in adult learning—the focus of her dissertation research:

> The space was animated with movement and social posturing. Doctoral core faculty members were working the room, chatting with people they appeared to know. As someone who didn't know anyone there, I had the distinct and uncomfortable feeling of being an outsider, wondering if I'd been sent an invitation by mistake. I tried not to stare as I postulated who these people were and what might be the socioeconomic range, not to mention the political affiliations of this somewhat conservative looking group. Did we have anything in common other than arriving in the same place at the same time? . . .
>
> "Let's get started," commanded the director. "We'll begin with introductions. Tell us your name, area of study, and why you have chosen to be in the doctoral program." Silence immediately spread through the room and everyone had a similar look of masked fear and deep concentration on their faces. It was apparent that most of us had not publicly divulged the details of our planned area of study since we had written it in our applications months ago. "Where should we start?" the director asked as he smiled. I didn't know whether it was a smile of compassion or of sadism as he probably could sense the cohort's level of nervous anticipation. The group on the couch volunteered while the rest of us rehearsed in our mind what we would say when it inevitably became our turn in the introduction ritual. . . .
>
> More than half way through the introduction, the Dean appeared at the door to welcome us. It was at that moment that all my fears and insecurities about being an adult thrown back into the role of student surfaced. Based on my past educational experience she represented authority and personified the esteem of the doctoral degree. As a student and a woman I had learned to genuflect when in the presence of either and here I was daring to achieve both. Self-doubtingly I thought, "Who am I trying to kid? What am I doing here?" . . .
>
> I was abruptly jarred from my introspective stupor by the program director. "We are really here to support you," he said, "and we are invested in increasing our program completion rate." For some reason, this piece of news did not sound encouraging. "Oh and also, be sure to make use of your cohort for support. For instance you can study for the comprehensive exams together," he added. It struck me as odd that I hadn't taken my first course yet and he was talking about exams. This, along with the fact that I wasn't sure what "the cohort" was left me wondering if I had missed something. . . .

Tillmann-Healy and Kiesinger (2001) combine autoethnography and narrative ethnography in their explorations into bulimia. Each first wrote autobiographically about her struggles with bulimia; then they interviewed each other about their experiences and wrote biographically about the other's experience; and finally, they responded to each other's writing (82). Of their work, they state, "we conducted our study as much with our hearts as with our heads" (103). The intense emotional work did not stop with data collection, but was fully a part of the writing: "each of us felt protective of the other, hoping our renderings would offer her tools for coping and not further pain" (104).

"Mystory" accounts are similar to autoethnography, but combine and collide various sources, including stories of the self, to critique some aspect of society. Mystory begins through the "sting of memory" (Denzin 2008, 123) such as a particular case of discrimination or a particular burden of guilt. The writer dramatically describes this memory and then begins to pull in associated pieces from the wider culture—academia, music, popular culture, etc. The text is shaped so that various "representations are contested, challenged" and eventually form a "montage text, cinematic and multimedia in shape . . . [and] locates itself against the specialized knowledges that circulate in the larger society" (Denzin 2008, 123). Mystory accounts work to present both critique and what Denzin (2008, 123) calls a "utopian vision" of what could be. Kelly Clark/Keefe (2006, 1180–1197) wrote a mystory (that she calls "ourstory") that included a re-created discussion with her mother on going to college:

Mom: So, will that be enough? How much did you say it is for both times?

Kelly: Well, it looks like here, that the first semester is more—it costs more—there's fees—something like what they're calling a "student health fee" and, uh, an "activity fee." And that's when, first semester, that's when I have to buy a meal card. *(shuffling through papers)* There was a separate letter from some company about that . . .

Mom: *(now standing up, facing the stove, scraping at the ground beef stuck to the skillet)* I don't like that you have to pay for all this food before you eat it. You probably—well, you probably could end up eating less than some other kids—you know, if you had to. *(pause)* But, I guess they don't let you do it that way?

Kelly: What?

Mom: Pay just for what you eat?

Kelly: Uh, I don't—Oh wait, here, Marriott Food Services. Here's that note, uh *(pause)* . . . It's expensive.

Mom: So how much for everything? *(sitting back down at the table)*

Kelly: First semester?

Mom: Yeah, I guess.

Kelly: Uh, like three-thousand, almost four-thousand . . . I think, with everything.

Mom: And you pay that two times, in one year, for how long?

Kelly: Well, it's a little less the second time that I go back—But yeah, so that, both times and if I stay in the whole time—it would be for four years.

(long pause)

Clark/Keefe juxtaposes her dramatized memories next to words from academic writers such as bell hooks describing her own experience as a first-generation college student from a working-poor background, lyrics to songs by Carpenter and Fogelberg, parts of interview transcripts, and more autobiographical vignettes. The pieces do not fit neatly together. Sometimes they support; sometimes they contradict, but as a whole they present to the reader the messy world of entering college from the perspective of a first-generation student from a working-class background.

Autoethnographic and mystory accounts relieve the writer (or give a reprieve) of speaking for the other (Richardson 2000). In contrast, poetic transcription—the next creative form to be discussed—depends heavily on the other's words with the researcher snipping and snipping, as Behar (1993) describes her work with Esperanza's *historias*, only to "patch together a new tongue" (19).

POETIC TRANSCRIPTION

In poetic transcription[1], the researcher fashions poem-like pieces from the words of interviewees (Glesne 1997; Richardson 2000, 2002). The writer aspires to get at the essence of what's said, the emotions expressed, and the rhythm of speaking. The process involves word reduction while illuminating the wholeness and interconnectedness of thoughts. Through shaping the presentation of the words of an interviewee, the researcher creates a third voice that is neither the interviewee's nor the researcher's but is a combination of both. This third voice disintegrates any appearance of separation between observer and observed.

Exhibit 9.1 shows some of the process I used in making a poetic transcription from transcripts of over 10 hours of interviews with a Puerto Rican educator, Dona Juana (Glesne 1997). The left column contains a portion of actual interview transcript. The right side begins with Version 1, a poetic rendering of the transcript in chronological order. The chronological rendering continued with other sections of the transcript that seemed related. Then I began eliminating words and moving them around to create the poem found in Version 2 on the right side of the figure.

Others have created poetic transcriptions from their research in ways that range from developing poetic reflexivity pieces from journal notes to compilations of interview voices. Katie Furney (1997) assembled the words of elementary school children to create a poetic transcription in which the children describe their school. At times, she changed tenses and pronouns, added lines at the beginning of the stanzas to give them some structure, and used conjunctions to hook similar comments from individual students together. Otherwise, the words are those the students spoke. Furney was researching practices in schools with a reputation for excellence in inclusion. She states that as she worked with the words of the students, "[I] heard echoes of the voices of teachers and administrators. I heard talk of engagement, caring relationships, students as active learners, and students who felt accepted and prized. I heard a sense of self-worth: the kind that comes from

TRANSCRIPT

C: If I asked you to use a metaphor to describe yourself as a professor, what would you say you were like? Someone I asked said that she was a bridge and then she told me why. What metaphor comes to mind for you?

J: **I would be a flying bird.**

C: A flying bird. Tell me about it. How are you a flying bird?

J: Because **I want to move so fast.**

C: Mm-hmmm. Cover a lot of territory.

J: Yes. Yes.

C: Are you any kind of bird or just any bird?

J: Well, any bird because I don't want to mention some birds, some birds here are destructive.

C: Are what?

J: Are destructive. They destroy and I don't want to …

C: No, you don't want to be one of them. No. You're just a bird that moves fast.

J: That moves fast and sees from the tops of trees. **So I can see quickly.**

C: See quickly, see everything.

I: **Everything.**

J: So you can see me?

C: I can. I can see you, a flying bird.

J: **I wish I could look at the world with the eyes of God.**

C: With the eyes of what?

J: Of God, of that spiritual power that can **give strength.**

C: That can give strength? Strength?

J: Yes, **to those that need.**

POETIC NARRATIVE

Version 1: Chronologically and linguistically faithful to the transcript.

I would be a flying bird.
I want to move so fast
so I can see quickly, everything.
I wish I could look at the world
with the eyes of God,
to give strength to those that need.

Version 2: Draws from other sections of the interviews, takes more license with words.

I am a flying bird
moving fast, seeing quickly,
looking with the eyes of God
from the tops of trees.

How hard for country people
picking green worms
from fields of tobacco,
sending their children to school,
not wanting them to suffer
as they suffer.
In the urban zone,
students worked at night
and so they slept in school.
Teaching was the real university.

So I came to study
to find out how I could help.
I am busy here at the university,
there is so much to do.
But the university is not the island.

I am a flying bird
moving fast, seeing quickly
so I can give strength,
so I could have that rare feeling
of being useful.

EXHIBIT 9.1   The Making of a Poetic Transcription

Source: From Glesne, C. 1997. That rare feeling: Re-presenting research through poetic transcription. *Qualitative Inquiry,* 3(2), 202–221

being cared for" (119–120). Furney's (1997, 120) poetic transcription portrays a school in which students, parents, and educators can take pride:

SCHOOL IS FUN—AND YOU LEARN A LOT TOO

I love school because it's cool
and I have lots of friends in school.
I have a lot of friends to spend time with
and they like school too.
If you didn't go to school you wouldn't know
as much as if you did go to school.
You learn stuff that you never knew before.

The teachers
usually listen to what you have to say.
They never ignore you and they let you
explain your own feelings.
They let you choose your own books
and your own topics in reading and writing.
They help us read and spell,
and they combine the stuff
that we are learning.

Sometimes you need help:
If you raise your hand quietly and ask
a question, your teacher will usually help you
get the right answer.
Our teachers help us work out and solve
our problems—
we can talk to our teachers.

Our teachers listen to us and respect
our privacy.
You don't just sit there all the time,
you get to do projects.
I like doing things with my hands,
like math on the computer,
helping other kids on the computer,
cleaning the classroom,
drama, breaks, recess,
my job.

There are some things that aren't so great:
there's never enough time to finish projects,
or to do math, reading, art, music and
library activities.
There's never enough food
or time to eat lunch.
The water fountain should be colder.
I hate getting into trouble and
I didn't like it when I broke up
with my girlfriend.

If I could change anything, I'd have
more projects, longer math and science classes, and
a longer school day to finish my work.
I'd like a bigger library with bigger books
and
a bigger bathroom for the teachers.
I would like more homework
(but I don't want any!)
I'd like a bigger playground, more sports,
a longer recess.
We should have more food, seconds every day.
I'd like them to put a different color of paint
on the walls—maybe something brickish.

Kids should run the school!
We would learn about space every day,
we'd watch Power Ranger videos,
and have pizza at every lunch.
All of the kids could pick up trash outside
of the school and get paid for it.

I like school—
I usually like all of my teachers
and they like me for how I am and I like that.
It's a cool school,
people should stay in school and be cool.

Carolyn Mears sought a way to document and learn from the tragedy at Columbine High School, a trauma that her son personally experienced as a Columbine student. To ground the research in lived experience and provide a contextual basis for her findings, Mears used a form of poetic transcription to communicate the emotions and diverse responses expressed by the parents in her study. The success of this approach, recognized in 2006 by the American Educational Research Association for its contribution to qualitative inquiry, led Meers to write a methods text describing her process, an approach she calls "gateway" because it "provides a means of connection, a way toward deeper understanding of a metaphorical 'community' of experience" (Mears 2009, 9). Her book provides many useful suggestions and examples for working with interview data to provide well-crafted interpretive displays as in this one with Lillian (Mears 2009, 197-198). Only the beginning of a much longer piece is reprinted here:

APRIL 20TH . . .
It was lunchtime. I was coming down Wadsworth.
All of a sudden,
Three cop cars going so fast—
About 6 feet apart.
It scared me to death—I thought,
Oh my gosh, there's been a wreck.
It has to do with high school kids.
You know how crazy the kids are in cars.

That's always been my biggest fear.

I decided to go past the school,
See what was going on.
The street was all blocked off.
I saw kids running.
One said, There's somebody inside shooting people up.
There's people dying in there.
I just went home—
     less that a mile—
Was Jenny okay?
I got home
Her car was in the driveway.
So the only horrible minutes I had,
     I am so lucky,
Was from Leawood to home.

Jenny was here.
          Other girls too,
               Jenny and her friends.
Jenny didn't open a book all through high school.
She didn't study.

They had lunch together—
     Gone to the mall to eat.
They were going to come back here to watch TV.
They had dropped a boy off at school.
He went in,
Into the library to study.
He was shot.

Source: From Mears, C. 2009. *Interviewing for Education and Social Science Research: The Gateway Approach.* New York: Palgrave Macmillan.

Laurel Richardson (1994, 2000, 2002) writes poetry and about poetic representation and other creative analytic practices. She also offers good advice to anyone beginning work in this area: Take classes and workshops in poetry writing, read poetry, listen to poetry, and "revise, revise, revise" (2002, 882). Richardson (2002, 882) reminds us that

A line
break does
not
a poem
make.

Richardson also discusses the use of imagery and metaphoric language—points to be emphasized. If you try to shape poetic representations out of abstract, general language, you will never succeed as well as if you use concrete observations, images, and metaphors to convey an idea or evoke an emotion.

Your poetic transcriptions may or may not arrive at the artistic sensibilities of a good poem. Never fear, poets often keep a file of "rich refusals" that they revisit periodically to rework until the words, rhythm, and feeling come together. Nonetheless, the process of doing poetic transcription can assist you as a writer and ethnographer to focus on what is essential to the story and to juxtapose items and concepts that you would not put together otherwise. Poetic transcription, as with drama, the next creative form to be discussed, also asks you to approach your data with an artistic eye, to let "ordering and invention coincide" (Dillard 1982, 56).

DRAMA

> If we were to inhabit the speech pattern of another, and walk in the speech of another, we could find the individuality of the other and experience that individuality viscerally.
>
> (A. D. Smith 1993, xxvii)

In representing data through dramatic portrayals, the researcher crafts interview transcripts into dialogue, and observation notes or documents into scenes and stage settings. The narratives are actual ones, although editorial license is taken to construct scenes or imply conversations among people who were not necessarily together. The following example is excerpted from Pam Kay's (1997, 15) reader's theater script entitled *Whose Child Is This?* The cast included Nancy, the parent; Carol, the teacher; and Pam, the researcher. *Reader's theater* refers "to a stage presentation of a piece of text or selected pieces of different texts that are thematically linked" (Donmoyer and Yennie-Donmoyer 1995, 406). Rather than act, presenters read text selections individually, and sometimes in chorus. Staging is simple, usually involving chairs or stools and perhaps a few props.

> **PAM (*to the audience*):**   We had our second parent-teacher action research meeting. Carol came in a little late, and she was upset.
>
> *Nancy and Carol face each other. Carol speaks angrily to Nancy.*
>
> **CAROL:**   Why aren't you giving Doug his medicine in the morning before he comes to school?
>
> **NANCY (*quietly*):**   We are all out of it. I was going to see Dr. Dave on Friday, but he is away for a week.
>
> **CAROL (*still angry*):**   The school nurse called the pharmacy, and the pharmacy says you should have 12 days supply left!
>
> **NANCY:**   Well, I don't.
>
> *Carol and Nancy turn away from the audience.*

Kay's piece explores tensions experienced by a parent and a teacher around a child's emotional and behavioral issues. Data for the script were taken from a case study that was part of a multisite inquiry into prevention of serious emotional disturbance, funded by the U.S. Department of Education. Kay shaped the script by sorting and selecting data gathered through individual interviews with Carol and Nancy, her field notes from team meetings, notebooks kept by Carol and Nancy, and field notes kept by a parent liaison employed by the project. Carol and Nancy's words are verbatim excerpts from the data. Pam used her own voice as narrator and stage director as a way of furnishing explanations and transitions. Following is another excerpt from Kay's script (1997, 16–17):

> *Pam sits down and turns to face Nancy and Carol, who again face each other.*
>
> **CAROL (***speaking carefully***):**   Nancy, may I bring up what Doug told me the other day?
>
> **NANCY:** Sure.
>
> **CAROL (***explaining to Pam***):**   There was trouble on the playground again. Doug got very angry. After he had calmed down, he told me that his father is dying.
>
> **NANCY (***in a low, husky voice***):**   The doctor has said that he can't do anything more for Walter. He can make him comfortable, that's all. I am always very honest with my children, so I told them how sick their father is. Also, Amy and her two babies have moved home because her boyfriend was abusive. So there is lots of anger in our house these days.
>
> **CAROL:**   He has had several bad days lately; he just wasn't Doug.
>
> **NANCY:**   He really interrupts me a lot and with the two little ones there, he had been jealous. He'll climb up on the table and jump off at me when I am holding one of the little ones. Of course, then I have to pay attention to him.

Using drama to portray the voices of everyday people is not new. Paolo Freire in Brazil created popular theater forums out of interviews and conversations as a means to both educate and politicize. Augusto Boal's (2006) Theatre of the Oppressed grew out of this work. Well-known playwrights also have created forms of ethnotheater. Anna Deavere Smith became known in the 1990s as she created documentary dramas based on her interviews with people involved in the 1991 Crown Heights riots in Brooklyn (*Fires in the Mirror*), and in the Los Angeles riots (*Twilight: Los Angeles 1992*).[2] Eve Ensler's work *The Vagina Monologues*, an annual Valentine's Day occurrence since 1998 that protests violence against women, is based on Ensler's interviews with more than 200 women from throughout the world. Moisés Kaufman and members of the Tectonic Theater Project (2001) created *The Laramie Project* out of hundreds of interviews, published news reports, and their own journal notes.

In the 1990s, researchers began transforming their data into dramas and performing them at national conferences. Health and social service professionals, in particular, turned to performance ethnography, or "ethnodrama," as a way to represent research. Their dramas, sometimes performed in collaboration with interviewees, were not only informative and instructive, but also cathartic. "Ethnodramatic performance allows victims of mental illness, sexual abuse or rape, substance abuse or plastic surgery, *in partnership with healthcare professionals and academics,* to explore and examine, through dramatic devices, what it is like from the inside looking out" (Morgan, Mienczakowski, and Smith 2001, 164). Mienczakowski has been particularly active in creating ethnodramas that are performed in a variety of theater spaces. His intent, he states, is to create "a form of public-voice ethnography that has emancipatory and educational potential" (Mienczakowski 1995, 364) by providing a forum for research participants to tell others about their health concerns, whether dependent upon alcohol or living with schizophrenia.

Johnny Saldaña also creates ethnodramas and writes about them. His edited text *Ethnodrama: An Anthology of Reality Theatre* provides nine examples of different approaches to dramatic portrayal of data. For example, Jose Casas's analysis of interviews resulted in the ethnodrama "14." He uses as his starting point fourteen deaths from a border crossing in Arizona. Although "14" was performed as a series of monologues, Casas used slides at the beginning of each new voice, giving the name of the interviewee, occupation, and hometown. Some pieces were performed in Spanish. He juxtaposed the pieces in strategic ways, putting the story of a woman who crossed the border with strangers, for example, next to that of an elderly rancher who declares, "listen I won't shoot at anything during the day . . . at night . . . that's a totally different story" (Casas 2005, 52). As another example, Jennifer Chapman, Anne Swedberg, and Heather Sykes created an ethnodramatic dialogue called "Wearing the Secret Out," based on interviews with gay, lesbian, and queer physical education teachers. They wrote their ethnodrama as a forum to provoke discussion about homophobia and heterosexism in schools.

Ethnodrama is a particularly good medium for highlighting tensions, conflicts, and differing perspectives. Creating an ethnodrama takes a special kind of thinking about what has been said in interviews and noted in observation journals. You have to find the *story line,* or "progression of events within the plot" (Saldaña 2005, 15). You have to consider the most appropriate way to present the material. Do you want one character telling the story in a monologue or several characters in dialogue? Do you want one person to take on the persona of several different characters? How will you divide the script into acts and scenes? You make analytical decisions about your data to create the story line for the play. Then you need to work with the transcripts and field notes, reducing them without changing the intent of what has been said. You choose the bits that are best for dramatic impact. And you need to think about what props, costumes, lighting, and technology you want to use. "Less is more," advises Saldaña (2005, 28). For example, rather than try to build a set, project a slide of a particular setting, as McCall (2000) did when she used slides of farm landscapes as the backdrop for her play based on interviews with fifty-two Midwestern women farmers.

Similar to poetic transcription, ethnodrama involves word reduction and reordering of text while striving to keep the narrator's voice. In Exhibit 9.2, Saldaña (2005, 21) provides an example of reducing words in an interview for a section of a monologue in his ethnodrama *"Maybe Someday, if I'm Famous . . ."*

JOHNNY SALDAÑA'S INTERVIEW WITH BARRY

BARRY: **And I remember going to see the shows.** I remember the interviews afterwards, sitting out on the grass, talking about what we thought about the shows, and what we thought about the longitudinal study. I remember always having interns sitting in the back of the class, watching us do drama.

JOHNNY: What shows do you remember?

BARRY: I remember **a lot of the Childsplay stuff.** [*Childsplay is a local professional touring theatre company for young audiences*]

JOHNNY: Any particular titles or images come to mind?

BARRY: I remember *Clarissa's Closet*, which was interesting because I performed that last year. And I was thinking, "You know I've seen this, I've seen this, it was Childsplay came did it." And I also remember one about, I recall an Oriental setting, there were masks, uh, I don't know much about it, like journeying something.

JOHNNY: Any other images?

BARRY: **I remember them coming out and taking their bows and then talking to us after the show, and the energy they had,** and just the raw energy and everything. **They were answering questions and they seemed to be having so much fun just being there, and I think that's when I first decided I wanted to be an actor.** So I saw that and **it was an amazing feeling,** there was just energy, you could see it, it was emanating from them, and just from having done this show. And it was just a show for a bunch of elementary kids, and yet it was still, it was a show, you know? And it was, **that was when** it first, **I first started thinking, "Hm, this is something I want to look into."**

ETHNODRAMATIC MONOLOGUE

BARRY: And I remember going to see the shows, a lot of Childsplay stuff. I remember them coming out and taking their bows and then talking to us after the show. And the energy they had! They were answering questions and they seemed to be having so much fun just being there. And I think that's when I first decided I wanted to be an actor. It was an amazing feeling! That was when I first started thinking. "Hm, this is something I want to look into."

EXHIBIT 9.2 The Making of an Ethnodrama

Source: From Saldaña, J. 2005. *Ethnodrama: An Anthology of Reality Theatre.* Walnut Creek, CA: AltaMira Press, 21.

Whether performed or read, ethnodrama can be used to juxtapose the voice of research participants, to present multiple perspectives together, and to exemplify the complexity of a phenomenon. To be sure, the researcher/writer shapes the drama but constructs it so that readers might understand more fully what it means to be, for example, the teacher *and* the parent of a child like Doug. As Saldaña (2005, 14) states, "Ethnotheatre reveals a living culture through its character-participants, and if successful, the audience learns about their world and what it's like to live in it."

SHORT STORY

Barbara Tedlock (2000) reminds us that the ethnographic novel or short story is not a new, postmodern invention. She cites examples. In 1890, Adolf Bandelier published *The Delight Makers*, a novel set among the Pueblo Indians. More widely known is Oliver LaFarge's 1929 novel *Laughing Boy*, based on his experiences among Navajo. Anthropologists and other social scientists have been writing poems, stories, and plays since the disciplines began. These creative works, however, were usually considered as something other than "academic." What is "new" is the increased acceptance of the blurring of genres.

In ethnographic drama and poetic transcription, writers artistically shape their representations, but they stay close to the data. In an ethnographic short story, researchers combine ethnographic insights and understandings with their own imaginations to tell good stories, drawing upon literary techniques such as flashback, characterization, dialogue, internal monologue, and action. For example, in *Drinkers, Drummers, and Decent Folk: Ethnographic Narratives of Village Trinidad*, John Stewart (1989) presents a series of ethnographic short stories that had their roots in his fieldwork in Trinidad. Stewart (1989, 13) states that writing up his research as short story allowed him to focus on an "anthropology of the inside":

> In an ethnography of the outside, that objective field to which most ethnographers are still grounded, social and cultural "structures" are the central concern. Not people. In an anthropology of the inside, how people fashion such "structures," how they manipulate, manage or are controlled by them, become the focus.

Phil Smith, while a doctoral candidate at the University of Vermont, was also seeking an anthropology of the inside. Working to understand issues of power and control in the lives of people with developmental disabilities, Smith (2000) wrote up some of his research as short stories and included them in his dissertation. The following is an excerpt from "Food Truck's Party Hat" (2000), another version of which Smith published in *Qualitative Inquiry* (1999):

> He looks at me again, grinning again, his head moving, his whole body, really, in constant motion, he never entirely stops, some part of him always racing beyond the rest of him, beyond his own body even, moving moving moving on, tapping swinging gliding always in continuous seamless never-ending can't-make-it-stop not-even-in-sleep motion. "Boy use jug," he says, and laughs, eyebrows raised, a question.
>
> No one knows, now, how Food Truck came to that phrase, or to the name Food Truck that he calls himself. He lived for over forty years at Langdon Training

School, where they used to lock up all the people they called morons imbeciles epileptics retards. Remember those words? Growing up, in school, some kid sitting next to you in class would do something dumb, drop their pencil and then step on it, break it, and you'd lean over so old Mrs. Whatever-her-name-was wouldn't hear, and whisper, "What a 'tard!" just loud enough so all the kids around you could hear and laugh. "You're such a retard!" and grin, the funniest thing you had said in weeks, beaming at your own joke. I said it lots of times, impugned my brother's intelligence if he walked in my room without knocking, or broke my model airplanes, or read my science fiction books without asking. "You retard!" I'd say angrily, the worst thing I knew to call him. I didn't know Food Truck then.

Food Truck grew up at Langdon, mostly. He spent his early childhood with his parents, and then they couldn't take care of him anymore, I think, or the family doctor said—as a lot of them did back then—"Well, you know, you really should send him off to Langdon, he'll be much happier there, with his own kind." So he went off to live at Langdon as a young boy, and that was his whole life, that's really all he's known, the back wards. Course he's out now, been out for four or five years, they're all out.

The ethnographic short story prompts the writer and the reader to seriously consider not only the line between shaping and fictionalizing, but also the purpose of the telling, the intent of the researcher/writer. If the intent of the writer is to represent the sense and feel, the complex emotions, and the dilemmas of everyday life, then the ethnographic short story can be an effective vehicle for entering that world.

TAKING RISKS

Meratus say that when God handed out the Holy Book, the Meratus ancestry ate his and thus ensured both internal inspiration and its essentially unarticulated script.

(Tsing 1993, 245)

While forms of writing dominate creative analytic practices, some researchers play with nonverbal representations, including dance (Blumenfeld-Jones 1995), painting (Clark 1999, Clark/Keefe 2002), and photography (Munoz 1995). This section provides brief examples from painting and some other representational strategies.

Kelly Clark (1999) explored painting as a way to synthesize data from her research with academic women from working-class backgrounds who were of the first generation in their families to attend college. The following painting (Figure 9.1) and explanatory narrative is excerpted from her dissertation. Clark created case studies of the women she interviewed. As she sat with the words of each woman, she picked up her paintbrush and began "synthesizing" their words into a painting, a process that, in turn, made her more deeply reflective on the emotional quality of their words. This example is from her work with Clementina, who was raised by a mother who worked as a night-shift waitress to support her four

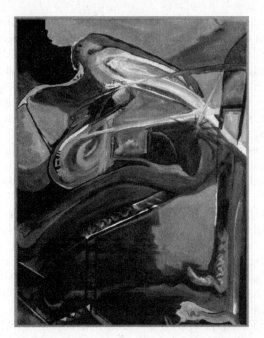

FIGURE 9.1 *Clementina* **by Kelly A. Clark/Keefe.**

children. By age 15, Clementina was determined "to not follow the same 'pattern' as that of her parents" (69). Clark (1999, 72–73) states:

> I decide her biographical rendering should reflect movement. It seems that any figural element should float above a sea of both definitive borders as well as less linear, more ambiguous horizons indicative of difference. An "H" pitched proudly on the hills behind her will pay metaphorical deference to her "Hollywood" sense of self—to her feelings, thoughts and imagination about the transformative power of heroes, heroines, role models, artists and educators. "Red" hair ("like [her] mom's") will be lined in black (like hers). It will flow down her back. . . . Placement of complementary colors in hues that reflect both the desert and the sea will attempt to draw viewers eyes around and around, in a solid (not scattered), circuitous motion. This will be a reflection of her ways of knowing her self, her world, and her spiritual connection to the harmoniousness of all life's music and its makers.

In Clark's example, as in other creative representations, the "essences (as understood by the artist) are extracted and represented in concrete, condensed forms" (Blumenfeld-Jones 1995, 392).

Researchers are also playing with "textual strategies" and the layout of text on the printed page. Ronai (1995) writes in a format she calls "the layered account" that, through the use of blank space or a row of periods or asterisks, allows the writer to integrate "abstract theoretical thinking, introspection, emotional experience, fantasies, dreams, and statistics" (395). Through writing short passages, the writer moves from one thought to another in a condensed way that requires the reader to supply transitions. Lather and Smithies (1997) use multiple genres and a split-text format to represent research with women living with AIDS. They split the page so that they could write different kinds of text, "a text at multiple levels, a double-coded text that is both broadly accessible and fosters brooding about the issues involved" (Lather 1995, 48). The top of the page focuses on the women and their stories, on dialogue between interviewee and interviewer, and social and cultural issues raised by AIDS; across the bottom of much of the book is commentary by Lather and Smithies regarding their experience of doing the research. They also insert what they describe as "factoid" boxes of information about AIDS, plus various forms of writing by some of the women.

In summary, as response to the crisis of representation, researchers engage in many different debates. Questioning the right to study and describe others has led to re-examination of research purposes and of researchers' obligations and responsibilities to communities in which they undertake inquiries. Some researchers choose to focus on historical, philosophical, or theoretical inquiry rather than become involved in fieldwork. Others turn their gaze onto themselves and use their own experiences as a forum for reflection on the larger society. Yet others struggle with how to do social science fieldwork and to share "findings" in ways that reveal the partial, incomplete, and particular state of their knowing. In considering for whom and for what purposes they write, many seek to make their work accessible to research participants and to others beyond the academic community. Doing so, means creating in forms that others will want to read, watch, or listen to, and in the process, feel and learn from the representations.

Creative forms and textual strategies help to provide options that counter many critiques of traditional reports—that they are authoritative, that they are boring or written for specialized audiences; that they do not evoke emotions and the senses; that they ignore the role of researcher; and that they neglect the political. "Take risks," urges Ellis. "Write from the heart as well as the head" (in Bochner and Ellis 1996, 42). Through experimenting with form, researchers seek to be open to how the medium is part of the message. Different mediums allow you to say (and to see) different things about the lives you seek to represent.

RECOMMENDED READINGS

Benson, P. (ed.). 1993. *Anthropology and Literature*. Chicago: University of Illinois Press.

Ellis, C. 2004. *The Ethnographic I: A Methodological Novel about Autoethnography*. Walnut Creek, CA: AltaMira.

Knowles, J. G., and A. L. Cole (eds.). 2008. *Handbook of the ARTS in Qualitative Research*. Thousand Oaks, CA: Sage.

Mears, C. L. 2009. *Interviewing for Education and Social Science Research: The Gateway Approach*. New York: Palgrave Macmillan.

Saldaña, J. (ed.). 2005. *Ethnodrama: An Anthology of Reality Theatre*. Walnut Creek, CA: AltaMira Press.

Van Maanen, J. 1988. *Tales of the Field: On Writing Ethnography*. Chicago: University of Chicago Press.

EXERCISES[3]

1. Explore some aspect of your research topic by writing a short autoethnography in which you use dramatic recall and images from your own life to situate your research in the personal and the social. Reflect upon what you learned about your topic, your research participants (even though they were not present in your story), and yourself through this exercise.

2. Work with interview transcripts from one person and create a poetic transcription. Use only the words, phrasings, and speaking rhythms of the interviewee. Reflect upon what you learned about your topic, the interviewee, and about yourself through poetic transcription.

3. Work with interview transcripts from several interviewees plus observation notes to create an ethnodrama. Reflect upon what you learned about your topic, about the interviewee, and about yourself through writing up your data as drama.

ENDNOTES

1. This section draws from my article "That Rare Feeling: Re-presenting Research through Poetic Transcription," published in 1997 in *Qualitative Inquiry*.
2. Watch Anna Deavere Smith perform by going to the following Web site: www.ted.com/index.php/talks/anna_deavere_smith_s_american_character.html.
3. Laurel Richardson (2000) suggests a series of writing practices in her chapter "Writing: A Method of Inquiry" in *Handbook of Qualitative Research*, including variations of those presented here.

CHAPTER 10

The Continuing Search

Learning to exist in a world quite different from that which formed you is the condition, these days, of pursuing research you can on balance believe in and writing sentences you can more or less live with.

(Geertz 1995, 133)

"Somehow you've got to put your heart and soul into it—not just for personal reasons, but to really understand what's going on. The more you allow yourself to fall in love with a place, the more you see the connections."

(student quoted in Wilson 1989, 17).

BECOMING QUALITATIVE RESEARCHERS: THE PERSONAL CONTEXT

The purpose of this text is to introduce one way of approaching qualitative research and to assist in the process of beginning a study. After an introduction to theories and philosophies associated with qualitative inquiry, the text focused on developing research questions and study design. It then concentrated on ethnographic methods for data production—in particular, observations and interviews. Chapters on field relationships and ethics raised considerations, debates, and dilemmas commonly associated with qualitative research, alerting you to think about the ways in which you want to interact with and give back to research participants. Information on data analysis focused on thematic organization and also introduced other ways to work with data. Chapters on writing provided suggestions and advice for getting started and keeping at the writing process, as well as ways to think about representing a study creatively.

At this point, if you have been doing a pilot study while reading this book, you know a great deal more about both your topic and the process of doing qualitative research. I assume that you also have more questions about both. I trust that one of your questions reflects Geertz and asks: What kind of research will you pursue that "you can on balance believe in?" Another question that I hope is on your list refers to both topic and process: Into what research can you put "your heart and soul?"

Qualitative research demands nearly total absorption. Researchers find their lives consumed by their work as they seek understanding and connections. Personal commitment, trust, and time are key to rich data and useful interpretations. Few anticipate the exacting demands of their research endeavors. For example, Toni set out in a pilot project to interview wives of medical interns about their sense of self. Six months later, she exclaimed:

> This project has really become bigger than me! It is everywhere. We talked about it in our social psych brown bag as we discussed feminist methodology. It comes up for me in almost all of my readings, at a conference I attended, in conversations . . . I have so much in my head and noted down somewhere that I have not had time to think about. . . . This project has consumed my life to the exclusion of almost all else.

Another student agreed: "I went to a conference the other day and kept taking notes for my research, and the conference was on a topic not even close to my project." Although, most likely, many of you do not have lives that adapt easily to the demands of qualitative research on your attention, it is when you find your "problem" everywhere that you can be assured you are getting somewhere.

Entering qualitative terrain can be lonely. Even though you may discuss your work with colleagues, friends, and research participants, in conventional qualitative research, you tend to be alone. You are alone in the role of researcher at your research site, alone with the ultimate responsibility of fitting the pieces together and finding meaning in the whole. You are alone as you struggle over writing sentences "you can more or less live with" (Geertz 1995, 133). Toni reflected on the loneliness of her work:

> Talk about isolation! I'm feeling it in many realms. One is working with the data, being overwhelmed by it all. I feel isolated at times when I talk about this [lives of spouses of medical interns] because people seem to get uneasy as though I am saying something I shouldn't about medicine. Additionally, I am wondering about how the women [interviewees] will react when they see it . . . and how I will react to how they react.

As Toni suggests, qualitative research can raise self-doubts. You worry that people won't want to talk with you or won't let you observe. You wonder if you are asking the right questions. You suddenly panic over whether your towering stack of notebooks, note cards, and computer files really tells you anything and, even if these records do, whether you are capable of putting the data bits together in a meaningful way. And you worry that perhaps you will not like what you bring to light.

That you do not know exactly what you search for contributes to periods of confusion and frustration. In the midst of analyzing data on a school in a rural transitional community, Carlton sighed, "I'm not sure if the data confuse me or if I confuse the data." Both surely occur in research projects. As surely, research projects require courage and integrity.

These discontinuities, the disturbing pieces that do not "fit," are actually what may give you clues to your more interesting realizations. You will need to learn to live with confusion, if not welcome it into your life—to see it as a harbinger of new mysteries to unravel. Bateson (1984) recognized this in the work of her parents, Margaret Mead and Gregory Bateson:

> Both Margaret and Gregory developed a style that involved collecting observational material in the expectation that, however rich and bewildering it might seem at first, they would arrive at points of recognition when things would "make sense" and fall into place. In the search for such moments of insight they would be dealing with points of congruence within the culture they were looking at and also points of personal response. (163)

Understanding involves getting at participants' perspectives, but it is more than that. It is reaching some collective understanding that includes self and others.

Although the research process is often exciting and meaningful, it can also be tiring. Exhaustion seems to hit hardest when one is trying to make sense of the data. Tina wrote,

> I felt extreme fatigue when the interviews were over. That fatigue made transcribing even more deadly. I remember many nights falling asleep for a few minutes at my computer during the transcribing process and thinking that I would never get to the last page. Somehow I did, but it was always a temptation to leave it until the next day.

Despite having nights when you fall asleep at your computer, you will have moments of insight, if not stretches of profound contentment. Holly described what the process of writing up research meant for her: "Transforming my thoughts into words not only allows me to reflect upon who I am and who I am striving to become, but also invites the reader to connect; to form a kind of relationship with me through the printed page." It is to the printed page and other outcomes of your research that I now turn.

APPLICATIONS OF QUALITATIVE RESEARCH: THE RESEARCH MANUSCRIPT

> What has practical relevance . . . depends not just, or even primarily, in finding "technological" solutions to discrete problems, but rather in forging new perspectives, new ways of looking at things.
>
> (Giddens 1995, 277)

When teachers conduct a study of new students' adaptations to middle school, when mothers map their families' past, or when students challenge the university food service, they all engage in research for a reason. The applications of research are as varied as the researchers and their sundry studies. When people talk about applying research, they generally refer to making use of the final report or manuscript: the research *product*. The research *process*, however, also has its own applications as discussed later.

The Possibilities of Words

Research manuscripts or texts can take you places that you have not had an opportunity to go, exposing you to other cultures and to unique aspects of your own culture. They help you adopt new perspectives, to see something from a different point of view, and to reexamine your own theoretical constructs. Texts can help to educate readers and to challenge stereotypes and assumptions. They can suggest avenues for policy change and the directions to pursue. Interpretative research can, as well, confront and augment theories about the myriad nature of human thought and interactions.

Interpretive inquiry means learning much about others and the ways in which they live their lives. Your perspective, however, is an interpretation. Barone cautions: "A text of qualitative inquiry is . . . better viewed as an occasion than as a tool. It is, more precisely, an occasion for the reader to engage in the activities of textual re-creation and dismantling" (Barone 1990a, 306). If you view the text as a tool, then you may too easily accept it as fact and ignore what went into the research process, including values of the researcher and problems in research design.

Instead of responding to research findings as though they represent an absolute truth, use the findings as an opportunity to think about the social world around you. Like the English teacher who said, "The beauty of a good story is its openness—the way you or I or anyone reading it can take it in, and use it for ourselves" (Coles 1989, 47), a good qualitative text invites you in. It encourages you to compare its descriptions and analyses to your own experiences and to, perhaps, think differently about your own particular situation.

Lorna was working on a study concerning the inclusion of children with special needs into public school classrooms. In the midst of analyzing and writing up her work, she reflected upon her text as an occasion for drawing others in, even though not every problem was "solved":

> There are so many questions I am leaving unanswered. Resisting the urge to delete the last half of my paper, I opened the day's *New York Times* magazine. I was drawn to an article about a single mother with AIDS searching for a new "mother" for her only child. In the midst of my tears, I couldn't help but recognize this as qualitative research, as a case study. The power and depth were apparent. And this author also left many questions unanswered.

The act of observing, listening, and recording can be a form of witnessing that brings attention to lives (plights and triumphs) of others. Scheper-Hughes

(1992) describes how the text can be an occasion for witnessing and giving voice to those who have been silenced or for providing a history of "people often presumed to have no history" (29):

> So-called participant observation has a way of drawing the ethnographer into spaces of human life where she or he might really prefer not to go at all and once there doesn't know how to go about getting out except through writing, which draws others there as well, making them party to the act of witnessing. (xii)

Witnessing sets the stage for conversations, dialogue, and systemic change. As Geertz (1988, 147) observes, "It seems likely that whatever use ethnographic texts will have in the future, if in fact they actually have any, it will involve enabling conversation across societal lines—of ethnicity, religion, class, gender, language, race. . . ." In addition, research from the standpoint of marginalized lives has the potential of generating valuable new questions that dominant groups have not considered, questions that could transform taken-for-granted conceptual frameworks (Harding 1998).

Qualitative research texts also assist in academic pursuits (i.e., hypothesis generation, theory development) and in creating solutions to practical problems. Toni's work with wives of medical interns extends a theory that explains the development of self in relationship to others. Her descriptive stories may also serve as a mode of support and awareness-raising for research participants and other wives of interns. As with many research texts, Toni's work has both theoretical and practical applications.

Undoubtedly, countless reports find their way into the forgotten corner of office shelves rather than become moving, transforming works, yet research reports have changed lives. Willis's (1977) research in England drew attention to the role of resistance in shaping the lives of working-class "lads" both in and out of school. Gilligan's (1993) work with the moral development of women paved the way for exploring the gender bias that had permeated theories of human development, which, for the most part, had been generated from male data. These studies are not without their problems, yet they and others have contributed to how we perceive and interact with the world.

Getting Published

A useful step toward getting published is to present your research at a conference where you can get feedback on assertions and representations. If you take time to construct a well-organized paper and from it prepare and practice a talk (or creative representation), you might even be approached by someone in the audience who asks you to send the paper to their journal for publication (this has happened). More likely, you'll meet people who have similar interests. Discussions may lead you to the writings of others and to consider aspects of your work differently.

Get information about the annual or regional meetings in your discipline so that you know when to send in a proposal to present. The American Anthropology Association, the American Association of Nursing, the American Educational

Research Association, and the American Sociological Association are all possibilities. Alternatively, you may prefer attending a conference that focuses only on qualitative research. For example, the International Congress of Qualitative Inquiry is held annually at the University of Illinois and both the Qualitative Health Research Conference and Advances in Qualitative Methods Conference are held annually at the University of Alberta in Edmonton, Canada.

The appearance of qualitative work in journals from various disciplines reflects the acceptance of interpretive, critical theory, and poststructural paradigms. Many journals within the social sciences review and accept for publication articles based on widely differing research methodologies (see Exhibit 10.1). Yet other journals specialize in qualitative research, such as *The International Journal of Qualitative Studies in Education (QSE)* and *Qualitative Inquiry (QI)*, and publish all kinds of approaches, including creative representations.

Publishing in a journal takes time and, often, perseverance. Because you should not send an article for review to more than one journal at a time, begin by finding a journal that best fits your purpose and writing style. Browse the journals in your library to see the kinds of articles each publish. Read their purpose statements and instructions for submission (generally inside the cover or on one of the first few pages). When you choose where to submit, follow carefully the journal's instructions for style and format and make your copy as well written and ready for publication as you can. Then, expect to wait for a couple months.

Most journals send each manuscript they receive to two to four "blind" reviewers who receive the paper without the author's name attached. The reviewers address a series of questions supplied by the journal editor and make comments on and suggestions for the manuscript. Reviewers don't get paid but generally take the job seriously and often enclose pages of remarks. Depending

American Educational Research Journal	*Journal of Social and Behavioral Sciences*
Anthropology and Humanism Quarterly	*Media, Culture and Society*
Criminal Justice Policy and Review	*Nursing Research*
Educational Studies	*Qualitative Health Research*
Feminist Studies	*Qualitative Inquiry*
Field Studies	*Qualitative Studies in Psychology*
Human Organization	*Qualitative Sociology*
International Journal of Qualitative	*Signs: Journal of Women in Culture*
Studies in Education	*and Society*
International Review of Sport Sociology	*Sociological Perspectives*
International Sociology	*Sociological Quarterly*
Journal of Contemporary Ethnography	*Studies in Symbolic Interaction*
Journal of Creative Inquiry	*Teaching Sociology*
Journal of Marriage and the Family	*Text and Performance Quarterly*
Journal of Popular Culture	*Western Journal of Nursing*

EXHIBIT 10.1   Examples of Journals That Publish Qualitative Research

upon how reviewers respond, the editor makes a decision about whether to publish your manuscript with limited edits, to ask you to revise based on reviewers' comments and resubmit, or to not publish your article.

If you receive the last response, don't be discouraged. It simply may not have been the right journal for your work. Consider seriously suggestions that were made, revise, and send your paper to another journal. If you receive the response to revise and resubmit, do so. If you attend to reviewers' comments, you are likely to have the manuscript accepted. Do not expect journal editors to say, "We want your piece just as it is; don't touch it," because they probably will not. Even though you may feel as though you cannot bear to rework your paper again, if you take the time, the manuscript will be better and will get published.

USING THE RESEARCH PROCESS

> The act of telling stories is powerful. I finally found something that can sustain me through my dissertation.
>
> (Vermont student)

Unlike the research text, which may be meaningful to people living thousands of miles away from the research site, the usefulness or application of the actual process of doing research is more limited to those involved. This, however, does not detract from its significance and contributions to improving practice, evaluation, policy, and understanding.

Unless asked to participate in someone else's funded research project, you will generally find yourself researching something within your academic or applied discipline (e.g., special education, nursing, social work, educational leadership). As you conduct research, you will invariably learn things that will improve your practice. Dorothy, with nearly 20 years of experience in clinical nursing, stated that she already knew "the value of a carefully placed 'go on,' a contemplative 'uh huh.'" Nonetheless, in her study of the process of committing a loved one to institutional care, she discovered that her interviewees "seem to yearn for a listening ear." Her open-ended, probing questions allowed participants to tell their stories. "For some," she stated, "I have the sense I am the first health professional to listen." In her research role, Dorothy learned more about her clients than she had in her nursing role. Seeing that her clients appreciated an extended opportunity to discuss difficult issues, Dorothy planned to incorporate longer, more probing interviews into her practice. Similarly, Aamodt (1989) discussed using qualitative interviewing techniques with children who have cancer in order to provide more personally meaningful care.

Dorothy also reflected on how the process of participant observation in qualitative inquiry expanded her concept of the potential usefulness of observation in nursing:

> Documenting observations comes as naturally to a nurse as listening. Attention to subtle detail is essential to comprehensive patient assessments. In nursing, however, the areas for observation are clearly prescribed. I know that observing

the rate and depth of respirations along with the color of fingernails and mucous membranes will allow me to reach conclusions about lung function. But what specific observations must I record to eventually understand family decision making? Would posture, level of enthusiasm, appearance of fatigue all be useful information? I now consider what I see in general. I describe the apparent uneasiness with which a son relates his inability to keep his dad out of the hospital.

By conducting qualitative research, Dorothy learned both skills and knowledge applicable to her nursing practice. Similarly, practitioner-researchers in other disciplines learn skills and knowledge that assist them in carrying out their practice, conducting program evaluations, and shaping policy.

In conventional ethnographic research, the participants may learn something about the conduct of inquiry. Also, the interview and observation process propels participants to become more reflective on aspects of their lives. In participant-oriented research (e.g., action research and, often, critical and feminist research), the research process is intended to assist participants. This kind of inquiry focuses upon issues of concern to those researched. The participants seek particular and localized solutions to some question or allow a researcher to work with them to address inequities or problems of some sort. The participants sometimes are co-researchers and may learn about research techniques as well as new ways to view or change their lives. When, for example, economically poor and isolated rural Vermont women in "Listening Partner" groups received the opportunity to regularly dialogue and collaboratively problem solve with women in similar situations, they began to look at and live their lives differently; and the relationships they formed through the learning circles rendered them less isolated (Belenky, Bond, and Weinstock 1997). The research *process* is as important as (or more important than) the *product* in participant-oriented research.

The processes involved in qualitative research—whether data collection, data analysis, or writing up—require expanses of time. A nursing administrator working on her doctorate reflected, "Usually I'm good at multitasking, but you can't make qualitative research another task on your list because qualitative research is a process of multitasking itself." Another student complained that her work kept interrupting her research. How long your research will take depends upon many variables, but particularly upon whether or not you must work at a full-time job and try to carry out your inquiry. Many foundations fund qualitative research, but your interests and the foundation's have to match *and* you have to begin the application process early, sometimes as much as a year before you plan to begin your research. Even with funding, some part-time students cannot leave their work. In this case, you can perhaps negotiate with your employer for release time for a limited period. If this is an option, consider requesting several hours a day rather than one full day a week. This allows you to attend to your research daily and forces you to use the limited time to the fullest, rather than dealing with the illusion of having a full day and then whittling away the time with other tasks and errands.

USING QUALITATIVE RESEARCH TO LEARN ABOUT YOURSELF

"I reached the wall," Charlie said. "I could not write another piece about the classroom. We were both tired—I of being there, and she of having me there." Charlie was in the midst of research on a multigrade classroom. He had been observing the classroom; interviewing children, parents, and school personnel; and discussing his thoughts in intense meetings with the teacher. After a short break, he returned to the classroom and was welcomed by the teacher and students; in the meantime, he had learned something useful about the process of doing research. Charlie began to schedule different kinds of breaks—reflective breaks that allowed him to take stock of his work, and absolute breaks that gave him a complete rest from the researcher role and gave his participants relief from the intrusion that a researcher, no matter how loved, represents.

The act of researching teaches you about yourself as a researcher. You may take pride in the way that you carefully listen and ask probing questions, but you may also realize that you are not as observant as you had hoped. You may need to develop better strategies to record and remember unspecified interactions. In addition to learning about yourself as a researcher, you may also learn more about yourself in general. Jill reflected, "By looking at what problems interest us and at what questions we ask, we may discover an avenue that leads us to a better understanding of what is important and of meaning to each one of us." Your research is autobiographical in that some aspect of yourself is mirrored in the work you choose to pursue. Figuring out where your interests lay leads you to a greater understanding of your core values and beliefs. Such understanding, in turn, can provide greater direction for future undertakings.

After a two-semester course in which students designed and conducted pilot studies, I asked for their advice to other beginning researchers. The following are Mary Lou's recommendations:

- Know your purpose—this is your anchor.
- Make a visual—if you find doing so difficult, think about your design some more.
- Critique your interview questions—do they provide the information you want?
- Always bring your interview questions to the interviews.
- Make sure your interviewee talks more than you do.
- Write notes so you can remember where you need to probe.
- Write in your journal every day.
- Email memos to yourself—date, subject, time. You can easily sort by subject.
- Sticky notes work well for initial coding—something about being able to move them around.
- You can learn things through qualitative research that cannot be learned any other way—perception is real.

CREATING AND DEEPENING RELATIONSHIPS

Terry Tafoya (1989), a Native American anthropologist, tells a story of Coyote who, through a series of events, loses his eyes. He is completely blind until Mouse gives him one of her tiny eyes and later, Buffalo gives Coyote one of his large eyes. Coyote does not learn how to balance these perspectives, however. Tafoya draws a moral for his readers: "To be a whole human (one might say, a complete Coyote) one must learn to switch back and forth between the eyes of not only Mouse and Buffalo, but those of Eagle, Bear, Cougar, and all the other animals of legend" (32).

Researchers need to learn to see (hear, feel) through different lenses. The act of researching, however, is fraught with problems because the conventional process situates the researcher as designer, sense-maker, and storyteller. And the researcher will never "see" through all the lenses needed to get it "right" for everyone. I will never fully understand what it means to be Mexican or gay or an Appalachian coal miner. Tierney (2000) reflects upon how he criticizes those who seek to "record the lives of those individuals on the border—Native American, lesbian and gay individuals, and the like," and yet how he also criticizes "the absence from traditional texts of those of us on the border" (547). He goes on to say that it's not that one should not study the "other," but "the researcher must begin with an understanding of the fragmented nature of identity and build a text that enables readers to see how the author/narrator/speaker has created a particular identity that is fraught with contested meanings" (548).

The work of qualitative researchers is to accentuate *complexity,* not the *norm,* and to emphasize that which contributes to plurality rather than to a narrowing of

Relationships within a group (whether co-researchers, researchers and participants, or traveling students) can unexpectedly become a greater opportunity for learning and growth than topics studied.

horizons. Moving out of the lone researcher model toward dialogue helps in this process. Through dialogue and learning from each other, we more easily see and examine the lenses upon which we rely. In dialogue, we do "not seek to win or to convince, but to search together from our different vantage points" (Panikkar 1995, 172). This process does not attempt to reduce a concept to shared understandings or to develop a new concept agreed upon by all participants. Rather, as Vashon (1995, 72) states, this kind of dialogue implies "harmony in our differences."

Many truths live side by side. This is not to say that one truth is as good as another, but rather that we need to become aware of the many truths throughout the world and in our own lives. The goal is not to weed out conflicting truths, but rather to reach new, deeper, and more complex understandings of multiple truths.

Through dialogue and collaborative research, we share ourselves as well, creating relationships and working with others rather than "on" or "about" them. Through moving together, we might begin to develop frameworks for actions that nurture "harmony in our differences." As Tsing (1997, 253) states, "We need frameworks that show how multicultural alliances do not filter, misuse, or distort original truths, but rather spark the creative contingencies in which all theory is built."

CONCLUDING WORDS

A naturalist said, "You can love a landscape for a lifetime, and it will still have secrets from you" (Wilson 1989, 18). Whether researching a village in Brazil, a Christian school in the Midwest, or the superintendency of a rural school district in Vermont, you will never understand it all, but you will know where next to look, what new questions to ask, and what sense it might have for yourself and others. As Lorna reflected upon her project, she stated:

> When I go back and look at my original purposes, I believe that I made some slight progress, small mini-steps, both in terms of understanding inclusion, and learning about and how to use qualitative research. I feel like I cracked open the door, and peeked inside. (It's an enormous room!) The vastness of what is left to explore is simultaneously intimidating and exhilarating. Trying not to feel overwhelmed, I'll remember what one teacher said, "You work and work and work and work and work. And . . . the child makes slow gains." I think she meant that mini-steps count.

Each step, no matter how small, contributes to understanding. Scheper-Hughes (1992) calls for the practice of a "good enough" ethnography, accepting that understandings always will be only partial. We can, however, "struggle to do the best we can with the limited resources we have at hand—our ability to listen and observe carefully, empathetically, and compassionately" (28).

Qualitative inquiry is a search that leads into others' lives, your discipline, your practice, and yourself. You cannot be sure of where you will end up, but you invariably get caught up in the search and make steps forward. Andrea's words convey the empathy, compassion, and respect that accompanied her work:

> There is so much I want to know. I feel as though each interview is a rosebud handed to me. As I take them home and transcribe them, they begin to bloom, and each petal is a new idea or a deeper understanding. Here I stand with three beautiful flowers in one hand and my other hand out-stretched.

> True research does not end. Instead, it points the way for yet another search.

RECOMMENDED READINGS

Denzin, N. and M. Giardina (eds.) 2009. *Qualitative Inquiry and Social Justice*. Walnut Creek, CA: Left Coast Press.

EXERCISES

1. Reflect upon the possible significance of your research. In what ways might it contribute to theory, policy, and/or practice? Write up these thoughts.

2. After completing your pilot, return to your research statement, your research design, and your interview questions. What modifications would you make?

3. Develop a research proposal and step forth onto the inquiry road.

APPENDIX A

Guide for Developing a Qualitative Research Proposal[1]

I. Title (Fashion a working title that gets at the heart of the study.)

II. Introduction to the Study
   a. Research purposes
   b. Research statement (Create a one-sentence statement that describes your intended inquiry. Make it clear, focused, and doable. Reuse this statement in your proposal whenever you discuss your plans.)
   c. Kind of study (ethnography, ethnomethodology, action research, etc.) and why appropriate

III. Study Context
   a. Relationship of study to existing theory and research
   b. Relationship of study to personal experience and knowledge
   c. Contributions of pilot study to your current thoughts and proposed approaches

IV. Research Questions
   a. Description of the major questions that your work seeks to understand/explore
   b. Relationship of your questions to prior research and theory, your own experiences, and research purposes

V. Research Methods (Describe and justify each selection, making use of qualitative research texts and articles to demonstrate your familiarity with the procedures you are proposing.)
   a. Description of research setting or social context
   b. Discussion of type of study (case study, grounded theory, ethnography, etc.)
   c. Sampling strategies (sites, persons, places, times, and other data sources)
   d. Data collection techniques
   e. Data analysis procedures
   f. Consideration of possible ethical issues

[1]This outline is meant as a guide, a possible template, not as a rigid framework.

   VI. Validity
- a. Potential threats to the study's trustworthiness
- b. How you are dealing with/will deal with these threats

  VII. Implications/Significance/Contributions
- a. Knowledge (What might your research contribute to knowledge or theory?)
- b. Policy (How might your research contribute to policy?)
- c. Practice (How might your research contribute to practice or to practitioners?)
- d. Participants (How might your research give back to research participants and/or the communities of which they are a part?)

 VIII. References

   IX. Appendices
- a. Timetable
- b. Lay summary
- c. Consent forms
- d. Interview questions

Glossary

Archival research: Document-based research. Documents may be historical or current and range from library archives to scrapbooks in people's attics.

Autoethnography: Research that inquires into the self as part of a sociocultural context. The resulting text tends to evoke the experience for the reader.

Backyard research: Inquiry into one's own institution, agency, or community.

Blog: An ongoing narrative published on the Internet, produced by an individual or group of users. Short for *Web log*.

CAQDAS: Acronym for computer-assisted qualitative data analysis software. These software programs assist in data analysis through computerized tools for organizing, coding, sorting, cross-referencing, building theory, displaying, and so on.

Case study: An intensive study of an individual, institution, organization, or some bounded group, place, or process over time.

Coding: Representing a characteristic, dimension, process, theme, and so on in a data set. In qualitative research, passages of text may be marked off by codes and thereby linked to like passages that are then studied to learn more about how an idea or theme is represented and expressed within the study group. See also *qualitative coding*.

Codebook: A list of codes and subcodes, along with their descriptors and any guidelines the researcher has made for their use.

Colonial research: A term sometimes applied to research that is imposed on a group of people by an outsider and/or a person of power. In research described as colonial, research purposes do not serve those who are researched, decisions are made and controlled by the researcher, and relational distance is maintained between the researcher and the researched.

Conceptual context: Theories, ideas, and definitions, often from multiple disciplines, that inform one's research. Together, these concepts can create a useful organizational schema for situating and posing inquiry questions.

Concientization: A consciousness-raising process through inquiry and dialogue, often used in participatory action research.

Constant case comparison: A procedure that comes from grounded theory research in which new data, particularly from new cases, are coded and continually compared to previously collected data to better refine theoretical categories and to assist the researcher in pursuing new cases or questions.

Creative analytic practices: A phrase coined by Laurel Richardson (2000) to describe the variety of nontraditional ways in which qualitative researchers represent inquiry, often drawing on literary traditions such as drama, poetry, and narrative.

Crisis of representation: Refers to "the uncertainty within the human sciences about adequate means of describing social reality" (Schwandt 2007, 48). Researchers give up the authoritative stance and accept that knowledge is always partial, situated in a particular context with specific historical understandings.

Critical race theory: A theory that focuses on ways in which racism is so embedded in society that it appears "normal" for many. It portrays race as a socially constructed means to identify and classify people.

Decolonizing research: Research in which the goals, methods, and uses of the research seek to challenge power relationships that serve to oppress and demean particular groups of peoples.

Deconstruction: A process of revealing contradictions and inconsistencies within texts (written or lived) that previously were assumed to be coherent or true. "The aim of deconstruction is not to decode a *text* to somehow reveal its meaning or truth but to displace or unsettle taken-for-granted concepts like the unity of the text, the meaning or message of the text, or the authorship of the text." (Schwandt 2007, 63).

Deductive reasoning: Reasoning that moves from the theoretical/general/abstract to the specific/concrete. Deductive reasoning is often contrasted with inductive reasoning.

Deontological: An ethical stance which posits that moral conduct can be judged independently of its consequences. The deontological framework holds up some standard, such as justice or respect or honesty, by which to evaluate actions.

Discourse analysis: "Method of investigating rules and structures that govern and maintain the production of particular written, oral, or visual texts" (Hay 2005, 281).

Embodiment: Fixed personal factors that are impossible or difficult to change and include attributes such as skin color, gender, age, size, physical disability, etc. Also referred to as *identity categories.*

Epistemology: A philosophy that deals with the nature of knowledge or the ways in which we know the world and justify our beliefs about the world.

Essentialism: The perspective that words and the objects they signify have fundamental meanings rather than socially constructed meanings.

Ethnodrama: A creative analytic practice in which researchers turn their data into dramas and perform them as a way to represent research.

Feminist communitarianism: A social ethic described as "communitarian, egalitarian, democratic, critical, caring, engaged, performative, social justice oriented" (Lincoln and Denzin 2008, 542).

Field journal: A notebook (or computer files) in which the researcher records observations of people, places, events, activities, and conversations, as well as ideas, reflections, hunches, notes about patterns that seem to be emerging, and personal reactions. Also referred to as a *field log.*

Field log: See *field journal.*

Fieldwork: Research that takes place in real-life situations rather than laboratories, usually involving participant observation, conversations, and interviews.

Focus group: A selected set of people gathered by a researcher with the purpose of facilitating a discussion on a particular topic.

Gatekeeper: The person or persons who must give their consent before a researcher may enter a research setting and with whom the researcher must negotiate the conditions of access.

Grand tour question: A request for the respondent to verbally take the interviewer through a place, a time period, or a sequence of events or activities or to describe some group of people or objects.

Grounded theory methodology: A research process of building theory that is grounded in research data through a continuous, reflexive process of gathering data, coding, identifying themes, and then seeking out more data.

Idealism: The perspective that reality does not exist independently of people's thoughts but is based on ideas that shape what and how we know.

Identity categories: See *embodiment.*

Inductive reasoning: Reasoning the moves from the specific or concrete to the general or abstract. This type of reasoning is often associated with qualitative research and contrasted with deductive reasoning.

Intersubjectivity: "The method of connecting as many different perspectives on the same data as possible" (Sunstein and Chiseri-Strater 2002, 119). Multiple sources are used to get different interpretations on the same account or behavior or situation, including the researcher's interpretation.

Intertextuality: Originally, the term applied to ways in which the meaning of written text was shaped by the meanings of other texts. The term has been extended to apply to oral and pictorial texts and "is a way of saying that individual accounts owe much of their structure and meaning to other accounts" (Gubrium and Holstein 2009, 185–186).

Interview schedule: A list of interview questions in which wording as well as order may be subject to change as the researcher becomes informed by interviewees.

Kinesis: Postures, positions, and movement that serve to communicate in some way.

Lay summary: A summary of the research purpose and procedures presented (written or oral) to participants. Lay summaries generally are required by Institutional Review Boards and accompany consent forms.

Life history inquiry: Research that focuses on the life experiences of one or several individuals, with data gathered primarily through interviews.

Liminal: A term used by Victor Turner in his work with rituals to refer to circumstances in which roles or identities are particularly uncertain or problematic. The term is often used to refer to aspects of identities that inhabit in-between spaces.

Local facilitator: A knowledgeable person local to the research site with whom a non-local researcher works closely in a variety of ways. Local facilitators are also sometimes referred to as *local consultants, collaborators,* or *informants,* although field relationships can vary within and across these terms.

Logical empiricism: A more moderate version of logical positivism that developed in the mid-twentieth century. "Logical empiricists hold that the aim of science is the development of theoretical explanations and that legitimate explanations, in turn, take the form of general (covering) laws . . ." (Schwandt 2007, 180).

Logical positivism: A paradigm which held that knowledge was "limited to what could be logically deduced from theory, operationally measured, and empirically replicated" (Patton 2002, 92). In the mid-twentieth century, logical positivism was basically replaced by a more moderate philosophy referred to as *logical empiricism.*

Material culture: The artifacts or physical materials found within a group or culture that hold or signify meaning, history, and values for members of the group.

Measures of accretion: Artifacts or physical materials that people create, such as graffiti, murals, drawings, notes, and songs.

Measures of erosion: Aspects of everyday life that people have worn away through patterned activities such as paths across the grass on college campuses or the shine on handrails in front of popular museum exhibits.

Memos: Notes to oneself about particular thoughts, insights, or questions jotted during fieldwork and data analysis. Sometimes referred to as *observer comments.*

Method: A technique or procedure that is used to generate or analyze data.

Methodology: A theoretical framework that guides how researchers come to know what they know. The methodological framework includes assumptions about what is of importance to study, what constitutes legitimate knowledge, and what counts as evidence for making knowledge claims.

Narrative analysis: A form of discourse analysis that focuses on the textual devices at work in the construction of oral or written narratives and that may include explorations of the everyday contexts in which the stories are told.

Objectivity: A belief that it is possible or a goal to approximate the separation of personal opinions, feelings, and biases from data collection and analysis. This term is often contrasted with *subjectivity.*

Observer comments: Analytic notes or recordings of things that occur to a researcher during moments of fieldwork. See also *memos.*

Ontology: Beliefs about the world, what makes up the world, and how those aspects interrelate. Ontology asks "What is the nature of reality, and what can be known about it?"

Oral history research: Interview inquiry that focuses on historical events, skills, ways of life, or cultural patterns that may be changing.

Paradigm: A philosophical or theoretical framework made up of interrelated assumptions and values that provide a way of seeing and inquiring into the world. The term *paradigm* became popular after its use by Thomas Kuhn (1962).

Participant observation: A research method that involves the researcher as an interacting observer in the everyday life of research participants. It sometimes is used as a synonym for *fieldwork,* including procedures of observation, interviewing, and document collection.

Participatory mapping: A group of people mapping or diagramming together some material aspect of their lives, usually with the assistance of a researcher/facilitator. Sometimes also referred to as *community mapping* or *ethnocartography.*

Photo-elicitation: Refers to "using photographs to invoke comments, memory and discussion in the course of a semi-structured interview" (Banks 2007, 65).

Pilot study: An abbreviated research project with the purpose of practicing and testing procedures that could be used in full-scale inquiry.

Poetic transcription: A creative analytic practice in which the researcher fashions poem-like pieces from the words of interviewees.

Positionality: "A researcher's social, locational, and ideological placement relative to the research project or to other participants in it" (Hay 2005, 290). Positionality is often influenced by embodied factors such as race or gender and positions such as class and formative experiences.

Postcolonialism: A theory that critiques ways in which Western thinking (liberal humanism and modernist ideals) dominates lives of people throughout the world. This theory works to bring the voices of the margins to the center, to displace Western hegemony.

Postmodernism: "A movement in the humanities and social sciences that . . . embraces the pluralism of multiple perspectives, knowledges, and voices rather than the grand theories of modernism" (Hay 2005, 290). Core concepts in postmodernism include fragmentation, indeterminacy, and heterogeneity.

Postmodernity: Indicates a break from modernity, a historical period of time marked, in part, by industrialization. Postmodernity is the new world order in the time of globalization, the decline of the nation-state, and an age of information technologies (Ahmed and Shore 1995).

Postpositivism: A term used by some to refer to *logical empiricism,* a less strict form of logical positivism, and by others to refer to anything other than logical positivism. In the latter use of the term, all paradigms other than early positivism would be forms of postpositivist thought.

Poststructuralism: A set of cultural theories that react to structuralism and closure of any kind. Associated with French scholars Derrida, Foucault, and others, poststructuralism asserts that "meaning is unstable, never fixed"; that "everything is a *text*—and all texts are interrelated" (Schwandt 1997, 122); and that deconstructionism is a strategy for revealing ways in which texts support and maintain beliefs that are often taken for granted and serve to legitimate dominant groups.

Praxis: A relationship between thought and action, between theory and practice. Praxis refers to more than putting theory into action; it also involves continual reflection on and inquiry into experience and the meaning of concepts used in everyday interactions.

Presupposition question: A question in which the interviewer presupposes "that the respondent has something to say" (Patton 2002, 369).

Problem statement: See *research question.*

Problematize: To question taken-for-granted assumptions, posit other possible interpretations of social phenomena, and/or draw attention to their complexity.

Proxemics: The study of how people communicate through their use of space, particularly social spaces.

Qualitative coding: Segregating data into like categories to discern themes, patterns, and processes and to make comparisons and build theoretical explanations. Also referred to as *indexing* or *categorizing.*

Qualitative research: A type of research that focuses on qualities such as words or observations that are difficult to quantify and that lend themselves to interpretation or deconstruction.

Quantitative research: A type of research that focuses on quantities, uses an instrument such as a survey, involves a large number of people, and is analyzed statistically.

Queer theory: A theory that focuses on the ways in which sexual and gender identity is socially and culturally constructed and on the shifting boundaries and ambivalences in these constructions. It challenges the concept of heteronormativity, the perspective that heterosexuality is/should be the normal (and legal) way for interactions.

Rapport: An attribute of accord or affinity that is instrumental to a variety of professional relationships, including research.

Reader's Theater: A form of creative analytic practices in which research data are shaped into dramas, sometimes with characters inserted to represent abstract notions such as "theory," "popular culture," and so on. Rather than memorize the script, presenters read text selections individually and sometimes in chorus. Staging is simple, usually involving chairs or stools and perhaps a few props.

Realism: The view that "reality" exists independently of the mind or the way people think about it.

Realist tale: A research representation in which the author minutely documents details of the lives of people studied, using closely edited quotations, to report how life really is for a person or some set of people. In a realist tale, the researcher is absent from much, if not all, of the text, taking a position of "interpretive omnipotence" (Van Maanen 1988, 51).

Reflection: Careful thought about some act, action, interaction, process, and so on in order to gain insight, understanding, and/or plan for the future.

Reflexivity: Critical reflection on how a researcher, research participants, a setting, and a phenomenon of interest interact and influence each other. This includes "examining one's personal and theoretical commitments to see how they serve as resources for generating particular data, for behaving in particular ways . . . and for developing particular interpretations" (Schwandt 2007, 260).

Relativism: The "view that different cultures define phenomena in different ways, so that the perspective of one cannot be used to judge or even understand that of another" (Gibbs, 2007, 151). Relativism is also used in an ethical sense to refer to the absence of universal moral principles for judging the rightness or wrongness of an act.

Representation: A description or portrayal of some aspect of the social world. How researchers use language to describe or depict others, however, is an area of much discussion in qualitative inquiry. Few would claim that their descriptions reproduce or mirror the social world, but many argue for making their representations evidence based. Poststructuralists bring all acts of representation into question.

Research purposes: Practical and intellectual (and possibly personal) goals for a specific research project.

Research question: A question or set of questions that serve to focus a study. Also referred to as a *problem statement.*

Semiotics: The study of signs and symbols—of things that stand for something else and, therefore, possess information.

Sign: A word or mark used to represent something else.

Social constructivism: A belief that knowledge is socially constructed or produced, including knowledge that appears to be "objective" or a "scientific truth." This view is usually associated with the idealist philosophy.

Stakeholders: Those with a stake in some process. This term is often used in action research.

Standpoint epistemologies: A belief that knowledge is politically situated and that prevailing concepts, even those that appear to be "neutral," serve interests of dominant groups. Standpoint epistemologies are positioned in the experiences, values, and interests of a group that has traditionally been oppressed or excluded (women, gays, lesbians, people of color, those who are colonized, etc.) and "are a means of deconstructing what has passed for knowledge, so as to expose its exclusions and dominant perspectives" (Schwandt 2007, 276).

Subject positions: Aspects of a person's life history and personal experiences that help to form her or his values.

Subjectivity: A term used in different ways in research texts. It can refer to aspects of one's personal history and attributes that form the basis for personal perspectives, beliefs, and feelings. It is sometimes used to refer to biases or prejudices, or to unwarranted claims. The term is often paired with *objectivity*. Poststructuralists claim that accounting for one's subjectivity is impossible because there is no such thing as a rational, knowable self.

Teacher research: Research carried out by teachers that involves inquiry into and reflection on their own practice.

Text: "Traditionally synonymous with the written page, but now used more broadly to refer to a range of source forms including oral texts (including semi-structured interviews and oral histories), images (including painting, photographs, and maps) as well as written and print texts (including newspapers, letters, and brochures)" (Hay 2005, 296). From a poststructuralist perspective, everything is a text and capable of being rewritten.

Theoretical sampling: A grounded theory technique in which the researcher refines concepts and theoretical constructs by finding gaps in data or holes in developing theories and then sampling specific cases that can contribute to the emerging theory.

Theoretical saturation: A grounded theory concept that refers to data seeming complete and integrated in that successive examination of sources yields redundancy and nothing new for the emerging theory.

Thick description: A term coined by Geertz (1973) that refers to "description that goes beyond the mere or bare reporting of an act (thin description), but describes and probes the intentions, motives, meanings, contexts, situations and circumstances of action" (Denzin 1989a, 39).

Triangulation: A term taken from surveying and navigation, it "is a means of checking the integrity of the inferences one draws" (Schwandt 1997, 163). Although the most common form of triangulation in qualitative research is through using multiple methods of data collection, triangulation may also refer to incorporation of multiple kinds of data sources (i.e., not just teachers but students and parents as well), multiple investigators, or multiple theoretical perspectives.

Utilitarian ethics: An ethical standard in which decisions are made on the basis of that which results in the greatest good for the greatest number. Also sometimes described as the "ends justify the means" approach.

Verisimilitude: A term that originally referred to getting as close to the truth, or reality, as possible. As used in qualitative research today, verisimilitude frequently refers to evocatively crafting an account with rich detail so that it has the appearance of reality and helps readers experience the perspectives or experiences of respondents (Schwandt 2007).

References

Aamodt, A. 1989. Ethnography and epistemology: Generating nursing knowledge. In J. Morse (ed.), *Qualitative Nursing Research: A Contemporary Dialogue* (pp. 29–40). Rockville, MD: Aspen Publishers.

Adler, P., and P. Adler, 1994. Observational techniques. In N. Denzin and Y. Lincoln (eds.), *Handbook of Qualitative Research* (pp. 377–392). Thousand Oaks, CA: Sage Publications.

Agar, M. 1973. *Ripping and Running: A Formal Ethnography of Urban Heroin Addicts.* New York: Seminar Press.

Agar, M. 1980. *The Professional Stranger.* New York: Academic Press.

Agar, M. 1995. Literary journalism as ethnography. In J. Van Maanen (ed.), *Representation in Ethnography* (pp. 112–129). Thousand Oaks, CA: Sage Publications.

Ahmed, A., and C. Shore. 1995. Introduction: Is anthropology relevant to the contemporary world? In A. Ahmed and C. Shore (eds.), *The Future of Anthropology: Its Relevance to the Contemporary World* (pp. 12–45). London: Athlone.

American Anthropological Association. 1995 (September). *Commission to Review the AAA Statements on Ethics Final Report.* Retrieved October 15, 2004, from www.aaanet.org/committees/ethics/ethrpt.htm.

American Anthropological Association. 1998. *Code of Ethics of the American Anthropological Association.* Retrieved October 15, 2004, from www.aaanet.org/committees/ethics/ethcode.htm.

Anderson, G., K. Herr, and A. S. Nihlen. 1994. *Studying Your Own School: An Educator's Guide to Qualitative Practitioner Research.* Thousand Oaks, CA: Sage Publications.

Anderson, N. 1923. *The Hobo: The Sociology of the Homeless Man.* Chicago: University of Chicago Press.

Anfara, V., Jr., and N. Mertz. 2006. Introduction. In V. Anfara, Jr., and N. Mertz (eds.), *Theoretical Frameworks in Qualitative Research* (pp. xiii–xxxii). Thousand Oaks, CA: Sage Publications.

Angrosino, M. 1998. *Opportunity House: Ethnographic Stories of Mental Retardation.* Walnut Creek, CA: AltaMira Press.

Ashton, P., and R. Webb. 1986. *Making a Difference: Teacher's Sense of Efficacy and Student Achievement.* New York: Longman.

Atkinson, R. 2002. The life story interview. In J. F. Gubrium and J. A. Holstein (eds.), *Handbook of Interview Research: Context and Method* (pp. 121–140). Thousand Oaks, CA: Sage Publications.

Ball, S. 1985. Participant observation with pupils. In R. Burgess (ed.), *Strategies of Educational Research: Qualitative Methods* (pp. 23–53). Philadelphia: Falmer Press.

Bandelier, A. F. 1971. *The Delight Makers: A Novel of Prehistoric Pueblo Indians.* New York: Harcourt Brace Jovanovich. (Original work published 1890.)

Banks, M. 2007. *Using Visual Data in Qualitative Research.* Thousand Oaks, CA: Sage.

Barone, T. 1990a. Using the narrative text as an occasion for conspiracy. In E. Eisner and A. Peshkin (eds.), *Qualitative Inquiry in Education: The Continuing Debate* (pp. 305–326). New York: Teachers College Press.

Barone, T. 1990b. *On the Demise of Subjectivity in Educational Inquiry.* Paper presented at the annual meeting of the American Educational Research Association, Boston.

Barone, T. 2008. Creative nonfiction and social research. In J. G. Knowles and A. L. Cole (eds.), *Handbook of the ARTS in Qualitative Research* (pp. 105–115). Thousand Oaks, CA: Sage.

Barrios de Chungara, D., and M. Viezzer. 1978. *Let Me Speak! Testimony of Domitila, a Woman of the Bolivian Mines* (V. Ortiz, trans.). New York: Monthly Review Press.

Bartunek, J., and M. R. Louis. 1996. *Insider/Outsider Team Research.* Thousand Oaks, CA: Sage Publications.

Bateson, M. C. 1984. *With a Daughter's Eye: A Memoir of Margaret Mead and Gregory Bateson.* New York: Morrow.

Bateson, M. C. 1990. *Composing a Life.* New York: Plume.

Bauman, Z. 2008. Afterthought on writing; On writing sociology. In N. Denzin and Y. Lincoln (eds.), *The Landscape of Qualitative Research,* 3rd ed. (pp. 507–518). Thousand Oaks, CA: Sage.

Baym, N., and Markham, A. 2009. Introduction. In A. Markham and N. Baym (eds.), *Internet Inquiry: Conversations about Method* (pp. vii–xix). Thousand Oaks, CA: Sage.

Becker, H. S. 1986a. *Doing Things Together: Selected Papers.* Evanston, IL: Northwestern University Press.

Becker, H. S. 1986b. *Writing for Social Scientists: How to Start and Finish Your Thesis, Book, or Article.* Chicago: University of Chicago Press.

Behar, R. 1993. *Translated Woman: Crossing the Border with Esperanza's Story.* Boston: Beacon Press.

Behar, R. 1995. Writing in my father's name: A diary of *Translated Woman's* first year. In R. Behar and D. Gordon (eds.), *Women Writing Culture* (pp. 65–82). Berkeley: University of California Press.

Behar, R. 1996. *The Vulnerable Observer: Anthropology That Breaks Your Heart.* Boston: Beacon Press.

Behar, R., and D. Gordon (eds.). 1995. *Women Writing Culture.* Berkeley: University of California Press.

Belenky, M., L. Bond, and J. Weinstock. 1997. *A Tradition That Has No Name: Nurturing the Development of People, Families, and Communities.* New York: Basic Books.

Benson, P. (ed.). 1993. *Anthropology and Literature.* Chicago: University of Illinois Press.

Benthall, J. 1995. From self-applause through self-criticism to self-confidence. In A. Ahmed and C. Shore (eds.), *The Future of Anthropology: Its Relevance to the Contemporary World* (pp. 1–11). London: Athlone.

Berg, B. 1995. *Qualitative Research Methods for the Social Sciences,* 2nd ed. Boston: Allyn & Bacon.

Berg, D. 1988. Anxiety in research relationships. In D. Berg and K. K. Smith (eds.), *The Self in Social Inquiry: Researching Methods,* 2nd ed. (pp. 213–228). Beverly Hills, CA: Sage Publications.

Berlinski, M. 2007. *Fieldwork.* New York: Picador.

Bernard, H. R. 1988. *Research Methods in Cultural Anthropology.* Newbury Park, CA: Sage Publications.

Bishop, P. 1998. *Portraits of Partnership: The Relational Work of Effective Middle Level Partner Teachers.* Unpublished doctoral dissertation, University of Vermont, Burlington.

Bishop, R. 2008. Freeing ourselves from neocolonial domination in research. In N. Denzin and Y. Lincoln (eds.), *The Landscape of Qualitative Research,* 3rd ed. (pp. 145–183). Thousand Oaks, CA: Sage Publications.

Bissex, G. 1987. Year-long, classroom-based studies. In G. Bissex and R. Bullock (eds.), *Seeing for Ourselves: Case-Study Research by Teachers of Writing* (pp. 31–39). Portsmouth, NH: Heinemann.

Bissex, G., and R. Bullock (eds.). 1987. *Seeing for Ourselves: Case-Study Research by Teachers of Writing*. Portsmouth, NH: Heinemann.

Bloom, L. 1998. *Under the Sign of Hope: Feminist Methodology and Narrative Interpretation*. Albany, NY: State University of New York Press.

Bloom, L. R., and P. E. Sawin, 2009. Ethical responsibility in feminist research: Challenging ourselves to do activist research with women in poverty. *International Journal of Qualitative Studies in Education*, 22(3): 333–351.

Bloor, M., and F. Wood, 2006. *Keywords in Qualitative Methods*. Thousand Oaks, CA: Sage.

Blumenfeld-Jones, D. 1995. Dance as a mode of research representation. *Qualitative Inquiry*, 1(4), 391–401.

Blumenfeld-Jones, D. 2008. Dance, choreography, and social science research. In J. G. Knowles and A. L. Cole (eds.), *Handbook of the ARTS in Qualitative Research* (pp. 175–184). Thousand Oaks, CA: Sage.

Boal, A. 2006. *Aesthetics of the Oppressed* (A. Jackson, trans.). New York: Routledge.

Bochner, A., and C. Ellis. 1996. Introduction: Talking over ethnography. In C. Ellis and A. Bochner (eds.), *Composing Ethnography: Alternative Forms of Qualitative Writing* (pp. 13–45). Walnut Creek, CA: AltaMira Press.

Bogdan, R., and S. Biklen. 2003. *Qualitative Research for Education*, 4th ed. Boston: Allyn & Bacon.

Bonfil Batalla, G. 1996. *Mexico Profundo: Reclaiming a Civilization*. Austin: University of Texas Press.

Bottorff, J. 1994. Using videotaped recordings in qualitative research. In J. Morse (ed.), *Critical Issues in Qualitative Research Methods* (pp. 244–261). Thousand Oaks, CA: Sage Publications.

Boyd, D. 2009. A response to Christine Hine. In A. Markham and N. Baym (eds.), *Internet Inquiry: Conversations about Method* (pp. 26–32). Thousand Oaks, CA: Sage.

Brady, J. 1976. *The Craft of Interviewing*. Cincinnati, OH: Writer's Digest.

Brooks, M. 1989. *Instant Rapport*. New York: Warner Books.

Bruner, E. 1984. Introduction: Opening up of anthropology. In E. Bruner (ed.), *Text, Play, and Story: The Construction and Reconstruction of Self and Society* (pp. 1–16). Washington, DC: American Ethnological Society.

Bruner, E. 1986. Experience and its expressions. In V. Turner and E. Bruner (eds.), *The Anthropology of Experience* (pp. 3–30). Urbana: University of Illinois Press.

Bruner, E.1993. Introduction: The ethnographic self and the personal self. In P. Benson (ed.), *Anthropology and Literature* (pp. 1–26). Urbana: University of Illinois Press.

Bruner, J. 1960. *The Process of Education*. Cambridge, MA: Harvard University Press.

Bruner, J. 1979. *On Knowing: Essays for the Left Hand*, rev. ed. Cambridge, MA: Belknap Press.

Bryant, I. 1996. Action research and reflective practice. In D. Scott and R. Usher (eds.), *Understanding Educational Research* (pp. 106–119). New York: Routledge.

Bulmer, M. (ed.). 1982. *Social Research Ethics: An Examination of the Merits of Covert Participation Observation*. London: Macmillan.

Burgess, R. 1984. *In the Field: An Introduction to Field Research*. London: Unwin Hyman.

Busier, H. 1997. *Beyond the Yellow Brick Road: Educational Portraits of Anorexic Women*. Unpublished doctoral dissertation, University of Vermont, Burlington.

Busier, H., K. Clark, R. Esch, C. Glesne, Y. Pigeon, and J. Tarule. 1997. Intimacy in research. *The International Journal of Qualitative Studies in Education*, 10(2), 165–170.

Butler-Kisber, L. 2008. Collage as inquiry. In J. G. Knowles and A. L. Cole (eds.), *Handbook of the ARTS in Qualitative Research* (pp. 265–276). Thousand Oaks, CA: Sage.

Cameron, J. 2005. Focusing on the focus group. In I. Hay (ed.), *Qualitative Research Methods in Human Geography*, 2nd ed. (pp. 116–132). New York: Oxford University Press.

Caro, R. 1988. Lyndon Johnson and the roots of power. In W. Zinsser (ed.), *Extraordinary Lives: The Art and Craft of American Biography* (pp. 199–231). Boston: Houghton Mifflin.

Carr, W., and S. Kemmis. 1986. *Becoming Critical: Education, Knowledge and Action Research.* London: Falmer Press.

Carspecken, P., and M. Apple. 1992. Critical qualitative research: Theory, methodology, and practice. In M. LeCompte, W. Millroy, and J. Preissle (eds.), *The Handbook of Qualitative Research in Education* (pp. 507–553). San Diego, CA: Academic Press.

Casas, J. 2005. Scenes from 14. In J. Saldaña (ed.), *Ethnodrama: An Anthology of Reality Theatre* (pp. 45–61). Walnut Creek, CA: Alta Mira Press.

Cassell, J. 1987. Cases and comments. In J. Cassell and S. E. Jacobs (eds.), *Handbook on Ethical Issues in Anthropology* (pp. 37–75). Washington, DC: American Anthropological Association.

Cassell, J., and S. E. Jacobs (eds.). 1987. Introduction. In *Handbook on Ethical Issues in Anthropology* (pp. 1–3). Washington, DC: American Anthropological Association.

Chapin, M., and B. Threlkeld, 2001. *Indigenous Landscapes: A Study in Ethnocartography*: Washington, DC: Center for the Support of Native Lands.

Charmaz, K. 2002. Qualitative interviewing and grounded theory analysis. In J. F. Gubrium and J. A. Holstein (eds.), *Handbook of Interview Research: Context and Method* (pp. 675–694). Thousand Oaks, CA: Sage Publications.

Christians, C. 2000. Ethics and politics in qualitative research. In N. Denzin and Y. Lincoln (eds.), *Handbook of Qualitative Research*, 2nd ed. (pp. 133–155). Thousand Oaks, CA: Sage Publications.

Christians, C. 2008. Ethics and politics in qualitative research. In N. Denzin and Y. Lincoln (eds.), *The Landscape of Qualitative Research* (pp. 185–220). Thousand Oaks, CA: Sage.

Clark, K. A. 1999. *Moving Beyond Recognition: Voices of Women Academics That Have Experience Being First-Generation College Students.* Unpublished doctoral dissertation, University of Vermont, Burlington.

Clark/Keefe, K. 2002. A fine line: Integrating art and fieldwork in the study of self-conceptualization and educational experiences. *The Alberta Journal of Educational Research*, XLVIII(3), CD-ROM supplement.

Clark/Keefe, K. 2006. Degrees of separation: An ourstory about working-class and poverty-class academic identity. *Qualitative Inquiry*, 12(6), 1180–1197.

Cochran-Smith, M., and S. Lytle. 1993. *Inside/Outside: Teacher Research and Knowledge.* New York: Teachers College Press.

Coffey, A., and P. Atkinson. 1996. *Making Sense of Qualitative Data: Complementary Research Strategies.* Thousand Oaks, CA: Sage Publications.

Coles, R. 1977. *Eskimos, Chicanos, Indians.* Boston: Little, Brown.

Coles, R. 1989. *The Call of Stories: Teaching and the Moral Imagination.* Boston: Houghton Mifflin.

Collier, J., Jr., and M. Collier. 1986. *Visual Anthropology: Photography as a Research Method*, rev. ed. Albuquerque: University of New Mexico Press.

Colvard, R. 1967. Interaction and identification in reporting field research: A critical reconsideration of protective procedures. In G. Sjoberg (ed.), *Ethics, Politics and Social Research* (pp. 319–358). Cambridge, MA: Schenkman.

Couch, J. 1987. Objectivity: A crutch and club for bureaucrafts/A haven for lost souls. *Sociological Quarterly*, 28, 105–110.

Cressey, P. G. 1932/2008. *The Taxi-Dance Hall: A Sociological Study in Commercialized Recreation and City Life.* Chicago: University of Chicago Press.

Creswell, J. 1998. *Qualitative Inquiry and Research Design: Choosing among Five Traditions.* Thousand Oaks, CA: Sage Publications.

Crisler, L. 1958. *Arctic Wild*. New York: Harper & Brothers.

Crotty, M. 1998. *The Foundations of Social Research: Meaning and Perspective in the Research Process*. London: Sage Publications.

Dalton, M. 1959. *Men Who Manage: Fusions of Feeling and Theory in Administration*. New York: Wiley.

Daniels, A. K. 1967. The low caste stranger. In G. Sjoberg (ed.), *Ethics, Politics and Social Research* (pp. 267–296). Cambridge, MA: Schenkman.

Davies, K. 1996. Capturing women's lives: A discussion of time and methodological issues. *Women's Studies International Forum*, 19(6), 579–588.

Davis, H. 2001. The management of self: Practical and emotional implications of ethnographic work in a public hospital setting. In K. Gilbert (ed.), *The Emotional Nature of Qualitative Research* (pp. 37–61). New York: CRC Press.

Davis, J. 1988. Teachers, kids, and conflict: Ethnography of a junior high school. In J. Spradley and D. McCurdy (eds.), *The Cultural Experience: Ethnography in Complex Society* (pp. 103–121). Long Grove, IL: Waveland Press. (Original work published 1972.)

Delamont, S. 1992. *Fieldwork in Educational Settings: Methods, Pitfalls and Perspectives*. Washington, DC: Falmer Press.

Delamont, S. 2002. Whose side are we on? Revisiting Becker's classic ethical questions at the *fin de siecle*. In T. Welland and L. Pugsley (eds.), *Ethical Dilemmas in Qualitative Research* (pp. 149–163). Burlington, VT: Ashgate Publishing.

Denny, T. 1978. *Storytelling and Educational Understanding*. Paper presented at the national meeting of the International Reading Association, Houston.

Denzin, N. 1989a. *The Research Act*, rev. ed. Englewood Cliffs, NJ: Prentice Hall.

Denzin, N. 1989b. *Interpretive Interactionism*. Newbury Park, CA: Sage Publications.

Denzin, N. 1997. *Interpretive Ethnography: Ethnographic Practices for a 21st Century*. Thousand Oaks, CA: Sage Publications.

Denzin, N. 2008. Interpretive biography. In J. G. Knowles and A. L. Cole (eds.), *Handbook of the ARTS in Qualitative Research* (pp. 117–125). Thousand Oaks, CA: Sage.

Denzin, N., and M. Giardina (eds.) 2009. *Qualitative Inquiry and Social Justice*. Walnut Creek, CA: Left Coast Press.

Denzin, N., and Y. Lincoln (eds.). 2000. *Handbook of Qualitative Research*, 2nd ed. Thousand Oaks, CA: Sage Publications.

Dickens, D., and A. Fontana (eds.). 1994. *Postmodernism Social Inquiry*. New York: The Guilford Press.

Dicks, B., B. Mason, A. Coffey, and P. Atkinson, P. 2005. *Qualitative Research and Hypermedia: Ethnography for the Digital Age*. Thousand Oaks: Sage Publications.

Didion, J. 1988. Interview on Fresh Air program, 19 January 1988. National Public Radio.

Diener, E., and R. Crandall. 1978. *Ethics in Social and Behavioral Research*. Chicago: University of Chicago Press.

Dillard, A. 1982. *Living by Fiction*. New York: Harper & Row.

Dillon, D. R. 1989. Showing them that I want to learn and that I care about who they are: A microethnography of the social organization of a secondary low-track English-reading classroom. *American Educational Research Journal*, 26, 227–259.

Dobbert, M. L. 1982. *Ethnographic Research: Theory and Application for Modern Schools and Societies*. New York: Praeger.

Dohan, D., and M. Sanchez-Jankowski. 1998. Using computers to analyze ethnographic field data: Theoretical and practical considerations. *Annual Review of Sociology*, 24, 477–498.

Donmoyer, R., and J. Yennie-Donmoyer. 1995. Data as drama: Reflections on the use of readers' theater as a mode of qualitative data display. *Qualitative Inquiry*, 1(4), 402–428.

Donmoyer, R., and J. Y. Donmoyer, 2008. Readers' Theater as a data display strategy. In J. G. Knowles and A. L. Cole (eds.), *Handbook of the ARTS in Qualitative Research* (pp. 209–224). Thousand Oaks, CA: Sage.

Douglas, J. 1976. *Investigative Social Research: Individual and Team Field Research.* Beverly Hills, CA: Sage Publications.

Douglas, J. 1985. *Creative Interviewing.* Beverly Hills, CA: Sage Publications.

Dowling, R. 2005. Power, subjectivity, and ethics in qualitative research. In I. Hay (ed.), *Qualitative Research Methods in Human Geography,* 2nd ed., (pp. 19–29). New York: Oxford University Press.

Ebbutt, D. 1985. Educational action research: Some general concerns and specific quibbles. In R. Burgess (ed.), *Issues in educational research: Qualitative methods* (pp. 152–174). Philadelphia: Falmer Press.

Eisner, E. 1981. On the differences between scientific and artistic approaches to qualitative research. *Educational Researcher,* 10(4), 5–9.

Eisner, E. 1990. *Objectivity in Education Research.* Paper presented at the annual meeting of the American Educational Research Association, Boston.

Eisner, E. 1997. The promise and perils of alternative forms of data representation. *Educational Researcher,* 26(6), 4–10.

Eisner, E. 2008. Art and knowledge. In J. G. Knowles and A. L. Cole (eds.), *Handbook of the ARTS in Qualitative Research* (pp. 3–12). Thousand Oaks, CA: Sage.

Eisner, E., and A. Peshkin (eds.). 1990. *Qualitative Inquiry in Education: The Continuing Debate.* New York: Teachers College Press.

Ellen, R. F. 1984. *Ethnographic Research: A Guide to General Conduct.* New York: Academic Press.

Ellingson, L. 2009. *Engaging in Crystallization in Qualitative Research.* Thousand Oaks, CA: Sage.

Ellis, C. 1995. The other side of the fence: Seeing black and white in a small southern town. *Qualitative Inquiry,* 1(2), 147–167.

Ellis, C. 2004. *The Ethnographic I: A Methodological Novel about Autoethnography.* Walnut Creek, CA: AltaMira.

Ellis, C., and L. Berger, 2003. Their story/my story/our story. In J. Holstein and J. Gubrium (eds.), *Inside Interviewing: New Lenses, New Concerns* (pp. 467–493). Thousand Oaks, CA: Sage Publishing.

Ellis, C., and A. Bochner (eds.). 1996. *Composing Ethnography: Alternative Forms of Qualitative Writing.* Walnut Creek, CA: AltaMira Press.

Ellis, C., and A. Bochner. 2000. Autoethnography, personal narrative, reflexivity: Research as subject. In N. Denzin and Y. Lincoln (eds.), *Handbook of Qualitative Research,* 2nd ed. (pp. 733–768). Thousand Oaks, CA: Sage Publications.

Elm, M. S. 2009. How do various notions of privacy influence decisions in qualitative internet research? In A. Markham and N. Baym (eds.), *Internet Inquiry: Conversations about Method* (pp. 69–87). Thousand Oaks, CA: Sage.

English, F. 1988. The utility of the camera in qualitative research. *Educational Researcher,* 17(4), 8–15.

Enright, S., and J. Tammivaara. 1984. *Tell Me More: The Elicitation of Interview Data in a Microethnographic Study of Multicultural Classrooms.* Paper presented at the annual meeting of the American Educational Research Association, New Orleans.

Ensler, E. 2001. *The Vagina Monologues.* New York: Villard.

Erickson, F. 1973. What makes school ethnography "ethnographic?" *Council on Anthropology and Education Newsletter,* 4(2), 10–19.

Erickson, F. 1986. Qualitative methods in research on teaching. In M. C. Wittrock (ed.), *Handbook of Research on Teaching*, 3rd ed. (pp. 119–161). New York: Macmillan.

Erickson, F., and G. Mohatt. 1982. Cultural organization of participant structures in two classrooms of Indian students. In G. Spindler (ed.), *Doing the Ethnography of Schooling: Educational Anthropology in Action* (pp. 132–174). New York: Holt, Rinehart & Winston.

Esch, R. 1996. *Conversation between Intimates, an Evening of Chamber Music: Girls' Friendship, Self, and Experience during the Transition from Childhood to Adolescence.* Unpublished manuscript, University of Vermont, Burlington.

Esteva, G., and M. S. Prakash. 1998. *Grassroots Post-modernism.* New York: Zed Books.

Farganis, S. 1994. Postmodernism and feminism. In D. Dickens and A. Fontana (eds.), *Postmodernism and Social Inquiry* (pp. 101–126). New York: The Guilford Press.

Feldman, M. S., J. Bell, and M. T. Berger. 2003. *Gaining Access: A Practical and Theoretical Guide for Qualitative Researchers.* Walnut Creek, CA: AltaMira.

Fetterman, D. 1998. *Ethnography: Step by Step*, 2nd ed. Thousand Oaks, CA: Sage Publications.

Finch, J. 1984. It's great to have someone to talk to: The ethics and politics of interviewing women. In C. Bell and H. Roberts (eds.), *Social Researching: Politics, Problems and Practice* (pp. 70–88). London: Routledge & Kegan Paul.

Fine, G. A. 1980. Cracking diamonds: Observer role in little league baseball settings and the acquisition of social competence. In W. Shiffir, R. Stebbins, and A. Turowetz (eds.), *Fieldwork Experiences: Qualitative Approaches to Social Research* (pp. 117–132). New York: St. Martin's Press.

Fine, G., and K. Sandstrom. 1988. *Knowing Children: Participant Observation with Minors.* Newbury Park, CA: Sage Publications.

Finley, S., and G. Knowles. 1995. Researcher as artist/Artist as researcher. *Qualitative Inquiry,* 1(1), 110–142.

Firestone, W. 1987. Meaning in method: The rhetoric of quantitative and qualitative research. *Educational Researcher,* 16(7), 16–21.

Flax, J. 1990. Postmodernism and gender relations in feminist theory. In L. J. Nicholson (ed.), *Feminism/Postmodernism* (pp. 39–62). New York: Routledge.

Flinders, D. 1987. *What Teachers Learn from Teaching: Educational Criticisms of Instructional Adaptation.* Unpublished doctoral dissertation, Stanford University, Stanford, CA.

Flinders, D. 1992. In search of ethical guidance: Constructing a basis for dialogue. *Qualitative Studies in Education,* 5(2), 101–115.

Flinders, D., and G. Mills (eds.). 1993. *Theory and Concepts in Qualitative Research: Perspectives from the Field.* New York: Teachers College Press.

Fonow, M., and J. Cook (eds.). 1991. *Beyond Methodology: Feminist Scholarship as Lived Research.* Bloomington: Indiana University Press.

Fontana, A. 1994. Ethnographic trends in the postmodern era. In D. Dickens and A. Fontana (eds.), *Postmodernism and Social Inquiry* (pp. 203–223). New York: The Guilford Press.

Fontana, A. 2002. Postmodern trends in interviewing. In J. F. Gubrium and J. A. Holstein (eds.), *Handbook of Interview Research: Context and Method* (pp. 161–175). Thousand Oaks, CA: Sage Publications.

Fontana, A., and J. Frey. 1994. Interviewing: The art of science. In N. Denzin and Y. Lincoln (eds.), *Handbook of Qualitative Research* (pp. 361–376). Thousand Oaks, CA: Sage Publications.

Fontana, A., and J. Frey. 2000. The interview: From structured questions to negotiated text. In N. Denzin and Y. Lincoln (eds.), *Handbook of Qualitative Research*, 2nd ed. (pp. 645–672). Thousand Oaks, CA: Sage Publications.

Fowler, F. 2006. Struggling with theory: A beginning scholar's experience with Mazzoni's arena models. In J. Vincent Anfara and N. Mertz (eds.), *Theoretical Frameworks in Qualitative Research* (pp. 39–58). Thousand Oaks, CA: Sage Publications.

Freilich, M. 1977. *Marginal Natives at Work: Anthropologists in the Field.* New York: Harper & Row.

Freire, P. 2000. *Pedagogy of the Oppressed.* New York: Continuum. (Original work published 1970.)

Fulwiler, T. 1985. Writing is everybody's business. *National Forum: Phi Kappa Phi Journal,* 65(4), 21–24.

Furney, K. 1997. *Caring as the Cornerstone of Change: A Cross-Case Analysis of Three Schools' Experience in Implementing General and Special Education Reform.* Unpublished doctoral dissertation, University of Vermont, Burlington.

Gall, M., W. Borg, and J. Gall. 1996. *Educational Research: An Introduction,* 6th ed. New York: Longman.

Galliher, J. F. 1982. The protection of human subjects: A reexamination of the professional code of ethics. In M. Bulmer (ed.), *Social Research Ethics* (pp. 152–165). London: Macmillan.

Gans, H. 1982. The participant-observer as a human being: Observations on the personal aspects of fieldwork. In R. Burgess (ed.), *Field Research: A Sourcebook and Field Manual* (pp. 53–61). London: George Allen & Unwin.

Geertz, C. 1973. *The Interpretation of Cultures.* New York: Basic Books.

Geertz, C. 1988. *Work and Lives: The Anthropologist as Author.* Stanford, CA: Stanford University Press.

Geertz, C. 1995. *After the Fact: Two Countries, Four Decades, One Anthropologist.* Cambridge, MA: Harvard University Press.

Gibbs, G. 2007. *Analyzing Qualitative Data.* Thousand Oaks, CA: Sage.

Giddens, A. 1995. Epilogue: Notes on the future of anthropology. In A. Ahmed and C. Shore (eds.), *The Future of Anthropology: Its Relevance to the Contemporary World* (pp. 272–277). London: Athlone.

Gilligan, C. 1993. *In a Different Voice: Psychological Theory and Women's Development.* Cambridge, MA: Harvard University Press. (Original work published 1982.)

Gitlin, A. (ed.). 1994. *Power and Method: Political Activism and Educational Research.* New York: Routledge.

Glaser, B. 1978. *Theoretical Sensitivity: Advances in the Methodology of Grounded Theory.* Mill Valley, CA: Sociology Press.

Glaser, B., and A. Strauss. 1967. *The Discovery of Grounded Theory: Strategies for Qualitative Research.* Chicago: Aldine.

Glazer, M. 1972. *The Research Adventure: Promise and Problems of Fieldwork.* New York: Random House.

Glazer, M. 1982. The threat of the stranger: Vulnerability, reciprocity, and fieldwork. In J. Sieber (ed.), *Ethics of Social Research: Fieldwork, Regulation, and Publication* (pp. 49–70). New York: Springer-Verlag.

Glesne, C. 1985. *Strugglin', but No Slavin': Agriculture, Education, and Rural Young Vincentians.* Unpublished doctoral dissertation, University of Illinois, Urbana.

Glesne, C. 1989. Rapport and friendship in ethnographic research. *International Journal of Qualitative Studies in Education,* 2(1), 45–54.

Glesne, C. 1997. That rare feeling: Re-presenting research through poetic transcription. *Qualitative Inquiry,* 3(2), 202–221.

Glesne, C. 1998. Ethnography with a biographic eye. In C. Kridel (ed.), *Writing Educational Biography* (pp. 33–43). New York: Garland Publishing.

Glesne, C. 2003. The will to do: Youth regenerating community in Oaxaca, Mexico. *Educational Studies,* 34(2), 198–212.

Glesne, C., and A. Peshkin. 1992. *Becoming Qualitative Researchers.* New York: Longman.

Gold, R. 1969. Roles in sociological field observations. In G. McCall and J. L. Simmons (eds.), *Issues in Participant Observation: A Text and Reader* (pp. 30–39). Menlo Park, CA: Addison-Wesley.

Gonzalez, N. 1986. The anthropologist as female head of household. In T. L. Whitehead and M. E. Conaway (eds.), *Self, Sex, and Gender in Cross-Cultural Fieldwork* (pp. 84–100). Urbana: University of Illinois Press.

Gorden, R. 1980. *Interviewing: Strategy, Techniques, and Tactics,* 3rd ed., Homewood, IL: Dorsey Press.

Goswami, D., and P. Stillman (eds.). 1987. *Reclaiming the Classroom: Teacher Research as an Agency for Change.* Upper Montclair, NJ: Boynton Cook.

Gould, S. 1989. *Wonderful Life: The Burgess Shale and the Nature of History.* New York: W. W. Norton.

Greene, J. 2000. Understanding social programs through evaluation. In N. Denzin and Y. Lincoln (eds.), *Handbook of Qualitative Research,* 2nd ed. (pp. 981–999). Thousand Oaks, CA: Sage Publications.

Griffiths, G. 1985. Doubts, dilemmas and diary-keeping: Some reflections on teacher-based research. In R. Burgess (ed.), *Issues in educational research: Qualitative methods,* (pp. 197–215). Philadelphia: Falmer Press.

Guba, E. 1990. The alternative paradigm dialog. In E. Guba (ed.), *The Paradigm Dialog* (pp. 17–27). Newbury Park, CA: Sage Publications.

Guba, E. (ed.), 1990. *The Paradigm Dialog.* Newbury Park, CA: Sage Publications.

Guba, E., and Y. Lincoln. 1994. Competing paradigms in qualitative research. In N. Denzin and Y. Lincoln (eds.), *Handbook of Qualitative Research* (pp. 105–117). Thousand Oaks, CA: Sage Publications.

Guba, E., and Y. Lincoln. 2008. Paradigmatic controversies, contradictions, and emerging confluences. In N. Denzin and Y. Lincoln (eds.), *The Landscape of Qualitative Research,* 3rd ed. (pp. 255–286). Thousand Oaks, CA: Sage Publications.

Gubrium, J. F., and J. A. Holstein. 2002. From the individual interview to the interview society. In J. F. Gubrium and J. A. Holstein (eds.), *Handbook of Interview Research: Context and Method* (pp. 3–32). Thousand Oaks, CA: Sage Publications.

Gubrium, J. F., and J. A. Holstein (eds.). 2002. *Handbook of Interview Research: Context and Method.* Thousand Oaks, CA: Sage Publications.

Gubrium, J. F., and J. A. Holstein. 2009. *Analyzing Narrative Reality.* Thousand Oaks, CA: Sage.

Hagedorn, M. 1994. Hermeneutic photography: An innovative esthetic technique for generating data in nursing research. *Advances in Nursing Science,* 17(1), 44–50.

Hammersley, M. 1992. *What's Wrong with Ethnography.* London: Routledge.

Hammersley, M., and P. Atkinson. 1983. *Ethnography: Principles in Practice.* New York: Tavistock.

Hamnett, M., and D. Porter. 1983. Problems and prospects in Western approaches to cross-national social science research. In D. Landis and R. Breslin (eds.), *Handbook of Intercultural Training* (pp. 61–81). New York: Pergamon Press.

Hansen, J. P. 1976. The anthropologist in the field: Scientist, friend, voyeur. In M. A. Rynkiewich and J. P. Spradley (eds.), *Ethics and Anthropology: Dilemmas in Field Work* (pp. 123–134). New York: Wiley.

Harding, S. (ed.). 1987. *Feminism and Methodology: Social Science Issues.* Bloomington: Indiana University Press.

Harding, S. 1998. *Is Science Multicultural? Postcolonialisms, Feminisms, and Epistemologies.* Bloomington: Indiana University Press.

Harker, R. 1993. *Searching for Trees in the Postmodern Forest: Tales of an Educational Dog.* Paper presented at the NZARE Annual Conference, University of Waikato, New Zealand.

Hay, I. (ed.). 2005. *Qualitative Research Methods in Human Geography,* 2nd ed. New York: Oxford University Press.

Henry, J. 1992. The paradox of friendship in the field: Analysis of a long-term Anglo-Japanese relationship. In J. Okely and H. Callaway (eds.), *Anthropology and Autobiography* (pp. 163–174). London: Routledge.

Hersey, J. 1988. Agee. *New Yorker,* 18 July, 72–82.

Higgs, C., and L. McAllister. 2001. Being a methodological space cadet. In H. Byrne-Armstrong, J. Higgs, and D. Horsfall (eds.), *Critical Moments in Qualitative Research* (pp. 30–43). Boston: Butterworth-Heinemann.

Higgs, J. 2001. Charting standpoints in qualitative research. In H. Byrne-Armstrong, J. Higgs, and D. Horsfall (eds.), *Critical Moments in Qualitative Research* (pp. 44–67). Boston: Butterworth-Heinemann.

Hockings, P. (ed.). 1995. *Principles of Visual Anthropology.* New York: Mouton de Gruyter.

Holliday, A. 2002. *Doing and Writing Qualitative Research.* Thousand Oaks, CA: Sage Publications.

Hollingsworth, S. (ed.). 1997. *International Action Research: A Casebook for Educational Reform.* Washington, DC: The Falmer Press.

Hollway, W., and T. Jefferson. 2000. *Doing Qualitative Research Differently: Free Association, Narrative and the Interview Method.* Thousand Oaks, CA: Sage Publications.

Homan, R., and M. Bulmer. 1982. On the merits of covert methods: A dialogue. In M. Bulmer (ed.), *Social Research Ethics* (pp. 105–124). London: Macmillan.

Hooks, B. 1984. *Feminist Theory from Margin to Center.* Boston: South End Press.

Horowitz, R. 1986. Remaining an outsider: Membership as a threat to the research report. *Urban Life,* 14, 409–430.

Howe, K. 1988. Against the quantitative–qualitative incompatibility thesis, or dogmas die hard. *Educational Researcher,* 17(8), 10–16.

Howitt, R., and S. Stevens, 2005. Cross-Cultural Research: Ethics, Methods, and Relationships. In I. Hay (ed.), *Qualitative Research Methods in Human Geography,* 2nd ed. (pp. 30–50). New York: Oxford University Press.

Huddle, D. 1991. *The Writing Habit.* Hanover, NH: University Press of New England.

Humphreys, L. 1970. *Tearoom Trade: Impersonal Sex in Public Places.* Chicago: Aldine.

Hustler, E., A. Cassidy, and E. C. Cuff (eds.). 1986. *Action Research in Classrooms and Schools.* Boston: Allen & Unwin.

Hyman, H. 1975. *Interviewing in Social Research.* Chicago: University of Chicago Press. (Original work published 1954.)

Hymes, D. H. 1982. What is ethnography? In P. Gilmore and A. Glatthorn (eds.), *Children in and out of School* (pp. 21–32). Washington, DC: Center for Applied Linguistics.

Jacob, E. 1988. Clarifying qualitative research: A focus on traditions. *Educational Researcher,* 17(1), 16–24.

Jacobs, S. E. 1987. Cases and solutions. In J. Cassell and S. E. Jacobs (eds.), *Handbook on Ethical Issues in Anthropology* (pp. 20–36). Washington, DC: American Anthropological Association.

Jansen, G., and A. Peshkin, 1992. Subjectivity in qualitative research. In M. LeCompte, W. Millroy, and J. Preissle (eds.), *The Handbook of Qualitative Research in Education* (pp. 681–725). New York: Academic Press.

Jeske, J. 1984. *Demystifying the Dissertation.* Los Angeles: University of California (ERIC document Reproduction Service no. ED 268 529; CS 209 648).

Johnson, C. 1982. Risks in the publication of fieldwork. In J. Sieber (ed.), *Ethics of Social Research: Fieldwork, Regulation, and Publication* (pp. 71–92). New York: Springer-Verlag.

Jorgensen, D. 1989. *Participant Observation: A Methodology for Human Studies.* Newbury Park, CA: Sage Publications.

Kaufman, M., and Members of the Tectonic Theater Project. 2001. *The Laramie Project.* New York: Vintage Books.

Kay, P. 1997. *Whose Child Is This? Reader's Theater Exploring the Sociocultural Tensions Experienced by a Parent and a Teacher around a Child's Emotional and Behavioral Issues.* Paper presented at the American Educational Research Association meetings, Chicago.

Kelly, A. 1985. Action research: What is it and what can it do? In R. Burgess (ed.), *Issues of Educational Research* (pp. 129–151). Philadelphia: Falmer Press.

Kemmis, S., and R. McTaggart (eds.). 1988. *The Action Planner,* 3rd ed. Waurn Ponds, Australia: Deakin University Press.

Kendall, L. 2009. How do issues of gender and sexuality influence the structures and processes of qualitative internet research? In A. Markham and N. Baym (eds.), *Internet Inquiry: Conversations about Method* (pp. 99–118). Thousand Oaks, CA: Sage.

Kinchelow, J., and P. McLaren. 2000. Rethinking critical theory and qualitative research. In N. Denzin and Y. Lincoln (eds.), *Handbook of Qualitative Research,* 2nd ed. (pp. 279–313). Thousand Oaks, CA: Sage Publications.

Kindon, S. 2005. Participatory Action Research. In I. Hay (ed.), *Qualitative Research Methods in Human Geography,* 2nd ed. (pp. 207–220). New York: Oxford University Press.

King, S. 2000. *On Writing: A Memoir of the Craft.* New York: Pocket Books.

King, T. 2008. The art of indigenous knowledge: A million porcupines crying in the dark. In J. G. Knowles and A. L. Cole (eds.), *Handbook of the ARTS in Qualitative Research* (pp. 13–25). Thousand Oaks, CA: Sage.

Kleinman, S., and M. Copp. 1993. *Emotions and Fieldwork.* Newbury Park, CA: Sage Publications.

Knowles, J. G., and A. L. Cole (eds.). 2008. *Handbook of the ARTS in Qualitative Research.* Thousand Oaks, CA: Sage.

Kopytoff, I. 1986. The cultural biography of things: commoditization as process. In A. Appadurai (ed.) *The Social Life of Things: Commodities in Cultural Perspective* (64-94). Cambridge University Press.

Kooser, T. 2004. *Delights and Shadows.* Port Townsend, WA: Copper Canyon Press.

Krieger, S. 1985. Beyond "subjectivity": The use of the self in social science. *Qualitative Sociology,* 8, 309–324.

Krieger, S. 1991. *Social Science and the Self: Personal Essays on an Art Form.* New Brunswick, NJ: Rutgers.

Kulick, D. 1995. The sexual life of anthropologists: Erotic subjectivity and ethnographic work. In D. Kulick and M. Wilson (eds.), *Taboo: Sex, Identity and Erotic Subjectivity in Anthropological Fieldwork* (pp. 1–28). New York: Routledge.

Kulick, D., and M. Wilson (eds.). 1995. *Taboo: Sex, Identity and Erotic Subjectivity in Anthropological Fieldwork.* New York: Routledge.

Kvale, S. 1996. *Interviews: An Introduction to Qualitative Research Interviewing.* Thousand Oaks, CA: Sage Publications.

La Farge, O. 1929. *Laughing Boy.* New York: Literary Guild of America.

Lamott, A. 1994. *Bird by Bird: Some Instructions on Writing and Life.* New York: Pantheon Books.

Lareau, A., and J. Shultz (eds.). 1996. *Journeys through Ethnography: Realistic Accounts of Fieldwork.* Boulder, CO: Westview Press.

Lather, P. 1991. *Getting Smart: Feminist Research and Pedagogy with/in the Postmodern.* New York: Routledge & Kegan Paul.

Lather, P. 1995. The validity of angels: Interpretive and textual strategies in researching the lives of women with HIV/AIDS. *Qualitative Inquiry*, 1(1), 41–68.

Lather, P. 1996. Troubling clarity: The politics of accessible language. *Harvard Educational Review*, 66(3), 525–545.

Lather, P., and C. Smithies. 1997. *Troubling the Angels: Women Living with HIV/AIDS.* Boulder, CO: Westview Press.

LeCompte, M. 1987. Bias in the biography: Bias and subjectivity in ethnographic research. *Anthropology and Education Quarterly*, 18, 43–52.

LeCompte, M., J. Preissle, and R. Tesch. 1993. *Ethnography and Qualitative Design in Educational Research*, 2nd ed. New York: Academic Press.

Leggo, C. 2008. Astonishing silence: Knowing in poetry. In J. G. Knowles and A. L. Cole (eds.), *Handbook of the ARTS in Qualitative Research* (pp. 165–174). Thousand Oaks, CA: Sage.

Lewin, E., and W. Leap (eds.). 1996. *Out in the Field: Reflections of Lesbian and Gay Anthropologists.* Chicago: University of Illinois Press.

Lewis, O. 1963. *The Children of Sanchez: Autobiography of a Mexican Family.* New York: Vintage Books.

Liebow, E. 1967. *Tally's Corner: A Study of Negro Streetcorner Men.* Boston: Little, Brown.

Lincoln, Y. 1990. Toward a categorical imperative for qualitative research. In E. Eisner and A. Peshkin (eds.), *Qualitative Inquiry in Education: The Continuing Debate* (pp. 277–295). New York: Teachers College Press.

Lincoln, Y., and N. Denzin. 2000. The seventh moment: Out of the past. In N. Denzin and Y. Lincoln (eds.), *Handbook of qualitative research*, 2nd ed. (pp. 1047–1065). Thousand Oaks, CA: Sage Publications.

Lincoln, Y., and N. Denzin. 2008. Epilogue: The eighth and ninth moments—Qualitative research in/and the fractured future. In N. Denzin and Y. Lincoln (eds.), *The Landscape of Qualitative Research*, 3rd ed. (pp. 539–554). Thousand Oaks, CA: Sage.

Lincoln, Y., and E. Guba. 1985. *Naturalistic Inquiry.* Beverly Hills, CA: Sage Publications.

Lincoln, Y., and E. Guba. 2000. Paradigmatic controversies, contradictions, and emerging confluences. In N. Denzin and Y. Lincoln (eds.), *Handbook of Qualitative Research*, 2nd ed. (pp. 163–188). Thousand Oaks, CA: Sage Publications.

Linden, R. 1993. *Making Stories, Making Selves: Feminist Reflections on the Holocaust.* Columbus: Ohio State University Press.

Lipson, J. 1994. Ethical issues in ethnography. In J. Morse (ed.), *Critical Issues in Qualitative Research Methods* (pp. 333–354). Thousand Oaks, CA: Sage Publications.

Lofland, J. 1971. *Analyzing Social Settings: A Guide to Qualitative Observation and Analysis.* Belmont, CA: Wadsworth.

Lofland, J., and L. Lofland. 1995. *Analyzing Social Settings: A Guide to Qualitative Observation and Analysis*, 3rd ed. Belmont, CA: Wadsworth.

Loving, C. 1997. From the summit of truth to its slippery slopes. *American Education Research Journal*, 34(3), 421–452.

Lugg, C. 2006. On politics and theory: Using an explicitly activist theory to frame educational research. In J. Vincent Anfara and N. Mertz (eds.), *Theoretical Frameworks in Qualitative Research* (pp. 175–188). Thousand Oaks, CA: Sage Publications.

Luke, C., and J. Gore (eds.). 1992. *Feminisms and Critical Pedagogy.* New York: Routledge.

Madison, D. S. 2005. *Critical Ethnography: Method, Ethics, and Performance.* Thousand Oaks, CA: Sage Publications.

Maguire, P. 1987. *Doing Participatory Research: A Feminist Approach.* Amherst: The Center for International Education, University of Massachusetts.

Maguire, P. 1996. Considering more feminist participatory research: What's congruency got to do with it? *Qualitative Inquiry*, 2(1), 106–118.

Malcolm, J. 1987. Reflections. *New Yorker,* 20 April, 84–102.

Malinowski, B. 1922. *Argonauts of the Western Pacific: An Account of Native Enterprise and Adventure in the Archipelagoes of Melanesian New Guinea.* New York: Dutton.

Malinowski, B. 1967. *A Diary in the Strict Sense of the Term.* New York: Harcourt, Brace & World.

Mann, C., and F. Stewart. 2000. *Internet Communication and Qualitative Research.* Thousand Oaks, CA: Sage Publications.

Marcus, G., and M. Fischer. 1999. *Anthropology as Cultural Critique: An Experimental Moment in the Human Sciences,* 2nd ed. Chicago: University of Chicago Press.

Markham, A., and Baym, N. (eds.). 2009. *Internet Inquiry: Conversations about Method.* Thousand Oaks, CA: Sage.

Markham, B. 1983. *West with the Night.* San Francisco: North Point Press. (Original work published 1942.)

Marshall, C., and G. Rossman. 1999. *Designing Qualitative Research,* 3rd ed. Thousand Oaks, CA: Sage Publications.

Martin, P., and C. Glesne. 2002. From the global village to the pluriverse? "Other" ethics for cross-cultural qualitative research. *Ethics, Place and Environment,* 5(3), 205–221.

Maxwell, J. 1996. *Qualitative Research Design: An Interactive Approach.* Thousand Oaks, CA: Sage Publications.

Maxwell, J. 2005. *Qualitative Research Design: An Interactive Approach,* 2nd ed. Thousand Oaks, CA: Sage Publications.

McCall, G., and J. L. Simmons (eds.). 1969. *Issues in Participant Observation: A Text and Reader.* Reading, MA: Addison-Wesley.

McCall, L. 2005. The complexity of intersectionality. *Signs,* 30(3), 771–880.

McCall, M. 2000. Performance ethnography: A brief history and some advice. In N. Denzin and Y. Lincoln (eds.), *Handbook of Qualitative Research,* 2nd ed. (pp. 421–433). Thousand Oaks, CA: Sage Publications.

McDermott, R. 1987. Achieving school failure: An anthropological approach to illiteracy and social stratification. In G. Spindler (ed.), *Education and Cultural Process: Anthropological Approaches,* 2nd ed. (pp. 173–209). Prospect Heights, IL: Waveland Press.

McMillan, J. 1989. *Focus Group Interviews: Implications for Educational Research.* Paper presented at the annual meeting of the American Educational Research Association, San Francisco.

McTaggart, R. (ed.). 1997. *Participatory Action Research: International Contexts and Consequences.* Albany: State University of New York.

Mears, C. L. 2009. *Interviewing for Education and Social Science Research: The Gateway Approach.* New York: Palgrave Macmillan.

Measor, L. 1985. Interviewing: A strategy in qualitative research. In R. Burgess (ed.), *Strategies of Educational Research: Qualitative Methods* (pp. 55–77). Philadelphia: Falmer Press.

Meho, L. 2006. E-mail interviewing in qualitative research: A methodological discussion. *Journal of the American Society for Information Science and Technology,* 57(10), 1284–1295.

Merriam, S. 1998. *Qualitative Research and Case Study Applications in Education,* 2nd ed. San Francisco: Jossey-Bass.

Michaels, A. 1996. *Fugitive Pieces.* New York: Vintage Books.

Mienczakowski, J. 1995. The theater of ethnography: The reconstruction of ethnography into theater with emancipatory potential. *Qualitative Inquiry,* 1(3), 360–375.

Mies, M. 1983. Towards a methodology for feminist research. In G. Bowles and R. Duelli Klein (eds.), *Theories of Women's Studies* (pp. 117–139). Boston: Routledge & Kegan Paul.

Miles, M., and A. M. Huberman. 1994. *Qualitative Data Analysis: An Expanded Sourcebook,* 2nd ed. Thousand Oaks, CA: Sage Publications.

Miller, J. 1990. *Creating Spaces and Finding Voices: Teachers Collaborating for Empowerment.* Albany: State University of New York Press.

Miller, S. M. 1952. The participant observer and "overrapport." *American Sociological Review,* 17, 97–99.

Mills, M., and P. Bettis, 2006. Organizational identity and identification during a departmental reorganization. In J. Vincent Anfara and N. Mertz (eds.), *Theoretical Frameworks in Qualitative Research* (pp. 73–84). Thousand Oaks, CA: Sage Publications.

Mitchell, C., and S. Allnutt, 2008. Photographs and/as social documentary. In J. G. Knowles and A. L. Cole (eds.), *Handbook of the ARTS in Qualitative Research* (pp. 251–263). Thousand Oaks, CA: Sage.

Mitchell, R., Jr. 1993. *Secrecy and Fieldwork.* Newbury Park, CA: Sage Publications.

Mohr, M., and M. Maclean. 1987. *Working Together: A Guide for Teacher Researchers.* Urbana, IL: National Center of Teachers of English.

Monk, J., and R. Bedford, 2005. Writing a compelling research proposal. In I. Hay (ed.), *Qualitative Research Methods in Human Geography,* 2nd ed. (pp. 51–66). New York: Oxford University Press.

Moorehead, A. 1959. *No Room in the Ark.* New York: Harper & Brothers.

Morgan, D. 1997. *Focus Groups as Qualitative Research,* 2nd ed. Newbury Park, CA: Sage Publications.

Morgan, S., J. Mienczakowski, and L. Smith. 2001. Extreme dilemmas in performance ethnography: Unleashed emotionality of performance in critical areas of suicide, abuse, and madness. In K. Gilbert (ed.), *The Emotional Nature of Qualitative Research* (pp. 163–178). New York: CRC Press.

Morse, J. 1994. Designing funded qualitative research. In N. Denzin and Y. Lincoln (eds.), *Handbook of Qualitative Research* (pp. 220–235). Thousand Oaks, CA: Sage.

Morse, J. 1998. What's wrong with random selection? *Qualitative Health Research,* 8(6), 733–735.

Munoz, V. 1995. *Where Something Catches: Work, Love, and Identity in Youth.* Albany: State University of New York.

Murray, D. 1986. One writer's secrets. *College Composition and Communication,* 37, 146–153.

Myerhoff, B. 1979. *Number Our Days: Culture and Community among Elderly Jews in an American Ghetto.* New York: Meridian.

Myrdal, J. 1965. *Report from a Chinese Village.* New York: Pantheon Books.

Nagel, P. 1988. The Adams women. In W. Zinsser (ed.), *Extraordinary Lives: The Art and Craft of American Biography* (pp. 91–120). Boston: Houghton Mifflin.

Naples, N. (ed.). 1998. *Community Activism and Feminist Politics: Organizing across Race, Class, and Gender.* New York: Routledge.

Nelson, A. 2002. *The Guys.* New York: Random House.

Nielsen, J. (ed.). 1990. *Feminist Research Methods: Exemplary Readings in the Social Sciences.* Boulder, CO: Westview Press.

Nisbet, R. 1976. *Sociology as an Art Form.* New York: Oxford University Press.

Noffke, S., and R. Stevenson (eds.). 1995. *Educational Action Research: Becoming Practically Critical.* New York: Teachers College Press.

Northcutt, N., and D. McCoy, 2004. *Interactive Qualitative Analysis: A Systems Method for Qualitative Research.* Thousand Oaks: Sage.

O'Reilly, K. 2005. *Ethnographic Methods.* New York: Routledge.

Oboler, R. S. 1986. For better or worse: Anthropologists and husbands in the field. In *Self, Sex, and Gender in Cross-Cultural Fieldwork* T. Whitehead and M. Conaway, 28–51. Chicago: University of Illinois Press.

Olesen, V. 2000. Feminisms and qualitative research at and into the millennium. In N. Denzin and Y. Lincoln (eds.), *Handbook of qualitative research*, 2nd ed. (pp. 215–255). Thousand Oaks, CA: Sage Publications.

Oliver, M. 1998. *Rules for the Dance: A Handbook for Writing and Reading Metrical Verse*. New York: Houghton Mifflin Company.

Pachter, M. (ed.). 1981. *Telling Lives: The Biographer's Art*. Philadelphia: University of Pennsylvania Press.

Panikkar, R. 1979. *Myth, Faith and Hermeneutics: Cross-Cultural Studies*. New York: Paulist Press.

Panikkar, R. 1995. *Invisible Harmony: Essays on Contemplation and Responsibility*. Minneapolis: Fortress Press.

Patton, M. 1990. *Qualitative Evaluation and Research Methods*, 2nd ed. Newbury Park, CA: Sage Publications.

Patton, M. 2002. *Qualitative Research and Evaluation Methods*, 3rd ed. Thousand Oaks, CA: Sage Publications.

Pelto, P. J., and G. H. Pelto. 1978. *Anthropological Research: The Structure of Inquiry*, 2nd ed. Cambridge, UK: Cambridge University Press.

Perreault, J. 1995. *Writing Selves: Contemporary Feminist Autography*. Minneapolis: University of Minnesota Press.

Peshkin, A. 1972. *Kanuri Schoolchildren: Education and Social Mobilization in Nigeria*. New York: Holt, Rinehart & Winston.

Peshkin, A. 1978. *Growing Up American: Schooling and the Survival of Community*. Chicago: University of Chicago Press.

Peshkin, A. 1982a. *The Imperfect Union: School Consolidation and Community Conflict*. Chicago: University of Chicago Press.

Peshkin, A. 1982b. The researcher and subjectivity: Reflections on ethnography of school and community. In G. Spindler (ed.), *Doing the Ethnography of Schooling* (pp. 20–47). New York: Holt, Rinehart & Winston.

Peshkin, A. 1985. From title to title: The evolution of perspective in naturalistic inquiry. *Anthropology and Education Quarterly*, 16, 214–224.

Peshkin, A. 1986. *God's Choice: The Total World of a Fundamentalist Christian School*. Chicago: University of Chicago Press.

Peshkin, A. 1988a. In search of subjectivity—One's own. *Educational Researcher*, 17(7), 17–22.

Peshkin, A. 1988b. Virtuous subjectivity: In the participant-observer's I's. In D. Berg and K. Smith (eds.), *The Self in Social Inquiry* (pp. 267–282). Newbury Park, CA: Sage Publications.

Peshkin, A. 1991. *The Color of Strangers, the Color of Friends: The Play of Ethnicity in School and Community*. Chicago: University of Chicago Press.

Pettigrew, J. 1981. Reminiscences of fieldwork among the Sikhs. In H. Roberts (ed.), *Doing Feminist Research* (pp. 62–82). Boston: Routledge & Kegan Paul.

Pfaffenberger, B. 1988. *Microcomputer Applications in Qualitative Research*. Newbury Park, CA: Sage Publications.

Pigeon, Y. 1998. *Among Adults: An Exploration of Adult–Student Learning Groups*. Unpublished dissertation, University of Vermont, Burlington.

Pillow, W. 2003. Confession, catharsis, or cure? Rethinking the uses of reflexivity as methodological power in qualitative research. *International Journal of Qualitative Studies in Education*, 16(2), 175–196.

Pink, S. 2007. Visual methods. In C. Seale, G. Gobo, J. Gubrium, and D. Silverman (eds.), *Qualitative Research Practice* (pp. 361–376). Thousand Oaks, CA: Sage Publications.

Plante, D. 1986. Profiles: Sir Steven Runciman. *New Yorker*, 3 November, 53–80.

Plummer, K. 1983. *Documents of Life.* Boston: Allen & Unwin.

Popkewitz, T. 1984. *Paradigm and Ideology in Educational Research: The Social Functions of the Intellectual.* New York: Falmer Press.

Potter, W. J. 1996. *An Analysis of Thinking and Research about Qualitative Methods.* Mahwah, NJ: Lawrence Erlbaum.

Prasad, P. 2005. *Crafting Qualitative Research: Working in the Postpositivist Traditions.* Armonk, NY: M.E. Sharpe.

Prosser, J., and Burke, C. 2008. Image-based educational research. In J. G. Knowles and A. L. Cole (eds.), *Handbook of the ARTS in Qualitative Research* (pp. 407–419). Thousand Oaks, CA: Sage.

Pugach, M. 1998. *On the Border of Opportunity: Education, Community and Language at the U.S.–Mexico Line.* Mahwah, NJ: Lawrence Erlbaum.

Punch, M. 1986. *The Politics and Ethics of Fieldwork.* Beverly Hills, CA: Sage Publications.

Punch, M. 1994. Politics and ethics in qualitative research. In N. Denzin and Y. Lincoln (eds.), *Handbook of Qualitative Research* (pp. 83–97). Thousand Oaks, CA: Sage Publications.

Purvis, J. 1985. Reflections upon doing historical documentary research from a feminist perspective. In R. Burgess (ed.), *Strategies of Educational Research: Qualitative Methods* (pp. 179–205). Philadelphia: Falmer Press.

Quantz, R. 1992. On critical ethnography. In M. LeCompte, W. Millroy, and J. Preissle (eds.), *The Handbook of Qualitative Research in Education* (pp. 447–505). San Diego, CA: Academic Press.

Rajchman, J. 1988. Foucault's art of seeing. *October,* 44(Spring), 89–117.

Rapley, T. 2007. Interviews. In C. Seale, G. Gobo, J. Gubrium, and D. Silverman (eds.), *Qualitative Research Practice* (pp. 15–33). Thousand Oaks, CA: Sage Publications.

Reason, P. 1994. Three approaches to participative inquiry. In N. Denzin and Y. Lincoln (eds.), *Handbook of Qualitative Research* (pp. 324–339). Thousand Oaks, CA: Sage Publications.

Reason, P. (ed.). 1988. *Human Inquiry in Action: Developments in New Paradigm Research.* Newbury Park, CA: Sage Publications.

Reed-Danahay, D. (ed.). 1997. *Auto/Ethnography: Rewriting the Self and the Social.* New York: Berg.

Reichardt, C. S., and T. D. Cook (eds.). 1979. Beyond qualitative versus quantitative methods. In *Qualitative and Quantitative Methods in Evaluation Research* (pp. 7–32). Beverly Hills, CA: Sage Publications.

Reinharz, S. 1992. *Feminist Methods in Social Research.* New York: Oxford University Press.

Richardson, L. 1990. *Writing Strategies: Reaching Diverse Audiences.* Newbury Park, CA: Sage Publications.

Richardson, L. 1992. The consequences of poetic representation, In C. Ellis and M. G. Flaherty (eds.), *Investigating Subjectivity: Research on Lived Experience* (pp. 125–137). Newbury Park, CA: Sage Publications.

Richardson, L. 1994. Nine poems. *Journal of Contemporary Ethnography,* 23(1), 3–13.

Richardson, L. 1997. *Fields of Play: Constructing an Academic Life.* New Brunswick, NJ: Rutgers.

Richardson, L. 2000. Writing: A method of inquiry. In N. Denzin and Y. Lincoln (eds.), *Handbook of Qualitative Research,* 2nd ed. (pp. 923–946). Thousand Oaks, CA: Sage Publications.

Richardson, L. 2002. Poetic representation of interviews. In J. F. Gubrium and J. A. Holstein (eds.), *Handbook of Interview Research: Context and Method* (pp. 887–891). Thousand Oaks, CA: Sage Publications.

Riley, G. (ed.). 1974. *Values, Objectivity, and the Social Sciences.* Reading, MA: Addison-Wesley.

Rist, R. 1977. On the relations among educational research paradigms: From disdain to detente. *Anthropology and Education Quarterly,* 8, 42–49.

Rivoli, P. 2005. *The Travels of a T-Shirt in the Global Economy: An Economist Examines the Markets, Power, and Politics of World Trade*. Hoboken, NJ: John Wiley & Sons, Inc.

Robson, K., and M. Robson. 2002. Your place or mine? Ethics, the researcher and the internet. In T. Welland and L. Pugsley (eds.), *Ethical Dilemmas in Qualitative Research* (pp. 94–107). Burlington, VT: Ashgate Publishing Co.

Roche, M. 2005. Historical research and archival sources. In I. Hay (ed.), *Qualitative Research Methods in Human Geography*, 2nd ed. (pp. 133–146). New York: Oxford University Press.

Rogers, C. 1942. The non-directive method as a technique for social research. *American Journal of Sociology*, 50, 279–283.

Ronai, C. 1995. Multiple reflections of child sex abuse: An argument for a layered account. *Journal of Contemporary Ethnography*, 23(4), 395–426.

Roorbach, B. 1998. *Writing Life Stories*. Cincinnati, OH: Story Press.

Rose, D. 1993. Ethnography as a form of life: The written word and the work of the world. In P. Benson (ed.), *Anthropology and Literature* (pp. 192–224). Urbana, IL: University of Illinois Press.

Rosengarten, T. 1985. Stepping over cockleburs: Conversations with Ned Cobb. In M. Pachter (ed.), *Telling Lives: The Biographer's Art* (pp. 105–131). Philadelphia: University of Pennsylvania Press.

Rubin, H., and I. Rubin. 1995. *Qualitative Interviewing: The Art of Hearing Data*. Thousand Oaks, CA: Sage Publications.

Runte, R. 2008. Blogs. In J. G. Knowles and A. L. Cole (eds.), *Handbook of the ARTS in Qualitative Research* (pp. 313–322). Thousand Oaks, CA: Sage.

Ryan, G. W., and H. R. Bernard. 2000. Data management and analysis methods. In N. Denzin and Y. Lincoln (eds.), *Handbook of Qualitative Research*, 2nd ed. by (pp. 769–802). Thousand Oaks, CA: Sage Publications.

Ryan, G. W., and T. Weisner. 1996. Analyzing words in brief descriptions: Fathers and mothers describe their children. *Cultural Anthropology Methods Journal*, 8(3), 13–16.

Ryen, A. 2007. Ethical issues. In C. Seale, G. Gobo, J. Gubrium, and D. Silverman (eds.), *Qualitative Research Practice* (pp. 218–235). Thousand Oaks, CA: Sage.

Rynkiewich, M. A., and J. P. Spradley (eds.). 1976. *Ethics and Anthropology: Dilemmas in Field Work*. New York: Wiley.

Saldaña, J. 2008. Ethnodrama and ethnotheatre. In J. G. Knowles and A. L. Cole (eds.), *Handbook of the ARTS in Qualitative Research* (pp. 195–207). Thousand Oaks, CA: Sage.

Saldaña, J. (ed.). 2005. *Ethnodrama: An Anthology of Reality Theatre*. Walnut Creek, CA: AltaMira Press.

Sandelowski, M. 1994. The proof is in the pottery: Toward a poetic for qualitative inquiry. In J. Morse (ed.), *Critical Issues in Qualitative Research Methods* (pp. 46–63). Thousand Oaks, CA: Sage Publications.

Sanjek, R. (ed.). 1990. *Fieldnotes: The Makings of Anthropology*. Ithaca, NY: Cornell University Press.

Savyasaachi 1998. Unlearning fieldwork: The flight of an arctic tern. In M. Thapar (ed.), *Anthropological Journeys: Reflections on Fieldwork* (pp. 83–112). New Delhi, India: Orient Longman Ltd.

Schaap, F. 2002. *The Words That Took Us There: Ethnography in a Virtual Reality*. Amsterdam, The Netherlands: Aksant Academic Publishers.

Schaeffer, J. 1995. Videotape: New techniques of observation and analysis in anthropology. In P. Hockings (ed.), *Principles of Visual Anthropology* (pp. 255–284). New York: Mouton de Gruyter.

Scheper-Hughes, N. 1992. *Death without Weeping: The Violence of Everyday Life in Brazil.* Berkeley: University of California Press.

Schram, T. 2006. *Conceptualizing and Proposing Qualitative Research,* 2nd ed. Upper Saddle River, NJ: Pearson Education, Inc.

Schuman, H. 1970. The random probe: A technique for evaluating the validity of closed questions. In D. P. Forcese and S. Rocher (eds.), *Stages of Social Research* (pp. 240–245). Englewood Cliffs, NJ: Prentice Hall.

Schwandt, T. 1989. Solutions to the paradigm conflict: Coping with uncertainty. *Journal of Contemporary Ethnography* 17: 379–407.

Schwandt, T. 1990. Paths to inquiry in the social disciplines: Scientific, constructivist, and critical theory methodologies. In E. Guba (ed.), *The Paradigm Dialog* (pp. 258–276). Newbury Park, CA: Sage Publications.

Schwandt, T. 1997. *Qualitative Inquiry: A DICTIONARY of terms.* Thousand Oaks, CA: Sage Publications.

Schwandt, T. 2000. Three epistemological stances for qualitative inquiry: Interpretivism, hermeneutics, and social constructionism. In N. Denzin and Y. Lincoln (eds.), *Handbook of Qualitative Research,* 2nd ed. (pp. 189–213). Thousand Oaks, CA: Sage Publications.

Schwandt, T. 2007. *The SAGE Dictionary of Qualitative Inquiry,* 3rd ed. Thousand Oaks, CA: Sage Publications.

Scott-Hoy, K., and C. Ellis, 2008. Wording pictures: Discovering heartful autoethnography. In J. G. Knowles and A. L. Cole (eds.), *Handbook of the ARTS in Qualitative Research* (pp. 127–140). Thousand Oaks, CA: Sage.

Scott, D. 1996. Methods and data in educational research. In D. Scott and R. Usher (eds.), *Understanding Educational Research* (pp. 52–73). New York: Routledge.

Scott, D., and R. Usher (eds.). 1996. *Understanding Educational Research.* New York: Routledge.

Seale, C. 2002. Computer-assisted analysis of qualitative interview data. In J. F. Gubrium and J. A. Holstein (eds.), *Handbook of Interview Research: Context and Method* (pp. 651–670). Thousand Oaks, CA: Sage Publications.

Seidman, I. E. 1998. *Interviewing as Qualitative Research: A Guide for Researchers in Education and the Social Sciences,* 2nd ed. New York: Teachers College Press.

Shaffir, W. G., R. A. Stebbins, and A. Turowetz. 1980. *Fieldwork Experience.* New York: St. Martin's Press.

Shaw, C. 1966. *The Jack Roller, a Delinquent Boy's Own Story.* Chicago, IL: University of Chicago Press. (Original work published 1930.)

Shostak, M. 1981. *Nisa: The Life and Words of a !Kung Woman.* New York: Vintage Books.

Shweder, R. 1986. Storytelling among the anthropologists. *New York Times Book Review,* 21 September, 1, 38.

Sieber, J. (ed.). 1982. *Ethics of Social Research: Fieldwork, Regulation and Publication.* New York: Springer-Verlag.

Silverman, D. 1993. *Interpreting Qualitative Data: Methods for Analyzing Talk, Text, and Interaction.* Thousand Oaks, CA: Sage Publications.

Sindell, P. 1987. Some discontinuities in the enculturation of Mistassini Cree children. In G. Spindler (ed.), *Education and Cultural Process,* 2nd ed. (pp. 378–386). Prospect Heights, IL: Waveland Press.

Sinding, C., R. Gray, and Nisker, J. 2008. Ethical issues and issues of ethics. In J. G. Knowles and A. L. Cole (eds.), *Handbook of the ARTS in Qualitative Research* (pp. 459–467). Thousand Oaks, CA: Sage.

Smith, A. D. 1993. *Fires in the Mirror: Crown Heights, Brooklyn, and Other Identities.* Garden City, NY: Anchor.

Smith, M. 1954. *Baba of Karo*. London: Faber.

Smith, P. 1999. Food Truck's party hat. *Qualitative Inquiry*, 5, 244–261.

Smith, P. 2000. *"I Know How to Do It": Stories of Choice, Control, and Power in the Lives of People with Developmental Disabilities*. Unpublished doctoral dissertation, University of Vermont, Burlington.

Soltis, J. 1990. The ethics of qualitative research. In E. Eisner and A. Peshkin (eds.), *Qualitative Inquiry in Education: The Continuing Debate* (pp. 247–257). New York: Teachers College Press.

Spradley, J. 1970. *You Owe Yourself a Drink: An Ethnography of Urban Nomads*. Boston: Little, Brown.

Spradley, J. 1979. *The Ethnographic Interview*. New York: Holt, Rinehart & Winston.

Spradley, J., and B. Mann. 1975. *The Cocktail Waitress: Woman's Work in a Man's World*. New York: Wiley.

Spradley, J., and D. McCurdy. 1988. *The Cultural Experience: Ethnography in Complex Society*. Long Grove, IL: Waveland Press. (Original work published 1972.)

St. Pierre, E. 2000. Poststructural feminism in education: an overview. *International Journal of Qualitative Studies in Education*, 13(5), 477–515.

Stake, R. 1995. *The Art of Case Study Research*. Thousand Oaks, CA: Sage Publications.

Stake, R. 2000. Case studies. In N. Denzin and Y. Lincoln (eds.), *Handbook of Qualitative Research*, 2nd ed. (pp. 435–454). Thousand Oaks, CA: Sage Publications.

Stewart, J. 1989. *Drinkers, Drummers, and Decent Folk: Ethnographic Narratives of Village Trinidad*. Albany: State University of New York Press.

Stoller, P. 1989. *The Taste of Ethnographic Things: The Senses in Anthropology*. Philadelphia: University of Pennsylvania Press.

Strauss, A. 1987. *Qualitative Analysis for Social Scientists*. Cambridge, UK: Cambridge University Press.

Strauss, A., and J. Corbin. 1998. *Basics of Qualitative Research: Techniques and Procedures for Developing Grounded Theory*, 2nd ed. Thousand Oaks, CA: Sage Publications.

Stringer, E. 1999. *Action Research: A Handbook for Practitioners*, 2nd ed. Thousand Oaks, CA: Sage Publications.

Strouse, J. 1988. The real reasons. In W. Zinsser (ed.), *Extraordinary Lives: The Art and Craft of American Biography* (pp. 163–195). Boston: Houghton Mifflin.

Strunk, W., and E. B. White. 1979. *The Elements of Style*, 3rd ed. New York: Macmillan.

Strunk, W., and E. B. White. 1999. *The Elements of Style*, 4th ed. Boston: Allyn & Bacon.

Stuhlmiller, C. 2001. Narrative methods in qualitative research: Potential for therapeutic transformation. In K. Gilbert (ed.), *The Emotional Nature of Qualitative Research* (pp. 63–80). New York: CRC Press.

Sullivan, G. 2008. Painting as Research: Create and Critique. In J. G. Knowles and A. L. Cole (eds.), *Handbook of the ARTS in Qualitative Research* (pp. 239–250). Thousand Oaks, CA: Sage.

Sullivan, M. A., S. A. Queen, and R. C. Patrick. 1958. Participant observation as employed in the study of a military training program. *American Sociological Review*, 23, 610–667.

Sultana, F. 2007. Reflexivity, positionality and participatory ethics: Negotiating fieldwork dilemmas in international research [electronic version]. *ACME: An International E-Journal for Critical Geographies*, 6, 374–385.

Sunstein, B. S., and E. Chiseri-Strater, 2002. *Field Working: Reading and Writing Research*, 2nd ed. New York: Bedford/St. Martin's.

Sze, M., and K. Wang. 1963. *The Tao of Painting*. New York: Pantheon Books. (Original work published 1701.)

Tafoya, T. 1989. Coyote's eyes: Native cognition styles. *Journal of American Indian Studies,* Special Issue (August).

Tedlock, B. 2000. Ethnography and ethnographic representation. In N. Denzin and Y. Lincoln (eds.), *Handbook of Qualitative Research,* 2nd ed. (pp. 455–486). Thousand Oaks, CA: Sage Publications.

Teran, G. 2002. *Conversations with Mexican Nomadic Storyteller Gustavo Esteva: Learning from Lives on the Margins.* Unpublished doctoral dissertation, University of Vermont, Burlington.

Tesch, R. 1990. *Qualitative Research: Analysis Types and Software Tools.* New York: Falmer Press.

Thomas, A. 2008. *Thinking about Memoir.* New York: Sterling Publishing.

Thomas, J. 1993. *Doing Critical Ethnography.* Newbury Park, CA: Sage Publications.

Tierney, W. 1995. (Re) presentation and voice. *Qualitative Inquiry,* 1(4), 379–390.

Tierney, W. 2000. Undaunted courage: Life history and the postmodern challenge. In N. Denzin and Y. Lincoln (eds.), *Handbook of Qualitative Research,* 2nd ed. (pp. 537–553). Thousand Oaks, CA: Sage Publications.

Tierney, W., and Y. Lincoln (eds.). 1997. *Representation and the Text: Re-framing the Narrative Voice.* Albany: State University of New York Press.

Tillmann-Healy, L. M., and C. E. Kiesinger. 2001. Mirrors: Seeing each other and ourselves through fieldwork. In K. Gilbert (ed.), *The Emotional Nature of Qualitative Research* (pp. 81–108). New York: CRC Press.

Tolman, D., and M. Brydon-Miller (eds.). 2001. *From Subjects to Subjectivities: A Handbook of Interpretive Participatory Methods.* New York: New York University Press.

Truss, L. 2003. *Eats, Shoots & Leaves.* New York: Gotham Books.

Tsing, A. L. 1993. *In the Realm of the Diamond Queen: Marginality in an Out-of-Way Place.* Princeton, NJ: Princeton University Press.

Tsing, A. L. 1997. Transitions as translations. In J. W. Scott, C. Kaplan, and D. Keates (eds.), *Transitions, Environments, Translations: Feminisms in International Politics* (pp. 253–272). New York: Routledge.

Tuhiwai Smith, L. 1999. *Decolonizing Methodologies: Research and Indigenous Peoples.* New York: Zed Books.

Turner, J. 1985. In defense of positivism. *Sociological Theory,* 3, 24–31.

Turner, R. 2008. *Embodiment, Positionality and Self-presentation: Informant Perceptions and Qualitative Data.* Paper presented at the 2008 Annual Meeting of the American Political Science Association, Boston.

Ueland, B. 1987. *If You Want to Write,* 2nd ed. St. Paul, MN: Graywolf Press.

Usher, P. 1996. Feminist approaches to research. In D. Scott and R. Usher (eds.), *Understanding Educational Research* (pp. 120–142). New York: Routledge.

Usher, R. 1996. A critique of the neglected epistemological assumptions of educational research. In D. Scott and R. Usher (eds.), *Understanding Educational Research* (pp. 9–32). New York: Routledge.

Van Galen, J., G. Noblit, and D. Hare. 1988–1989. The art and science of interviewing kids: The group interview in evaluation research. *National Forum of Applied Educational Research Journal,* 1(2), 74–81.

Van Maanen, J. 1983. The moral fix: On the ethics of fieldwork. In R. Emerson (ed.), *Contemporary Field Research* (pp. 269–287). Boston: Little, Brown.

Van Maanen, J. 1988. *Tales of the Field: On Writing Ethnography.* Chicago: University of Chicago Press.

Van Maanen, J. 1995. An end to innocence: The ethnography of ethnography. In J. Van Maanen (ed.), *Representation in Ethnography* (pp. 1–35). Thousand Oaks, CA: Sage Publications.

Van Maanen, J. (ed.). 1995. *Representation in Ethnography.* Thousand Oaks, CA: Sage Publications.

Vashon, R. 1995. Guswenta or the intercultural imperative. *International Journal of Intercultural and Transdisciplinary Research,* 28, 1–73.

Véa, A. 1993. *La Maravilla.* New York: Plume.

Vidich, A., and J. Bensman. 1968. *Small Town in Mass Society,* rev. ed. Princeton, NJ: Princeton University Press.

Vidich, A., and S. Lyman. 2000. Qualitative methods: Their history in sociology and anthropology. In N. Denzin and Y. Lincoln (eds.), *Handbook of Qualitative Research,* 2nd ed. (pp. 37–84). Thousand Oaks, CA: Sage Publications.

Waitt, G. 2005. Doing discourse analysis. In I. Hay (ed.), *Qualitative Research Methods in Human Geography,* 2nd ed. (pp. 163–191). New York: Oxford University Press.

Wang, J. 1995. *Comparisons of Research Methods in China and United States from Personal Experience.* Unpublished manuscript. University of Vermont, Burlington.

Wax, M. 1982. Research reciprocity rather than informed consent in fieldwork. In J. Sieber (ed.), *Ethics of Social Research: Fieldwork, Regulation, and Publication* J. (pp. 33–48). New York: Springer-Verlag.

Wax, R. 1971. *Doing Fieldwork: Warnings and Advice.* Chicago: University of Chicago Press.

Weber, S. 2008. Visual images in research. In J. G. Knowles and A. L. Cole (eds.), *Handbook of the ARTS in Qualitative Research* (pp. 41–53). Thousand Oaks, CA: Sage.

Webster's Third International Dictionary. 1986. Springfield, MA: Merriam & Webster.

Weis, L., and M. Fine, 2004. *Working Method: Research and Social Justice.* New York: Routledge.

Weitzman, E. A. 2000. Software and qualitative research. In N. Denzin and Y. Lincoln (eds.), *Handbook of Qualitative Research,* 2nd ed. (pp. 803–820). Thousand Oaks, CA: Sage Publications.

Weitzman, E., and M. Miles. 1995. *Computer Programs for Qualitative Data Analysis: A Software Sourcebook.* Thousand Oaks, CA: Sage Publications.

Welch, D. D. 1994. *Conflicting Agendas: Personal Morality in Institutional Settings.* Cleveland, OH: Pilgrim Press.

West, J. 1945. *Plainville, U.S.A.* New York: Columbia University Press.

Whitehead, T., and M. Conaway (eds.). 1986. *Self, Sex, and Gender in Cross-cultural Fieldwork.* Chicago: University of Illinois Press.

Whyte, W. F. 1984. *Learning from the Field: A Guide from Experience.* Beverly Hills, CA: Sage Publications.

Whyte, W. F. 1993. *Street Corner Society: The Social Structure of an Italian Slum.* Chicago: University of Chicago Press. (Original work published 1943.)

Whyte, W. F. (ed.). 1991. *Participatory Action Research.* Newbury Park, CA: Sage Publications.

Wieder, A. 2004. Testimony as oral history: Lessons from South Africa. *Educational Researcher,* 33(6), 23–28.

Wildavsky, A. 1993. *Craftways: On the Organization of Scholarly Work,* 2nd ed. New Brunswick, NJ: Transaction.

Wilkins, L. T. 1979. Human subjects—Whose subject? In C. B. Klockars and F. W. O'Connor (eds.), *Deviance and Decency* (pp. 99–123). Beverly Hills, CA: Sage Publications.

Willis, J. 2007. *Foundations of Qualitative Research.* Thousand Oaks, CA: Sage.

Willis, P. 1977. *Learning to Labor: How Working Class Kids Get Working Class Jobs.* New York: Columbia University Press.

Wilson, S. May 1989. Alaskan journal. *Vermont Quarterly,* 13–18.

Winchester, H. P. M. 2005. Qualitative Research and its place in human geography. In I. Hay (ed.), *Qualitative Research Methods in Human Geography,* 2nd ed. (pp. 3–18). New York: Oxford University Press.

Wincup, E. 2001. Feminist research with women awaiting trial: The effects on participants in the qualitative research process. In K. Gilbert (ed.), *The Emotional Nature of Qualitative Research* (pp. 17–35). New York: CRC Press.

Wolcott, H. 1973. *The Man in the Principal's Office: An Ethnography.* New York: Holt, Rinehart & Winston.

Wolcott, H. 1975. Criteria for an ethnographic approach to research in schools. *Human Organization,* 34, 111–127.

Wolcott, H. 1981. Confessions of a trained observer. In T. S. Popkewitz and B. R. Tabachnick (eds.), *The Study of Schooling* (pp. 247–263). New York: Praeger.

Wolcott, H. 1990. *Writing Up Qualitative Research.* Newbury Park, CA: Sage Publications.

Wolcott, H. 1992. Posturing in qualitative research. In M. LeCompte, W. Millroy, and J. Preissle (eds.), *The Handbook of Qualitative Research in Education* 3–52. San Diego, CA: Academic Press.

Wolcott, H. 1994. *Transforming Qualitative Data: Description, Analysis, and Interpretation.* Thousand Oaks, CA: Sage Publications.

Wolcott, H. 1995. *The Art of Fieldwork.* Walnut Creek, CA: AltaMira Press.

Wolcott, H. 2001. *Writing up Qualitative Research,* 2nd ed. Thousand Oaks, CA: Sage Publications.

Wolff, G. 1981. Minor lives. In M. Pachter (ed.), *Telling Lives* (pp. 56–72). Philadelphia: University of Pennsylvania Press.

Woods, P. 1985. New songs played skillfully: Creativity and technique in writing up research. In R. Burgess (ed.), *Issues in Educational Research* (pp. 86–106). Philadelphia: Falmer Press.

Woods, P. 1986. *Inside Schools: Ethnographic Approaches and Methods.* New York: Routledge & Kegan Paul.

Woolfson, P. 1988. Non-verbal interaction of Anglo-Canadian, Jewish-Canadian and French-Canadian physicians with their young, middle-aged, and elderly patients. *Visual Anthropology,* 1, 404–414.

Wright, R., and S. Decker. 1997. *Armed Robbers in Action: Stickups and Street Culture.* Boston: Northeastern University Press.

Yoors, J. 1967. *The Gypsies.* New York: Simon & Schuster.

Young, B., and C. Tardif. 1988. *Interviewing: Two Sides of the Story.* Paper presented at the annual meeting of the American Educational Research Association, New Orleans.

Zigarmi, D., and P. Zigarmi. 1978. *The Psychological Stresses of Ethnographic Research.* Paper presented at the annual meeting of the American Educational Research Association, Toronto.

Zinsser, W. 1988. *Writing to Learn: How to Write and Think Clearly about Any Subject at All.* New York: Harper & Row.

Zinsser, W. (ed.). 1986. *Extraordinary Lives: The Art and Craft of American Biography.* Boston: Houghton Mifflin.

Zorbaugh, H. W. 1929/1983. *The Gold Coast and the Slum: A Sociological Study of Chicago's Near North Side.* Chicago: University of Chicago Press.

Zuber-Skerritt, O. (ed.). 1996. *New Directions in Action Research.* Washington, DC: Falmer Press.

Name Index

Subject Index